THE
GREAT WAR
HANDBOOK

THE
GREAT WAR
HANDBOOK

GEOFF BRIDGER

FOREWORD BY
CORRELLI BARNETT

Pen & Sword
FAMILY HISTORY

First published in Great Britain in 2009
Republished in this format 2013 by
PEN & SWORD FAMILY HISTORY
an imprint of
Pen & Sword Books Ltd
47 Church Street
Barnsley
South Yorkshire
S70 2AS

ISBN 978 1 78346 176 9

A CIP catalogue record for this book is
available from the British Library.

Typeset in Palatino and Optima by
Chic Graphics

Printed and bound in England by
CPI Group (UK) Ltd, Croydon, CR0 4YY

Pen & Sword Books Ltd incorporates the imprints of
Pen & Sword Aviation, Pen & Sword Family History, Pen & Sword Maritime,
Pen & Sword Military, Pen & Sword Discovery, Wharncliffe Local History,
Wharncliffe True Crime, Wharncliffe Transport, Pen & Sword Select,
Pen & Sword Military Classics, Leo Cooper, Remember When,
The Praetorian Press, Seaforth Publishing and Frontline Publishing

For a complete list of Pen & Sword titles please contact
PEN & SWORD BOOKS LTD
47 Church Street, Barnsley, South Yorkshire, S70 2AS, England
E-mail: enquiries@pen-and-sword.co.uk
Website: www.pen-and-sword.co.uk

CONTENTS

LIST OF TABLES

FOREWORD

I warmly recommend *The Great War Handbook* to all those wishing to brief themselves factually about this titanic conflict. It will prove especially valuable as background information to families researching into the wartime service of an ancestor. It will act as an essential resource for those either teaching in school about the war or guiding school parties round the battlefields and war cemeteries. For young people, *The Great War Handbook* will provide a fascinating but objective starting-point for their reading.

Geoff Bridger has done us all – professional historians included – a great service.

Correlli Barnett CBE
National President, the Western Front Association.

*   *   *

ACKNOWLEDGEMENTS

Much of the material for this book comes from my own research notes for talks I have been giving for very many years. And much of that, in turn, originated from veterans of the Great War. I have been most privileged to speak to many former soldiers, sailors and airmen – some relations, some friends of my father who served from 1 September 1914 until 19 February 1919 and other veterans who kindly tolerated my persistent questioning. Those priceless interviews took place over several decades, mostly whilst the veterans were still relatively young and their memories fresh and accurate. Many kindly gave me copies of their precious photographs and documents at the time and some are reproduced in this book.

There are various institutions without whose help and cooperation a book of this kind would be impossible. During the course of my research I visited many archives, institutions, libraries and museums but wish to specially mention: The National Archives at Kew, The Commonwealth War Graves Commission, The Imperial war Museum, Lambeth, London, The National Army Museum, Chelsea, London. The staff of all these organizations are always most professional and unstinting with their help.

I wish to thank for their help: The eminent military historian Correlli Barnett for kindly agreeing to write the foreword and for many invaluable suggestions to improve the book; Rupert Harding, my commissioning editor, for general guidance, tolerance and encouragement; Jane Robson, my copy-editor, for her expertise in spotting and correcting my non-deliberate mistakes; Sue Rowland for whose cartographic skills I am indebted – she has modified and made readable old maps and converted my scribbles into useful graphics; Julian Sykes, for information on his specialist subject – mortars; Terry Whippy for supplying items and photographs from his collection for examination and photographing; Bill Fulton and the Machine Gun Corps Association for help in defining the Corps – not the simplest of tasks.

And my thanks to many friends for words of wisdom, encouragement and advice on several subjects. They include: Chris Buckland, Gary Buckland, Terry Cave, Gary Cooper, Bernard Delsert, Meurig Jones, Henry Lequien, Hilary Llewellyn-Williams, Julian Putkowski, Guy Smith, Angela Wiseman and Paul Yates.

I am especially indebted to my old friend Paul Reed. He and I have trudged many a battlefield over the years and his knowledge and expertise on matters concerning the Great War are truly formidable. He kindly glanced over my manuscript and made several helpful and valuable suggestions. I naturally accept full responsibility for any residual faux pas, errors and omissions.

Writing a book is, in my case, a long and laborious task, which has been made so much easier by the willing cooperation and unstinting help of my wonderful wife and friend Anna-May. She has been totally supportive in my endeavours and encouraged me to continue on those 'dark days'. She has offered many valuable words of advice concerning my phraseology; excused unfortunate phraseology levelled at my temperamental computer and accepted my excuses for not helping with the housework or garden for a long time. Thank you Anna-May. I could not have done it without you.

DEDICATION

This book is dedicated to all the soldiers, sailors and airmen of the Great War who faithfully served their country in time of crisis.

I would especially like to remember my cousin, Lance-Corporal Harry Bridger, 2/Essex Regiment, who was killed in action on 18 November 1914.

Lance-Corporal Harry Bridger, 2/Essex Regt.

INTRODUCTION

This book is not another history of the Great War, although it does include a brief account of its origins and main events. As its title suggests, it is primarily designed to answer many of the basic questions newcomers, and indeed experienced historians, often ask when confronted by this enormous and challenging subject. With so many books and other media being available on specific aspects of the Great War, this guide should prove to be useful for students, family historians, teachers and anyone who is eager to gain an all-round understanding of the nature of the conflict. Existing books, many excellent in themselves, tend to concentrate on regiments, individuals, places or battles. Rarely do they explain what it was like to be in the firing line.

The handbook will help provide a greater understanding of what servicemen went through. It can be used either on its own or as a companion to other material you may be studying, to help interpret the many terms and jargon used. It covers not only what happened and why, but what the Great War was like for ordinary soldiers who were, often unwillingly, caught up in it. Sections describe the conditions soldiers endured, the deadly risks they ran, their daily routines and the small roles they played in the complex military machine they were part of. Most aspects of the soldier's life, from recruitment and training, through life in the trenches, the equipment they used, to the experience of battle and its appalling aftermath are considered. It does not however go into the minutiae of equipment nor give details of battles or the battalions that fought them. The contents show exactly what is covered and, if desired, the reader can go straight to the subject on which they seek clarification.

Most measurements are quoted in imperial, as used at the time, but as so many modern students are more accustomed to metric I have added the *approximate* equivalent in parentheses where thought appropriate. As will be seen from the weights involved, the Army did not 'do light'. Everything was built to be 'soldier proof' and very durable. Soldiers had a great deal of heavy equipment to carry about.

When describing certain pieces of equipment, to save space I often give examples of perhaps two of the most commonly encountered items. The interested reader wishing to know more about other variations should refer to the many excellent specialist publications available on the market. Some of these are referred to in the Bibliography. Aspects of a subject may appear in more than one chapter so it is always worth consulting the index.

As with everything else in life there are exceptions to many rules and I ask for the indulgence of any specialist who challenges any unqualified statement of mine as necessarily definitive. For example, I refer to sappers being trained to fight if necessary. Some miners (sappers) went straight to the front, or rather beneath it, with little or no military training. It is not always practical to list every exception.

From the British perspective the 1914–18 war was the first ever conflict to involve virtually everybody in the country. In one form or other the First World War was just that. It spanned most of the globe. And our gallant servicemen died on operations that reached from the Falklands in the South Atlantic to north China in Asia. However, by far the greatest number who served – and perhaps were wounded or died – did so on the Western Front upon which this work concentrates. It is also weighted towards the army and especially the infantry, as it was after all they, with a lot of help from chums in many other units, who won the war! Nevertheless, the various other theatres of war are considered and brief details of the activities there are recounted. We must not forget the sailors and airmen who contributed to the Allied victory and so often lost their lives or limbs in the process. Consequently a very brief summary of their part in the conflict is also included.

The weapons of war were specifically designed to kill as efficiently as possible and were used with equal effect on land, sea and air no matter where on earth fighting occurred. The terrain, weather and conditions varied of course but suffering and casualties, both human and animal, are the inevitable outcome of the war. Despite its full title 'The Great War for Civilisation' there is no such thing as a civilized war.

The conditions for men and animals were, by today's standards, harsh or even brutal. Punishment for wrongdoers was swift and uncompromising. But, as amplified in Chapter 3 we must accept that the men and women who served in our armed forces, and indeed in the munitions factories at home, did so in a very different environment from that prevailing today. And, not having the benefit of our hindsight, did so more or less willingly. That is not to say there were no disputes. There were, but with a few exceptions these mainly related to pay and not the conditions of the time.

Today the First and Second World Wars are taught in schools as history, not as recent memory. The teachers and pupils can have no first-, or

The thirteenth-century Cloth Hall in Ypres was totally destroyed by shell fire by 1918.

probably even second-hand, experience of the Great War. Reminiscences of veterans, if not already recorded, have been lost forever. But that does not mean all evidence is gone – far from it. Family history is one of the most popular pastimes of our age, with so much information from old records being transcribed and made available either on the internet or other easy access forms. Family history societies abound and have large libraries of data for their members. Our quest for information about our forefathers seems unlimited. For the greater part, however, all we can discover are basic facts such as dates and places of birth, marriage and death. It is rare to be able to discover what sort of life our forebears led. We do though know what conditions were like during the Great War and if, as is the case in the majority of British families, a member served in the armed forces we can discover what it was like to be there.

Research sources will be covered later but if you are investigating a particular individual or unit then it is best to adopt certain basic techniques at an early stage. Gather whatever evidence is available and record it systematically. The trusted notebook and pencil are essential tools. Even second-hand stories from the children of veterans have their place. But be prepared to challenge everything you have recorded. Even official documents and records contain errors. Demand evidence but do not be disappointed if it is not immediately available. Put it in the temporary 'unproven but interesting if only it is true' file. Hopefully much of it will slot into place eventually.

Do not give up hope in your research, for unexpected gems resurface every so often to provide that missing piece of family history. It is worth checking exactly what relevant items are hidden away in the attic of any descendants of Great War soldiers, sailors or airmen. Items such as photographs, documents, letters from the Front and medals were often thought worthless just after the war and put away and forgotten. They can be vital to your quest and advice on interpreting them and other heirlooms and artefacts will be offered. It may well be beneficial to join your local family history society to not only gain tips on research, but also to share with their members your own story and any treasures you have discovered.

Although many sources of information are available and can be consulted, unfortunately large numbers of records have been irretrievably lost or destroyed over the years. Additionally it is appropriate to say here that no record of what each soldier did on a day-by-day basis exists or ever has existed. Where service documents survive they commonly indicate physical descriptions and family details, together with limited health and discipline notes and sometimes movement between units. Perhaps surprisingly, for those who died there is often more information available than for those who lived. It is however quite reasonable to assume that a soldier in any particular unit enjoyed the same conditions and privations as his chums. And many of these have been chronicled in considerable detail over the years. It is from the plethora of books, documents, photographs and official records that much of the data in this book is condensed. Other sources include my own background notes to talks I have been giving for very many years.

Vital information, perhaps seemingly trivial but still essential to the greater understanding of what it was really like, has been derived from the statements made by veterans. And that includes my own father. Whereas the correct use of the bayonet is described in detail in infantry training manuals, I know of no contemporary publication, official or otherwise, that describes accurately how it felt to be infested with lice. 'How to scratch' was most definitely not covered in King's Regulations. The fact that toilet paper was not issued to the ordinary soldier failed to be mentioned in the surfeit

Re-examination of the negative with a magnifying class reveals parts of the inscription. Searching Soldiers Died in the Great War *shows the casualty to be Sapper Frank Vickery, killed in action, 16 Aug. 1917.*

of, often quite useless, forms and instructions that were regularly sent to the front line every day. But perhaps those forms were rather useful after all!

Throughout the book the terms, 'men', 'soldier', 'serviceman', 'troops', are used, which seems to imply that only males were involved in the Great War. That is simply not true. If it were not for the millions of women involved at home in hazardous war-related jobs, the conflict could not have continued. We must also remember with pride the thousands of women who were in war zones engaged in nursing and related occupations. Several lost their lives in the process; many more caught nasty illnesses or were injured. And all were in danger. During the First World War women did not fight in a combat role in the British Forces and it is not therefore appropriate to use such modern terms as 'serviceperson'. The soldiers were men after all. In addition, unless separately amplified, the terms 'men', 'soldier', etc. include both officers and other ranks.

The First World War was a learning war. In the majority of earlier conflicts the generals could control the battle from a central position by signalling their intentions. Adequate communication was simply not possible over the large broken battlefields. Portable radio equipment was awaiting invention. And hindsight did not exist. Technology was advancing at an alarming rate, as it invariably does in wartime, but no experience existed as to the best ways to employ it. The eminent military historian John Terrain summarized the situation: 'It was the only war that has ever been fought without voice control. Generals became impotent at the very moment when they would expect and be expected to display their greatest proficiency.'

We must never forget it was also a deadly war. In simplistic terms, one out of every five soldiers who served at the Front was killed and a further two were injured during the war.

We will Remember them.

Chapter 1

PROLOGUE AND OVERVIEW OF THE WAR

The history of the Great War, especially its famous battles, has already been well chronicled by eminent historians. In consequence I here place greater emphasis on the less well-publicized origins and opening moves rather than the overall cataclysm. The full political considerations and military operations of the war are naturally outside the scope of this book anyway.

The fighting in the various theatres of war other than France and Belgium was often intense and cost many lives. And yet the final outcome of the war would only be decided on the Western Front. Whilst the other theatres of war (often called, I feel disrespectfully, 'side-shows') are briefly covered, the main emphasis in this short narrative is devoted to the Western Front. With the full realization that it was a world war involving so many nations, the main focus is on the British involvement because of space constraints. Sadly, even then only a very brief summary is possible.

Prelude to War

The name Gavrilo Princip will be familiar to many students of the Great War. It was he after all, a disaffected 19-year-old consumptive youth, who fired those fatal shots in Sarajevo on 28 June 1914.

Princip was part of a disparate Serbian nationalist gang optimistically recruited, armed and despatched by Colonel Dragutin Dimitrijević, head of the Serbian military intelligence and the terrorist group 'Black Hand'. Their

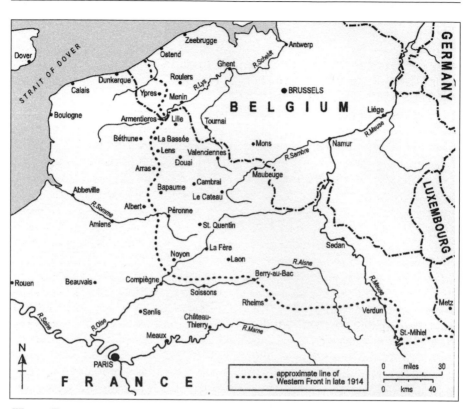

Western Front. Sue Rowland

mission was to assassinate Archduke Ferdinand, the heir presumptive to the Austrian-Hungarian Empire and a man deeply opposed to Serbian nationalism. Sophie, the Archduke's wife, was also shot dead – an unnecessary act for she had no political or royal standing at all.

The spectacular assassination has been called the 'fuse that set Europe ablaze' but that was a slight exaggeration in terms. It certainly did not calm the situation but it was by no means the sole or even principal cause of the First World War. One has to look further back and further afield than that.

What is true is that the immediate origins of the First World War stem from the volatile area we loosely call 'the Balkans'. It was (and still is) populated by very many different ethnic groups, which basically did not get on with each other for numerous historical reasons that dated back centuries. The same was true of the once great Austro-Hungarian Empire, which by 1914 was losing its grip on power, but still had ambitions in the region where many alliances and much intrigue prevailed. Those ambitions were really above its military capability, for its standing army by 1914 had dwindled to about 400,000 – small by European standards of the day. It was not very well equipped with modern field artillery either. Because of internal politics between Austria and Hungary the army had not expanded adequately to keep pace with European rivals and its reserves were small. Along with recently semi-independent Balkan states it wanted a share of the retreating Ottoman Empire, most especially towards the southeast. Unfortunately, Serbia was in the way.

Austria-Hungary had already antagonized the Russians by arbitrarily annexing Bosnia-Herzegovina in 1908. Russia, still weak after losing the Russo-Japanese War of 1904/5 could do little more than protest and harbour resentment on that occasion. Serbia too disliked the colonization, which blocked its own aspirations for an Adriatic port. As Bosnia had a large Slav population, Serbia considered she, and not Austria-Hungary, should rule there. Serbia was already an expanding and antagonistic state as a result of two Balkan Wars in 1912 and 1913 and was not frightened by its large neighbour to the north that had kept out of those conflicts. Austria-Hungary, by contrast, was nervous of potential conflict and the wider implications of regional war without the full support of a powerful backer.

The assassination of Archduke Ferdinand by Serbian terrorists was largely an attempt to show solidarity with the Serbs in Bosnia-Herzegovina. It was also to raise the profile of Serbia, whose ambitions were to reclaim as much as possible of its old empire, which had been lost to the Ottoman Empire long before. Tensions were running high.

Earlier policy decisions to implement fresh alliances for Austria-Hungary were delegated to ambitious and volatile Foreign Ministry officials, among whom were Franz von Matscheko and Alexander Graf von Hoyos. The initial policy document was not too confrontational, but matters escalated considerably following the assassination of the Archduke. The whole blame for that was laid fairly and squarely upon Serbia and the greatest proponent for swift retaliatory action against it was the chief of the general staff, Franz Conrad von Hötzendorff. He was a man of great ambition and personal drive but limited intellect. Diplomatic meetings between Austria-Hungary and Germany were hurriedly arranged and much spin was brought into the situation. The actions of Dimitrijević's men at Sarajevo did not represent the Serbian government's official position, although there was much public support for the assassination.

Central Powers

By the time of the First World War there were already two powerful alliances or understandings that had evolved in Europe. One was between Germany and Austria-Hungary – sometimes called the Central Powers. It was signed in 1879 to provide mutual support in case a peeved France or an unstable Russia attacked either country. France was still peeved following its loss of the provinces Alsace and Lorraine in 1871 after its defeat in the Franco-Prussian War of 1870/1. Russia wanted to expand into the Balkans. Italy joined Germany and Austria-Hungary to form the Triple Alliance in 1882. It joined because France had seized Tunisia, in which Italy had considerable interest, the previous year. As a latecomer, Germany lacked much in the way of overseas colonies when compared to France, Britain and other colonial powers. It was disturbed by the potential of the Royal Navy to cut off its supply of vital materials from neutral countries in the event of hostilities. Germany was however a rapidly expanding industrial country, most especially since the unification of its various states in 1871. Its steel and coal production had increased far more than that of its rivals. Much of this was used in the armaments industry to create a first-class, well-organized, well-equipped and well-trained army and also rapidly increase the size and quality of its fleet – the last element a cause of great concern to the British.

The ambivalent Italy used a technicality to avoid actual fighting on behalf of the Triple Alliance of which she was a member. Instead she declared neutrality in August 1914 and waited to be tempted with promises of territory by the Allies in May 1915 before joining them. She declared war on Turkey on 20 August 1915 but waited until 27 August the following year before declaring war on Germany.

Turkey too was somewhat ambivalent until very late in the day. Both Britain and Germany had input in the region mainly for economic and political rather than militaristic reasons. Turkey was not considered initially by either Britain or Germany as a good military partner. Turkey however needed an ally in the area to bolster its own prestige. Then, in 1914, Britain made a series of diplomatic blunders which offended Turkey, whilst Germany made all the right noises – and backed these up with arms and naval supplies. Finally, antagonized by Britain, Turkey decided to join the Great War on the side of the Central Powers.

The Allies

The other European grouping was the Triple Entente. This grouping was often referred to as the 'Allies' that other countries, such as the United States of America, joined in due course. It started as an alliance between

France and Russia in 1894 to confront the Triple Alliance after the latter's formation in 1882. Britain joined with France in 1904 to form the Entente Cordiale – mainly to combat the perceived menace from the expanding German fleets. Britain finally linked up with Russia in 1907 and the Triple Entente was formed. Britain also had a treaty with Japan that released British warships from the Pacific region. It was left to the Japanese Navy to deal with any enemy merchantmen and warships that wished to trade and roam there. There were other, earlier alliances between the various nations that have little bearing on the Great War and are not discussed here.

The German and French nations by 1914 were disproportionate in the size of their populations. France had about 40 million people whereas Germany, at around 65 million, had over one third more. The difference gave Germany a considerable advantage in the number of men it could potentially recruit into its armed forces. Perhaps surprisingly, in 1914 both countries had similarly sized armies at around 3 million men each, once reservists were recalled. But this ratio was unsustainable in the long term.

The prospect of Germany having to fight on two fronts was highly likely in view of the alliance between France and Russia. We must also remember that, as Poland had effectively been annexed by Russia, the distances between the outer Russian borders and France through Germany had shrunk to around 520 miles – a day's troop-train journey. Despite naval rivalries, and diplomatic incidents, war with Britain was not considered too likely. Britain was rather preoccupied with problems in Ireland where home rule was the major issue and had the potential for violence. It had a very small army and was not too concerned with developments in the Balkans, which would probably be localized. Germany was however concerned about France, especially as two incidents in Morocco had raised the tension between those countries. A further incident at Agadir in 1911 did nothing to lessen the tension and had the potential to involve Britain, as intimated by Lloyd George's Mansion House speech that year. The competitive search for sustainable overseas markets by the European powers did nothing to ease the background tensions.

Austria-Hungary might be able to defeat Serbia but she could not survive unaided if Russia intervened on behalf of her Slavic kin. She sought help and backing from Germany if she was challenged by Russia. And got it. The so-called 'blank cheque', evidently approved by the Kaiser and senior ministers, was soon to be cashed by Austria-Hungary. Meetings were rapidly arranged between von Hoyos and various ministers from Austria and Hungary. They were often fed cleverly distorted versions of the true nature of German support. Eventually agreement upon the next course of action, war against Serbia, was approved. A forty-eight-hour ultimatum was sent to Serbia, the terms of which, it was believed, would give Serbia no option but to reject them and thus commit her to war. Intelligence sources were of the opinion that Russia was not yet militarily ready for war. There was also the naively optimistic idea that the slightly fragile Triple Entente might not hold together. There were yet other nationalistic reasons why Germany was not particularly opposed to a limited war which might increase its world influence and at the same time unite factions at home, where socialist unrest threatened disorder.

In fact Serbia accepted virtually all of the conditions of the ultimatum. It therefore gained a slight diplomatic advantage to help counteract the negative international feelings towards it following the assassination of the grand duke. On 24 July 1914, as well as protesting her innocence in the assassinations, Serbia made a direct appeal to the Tsar for Russian assistance. Amazingly, in an official statement on 27 July 1914, Sir Edward Grey, the British Foreign Secretary, sided fully with Austria, to the extent of stating that he regarded the Serbian response as inadequate and would not blame Austria-Hungary for any military action they might take. In view of the tension, and as a precaution against a pre-emptive Austria-Hungarian strike, Serbia set about mobilizing its own forces. Austria-Hungary was so convinced that their ultimatum would be rejected out of hand, thus wrong-footing Serbia, that they too ordered mobilization. Last-minute efforts by Germany to exercise restraint went unheeded and Austria-Hungary declared war and then, without more ado, opened fire on Serbia on 28 July 1914.

In earlier times countries often mobilized – that is, got ready for war but did not actually fight – as a means of posturing and brinkmanship. That was all very well between small countries in localized situations. It was not so easy when maybe millions of men were involved. It took time for a country to get ready for war. The standing army had to be reinforced with reserves. Reservists were trained soldiers who had served their time in uniform, were released to their homes and civilian occupations, but subject to recall at times of crisis. Men could be on a reserve or recall list for thirty years or more and this feature of continental armies meant that huge forces could be assembled relatively quickly. The reservists however had to be notified and respond to their call-up, taken to their assembly areas, given uniforms, equipment and arms. And possibly retrained. Then the reinforced armies had to proceed to their designated concentration areas ready for war. If war did not occur, the country would have been severely disrupted at considerable unnecessary expense. In practice by 1914, general mobilization was tantamount to war. If your hostile neighbour was ready and poised across the border, that threat could not be ignored and had to be countered. All that was required was the formal declaration. Existing treaties and alliances virtually ensured that once one country started mobilization or offensive action against another the domino effect would soon set in.

War, from Britain's perspective, was becoming increasingly likely day by day but the weak Liberal Government needed to be persuaded it was inevitable. The Cabinet was split on whether to fight or not. Much last-minute diplomacy by Sir Edward Grey was conducted, until finally the German invasion of Belgium gave Britain the valid reason it required to declare war on Germany. Many countries including Britain and indeed Prussia (Germany) had pledged support for Belgian neutrality as far back as 1839. The violation of her neutrality was the last straw. Germany had not thought Britain would oppose its actions in Belgium, which it regarded as fundamental in its battle with France. It was surprised and dismayed that Britain did not agree. The First World War, in all its horrors, finally commenced from a British perspective at 11pm (midnight in Berlin) on 4 August 1914. Last-minute ultimatums to Germany to withdraw from Belgium were rejected.

As we have seen in the birth of the two major alliances, the causes of the unease and suspicion that prevailed in pre-war Europe did not all come from the Balkans, even though it was there that hostilities commenced. Indeed friction in Europe went back many more years but here we are only considering the most recent causes of the war. Once a stone is cast into a pond it is virtually impossible to stop the ripples spreading outwards until the bank is reached or breached.

And as for Princip – the man accused of starting it all – he was thwarted in a suicide bid after the shooting, arrested and subjected to forceful handling. His trial and conviction for murder soon followed. As he was too young to be executed he received a twenty-year prison sentence to be served under very harsh conditions. His health soon failed, an arm had to be amputated, and he died of tuberculosis on 28 April 1918 still in prison. His grave was not marked.

The gun used by Princip now reposes in the Heeresgeschichtliches Museum in Vienna, Austria, together with the car in which the victims were shot. That fateful car had a very chequered career before ending its days in the museum. What is rather poignant is its registration number: 'A 111 118'. With a little imagination that translates to A (perhaps for Armistice) 11 11 18 or 11 November (19)18 – the date of the Armistice, and when the shooting in Europe ended. So, the car that arguably witnessed the first shots of the Great War bears the date of the last shots!

The Western Front – Plans

Germany's war plans were to rapidly defeat France and then, using its superb railway network, switch troops to the east to fight Russia. To beat France it was intended to implement the Schlieffen Plan, first drawn up in 1905 but then diluted many times. By 1914, under Schlieffen's successor von Moltke, two key elements of the original plan were no longer an option. In very simple terms the original plan involved invading France in the north by penetrating neutral Belgium via the southern appendage of equally neutral Holland. The heavily fortified and defended frontier separating France and Germany would therefore be by-passed. The northern German armies would be massively weighted in favour of their sweeping invasion leaving weaker forces to face the French across their joint frontiers further south. It was originally assumed the French would, once war had commenced, push their armies directly into Germany through Alsace and Lorraine. The intention was that the weaker German forces there would give ground, as expensively in French lives as possible, whilst occupying the attention of the bulk of the French armies.

Meanwhile the overwhelmingly powerful attack to the north would rapidly sweep in an arc around Paris and end up behind the French forces, thus trapping them between the two German army groups. This plan evolved in two major and vital ways. First, it was decided not to invade through Holland, so that Germany would continue to have access to world markets during the war via a neutral country. That was a good idea but meant that the invading Germans had much further to travel. They now had to journey round the protruding Limburg appendage to avoid infringing Holland's territory. And we must remember this was largely a pedestrian war. The second important change to the original plan was that the defensive armies facing the French across Alsace and Lorraine should not give ground after all but face up to the French. They were to be reinforced by taking soldiers from the northern invading armies. The net result was that the northern invading armies were not strong enough to fulfil their mission. This defeated the very purpose of the invasion, although vast numbers of French soldiers were killed attempting to force through the German lines in Alsace and Lorraine using their Plan XVII.

FIRST CONTEMPTIBLE : "D'you remember halting here on the retreat, George?'
SECOND DITTO : "Can't call it to mind, somehow. Was it that little village in the wood there down by the river, or was it that place with the cathedral and all them factories?"

With villages razed to the ground, how true the sentiment is.

The French War Plan XVII was no better than the previous sixteen plans. In fact it was a catastrophe. It involved sending four-fifths of all available French soldiers in frontal attacks against well-defended German positions in Alsace, Lorraine and in the southern Ardennes. Their objective was to recapture provinces lost to Germany in 1871. The optimistic idea was to pin the Germans against the Rhine and slaughter them. But that did not happen, for the Germans were far too strong. The only tactic was élan – the bold, almost suicidal, dash into combat expected from the French soldiers against a formidable foe. The disastrous action became known as the Battle of the Frontiers and cost France dearly. By the end of November 1914 France had lost 454,000 dead – one third of their total dead for the entire war, as examination of war memorials in France will testify. Disastrously, during that time, a high proportion of all available French officers were killed or wounded, which robbed France of much needed leadership in the years to come.

The Western Front – War

On the Western Front the Great War actually commenced on 4 August when the first German soldiers violated Belgian territory. That action overshadowed the conflict in the Balkans and finally set Europe ablaze.

Britain sent an expeditionary force to war in France under the command of Field Marshal Sir John French. It consisted of one cavalry and four infantry divisions, comprising around 81,000 men. Reinforcements rapidly followed. It was to concentrate on the left of the French Fifth Army near the town of Maubeuge, close to the Belgian border and less than twelve miles south of Mons.

Although it had been observed during the Russo-Japanese War of 1905, the possibility of trench warfare in France was considered most unlikely in 1914. Long-range, accurate rifle fire by the infantry, supported by light field guns and the cavalry, seemed the most likely course of events.

The British Expeditionary Force (BEF) moved to intercept German units approaching Mons and was soon in action. Faced with overwhelming odds the British first fought, then delayed, then were forced to retreat from massed German battalions, which had already overcome spirited Belgian resistance. And that despite having marched several hundreds of kilometres from their bases in Germany. The retreat started on 23 August 1914 and lasted until 5 September, during which time the British soldiers were fighting rearguard actions and surviving as best they could. They crossed the River Aisne and then the River Marne before halting, tired, hungry and footsore, within twenty miles of Paris.

Poorly equipped British sailors, in the recently formed Royal Naval Division, attempted unsuccessfully to aid Belgian forces in the defence of Antwerp in October 1914. Many escaped to the Netherlands where they were interned for the rest of the war.

Any invading army is at a disadvantage when it comes to resupply. It can only carry limited amounts of food, fuel and munitions. Fresh stocks have to be brought through hostile territory over an ever-increasing distance. The transport system itself uses fuel and food even if it does not have to fight. A retreating army within its own country falls back on rear-based supplies and the population is generally friendly. The Germans effectively advanced, over the River Marne, to the point of exhaustion. They were low on munitions, food and other essential materials. Even the soldiers' boots were worn out. Their retreat to a place of entrenchment was inevitable. They chose to fall back on the north bank of the River Aisne and stand their ground in an easily defensible position. After a brief but bloody battle the

Infantryman 1914 (front).   *Infantryman 1914 (profile).*

British Expeditionary Force entrained for the Ypres Salient in Belgium leaving the French to face the enemy across the Aisne. The BEF, still small in numbers, took over part of that infamous salient and remained there for the rest of the war. Gradually it assumed responsibility for more and more of the front-line in Belgium and France. Thus the periods of stagnation, which became known as 'trench warfare', commenced. The length of the front-line in France and Belgium for which the British were responsible varied from an average of 25 miles in 1914 to over 123 miles in 1918. To carry the vast amounts of war materials required from dockside to railheads, nearly 5,000 miles of railway track were laid, including over 3,000 miles of broad gauge. Great use was also made of the canal system in Northern France for moving supplies.

Following Britain's declaration of war, the Dominions and Colonies, including Australia, Canada, India, Newfoundland, New Zealand, South Africa and other parts of the old empire, rapidly sent contingents of fighting men to help. Not all fought initially on the Western Front but all made great sacrifices during the course of the war.

By mid-October 1914, both sides were busy creating a fortified system of trenches and other obstacles that was to stretch from the North Sea to the Swiss border. From then until 21 March 1918, when the Germans launched their Spring Offensive, the opposing armies faced each other across No Man's Land. The line they created was designed to be impregnable and was defended by literally millions of well-armed and determined men. Each side launched battles against the other in an attempt to break the deadlock and it cost them dearly. None was sufficiently decisive to force the other out of the war. A list of those battles involving British forces appears in Chapter 11 and they can be studied in depth in other publications. During that period of the war hundreds of thousands of lives were lost or ruined by fighting that achieved remarkably little else. But what was the alternative?

Generals are criticized for those casualties, but the ability to foresee the future, and the technology it would bring, was impossible. And our gift of hindsight was not available to the leaders of the time! Let us briefly examine the situation. The Allies wanted the Germans out of their territories and the Germans wanted to stay. Neither was prepared to compromise. Any negotiated ceasefire during the war would effectively have resulted in a German 'win'. True they might have stopped fighting but they would not have retreated to their own borders. Why should they? They were in situ in France and Belgium and not intending to return home empty-handed. The Allies were faced with the situation of forcing them to retreat or surrender. But the German armies were well trained, well armed, well motivated, well entrenched and enshrined in the belief embossed on their belt buckles, 'Gott Mit Uns' (God with us). There were many problems in trying to force them to leave that need to be considered:

- By diplomacy: we have already considered this – unlikely to succeed.
- By the blockade of Germany: yes, this works and was adopted from the start, but Germany was or became largely self-sufficient in most things and it takes a very long time to starve a whole country into submission.
- Attack in other areas such as the Mediterranean and the Middle East: this was tried and found wanting. The only decisive area of conflict remained the Western Front.

• Go round the German lines. But where? Before the trench lines were finally established each side had attempted to outflank the other. The barrier was however completed and stretched, effectively unbroken, for around 450 miles (720km). It is difficult to be precise as it did not follow roads or easily measured features of the land. It evolved wherever the fighting stalled and men dug in. It zigzagged around natural obstacles, formed salients and changed considerably during the war.

To the north was the North Sea. Invasion by seaborne landing craft was considered but abandoned as impractical. It is immensely difficult to land a large army from the sea without purpose-built ships and massive preliminary destruction of the enemy coastal defences. Landing craft, as used in the Second World War, had yet to be invented. Then there is the problem of rapid movement if and when ashore and the whole question of resupply.

To the south was Switzerland, a fiercely neutral and easily defended mountainous country completely unsuitable for rapid movement of invading troops. If it were easy the Germans would have tried it! As it happened neither side wanted to even consider the possibility. Switzerland was far too valuable as a neutral country with which to trade and exchange men, messages and espionage.

• By tunnelling underneath No Man's Land into German-held territory. We did extensive tunnelling on the Western Front but those tunnels were mostly narrow excavations designed for the placing of mines to destroy specific targets. They were totally unsuitable for the movement of hundreds of thousands of invading soldiers carrying all sorts of weapons and equipment. And each side could usually detect the other's tunnelling activities and take countermeasures.

• By going over the lines. How? Paratroops were way into the future. Even if the idea had occurred to someone, the parachutes of the day were unsuitable for carrying heavily armed men. And the aeroplanes were not powerful enough to carry much weight.

So what are we left with? We cannot go round the enemy. We cannot go beneath him. We cannot drop soldiers behind him. Surely the only other way remaining is to go through him! As we have seen, the lines were strong and heavily defended. Any frontal attack, with the weapons, equipment and communications (or rather lack of) at the time was inevitably going to be very costly in human lives. Once a preplanned attack commenced there was no quick or practical way for high command to communicate with its own forces. Truly portable radios and mobile phones did not exist. A local commander could not quickly call off or redirect an artillery barrage from his forward position. He could not get reinforcements to his aid without much delay. He could not retreat without endangering adjacent battalions. He probably could not even call his own men above the din of battle. He had to make do with what had been planned and with what he had available. Even when allowed to use his own initiative and deviate from the plan (not always a good idea, for units on either side would be unaware of the change) he had little scope beyond minor local skirmishes.

New weapons and tactics evolved as the war progressed. Poison gas, flamethrowers and tanks were born here but none was capable of winning the war. Aircraft design leapt forward at an amazing pace. Suitable countermeasures were found. War is a great time for rapid advances in technology and this growth really began with the Great War. It was a learning war, for nothing like it had ever occurred before. The British Army had effectively been a police force keeping order throughout the Empire before the war. Britain expected the war to be mobile, as experienced in the South African War. We had no experience or training for a continental war involving millions of men dug in and resisting eviction. Our Belgian and French allies, later joined by American troops, fought alongside us in many brave and costly actions such as that at Verdun.

Scene of devastation in Chateau Wood, Oct 1917. The duckboards were essential. Many men drowned in this type of quagmire.

What broke the stalemate? Well it was actually the Germans. They had been fighting a war on two main fronts more or less simultaneously until the Russians sought peace at the end of 1917. There had been little fighting on the Eastern Front between March and September 1917, in anticipation of Russian capitulation in an atmosphere of Revolution. An armistice was agreed in December 1917 and was followed by a Peace Treaty between Russia and the Central Powers in March 1918. This treaty wrested vast territories from Russia but necessitated Germany keeping a considerable number of troops in the area as insurance against resumed hostilities. Nevertheless around one million men were released for service on the Western Front in preparation for the coming offensive.

Germany was well aware that, whilst Britain and France were fatigued, American forces were growing stronger in France by the day. The USA had declared war upon Germany in April 1917 but declined to bolster weakened Allied divisions in a piecemeal fashion. Under General Pershing, America decided to fight as an independent force and would not be pressurized into action until they had sufficient numbers of trained troops to achieve that ambition. Thousands of fit, young Americans began arriving each month.

It could only be a matter of time before the Allied armies were sufficiently strong to finally crush the German defences and drive them back. And perhaps even invade their beloved homeland. They decided to strike and hopefully drive a wedge between the British and French armies. It had been politically decided to keep back over one million new British soldiers from the fighting and so, in March 1918, we were not as strong as would have been desired. The French armies were still recovering from mass mutiny in 1917 – although somehow the Germans seemed unaware of its extent. New German tactics were tried and these, combined with surprise, massive artillery bombardments, foggy weather (which prevented aerial observation) and huge concentrations of soldiers, enabled the Germans to break through our lines in several places.

There were five main attacks in Operation Kaiserschlacht (the Kaiser's Battle). They began on 21 March 1918 with the Michael Offensive against a weak British 5th Army, east of the old Somme battlefields. The British retreated, losing much ground, material and men. Other attacks followed from April to July, in areas ranging from the British areas south of Ypres to the French Marne sectors. The Germans kept up the pressure until August 1918 when, in essence, their attack 'ran out of steam'.

Deep inside enemy territory the German armies were low on supplies and exhausted from fighting an ever-stiffening British and French defence.

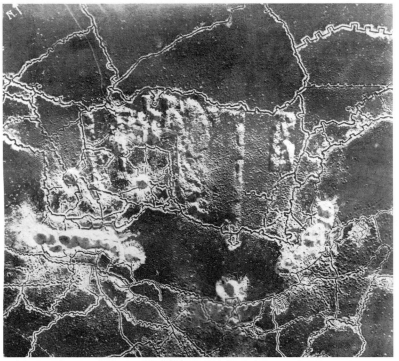

Aerial photograph of area east of Vermelles (Map 36C NW3 G11 and 12). The trench castellations show clearly in the top right.

Official interpretation of features in aerial photograph 36C G11 and 12.

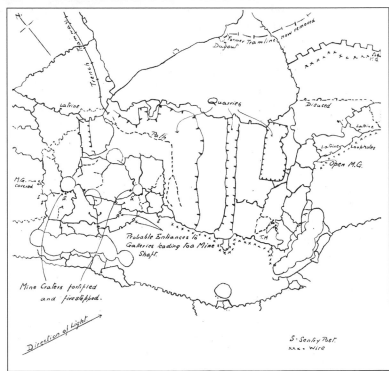

The naval blockade on Germany was biting and her population undernourished. Although higher quality food was diverted to the army it was not really sufficient or very exciting. Ersatz, meaning substitute, was the norm. For example, coffee was synthetic. It was made from ground acorns and other nuts. Bread was adulterated with sawdust to eke out the meagre grain supplies. Life was not luxurious for the German soldier. Even his boots were of inferior quality as leather was scarce. Indeed that is the reason why so many photographs of dead Allied soldiers show them without boots. They were 'salvaged' by their killers. When the German conquerors came across British supply dumps they could not

Bystander copyright.
THE DUD SHELL—OR THE FUSE-TOP COLLECTOR
"Give it a good 'ard 'un, Bert; you can generally 'ear 'em fizzing a bit first if they are a-goin' to explode."

A sardonic but apt cartoon by Bairnsfather. Many soldiers were killed tinkering with munitions.

believe their eyes. They were crammed with the luxuries of life such as real food, real coffee, real soap, wool blankets, proper clothes and alcohol. They were totally demoralized by the extent of the British supplies, much of which came from America. In consequence very many German soldiers literally took 'time out' to loot and gorge and get drunk.

With the onslaught finally halted just outside the vital town of Amiens in August 1918 the Allied steamroller, led by Britain and her Commonwealth Allies, commenced. It was open warfare at last. Communications had improved. New tactics, aided by tanks and masses of aircraft, to attack German positions and troop concentrations, wreaked havoc. During that time various vicious and vital actions were also fought by French and American Divisions with the help of their airmen. The famous 'last 100 days' of the war were under way and the German armies were finally beaten into submission and the Armistice.

Other Theatres Involving British Forces

China: Tsing-Tau

The Germans had a naval base at Tsing-Tau in north China. It was home to Vice-Admiral Graf von Spee's German East Asiatic Squadron that had set sail to peacefully visit far-flung parts of empire in June 1914. With war declared, it was subsequently to wreak havoc in the Pacific before being finally destroyed itself at the Falklands in December 1914. As the German naval base was a threat it was decided to mount a joint amphibious assault on it in conjunction with Japanese forces. After a naval bombardment the forces landed unopposed eighteen miles from Tsing-Tau on 23 September and moved, with much difficulty, into position. Following artillery bombardments to break the siege, and after fierce fighting, the German garrison surrendered on 7 November 1914.

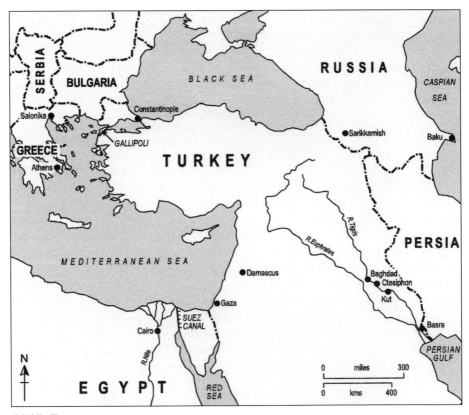

Middle East. Sue Rowland

Middle East – Introduction:

The various theatres of war, which grew in the Middle East, developed from a simple concept. In late November 1914 an idea was mooted by Churchill to the War Council that involvement in the region would serve several purposes. If the Dardanelles could be forced by the navy, at that time not heavily engaged elsewhere, then Constantinople might well be seized or at least dominated. That would demoralize the Turks, following a declaration of war against them on 5 November 1914. It might persuade other states in the region towards the Allied cause. There was always a possibility that Turkey might capitulate or even join the Allies – after all, it was not clear in August 1914 which way she would lean. That would have made defending the vital Suez Canal very much easier. Another major consideration was that a successful operation, resulting in free passage through the Dardanelles to the Black Sea, would open up an all-seasons route to Russia for the transportation of weapons and materials; she was already in desperate need of these. Britain also had to guard its oil supplies from the Middle East.

As we shall see, the Dardanelles was not forced. The invasion of the Gallipoli Peninsula was a failure and the actions at Salonica were unproductive. Mesopotamia was not initially a success either. However the Suez Canal was successfully defended and the Egyptian campaign the only real accomplishment.

Gallipoli

Those who served in both Gallipoli and in France regarded the former as many times worse. Apart from the normal privations of warfare against a relentless enemy, the climatic conditions were merciless to the British, Commonwealth and French troops who landed there.

Flies covered everything in sight, including each mouthful of food, with the result that dysentery was prevalent. Most men were subject to the 'Turkey Trot' but stayed at their posts until (almost) too weak to walk to the latrine unaided. Some fell into the latrine and drowned there.

This theatre of war really commenced on 19 February 1915 with a joint British and French naval bombardment of Turkish forts. The plan was to force a way through the straits by sheer power of arms by naval forces alone. It was not successful and several ships were sunk or damaged, with considerable loss of life. During the campaign six battleships and many other smaller vessels were lost, with over 600 perishing in the French battleship *Bouvet* alone. Almost as many British sailors died when HMS *Coliath* was torpedoed on 13 May. Seaborne landings, mostly violently

Table 1. Total military deaths at Gallipoli (killed in action, died of wounds and died of other causes)	
British Army	29,134
Royal Naval Division	2,409
Australian Forces	8,709
New Zealand Forces	2,721
Newfoundland Regiment	49
Indian native troops	1,358
French Army (estimated)	10,000
Turkish Army (estimated)	more than 60,000

opposed, were undertaken by British, French, Newfoundland, Indian, Australian and New Zealand troops.

Despite great heroism and considerable loss of life, it was not possible to conquer the peninsula and advance north, as had been planned, to open a viable second front against Turkey and the Central Powers. Eventually most troops were evacuated in December 1915, with the remainder leaving the Cape Helles zone on 8 January 1916. The campaign was finally abandoned.

Although the loss of life by the ANZAC (Australia New Zealand Army Corps) was not as great as the British or French, proportionate to their small populations, it was seen as catastrophic. To commemorate their war dead a public holiday on 25 April in both countries marks the day of the landing of their forces at Anzac Cove on the west of the Gallipoli Peninsula.

Whereas extraordinary figures for dead and injured in this campaign are sometimes suggested, the approximate numbers, using official sources where possible, are shown here. Unfortunately those official sources tend to disagree with each other – especially for British casualties. Most sources give the number of British officers and men who died at around 22,000. Investigation by Gallipoli Association members produces very different figures and it is their well-researched total that is quoted here for the British Army. The differences could be accounted for by the subsequent deaths of those who left the area sick or wounded. Over 410,000 British and Commonwealth military personnel took part in the operation. There were in addition over 80,000 French soldiers and thousands of British and French sailors. Disease was rife during the campaign and nearly half those sent were affected by it, with almost 2,000 dying from non-battle causes. Well over one thousand sailors were killed or drowned. When considering the deaths we must remember that more than twice these numbers were seriously wounded.

Italy

Having at last been persuaded, by promises of territories when victorious, to join the Entente, Italy at last declared war on Austria-Hungary on 23 May 1915. Under Generalissimo Luigi Cadorna the Italians lost a great many men in fruitless frontal assaults against well-defended, yet numerically inferior, Austro-Hungarian positions in an extremely difficult terrain for fighting. Little ground was gained and a stalemate situation ensued with neither side gaining the advantage.

The overall objective of the Italians was the strategic port of Trieste but war raged from the high Tyrol to the shores of the River Isonzo, where altogether twelve punishing battles were fought between June 1915 and November 1917. Following the Italian declaration of war on Germany on 27 August 1916, elite mountain troops, some led by then acting Major (later Field Marshal) Erwin Rommel, took to the offensive and forced mass retreats and surrenders by the Italians.

To bolster its ally, Britain and France each sent sizeable expeditionary forces in late 1917. Their responsibility moved from a supporting role to fierce fighting, in rather mountainous terrains in the Piave and adjacent regions, not previously experienced by the British during the war. In excess of 80,000 British combat troops served, and well over 1,000 British officers and men died on the Italian front. American troops were also deployed in this region but saw very little action.

Mesopotamia

This is the area, formerly part of the Ottoman Empire, now known as Iraq. Following a naval bombardment and landing a small force, a joint Anglo-Indian 'Force D' invaded, almost unopposed, in November 1914. With war against Turkey declared on 2 November 1914, its purpose was to 'show the flag', ostensibly protect vital oil installations, and safeguard the Shatt-al-Arab waterway. That was the name given to the united streams of the Tigris and Euphrates rivers flowing into the Persian Gulf below Basra. The ease of the operation in the early days, which included the taking of Basra as forward base, lulled Force D into overconfidence in its own powers. The Turkish army, a formidable power to be reckoned with, was totally underestimated. Turkish soldiers had launched inconclusive offensives and raids against oil pipelines but had done nothing, so far, to unduly worry the Anglo-Indian force.

A mission was despatched to conquer Baghdad some 400km to the north. It was launched with inadequate intelligence and insufficient resources. After getting to within 40km of its target, the column was attacked by some 20,000 well-armed and determined Turks and lost heavily in the engagement. Retreat to the town of Kut-al-Amara, lying inside a large loop of the River Tigris, followed. Force D was besieged there for nearly five months, losing many men through disease and even starvation, as the several attempts to rescue them by land and by river failed. Even airdrops of food and ammunition were attempted.

With summer temperatures regularly exceeding 50 degrees Celsius, it would be a further year before Baghdad fell. Eventually over 250,000 Allied soldiers were deployed against a Turkish force one-fifth their size. But disease and the hostile terrain favoured the enemy. Operations, with limited success, in the region continued right up to the armistice with Turkey on 30 October 1918.

Egypt and Palestine

Predominant in this region was the Suez Canal – a vital artery through which essential war supplies of men and materials, including food and oil, reached the Allies from the Middle East, India and the Far East. It had to be defended at all costs from the hostile Turkish forces, bolstered by some German units and officers, already ensconced in the area. Muslim Egypt was heavily influenced by the Ottoman Empire, while to the east lay vast tracts of Turkish territory. The many disparate Arab factions in the Middle East were gradually united in their cause against the historical conqueror of their lands. Encouraged by Britain, especially Colonel T E Lawrence, they eventually engaged the Turks in guerrilla warfare. Egypt became the headquarters of the Mediterranean Expeditionary Force. However, its divisions were regarded by London as a strategic reserve for other theatres of war if necessary, besides defending the local area.

Britain and her allies, most notably India, Australia and New Zealand and with help from the French, conducted a very successful campaign. Turkish attacks against the canal were thwarted. The terrain was ideally suited to cavalry operations (both horse and camel) and aircraft played their part in reconnaissance and ground-attack. Operations to press north towards Syria initially met with limited success. Eventually, aided by reinforcements of men and supplies, and with good leadership, the Allies

Privately made identity discs. Those from Salonica and Baghdad illustrate boredom.

advanced in September 1918 to take Aleppo, not far from the Turkish border itself. Fighting ceased, as it did in Mesopotamia, with the armistice with Turkey on 30 October 1918.

Macedonia (Salonica)

Macedonia was an area of land through which ran a railway line linking the strategically important Greek port of Salonica on the Aegean Sea with Belgrade, capital of Serbia. When Bulgaria joined the Central Powers in September 1915, the Allies, at the invitation of the Greek government, landed troops at Salonica with the idea of supporting Serbia. Moving slowly north, they arrived too late to aid the Serbs, and the poorly equipped Anglo-French force retreated to a defensive position around the port of Salonica. They were surrounded on the landward side by large contingents of Bulgarian and German soldiers and, despite minor actions, effectively remained trapped in their enclave from November 1915 until September 1918. Much intrigue ensued involving the Greeks and it was not always clear whose side they were really on. Reinforced by fresh British, French and Serbian troops by sea, breakout was finally achieved and Bulgaria invaded. It was hardly a victory, for by then the German stiffening had been withdrawn to the Western Front and Bulgaria offered little resistance. Altogether over one million Allied soldiers were deployed in the area at one time or other and perhaps half fell victim to malaria and other diseases in this unhealthy place. The soldiers could arguably have been better deployed elsewhere and Macedonia had the unenviable reputation of being 'Germany's biggest internment camp'.

Africa

Germany had colonies in East Africa, South West Africa, the Cameroons and Togoland. The small German garrisons in all but East Africa (essentially present-day Tanzania) surrendered in 1914 or 1915. Conversely, the small East African forces under Colonel (later General) von Lettow-Vorbeck fought a successful guerrilla campaign against numerically superior British, Indian and African forces. The German territory, despite being blockaded to cut off supplies, kept going by using captured weapons and ammunition and husbanding its own resources. Intermittent skirmishes ranged over a vast area of eastern Africa and involved British East Africa (Kenya and Uganda), Northern Rhodesia (Zambia), Belgian Congo and Mozambique. The tactics used by von Lettow-Vorbeck tied down the British Empire forces for the whole war. Most of the casualties on both sides were the result of disease rather than enemy action, although hundreds were nevertheless killed in action. An attempt to resupply von Lettow-Vorbeck by Zeppelin from a base in Bulgaria failed after the airship turned back following false reports that he had surrendered. In fact, unaware that the war was eventually over, he did not surrender until 25 November 1918.

Russia

At the time of the Great War, Russia was a highly complex nation that warrants extensive study. The British involvement with it was mainly confined to sending massive aid in war materials. They did however get embroiled in fighting in mainland Russia, partly to protect their own interests in the Artic and partly to support the White Armies against the Communist Red Army. Britain was not alone. France, the United States of America and Japan also sent soldiers. They were in actions across much of Russia, ranging from Archangel in the north, to Vladivostok in the east of that vast nation. The allies slowly lost ground against the Red Army and they finally withdrew on 10 October 1919.

Other Areas Not Involving British Forces

As well as the areas involving British and Empire forces there was extensive warfare in Eastern Europe. Although it principally concerned Germany with Austria-Hungary fighting Russia and Serbia, several other nations, such as Romania and Bulgaria, were involved. The battles covered huge areas, much of it in Poland and East Prussia, and a great many lives were lost. Although not as well covered by English-language books as the Western Front, there are several that deal adequately with this aspect of the Great War.

Following the Armistice there was continued unrest and fighting in parts of the Middle East. For example, Turkey was in turmoil and in conflict with Greece until October 1922, which involved mass population exchanges. The RAF was used to police the region and sometimes ground troops were involved as well in maintaining law and order in Iraq and Persia for many years after the war.

Royal Navy

Whereas most soldiers engaged in fighting were able, albeit perhaps unwillingly, to see what was going on, few in the Royal Navy witnessed the actions their ships fought. Most were entombed within the steel cladding of their pitching warship, doing their job amid noise and smoke, but unable to see beyond their action station. Certain officers and lookouts were often the only ones to actually see an enemy vessel – and then usually only at several miles distance. Many sailors were never in action. Some remained in shore stations, affectionately called concrete battleships, or spent the war swinging around the anchor in harbour. Others were sent, as part of the Royal Naval Division, to fight alongside the army ashore.

From the very beginning of the war the Royal Navy blockaded Germany. It was not a close blockade but maintained at a distance to stop and capture or sink merchant vessels and so slowly starve Germany. The Imperial German Navy was largely impotent and unable to defend its merchantmen whereas the Royal Navy, together with the ships of our allies, literally ruled the waves. This blockade contributed considerably to the downfall of Germany.

Various famous actions were fought about which much has been written over the decades and it is not necessary to repeat the details here. The words

The mighty battleship was to be outclassed by the invisible submarine.

Heligoland Bight, Dogger Bank, Coronel, Jutland and actions such as that at Zeebrugge, are on the lips of everyone who has read about the war at sea. Ships put to sea and shore batteries engaged German ships bombarding northeast coastal towns. Cruisers patrolled the oceans, keeping Allied shipping lanes free from German raiders. Most big ship actions were indecisive and yet many lives were lost. The vast majority of casualties at sea, in all branches of shipping, remain at sea. It is their grave.

During the First World War the battleship theoretically reigned supreme. Improvements in guns, gunnery, protective armour and speed were made all the time. The fleets were huge and the cost of producing and maintaining them immense. They required colossal manpower and yet the most powerful elements of all fleets, those massive battleships, saw relatively little action. In truth it was submarines on both sides that decided the course of the war at sea. Both sides sank a huge tonnage of shipping with much loss of life.

One of the most controversial actions of the Great War was the sinking of RMS *Lusitania* on 7 May 1915, which resulted in 1,198 deaths. It was sunk by U-20, one of a fleet of submarines that altogether sank nearly 13 million tons of Allied shipping. This resulted in severe shortages of supplies for Britain. Of over 350 submarines built, the Imperial German Navy lost over 200 during the course of the war. By comparison, of the total British submarine fleet of over 200 boats – some of which were obsolete, 54 were lost. Submarines are traditionally referred to as 'boats' – not ships! The German name for a submarine was 'unterseeboot', or U-boot (U-boat) for short.

The badge of the Mine Clearance Service.

Another weapon of naval warfare employed by both sides was the sea mine. It was tethered to a weight on the seabed and floated a few feet below the surface. It was detonated by direct impact with a passing ship or submarine. Various areas of the seas around Britain and the continental shelf were mined to prevent unauthorized access by each side. Generally one's own minefields were well charted with safe passages noted but mines often broke free from their moorings and drifted away from their planned positions. It was a mine that sank HMS *Hampshire* en route to Russia on 5 June 1916. Almost everybody on board was lost including Field Marshal Kitchener. Another famous incident was when Turkish mines guarding the Dardanelles stopped it being forced by British and French fleets in March 1915. Fleets of small ships were eventually equipped to counter the mine threat and were very successful, but many mines remain in the seas to this day – a legacy of the Great War.

Merchant Navy

These were the brave men who fought not only the enemy but also the elements, in ships not always of the highest quality. If armed at all it was with a few surplus or obsolete guns, manned, usually, by Royal Navy personnel. Without the merchant fleets, and also the fishing fleets, Britain would have starved. It was not self-sufficient in food or war materials and needed to import a great deal. Before the days of the convoy system merchantmen sailed alone, and were easy prey to surface raiders and submarines that attacked them at will. With convoys, whereby a large number of merchant ships were grouped together and protected by escorting warships, the dangers receded but never passed. It was still easy for a torpedo to be aimed at a ship unseen from beneath the waves. Some 3,305 British merchant ships were sunk during the Great War, with more than 17,000 officers and sailors being killed. Most have no known grave and are commemorated on a special memorial at Tower Hill in London.

The Air Services (RFC, RNAS and RAF)

Although their stores and main personnel travelled to France by ship, most aircraft of the original Royal Flying Corps contingent of just four squadrons took to the air and flew across the Channel. The first to arrive did so on 12 August 1914. Their initial job was reconnaissance to determine the location of the German invaders. The eye in the sky had arrived. On 22 August the first contact was made and a German column identified. The aircraft was unfortunately shot down by ground fire and became the first ever to be lost due to enemy action. See Chapter 10 for details.

From that small beginning the Corps expanded rapidly. Because of the limitations of early aircraft no fixed armaments were carried and only lightweight officers were accepted as pilots. As their primary role was reconnaissance, it ideally suited former cavalry officers used to the 'light-touch' required to control horses and essential to fly the delicate flying machines of 1914. Overall about one-third of deaths among flyers were caused by accidents.

Once more powerful machines were developed each side tried to deprive the other of air space. After five confirmed aircraft 'kills' (balloons counted as a half-kill) a pilot was known as an 'ace'. Despite the highly publicized exploits of those aces, on both sides, they had little real effect upon the war.

Spotting the fall of shots for the artillery became commonplace. Contact with the ground was usually one way only. Initially, messages placed inside weighted streamers were thrown out. Later primitive transmitting radios were used.

First the Royal Naval Air Service, then the Royal Flying Corps and later the Royal Air Force deployed large numbers of fixed kite balloons for observation over enemy lines. They were usually either the Drachen or the French Caquot types. Beneath each canopy was slung a wickerwork basket that held two observers, typically an officer and an NCO. The men were attached, whilst airborne, to prepacked parachutes that were contained in inverted cones attached to the outside of the basket. Initially only home-made harnesses were available. In an emergency the act of jumping from

Launching a kite balloon.

the basket pulled the parachute free from its container and deployed it and over 400 lives were thus saved during the war. Although defended by anti-aircraft guns sited on the ground, most often the observers went aloft unarmed in the fond hope that enemy aircraft would only shoot at the balloon and not at its crew. The balloons were tethered to a tender (lorry) by a cable that was unwound to allow the balloon to ascend to above 6,000 feet (1,800m) altitude. It could be rapidly rewound on a drum mechanism if attacked. Communication with the ground was by telephone along a separate cable to that supporting the hydrogen-filled balloon. To distinguish their status qualified observers wore a special single winged badge with the letter 'O' attached.

Bombing of strategic targets, such as Zeppelin sheds and railway junctions, was undertaken with limited success, due to the primitive methods of aiming the bomb. Tactics to bomb and strafe (machine gun) troops on the ground were slowly improved and caused much damage and consternation, especially in the latter part of the war.

Ships were escorted, usually by the Royal Naval Air Service, and that arm also undertook anti-submarine searches and attacks. For these missions

Bristol Fighter of the Royal Flying Corps, 1917.

the RNAS frequently flew highly manoeuvrable airships of various designs.

Squadrons of aircraft were kept in Britain to protect us from air raids by Zeppelins and German bombers. Attempts failed to shoot down any airship, some of which bombed with apparent immunity from heights of up to 19,000 feet, until Lieutenant Leefe Robinson shot one down on 3 September 1916 over Cuffley in Essex. It was technically not a Zeppelin but a wood-framed Schutte-Lanz airship. Of whatever design, all the hydrogen-filled hulls were very vulnerable to the new incendiary bullets and airship raids soon ceased.

Late in the war long-range bombing was undertaken. Various bombs, culminating in the 1,650lb (750kg) heavy bomb carried by the Hanley Page O/400 late in 1918, were carried to cities in western Germany in an attempt to interrupt armament production. Although judged to be of military importance, the success of those air raids was minimal.

As an independent air force the Royal Air Force was formed on 1 April 1918. It encompassed the Royal Flying Corps and the Royal Naval Air Service and had a separate command structure from the military and navy. From a tiny beginning, by the time of the Armistice the RAF possessed, albeit not all in good order, many thousands of flying machines of one kind or other. Later, the navy re-established its own airborne branch and became separate again in 1937.

Aircraft carriers as such did not play much of a role in the Great War. It is true that several ships were converted as seaplane launchers – indeed, one was used to spot for the capital ships guns in the Dardanelles. In addition many larger warships carried seaplanes. Some could be launched from the parent ship, being flown off temporary platforms built over forward gun barrels. Others were lowered over the side to take off. All were recovered by crane after landing at sea. It was not until after the war that the modern conception of an aircraft carrier emerged.

Attacks on Britain

Most, but not all, of the German airmen who died and were buried in the UK were exhumed and are now interred at the German War Cemetery at Cannock Chase, in Staffordshire.

Table 2. Attacks on Britain			
Type	Number of raids	Killed	Injured
Airship raids	48	556	1,357
Aeroplane raids	59	857	2,050
Coastal bombardments	12	157	634

Armistice Details

The Armistice (a ceasefire only – not a peace agreement) was agreed at 5am on 11 November 1918 in a railway carriage in the Forest of Compiègne and came into effect at 11am, Paris time. It was signalled to units thus:

> Hostilities will cease at 11.00 on November 11th. Troops will stand fast on the line reached at that hour which will be reported by wire to GHQ. Defence precautions will be maintained. There will be no intercourse of any description with the enemy until receipt of instructions from GHQ. Further instructions will follow.

The principal signatories of the Armistice were Marshal Foch for the Allies, and Matthias Erzberger, the German representative. That effectively brought the Great War to an end in most of Europe. There were several armistices to end fighting between the various belligerents and not all were adhered to. For example, fighting resumed between the Central Powers and Russia after an earlier ceasefire in December 1917 and much Russian territory was (temporarily) lost. Most combat ceased towards the end of 1918 but continued in parts of Russia, the Middle East and between Greece and Turkey. Parts of Germany were occupied by Britain, France and America for several years, which caused much resentment.

The Kaiser went into exile at Huis Doorn in the Netherlands and remained there. He died on 4 June 1941 and is buried in the grounds of the chateau.

The Aftermath

Among the many tragedies of the Great War were the hundreds of thousands of eligible young women destined to forever remain single. Britain, before the war, already had a surplus of over half a million more women than men. With so many young men killed or crippled for life, well over a million women were doomed to never marry – the one thing that, above all else, most women of that generation aspired to. Fortunately nature seems to have stepped in and the post-war birth rate shot up to restore most of our lost youth during the next two decades. A not dissimilar situation existed in France and Germany, and indeed in every other country, where the scythe of war had cut down so many young men.

Unemployment hit Britain soon after the war and jobs became scarce. The vast quantities of war materials were no longer required and the country's industry rapidly returned to peacetime production. During the war around one million women took over jobs traditionally done by men. When the boys came home they were not anxious to return to their earlier drab and poorly paid existence. They expected better. In 1929 the Wall Street crash brought unemployment and misery to many of those who had found work. For those still out of work it made life harder still. It was not a happy time for the men who had expected to return home to a grateful government and a land fit for heroes. Much discontentment prevailed, not just in Britain, but around the world. It became the excuse for extreme government on both sides of the political divide and was to culminate in another world war.

Chapter 2

THE ARMY

Structure of the British Army in 1914

By 1914 the soldiery of the army was quite complex and comprised Regular, Reserve and Territorial Force officers and other ranks. Men in the Regular Army usually enlisted for twelve years. They most often served about seven years with the Colours (that is, as 'armed' soldiers in uniform) followed by five years in one or more classes of Reserve.

It was possible for the ratio of Regular and Reserve Service to vary considerably but the man was not totally free from military jurisdiction for the full twelve years. There were different categories and subcategories of Army Reserve Service depending upon the conditions of the soldiers' release from Regular Service. When war was declared the entire British Army was comprised of 247,482 Regular officers and men, 316,094 Territorials and 228,120 conventional Reservists that included 3,000 ex-Regular officers on reserve. The above figures include staff and other non-effective appointments not available for deployment to theatres of war. By November 1918 the overall total then serving had risen to nearly three and a half million.

Typical British Tommy in 1914. A soldier of 4th Middlesex Regt near Mons.

In 1908 the Militia (an earlier type of territorial army that had evolved in a rather disjointed way over hundreds of years) was partially disbanded and the remainder formed sections of the Special Reserve and Territorial Force. The Special Reserve was part of the first class of the Army Reserve. It included cavalry, corps troops and infantry – of which there were seventy-four Special Reserve battalions and twenty-seven Extra Special Reserve battalions. Former regular soldiers could also join the Special Reserve and after retraining return to civilian life, subject to recall in an emergency. The conditions for service in all reserve units were numerous and are detailed in the *Manual of Military Law 1914*.

Infantry reservists were allocated to certain battalions of their regiment but not physically attached to those battalions unless called up. Those reserve battalions were, in peacetime, the Depot or recruiting battalions and often numbered three in the regimental order. Each such battalion was staffed by around 100 regular officers and men for recruiting and training purposes. In peacetime, the newly trained soldier would not have stayed with the Depot but would have been posted to one of the regular battalions (generally the first or second battalions). Any surplus reservists on call-up not required to reinforce the regular battalions would be assigned as Special Reservists to the reserve (Depot) battalion. There, they would train recruits or be reassigned to the regular battalions when vacancies (casualties) occurred. Some went as instructors to the New Armies. They also took over the duties of regular garrisons at home. In 1914 there were 101 Reserve and Extra Reserve infantry (but not guards) battalions.

The National Reserve consisted of former trained servicemen who were no longer in any other type of reserve unit. They could elect, subject to conditions, to register to serve in an emergency. They were generally older men and were paid an annual grant depending upon which category they joined.

The Territorial Force was extensive and comprised infantry, artillery, engineer, transport, medical and veterinary units. It was originally intended for home defence. Men enlisted initially for four years and could re-engage subject to certain conditions. Preliminary training was given and then men were required to attend a number of drills and annual training camps. They were subject to call-up to full-time service in an emergency (embodiment) but, unlike the Special Reserve, were not obliged to serve overseas; they could however volunteer to do so.

Reservists were paid to compensate them for training times and continuing commitment. Officers as well as men served in all reserve units and were subject to Military Law.

It was technically possible for regular soldiers and reservists to complete their full period of commitment during a crisis – or even during a war. They were then discharged and free to leave. But when compulsory service came into force they could be conscripted back into the army – assuming they had not already volunteered to stay on!

Various other reserve classes were created during the war to encompass men who could be called up but were temporarily, at least, more valuably engaged in their civilian occupation. Those classes were P, T and W and it depended upon the man's job and medical category as to which he was allocated. It was not uncommon for a man to serve in the field, be transferred out of the army to a reserve class and then be recalled to the Colours later.

When the war was over most men were not immediately given their complete freedom but were transferred to Class Z Reserve on demobilization. That meant they could be recalled should an emergency arise – such as a resumption of hostilities by Germany. They were not finally released until 31 March 1920.

All figures quoted in the following sections are for the prescribed war establishment and assume full strength. It must be realized that all units were rarely at full strength.

Ole Bill Bus, once used to transport troops, carrying veterans in London.

Army Command

All members of the armed forces swore allegiance to the King. On his behalf the Army was administered by the Army Council. That in turn was chaired by the Secretary of State for War, as minister responsible for the War Office. The council was comprised of both military and civilian members. Its military adviser was the Chief of the Imperial General Staff (CIGS).

Various forces were set up during the war. They came under the jurisdiction of a command structure, which was known as either General Headquarters (GHQ) or sometimes Headquarters (HQ) – depending on the rank or seniority of the general in local command. At various times during the war the following GHQ were established:

Home Forces
British Expeditionary Force (BEF) France and Flanders and later Italy
Egyptian Expeditionary Force (EEF)
Mediterranean Expeditionary Force (MEF)
Mesopotamia
British Salonica Army
East Africa

Going to War

In early August 1914 the British Expeditionary Force sailed for France. It comprised two Army Corps consisting of four infantry divisions. (A third corps was held back by Kitchener for home defence.) There were also two cavalry divisions – a grand total of 81,000 officers and men. Reinforcements in the shape of reservists, regular soldiers returning from overseas stations, Indian soldiers and territorials, followed rapidly. By mid-December 1914 the BEF numbered 269,711 officers and men. To that number must be added over 22,500 officers and men who had already been killed by December, plus tens of thousands more wounded. By November 1918 those original two Army Corps had expanded somewhat as can be seen in Table 3.

During the course of the war, divisions frequently moved between Army Corps and the composition of all echelons changed to suit the demands of High Command. The *Orders of Battle* (see Bibliography) chronicles these changes.

Table 3. Higher formations of the British Expeditionary Force

August 1914

Commander in Chief	Field Marshal Sir John French.
I Army Corps	Lieutenant-General Sir Douglas Haig, 1st and 2nd Divisions.
II Army Corps	General Sir Horace Smith-Dorrien, 3rd and 5th Divisions.
III Army Corps	Major General William Pulteney, 4th and 6th Divisions. (Formed in France, 31 August 1914)

November 1918

Commander in Chief	Field Marshal Sir Douglas Haig.
First Army	General Sir Henry Horne.
VII Army Corps	Major-General Sir Robert Whigham (reserve June 1918).
VIII Army Corps	Lieutenant-General Sir Aylmer Hunter-Weston, 8th, 12th (Eastern), 49th (West Riding) and 52nd (Lowland) Divisions.
XXII Army Corps	Lieutenant-General Sir Alexander Godley, 4th, 11th (Northern), 51st (Highland), 56th (London) and 63rd (Royal Naval) Division.
Canadian Army Corps	Lieutenant-General Sir Arthur Currie, 1st, 2nd, 3rd and 4th Canadian Divisions.
Second Army	General Sir Herbert Plumer.
II Army Corps	Lieutenant-General Sir Claud Jacob, 9th (Scottish) and 34th Divisions.
X Army Corps	Lieutenant-General Reginald Stephens, 29th and 30th Divisions.
XV Army Corps	Lieutenant-General Sir Henry de Beauvoir De Lisle, 14th (Light), 36th (Ulster) and 40th Divisions.
XIX Army Corps	Lieutenant-General Sir Herbert Watts, 31st, 35th and 41st Divisions.
Third Army	General Hon. Sir Julian Byng.
IV Army Corps	Lieutenant-General Sir George Harper, 5th, 37th, 42nd (East Lancashire) and the New Zealand Divisions.

V Army Corps	Lieutenant-General Cameron Shute, 17th (Northern), 21st, 33rd and 38th (Welsh) Divisions.
VI Army Corps	Lieutenant-General Sir James Haldane, Guards, 2nd, 3rd and 62nd (West Riding) Divisions.
XVII Army Corps	Lieutenant-General Sir Charles Fergusson, Bt., 19th (Western), 20th (Light), 24th and 61st (South Midland Divisions).
Fourth Army	General Sir Henry Rawlinson, Bt.
IX Army Corps	Lieutenant-General Sir William Braithwaite, 1st, 6th, 32nd and 46th (North Midland) Divisions.
XIII Army Corps	Lieutenant-General Sir Thomas Morland, 18th (Eastern), 25th, 50th (Northumbrian and 66th Divisions.
Australian Army Corps	Lieutenant-General Sir John Monash, 1st, 2nd, 3rd, 4th and 5th Australian Divisions.
Fifth Army	General Sir William Birdwood.
I Army Corps	Lieutenant-General Sir Arthur Holland, 15th (Scottish), 16th (Irish) and 58th (London) Divisions.
II Army Corps	Lieutenant-General Sir Richard Butler, 55th (West Lancashire) and 74th (Yeomanry) Divisions.
XI Army Corps	Lieutenant-General Sir Richard Haking, 47th (London), 57th and 59th Divisions.
Portuguese Corps	General Garcia Rosado, 1st and 2nd Portuguese Divisions.

Note: There were additionally cavalry divisions and others in lines of communication.

Enlistment

Volunteers

Field Marshal Lord Kitchener, as Minister of State for War, persuaded the Cabinet that the war against Germany would not be quickly or easily won. He considered it would take at least three years to defeat the highly efficient and well-equipped German Armies. Kitchener therefore encouraged mass recruitment and the country responded to the call.

The men who flocked to the Colours were all volunteers and they were largely assigned to new formations. These were created specifically to cater for the rapid enlargement of the army necessitated by the war. Some men intentionally joined the Territorial Force but this was not encouraged. Kitchener decided it was best to build entirely new armies rather than expand the existing one. He was of the opinion it would be a long war, which could only be won by large, well-organized and well-trained forces. The existing army structure was totally inadequate to allow for massive expansion. Many new divisions were required to accommodate the numbers of men deemed necessary to win the war. Kitchener did not consider the territorials were sufficiently highly trained to bolster the regulars and was not sure they would volunteer for overseas service in sufficient

The famous poster depicting the accusing finger of Field Marshal Kitchener.

numbers. In the event their training proceeded apace and most agreed to fight overseas – many serving with great distinction.

Those responding to the 'call' could largely choose their regiment and were subject, in theory at least, to the same physical fitness and age constraints that applied to the regular army. For it was indeed the regular army they were joining, even if not entirely on the same terms. They mostly signed up for three years or the duration of the war. The idea was that these men would be trained and then sent into battle as complete units. Some were however required as soon as possible to fill gaps in the ranks of existing battalions. Eventually five New Armies were to be created and, popularly known as Kitchener's Army, were numbered from K1 to K5. These armies mostly contained six divisions (K5 had seven), each of twelve battalions.

Officers who had left the army years before were 'dug out' of retirement and many old soldiers re-enlisted and were promoted to train new recruits. Some were better than others at their new tasks. Both officers and NCOs who had been wounded in France were eagerly sought after on their recovery for the New Armies. Recent experience was desperately needed.

The tide-swell of men coming forward voluntarily gradually diminished and to maintain the flow other measures were necessary. Upper age limits were increased but that did not produce enough men. It was decided to see how many men were theoretically available for the armed forces. A census was conducted under the National Registration Act of 1915 to establish the numbers, ages and trades of the male population.

Enlistment expanded with the introduction of conscription and the traditional regimental system became overloaded. From September 1916, Training Reserve Brigades comprising three, four or five Reserve Battalions were formed. Further changes from May 1917 resulted in Graduated and Young Soldier Battalions being formed. Young Soldier battalions recruited men aged 18 and after basic training these soldiers were transferred to Graduated Battalions. They were then ready for home service and, if required, for overseas service. The battalions were eventually attached to existing regiments and their deployment can be traced in the *Order of Battle of Divisions* and other sources.

One effect of the rush to volunteer was that, once in, it was difficult to get out again. Captains of industry often pleaded in vain for the release of men whose expertise was vital to the war effort at home and currently being 'wasted' in the trenches.

Derby Scheme

In October 1915 Lord Derby was appointed Director General of Recruiting. He introduced a system, which became known as the 'Derby Scheme', whereby males between 18 and 40 were asked to either enlist or register for call-up if required. They were told that the chance to volunteer and thus have some choice of regiment etc. was soon to end. Compulsion loomed! Those on the register were classified, depending upon age and marital status, as ready for enlistment when required. There were many exemptions from potential call-up, for example, because of special job skills. The process produced well over two million actual and potential recruits but many did not register before the scheme closed on 15 December 1915 and so the next step was taken. Often those on the register were not actually attested for many months.

Conscription

The Military Service Act, which came into effect from 2 March 1916, was extended and modified in May 1916 to include married men, and made enlistment into the armed forces compulsory. Men could no longer choose their regiment etc. Again there were many exemptions and various tribunals heard appeals against service. These appeals were generally reported in the local press for all to see the excuses offered. If exemption was granted it was often conditional. For example, if the man left a reserved occupation he was immediately liable for service. Other authorities, such as government departments, could approve exemption from call-up. When a notice of call-up was issued, usually with a railway warrant for free travel, the recipient had to report to a specific recruiting office at the time stipulated – usually about two weeks later. By April 1918 age limits were again extended – this time to those between 18 and 50.

Officers

When the war started so many new officers were required that the supply could not equal the demand. Potential reserves of officers were soon exhausted. Officers Training Corps attached to universities, public schools and certain similar establishments, whose role it was to train young men to the standard whereby they could receive commissions, produced insufficient numbers. The appalling casualty rate among junior officers was proportionally was far higher than that of their men. With so many new officers urgently required, the pre-war standards of training before commissioning had to be condensed. The young men arriving in France to command platoons were often held in scant regard by their men. Officers promoted from the ranks fared better. Any lack of 'public school' polish was more than compensated for by recent experience in the field of battle.

2/Lt Eric Heaton, 16th Middlesex, killed in action 1 July 1916. Private collection

Definition of Army Formations

British Expeditionary Force (BEF)

This is a global term for all the British Army units in France, Flanders and Italy in the Great War. There were only ever two commanders-in-chief. Until 19 December 1915 Field Marshal Sir John French commanded it. From noon that day General (later Field Marshal) Douglas Haig took over and remained in post for the remainder of the war.

Lines of Communication (Troops)

This term referred to the vast number of soldiers, in hundreds of units in rear areas, dealing with the transport and supply of materials for the fighting soldiers. Their jobs involved working in, at or on: docks, quarries, roads, forestry, railways, repair workshops, general provisions and petrol supply, hospitals, prisons, ambulance trains, hospital ships, etc. The actual lines of communication were the systems of rail, road and navigable waterways linking the army and its base or bases.

Army

An army was an organized body of men armed for war and commanded by a general. It consisted of two or more corps and other supporting units and services including artillery, engineers, medical personnel, veterinary services and transport. By March 1915 there were two armies in the BEF. By 1918 this total had risen to five.

Corps

This was a formation consisting of two or more divisions and also supporting forces, responsible to the lieutenant-general in charge. An army corps's identifying numbers were in Roman numerals.

It is also the name used by units such as Army Service Corps, Royal Army Medical Corps, etc. These two uses of the word 'Corps' must not be confused.

Division

This was almost a miniature army under the command of a major-general. Besides three brigades of combat soldiers, it contained all necessary support units to enable it to fight independently. Such units would include, for example, artillery, ambulance, engineers including a signalling section, and transport. Divisions were frequently moved during the war and came under the command of different corps or armies. There were also cavalry divisions. The regular army in 1914 was comprised of eight divisions, numbered one to eight, but subsequently four more were formed from reservists and men returning from overseas stations. They became the 9th, and 27th to 29th Divisions. Full details of the composition of each division are in the *Order of Battle of Divisions*.

When out of the line a division was usually at rest and/or training. It was re-sorted, reinforced and re-equipped prior to being reassigned to another, perhaps quieter or perhaps not, sector of the front. Brigades were sometimes switched between divisions to bolster a weaker one or to assimilate less experienced troops into a more seasoned one.

Medium and heavy mortar batteries came under divisional control and were operated by men of the Royal Field Artillery. These batteries were usually numbered to correspond to the parent division. For medium batteries, there were normally three, that number was prefixed by X, Y or Z. For the heavy battery the prefix was V.

Brigade (Infantry)

In 1914 it was a formation of four battalions commanded by a brigadier-general and assisted by headquarters staff. A further territorial battalion would sometimes be attached to a brigade. Machine gun and light trench mortar units were controlled at brigade level. Around March 1918 the brigades were reduced in strength from four to three battalions because of shortages of manpower. Several battalions were amalgamated at the same time for the same reason.

Note that the 'Rifle Brigade' is the title of an infantry regiment and consisted of many battalions – it is not a separate brigade. See below.

Regiment

Many soldiers feel they owe allegiance to their regiment. But what exactly is a regiment? It is rather hard to define but simplistically it could be said to be an umbrella organization, steeped in tradition, commanded by a colonel and comprised of battalions of soldiers plus the Depot, regimental silver and the goat or other mascot. Unlike Germany, British regiments never fought as a body. Its battalions were dispersed across the divisions. In peacetime the regular battalions were often on overseas stations and its territorial battalions were spread across their recruiting areas in their respective companies. Only the Depot, with perhaps 100 men, the colonel, goat, etc., remained in the main barracks in its garrison town. But that is where the *esprit de corps* was centred. Soldiers spoke with pride of their regiment and then added that they were in a particular battalion.

Battalion

The infantry battalion was the principal fighting unit of the British Army during the Great War. As part of a brigade, which was in turn part of a division, a battalion was ordinarily commanded by a lieutenant-colonel. He was assisted by twenty-nine officers and a further 977 men made up his command. Thus, notionally, a battalion had 1,007 officers and men. The reality was somewhat different, for battalions often went into battle fielding but a few hundred in total. In addition to the men, a battalion had under its command many horses, wagons and carts to carry ammunition and supplies. The diminutive machine gun section was radically altered as the war progressed. (For details see the Machine Gun Corps.) Infantry battalions frequently moved between brigades during the war. Each battalion was divided into four companies.

New Army battalions were assigned to existing regiments and numbered from where the regular, reserve and territorial battalions ceased, but with the addition of the word 'Service' to their number. Territorial battalions often, but not always, started in the numbering sequence at four and there were often at least two of them. As recruits often elected to join the territorials rather than the regular army (new armies) there were more men than places available. To accommodate this situation new battalions were created and given the same number as the original but with the addition of a prefix. Thus one finds the 1/5th (originally just the 5th), 2/5th and even the 3/5th. Altogether including regular, reserve, territorial, new army, etc. there were 1,743 British infantry battalions during the Great War, but many did not serve overseas.

Not all battalions were primarily comprised of fighting soldiers – although all were armed and fought if required. Several battalions were designated for pioneering or labouring tasks whilst others guarded important installations at home and abroad.

For more information see *British Regiments 1914–1918* (details in Bibliography).

Pals Battalions

It was thought men might more readily enlist if they knew they could serve with their chums – maybe from work or neighbourhood. Men like Lord Derby and the then Major-General Sir Henry Rawlinson appealed for like-minded groups to enlist together. Lord Derby, known as 'England's best recruiting "sergeant"', coined the term 'Pals' when he was recruiting in Liverpool on 28 August 1914. He said: 'this should be a battalion of pals, a battalion in which friends from the same office will fight shoulder to shoulder for the honour of Britain and the credit of Liverpool'. Many similar Pals battalions were formed, with arguably the Accrington Pals being the most well known. Unfortunately, if a Pals Battalion suffered heavy casualties in a battle it meant that a small community at home or at work was particularly hard hit. Whole streets could lose their men-folk overnight.

Cadre

The cadre was a basic unit of a few officers, NCOs and men kept out of the battle, usually with the transport, to form a nucleus for expansion or recovery when necessary, such as when the battalion had devastating losses in battle. The term 'decimated' is often incorrectly used to suppose massive losses; indeed some confuse it with the phrase 'wiped out'. It actually means one man in ten being a casualty. Many units suffered far heavier losses than that.

Company

As one quarter of the fighting arm of a battalion, the company notionally comprised six officers and 221 men. A major or a captain ordinarily commanded the company. Each company was usually titled A, B, C or D. Some battalions however used instead the letters W, X, Y and Z.

Platoon

The platoon was one quarter of a company. A lieutenant or second lieutenant usually commanded it. But frequently in battle an NCO would assume command if the officer was killed.

Section

Each platoon was divided into four sections, each commanded by an NCO.

Artillery (see also Chapters 6 and 8)

The artillery was divided into the Royal Horse, Royal Field and Royal Garrison Artillery. Their batteries were usually classified according to its guns or howitzers. For maximum mobility the Royal Horse Artillery was armed mostly with light guns firing shells weighing 13 pounds. The Royal Field Artillery used slightly heavier 18-pounder field guns plus 4.5" howitzers and some medium artillery pieces. The Royal Garrison Artillery was responsible for heavy guns. There were many titles for these batteries such as horse, field, mountain, garrison, siege, heavy, anti-aircraft and railway. There were also mortar batteries.

Artillery Brigade

An artillery brigade was a grouping of three or four batteries of guns or howitzers commanded, at full strength, by a lieutenant-colonel. To distinguish it from an infantry brigade it was numbered in official writings in Roman numerals. There were usually four or six guns in a battery – sometimes less if the guns were above 12" calibre.

Cavalry

In 1914 there were thirty-one cavalry regiments. They comprised three Household, seven Dragoon Guards, three Dragoons, six Lancers and twelve Hussar Regiments. Technically the dragoons were mounted infantry. In addition there was the Yeomanry, the mounted arm of the Territorial Force. The yeomanry (in a similar fashion to the territorial force) raised second and third line units to reinforce their main regiment. Most of these were later broken up or converted to cyclist or reserve units in 1917, with the men released being retrained accordingly. There was also the Imperial Camel Corps established in 1916, mainly from former Gallipoli veterans.

One cavalry division of four brigades, each comprising three regiments, sailed with the Expeditionary Force in August 1914 but the number of brigades per division was soon reduced to three. Reinforcements for France and Belgium rapidly followed and eventually five cavalry divisions, which incorporated the two Indian divisions, were formed. Three of these remained in service throughout the war. There were additionally dismounted cavalry units.

The regiment was the principal fighting unit of the cavalry. It was commanded by a lieutenant-colonel and comprised around 550 officers and men organized into three squadrons, each of four troops. (The Household Cavalry had four squadrons.) Each regiment also had a two-gun machine gun section and all the men were trained to fight dismounted if necessary. The men were usually armed with the 1908 Pattern Sword plus either a pistol or rifle. A few lancers, as their name implies, still carried eight-foot long lances. Indeed they were used in action at High Wood on the Somme on 14 July 1916.

Medals

These come in two main categories. Campaign medals, or medals for 'being there' and gallantry medals for special deeds of bravery. There were also medals for long service and good conduct, given to men who had served in the armed forces for eighteen years and whose record of service was exemplary. Pre-war regular soldiers often had medals relevant to earlier campaigns such as the 'Boer War' or perhaps, for general service in India.

The precise conditions for the entitlement to any medal, including those briefly mentioned here, are most complex and the subject of specialized books, so these comments are only intended to give general guidance. Again, as with most things in life, there are exceptions to many rules – often because a mistake has been made!

Campaign Medals and Entitlement

For the Great War, each soldier, sailor, airman and certain civilians who served in a defined theatre of war against Germany or her allies was entitled to one or more campaign medals. Where the recipient had been killed, the medals were sent to the next of kin.

The first medal is the bronze 1914 Star that was awarded to those who served in France or Belgium between 5 August and midnight on 22/23 November 1914. Where the serviceman was actually within range of the enemy guns a small bronze bar, to be attached to the medal ribbon, was also awarded. It follows that all those 'Old Contemptibles' killed in action between the above dates in France and Belgium were entitled to the bar. This medal is popularly, if incorrectly, called the Mons Star. Around 378,000 such stars were issued but many, such as those who never left rear areas, were not entitled to the bar.

For those who served in a different theatre of war to that required for the 1914 Star (with or without a bar) or those who did not go to France or Belgium until after 23 November 1914 the appropriate award was a 1914–15 Star. This is very similar to the 1914 Star but was never awarded with a bar to distinguish those who actually served under fire from those

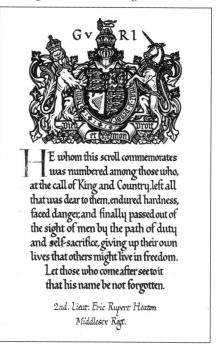

2nd. Lieut. Eric Rupert Heaton
Middlesex Regt.

Memorial scroll to 2/Lt Eric Heaton, 16th Middlesex, killed in action 1 July 1916. Private collection

who worked away from the enemy lines. Only one Star could be held and the 1914–15 Star ceased to be given to anybody who arrived in their theatre of war after 31 December 1915. Members of the Royal Navy, even if killed in the first few days of the war, could only receive the 1914–15 Star unless they served ashore in France or Belgium before 23 November. An example of such service would be with the Royal Naval Division fighting at Antwerp. The medal was made of bronze and approximately 2,366,000 were issued. Of these some 283,500 were for Royal Navy personnel.

A person receiving a 1914 or 1914–15 Star would also be awarded two further campaign medals. The first is the British War Medal, which is made of silver. The criteria for issue were similar to that of the 1914–15 Star but the time in which qualifying service had to count was extended to at least 11 November 1918. In certain theatres this date was extended to as late as 1920 (for example for mine clearance), but the medal is dated 1914–1918.

Memorial plaque to Eric Heaton.
Private collection

Those who were sent abroad on or after 1 January 1916 were only eligible for this and the Victory Medal described below. Unless that is, gallantry, long-service awards or special Territorial Force medals were earned. Around 6½ million British War Medals were issued in silver and a further 110,000 in bronze, most often but not always in conjunction with the Victory Medal. The bronze issue was for Chinese, Indian and some other overseas Labour Corps and similar personnel who were paid by the military authorities.

The last campaign medal generally awarded was the Victory Medal, which was cast in bronze to commemorate the Allied victory. Around 5¾ million Victory Medals were despatched. The dates impressed, 1914–1919, reflect the continued fighting in the Middle East, India and Russia into 1919, and the signing of the Peace Treaty at Versailles on 28 June that year.

All campaign medals are named to the recipient and also show his rank/rating and number (unless to an officer, as First World War officers did not have a number), together with the name of his regiment or arm of service. There was no distinction between officers and other ranks regarding the issue of campaign medals.

The medals were sent automatically to the latest address known to the armed forces. It was not necessary to claim them – unlike medals for the Second World War. When the medals were sent to the next of kin because the recipient had been killed, two further items were included. One was a large bronze plaque bearing the dead person's name and inscribed with the words, *He* [or *She*] *Died For Freedom And Honour*. Some 1,355,000 plaques were issued in respect of those who fell during the period 5 August 1914 to 10 January 1920. These were sometimes called 'A Dead Man's Penny'. The other item was a scroll, identical for both officers and men, individually named with additionally rank and regiment.

Silver War Badge

Sometimes called the silver wound badge, it was issued to servicemen honourably discharged from the forces under King's Regulations after September 1916, because of wounds or sickness. Around the front of each badge is written, *For King and Empire. Services Rendered.* Each badge carries a unique number and it is possible to trace the recipient from that number. It was issued as a form of recognition to the men who no longer wore a uniform and were being mistaken for those who had never joined up.

Silver war badge.

Gallantry Medals, etc.

There were many instances of gallantry during the Great War. For the deed to be rewarded with a suitable medal or award the recipient usually had to survive the incident. There were certain exceptions. The Victoria Cross and the Albert Medal (the latter for saving or attempting to save life – not necessarily during war) could be awarded posthumously. Details of the heroism are chronicled in the *London Gazette* and are worthwhile reading. Unfortunately the deeds that resulted in the award of the Military Medal were not published in the *Gazette*. There were, no doubt, many other unrecognized acts of heroism, either because the man was killed or because there were no qualified witnesses. If the recipient earned a second (or more) award then a bar(s), to be attached to the ribbon, was given. A brief description of some of the more famous British medals follows but alas space limits me to but a few examples.

Victoria Cross (VC)

It is the premier award for all ranks for supreme acts of gallantry in the face of the enemy. Made from the metal of guns captured from the Russians in the Crimean War, it is simply inscribed with the words, *For Valour.* On the reverse is the date of the deed and on the suspender the recipient's name and unit are engraved. In total 633 Victoria Crosses, including it is believed 293 posthumous awards, were made for the Great War. Only one recipient received both the Victoria Cross and a bar for actions in the First World War. He was Captain Noel Chavasse and he died of his injuries on the second occasion.

Distinguished Service Order (DSO)

First instituted in 1886, it is a decorated, enamelled cross with a crown and laurels in the centre. By the time of the First World War it was more usual for it to be awarded to officers of major (or equivalent rank) and above for distinguished services, usually under fire. Rather less than 9,000 first awards were given to army officers and there were a further 786 bars, including seventy-one second and seven third bars. Naval and Air awards were, in total, 882 and 61 respectively. Both the latter figures include bars. It was not named when issued.

Military Cross (MC)

Instituted on 28 December 1914 and made of silver, it was for captains and lower rank officers and warrant officers, in (Royal) appreciation of 'distinguished and meritorious service in time of war'. Over 37,000 crosses and 4,123 bars – several second and four third bars – were presented. It was not named when issued.

Distinguished Conduct Medal (DCM)

First instituted in 1854, it is a highly regarded decoration for 'other ranks', 'for distinguished conduct in the field'. It ranks below the Victoria Cross but above the Military Medal in prestige. The medal, made of silver, bore the name, rank and number and unit of the recipient and approximately 25,000 (including 470 bars and ten second bars) were awarded during the Great War.

Distinguished Conduct Medal with 1914 Star and Bar, British War and Victory Medals to Sapper Thomas Jones, Royal Engineers, who died of wounds on 15 March 1915. Private collection

Military Medal (MM)

It was felt there was need to reward lesser acts of bravery, for other ranks, than that envisaged for the Distinguished Conduct Medal. In consequence on 25 March 1916 the Military Medal was instituted. It was primarily prescribed 'for bravery in the field' but could also be awarded to women for their bravery. For nearly two months retrospective awards were considered and a few granted. The medal was in silver and bore the name, rank, number and unit of the recipient on the rim. Over 115,000 Military Medals were awarded for the Great War, together with nearly 6,000 bars, including not only 180 second bars but also one third bar – the latter to Corporal E A Corey, 55 Australian Infantry.

Indian Order of Merit (IOM)

Founded in 1837 by the Honourable East India Company, it is the oldest gallantry award of the British Empire. There were two military classes by the time of the Great War. The second class was equivalent to the Distinguished Conduct Medal.

Mentioned in Despatches (MiD)

A 'reward' given by the naming of the recipient in the commander's despatch to higher authority and then published in the *London Gazette*. Along with the Victoria Cross and Albert Medal, and unlike the other awards, the MiD could be made posthumously. To symbolize the Mention a sprig of bronze oak leaves was worn on the ribbon of the Victory Medal and a special certificate was issued. Nearly 140,000 army personnel were 'Mentioned in Despatches' for the First World War.

Regimental Numbers

At the beginning of the Great War – and indeed before it – many soldiers were issued with an identical service number to that already in use by men from other units. Unique army numbers were not issued until at least 1920 (and then only for the Army Reserve and new soldiers) and only an overview of the Great War numbering system is possible here. Essentially each army corps, e.g. Royal Engineers, Royal Artillery, etc., and each infantry battalion was allocated a block of numbers to issue, ranging from one to several thousand. As regiments usually had more than one regular battalion, duplication occurred even within that regiment. Sometimes a number prefix was used to distinguish the battalion (e.g. 3/3321) but that practice was not universal. It was also confusing where a man changed battalions within a regiment but often kept his old number! If he moved to another regiment he was allocated a new number. It is obvious therefore that much duplication occurred. Indeed, using *Soldiers Died in the Great War* as a reference source, it is noticed that even the number 'one' had been issued to eight different soldiers who died. Although not having the highest instance of overall repetition, when compared with some other numbers, over 220 British soldiers were issued with the number 1883. And of those thirty-seven died during the war – more than with any other number.

Territorial battalions followed a similar system until 1 March 1917 when they were renumbered using six-figure numbers, starting at 200,001 under the provisions of Army Council Instruction 2414 of December 1916. Unfortunately even after this exercise much duplication occurred, as each army administrative record office seems to have issued blocks of numbers that replicated those issued by other record offices. Even the number of 200,001 appears to have been issued to seventy-eight soldiers. The problem of insufficient unique numbers was not properly addressed and we were not much better off than before.

Various prefixes were added to numbers and each had different meanings. Concerning the infantry, not all regiments used all of the prefixes and there were variations and errors by record offices when issuing numbers. There were many other letters used and in consequence the following is only a guide and is certainly not complete.

L	Regular Army – line regiments
G	General
GS	General Service
GSSR	General Service Special Reserve
SR	Special Reserve (former regular soldiers)
S	Similar to GS prefix and mainly, but not exclusively intended for Scottish Regiments
TF	Territorial Force

The Army Service Corps especially used prefixes to indicate the branch of the Corps to which a man was attached. The main branches and number prefixes were:

Remount	R/
Supply	S/
Horse Transport	T/
Mechanical Transport	M/

A second letter prefix was frequently added to indicate the trade or other subcategory to which the man belonged.

Other prefixes were used by battalions of certain regiments to indicate the original recruiting source. For example:

SD   Southdown Battalions (11, 12 and 13/Royal Sussex Regiment).

PS   Public Schools Battalion (16/Middlesex Regiment.

STK Stockbrokers Battalion (10/Royal Fusiliers)

Sadly, because of the duplication referred to earlier, it is rarely possible to positively identify a First World War soldier from his basic number alone if that is all you have.

Chapter 3

THE NEW SOLDIER

Why Enlist?

Life in Britain for most people, just before the Great War, was not easy. Many children died young and the male life expectancy was only 50. Health and safety laws scarcely existed and thousands died each year in industrial and agricultural accidents. Trade unions had little muscle and it was rare for any compensation to be paid to widows or mutilated survivors. With no wireless (radio) in the home, newspapers reigned supreme over the distribution of information, which was not entirely unbiased. Wages were poor, malnutrition commonplace and any entertainment mostly home-grown.

Is it any wonder men were eager to escape their dull and drab existence for the adventure the army was offering? They were assured a dependable, if not generous, wage; they were regularly fed with often far better food than at home; they were clothed and housed. And, perhaps for the first time in their lives, adventure beckoned. They could travel to foreign parts and become part of the infectious patriotic surge that was sweeping the land.

These men were not natural heroes but they were certainly not cowards either. Their country needed them – all the newspapers, billboards and propaganda told them so. Their conditions at home were not exactly wonderful. And so they flocked to the Colours in their hundreds of thousands. The famous pointing finger of Lord Kitchener advising people that 'Your country needs you' drew in recruits for the army; other posters set about attracting men to the navy. One thing Britain has always been good at is propaganda and in wartime it excels itself.

Attestation

Attestation is essentially an oath of allegiance to the monarch and country. Pre-war, to join the regular army, the would-be soldier had to comply with certain formalities including fairly strict physical requirements. He had to be aged between 19 and 38, at least 5 foot 3 inches tall, and physically fit. He could generally choose his regiment and committed himself for twelve years service with the Colours and on Reserve. There were other avenues into the army such as the Territorial Force or Special Reserve.

When war broke out, the flood of volunteers initially overwhelmed the system and shortcuts were taken. The man had to pass a rudimentary interview by the recruiting sergeant and then, after a basic medical examination, fill in an attestation form in duplicate. It was commonly, but not exclusively, Army Form B.111 that committed the soldier to serve 'until the War is over'. He then swore an oath of allegiance to the King before an officer. The wartime medical was not usually too demanding and the Army Form B.178, completed by the medical officer, included a physical description of the soldier. Another officer then certified his approval and at that stage the man was deemed to be a soldier subject to the King's Regulations. He then received a shilling. Usually the recruit was sent home to await call-up for training.

THE WATCHERS OF THE SEAS.

THE NAVY NEEDS BOYS AND MEN FROM 15 TO 40 YEARS OF AGE.

APPLY: 7, WHITEHALL PLACE, S.W.

Royal Navy recruiting poster dated 1915 (by L. Raven-Hill).

Soldiers were classified into medical groups depending upon their health and age. The basic categories were A, B, C or D with subcategories added in numbers, e.g. A1, B2, C1, etc. Essentially all A group were medically fit for active service overseas. Those in group B were fit for lines of communication duties overseas; those in group C were assigned to home service duties, whilst those in group D were, at least in the short term, considered unfit for any normal military duties but could work in depots at home. The precise criteria, including height restrictions, became somewhat blurred during the course of the war to suit manpower requirements. Indeed Bantams battalions were soon created to cater for shorter but fit men over 5 feet tall.

Over/Under Age and Aliases

There are so many accounts of men attesting under age that either there is mass hysteria on the subject or some truth in it! The army did not officially encourage under-age enlistment but, on the other hand, did not insist on proof of age at the recruiting centre. On the Military History Sheet age is referred to as 'Apparent Age' and on Army Form B.178 (Medical History) it is described as 'declared age'. The subject does not appear to have been of vital importance to the military. Interestingly, of the seventeen questions on army attestation Form B.111, only eleven were subject to a penalty (two years hard-labour) if a false

The grave of Henry Webber, one of but by no means the oldest soldier to die for his country.

statement was made. The first six questions, which included name, nationality and age, were exempt from that penalty if untruthfully answered. And those are the main areas where lies were told. Indeed, over 6,000 British Empire men died under an assumed name and the number enlisting under or over age is totally unknown but not inconsequential.

Aside from a few '(very) old soldiers' serving in the United Kingdom, probably in an administrative capacity, the proven extremes for those who died on active service are 15 and 69. (The true age of a famous 14-year-old casualty is not proven.) But then we have Field Marshal Lord Roberts VC who died whilst inspecting his troops in France at the age of 82.

Pay and Allotment

The basic rate of pay for a private soldier was one shilling per day. This could be increased by earning proficiency pay in various skills, such as marksmanship. An increase of one (old) penny was paid when in a war zone. From 29 September 1917 a further three (old) pence per day was given by way of a pay increase. If the soldier was in one of the corps, such as Royal Engineers or Army Service Corps, then he would have been paid more for his specialist skills such as mining or mechanical vehicle driving. If the soldier was married it was usual for an allotment or compulsory

Notification under A.O. 1, of 4-12-17 of alteration
of the net rate of pay issuable to a soldier
from the 29th September, 1917.

(To be inserted in front of page 3 of A.B. 64.)

Soldier's Name..

Regtl. No. and Rank...**Pte 51217**

Unit...**ROYAL FUSILIERS**

	s.	d.
Regimental Pay (including the extra 3d. a day authorised for Warrant and N.C.Os. of certain arms)	1	—
Proficiency Pay		3
Service Pay		
Engineer or Corps Pay		
Difference (if any) to make up the minimum under the Army Order		3
War Pay		1
Deduct Voluntary Allotment		
Compulsory Stoppage		
† NET DAILY RATE FOR ISSUE:		
(Words)..One Shg Sevenpence..	1	7

............................Regimental Paymaster.

..........Date. ....Station.

† Subject to Promotions, Reductions, etc., since 29th Sept., 1917.

[M40011 W2683/G331 Mod 12/17 ...

Page of soldier's pay book (Army book 64).

stoppage of six (old) pence per day to be paid to his wife. This was supplemented and the wife of a private or corporal received 12/6d per week, with more for children. If he was not married he could nominate one dependent relative to receive (a lesser sum of) money. Many conditions were imposed. More was paid for sergeants and warrant officers but they had to contribute more as well.

Currency Guide (Approximate)
1 shilling = 12 (old) pence or 5 (new) pence (one shilling was shown as 1/-)
1 (old) penny = ½ (new) pence (one old penny was shown as 1d)
Thus 1/6½d was one shilling and six pence ha'penny (8 (new) pence) and 12/6d was twelve shillings and six pence (62½ (new) pence).

We must however realize that one shilling in 1914 was worth approximately £3.44 in today's values – a sixty-nine-fold increase due to inflation. The average weekly unskilled wage was then £1/5/0d, equal to £86.25 in 2008. However his rent took less than a quarter of his wage and he could buy a kilo (2.2lbs) of flour for around three old pence and beef was cheap at nine old pence a kilo. Good beer was six old pence a pint and cigarettes three old pence for a packet of twenty!

Training

Basic training for the new recruit was divided into two unequal parts. The soldier had to become fit, learn about his equipment, and be taught how to shoot and fight with a bayonet, as well as learn the basic skills to prepare him for war. Initially, however, the most intensive part of his training was designed to instil unquestioned discipline and build up his physique. For this, seemingly endless marching, drill and polishing of equipment were imposed. The precise method of saluting was judged to be of prime importance. The soldier had to obey orders unchallenged and immediately as if it were second nature. Accurate drill requires immediate response to a word of command and, if repeated often enough, men became accustomed to the routine of blind obedience. Individual initiative was most certainly discouraged at this level of training. Minor transgressions resulted in extra drill or fatigues. More serious breaches of discipline resulted in detention in one form or other.

Formal marching, with arms raised shoulder height on every step, is considered by the army to be excellent overall exercise. To toughen them up, men went on route marches of from fifteen to twenty-five miles a day, carrying their full pack and rifle or, in the parlance of the day, 'full marching order'. The usual pace or step for marching was thirty inches and troops marched at the rate of three miles per hour with short halts being permitted. Rivers were considered fordable up to a depth of three feet. No allowance at all was made for wet clothing and boots afterwards!

The second part of the training was spent learning the basics of army life. Particular attention was paid to the correct use of the bayonet and elementary shooting skills were practised on the rifle ranges. Fire discipline – when and what and how to shoot was taught. The pre-war standards of marksmanship (fifteen accurately aimed shots per minute) had to be abandoned for new recruits, as time was critical. After 1914 some instruction was given on trench digging and on life in the trenches.

More advanced training was often carried out in the theatre of war – especially so if it were France and Flanders. Soldiers usually spent many unhappy hours in training camps such as the famous Bull Ring at Etaples. It was in such places that they learnt some of the finer arts of trench warfare and were subject to even more rigorous drill routines to hone their discipline. Courses were given to newly arrived men on the art of killing without being killed, by soldiers with recent practical experience. Specialist courses were also run from bases such as Rouen, Harfleur, Havre and Etaples for newly appointed NCOs and officers on matters as diverse as bombing, machine-gunning, mapping, signalling, etc. Before major offensives, rehearsals were sometimes practised in specially constructed training battlefield areas.

The minutiae of killing were taught, as the following extract from a 1918 War Office training pamphlet on the use of the bayonet illustrates:

> If possible the point of the bayonet should be directed against the opponent's throat, especially in corps-d-corps fighting, as the point will enter easily and make a fatal wound on penetrating a few inches and, being near the eyes, makes an opponent 'funk'. Other vulnerable and usually exposed parts are the face, chest, lower abdomen and thighs, and the region of the kidneys when the back is turned. Four to six inches' penetration is sufficient to incapacitate and allow for a quick withdrawal, whereas if the bayonet is driven home too far it is often impossible to withdraw it. In such cases a round should be fired to break up the obstruction.

Embarkation

Infantry battalions were gradually formed into divisions and they assembled ready for deployment to a theatre of war by troopship, usually from one of the Channel ports. There are published lists showing their initial date of arrival. If the soldier went to war before 31 December 1915 the area he was sent to and the date of arrival should be shown on his Medal Index Card.

Wills

A soldier on active service was able to make a simple will in his pay book. It did not need to be witnessed and was usually honoured.

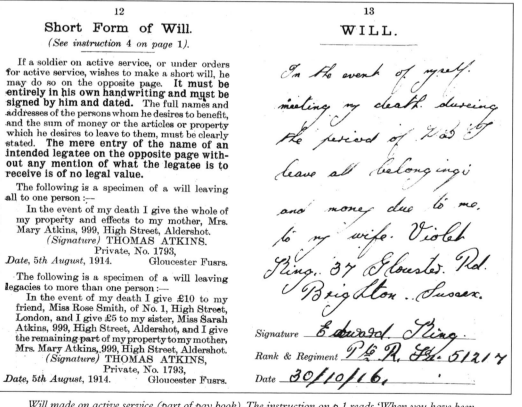

Will made on active service (part of pay book). The instruction on p.1 reads 'When you have been placed under orders for active service (and not before) you may make your will, if so desired.'

Uniforms and Accoutrements

Because of the huge influx of men in 1914 it was not possible to clothe and arm them to current specifications straight away. Around 500,000 recruits wore improvised uniforms during training, made from blue serge, and popularly known as 'Kitchener's Blues'. Blue was substituted as the traditional khaki dye came from Germany, whose chemical industry specialized in dyes. It was naturally unobtainable once war commenced and it took a while to find a replacement. Many varieties of 'uniform' and other kit existed, especially early in the war when much was purchased hurriedly from America and Canada. Even the manufacture of the tunic was simplified for mass production but all had a field dressing enclosed in a special inside pocket. Headgear also changed from the formal cap to much more comfortable hats. The 'Gor Blimy' soft cap, with flaps to keep the ears warm, was very popular, but was gradually replaced by a new soft cap in 1916.

Old rifles and other items were unearthed from reserve stores and issued to fill the gap until more could be made. The term 'accoutrements' is defined as comprising those items, other than weapons, carried outside the clothing. It consisted of belts, pouches, bandoliers, slings, mess tins, haversacks, water bottles and similar articles. Some of this is technically called 'equipment', i.e. the harness and containers used to carry all the items a soldier needed. It had been made of webbing since 1908 but was complex to produce rapidly, so leather items were substituted.

The full kit list for a soldier was most impressive and covered items from his studded boots to his cap. When marching during training he carried over 61 pounds (28kg) of clothing, weapons and equipment. Everything seemed heavy. The rifle, bayonet and 150 rounds of ammunition weighed almost 20lbs (9kg). Even his woollen underpants (drawers) weighed over one pound (500g). And that was when they were clean and fresh on! Occasionally as much as a month would elapse between changes. Here kilted regiments gained – they were not issued with any. Additional items, such as a steel helmet and respirator, were added as time went by.

Marching: Time and Distance

For the infantry soldier the usual mode of transport was his feet. Only rarely did he get a ride. Indeed, during the course of the war the British army wore out over 40 million pairs of boots!

The usual infantry marching speed was at the rate of 98 yards per minute or three miles per hour. That allowed for a six-minute halt every hour. Infantry soldiers marched in columns of four abreast and each battalion (notionally 1,007 officers and men) took up 590 yards of road space for the fighting portion, with a further 210 yards allocated to their first line transport. A battalion therefore occupied 800 yards of road – not far short of half a mile – while on the move. In 1914 a division, which was home to around 18,000 officers and men, plus 5,000 horses and hundreds of wagons and carts took up nearly fifteen miles of road space if it ever moved as a complete unit. Small columns of seasoned troops could cover twenty-five miles a day in favourable conditions. Larger groups, hampered by transport wagons, were expected to travel fifteen miles per day.

Column of soldiers moving by the usual means of transport – marching. Paul Reed Archives

Identity Discs

The British Army issued official identity discs from at least 1906. Initially the single disc was made of aluminium and then, from 1914, a red compressed fibre disc gradually superseded it. By September 1916 it was decided two discs were required. A round disc, whether the earlier aluminium or later red fibre type, was to remain on the body after burial. The second fibre disc, which had eight sides and was dull green in colour, was to be removed in the event of death and the details recorded. The information stamped into the discs was basically surname, initials, number, unit and religion but variations appeared. Each belligerent nation had a different design of identity disc. The fibre discs endured for a long time in the ground. But no one expected them to last for around a century, which is one reason why recently discovered bodies can rarely be identified. The term 'dog-tag' was not used in the Great War. Soldiers referred to the identity disc as a 'cold meat ticket'. Many soldiers had private identity discs or bracelets made from all manner of materials, but coins seem to have been the most popular.

Examples of official identity discs.

Home Leave

This was at the discretion of the officer commanding the unit and depended for other ranks on the manpower available and to a large extent on the soldier's service record. Denial of home leave was used as a punishment for transgressions. There do not seem to have been any fixed criteria until mid-1917 but it was not unusual for a couple of years to elapse before leave was granted. Transport by train and boat was free but there was a problem. Any leave pass was for a fixed number of days, often as few as five, and the amount allotted included the time it took to travel to and from home. That was fine for a soldier who lived in Dover but not so good for the man whose address was in Scotland. And getting from the trenches to the railway station could be time-consuming. Officers seem to have received a more generous allowance.

All kit, including his rifle but not usually ammunition, was taken home by the soldier. This was because his unit may well have moved by the time of his return and there were no facilities to store and transport extra kit. Any spare space in his pack was usually crammed with souvenirs, such as cap badges, *pickelhaubes*, fuse caps, etc., picked up on the battlefields. It was not unusual for more deadly items to be brought back. Among the souvenirs was often a lice-infested uniform for his mother to launder.

Chapter 4

THE TRENCH

Trenches: Summary

A trench was effectively a slot dug into the ground. Its purpose was to limit the effect of different projectiles and the blast effect of high explosive shells. They were the most common type of defensive position on the battlefields. The first real trenches, which were to form the opposing lines for well over three years of siege warfare on the Western Front, were constructed in September 1914 following the Allied Advance to the Aisne. Before that, during the period of mobile warfare, when necessary individual soldiers dug hollows in the ground with their entrenching tools to get some protection from incoming small arms and artillery fire. (An entrenching tool is a personal issue small spade that frequently incorporated a short pick.) The ideal textbook front-line trench was about 3 feet 4 inches wide at the top, around 7 feet deep with the sides cut as steep as possible, and tapering to about 3 feet wide at the bottom. It had raised areas at the front and back, known respectively as a parapet and a parados. About 18 inches of the width at the bottom incorporated a raised fire-step on the side facing the enemy. It did not leave much actual floor space for movement. The exact construction varied considerably and was heavily dependent upon the soil conditions. Often the sides were reinforced with corrugated iron, wickerwork hurdles, wire netting, timber or other convenient materials scavenged locally. Where sandbags were used, they were laid to precise specifications and stakes were driven through them at intervals to add strength and avoid collapse. Sandbags were normally only used where speed of construction was the first priority as they rotted after a while and in consequence their contents spilled out into the trench. In general terms

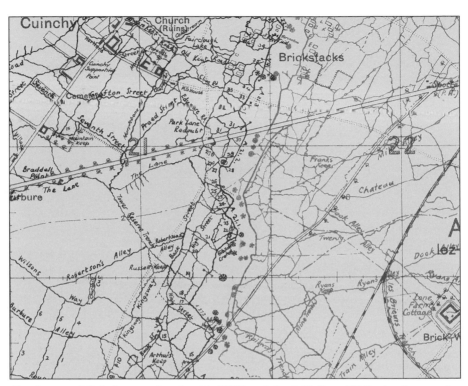

Trench map of Cuinchy area (number 36c NW1 and dated 10 June 1916), showing opposing lines. Note craters in NML.

the narrower the trench, the more protection it offered. After the lessons learnt at the beginning of the war, the trench bottoms were often floored with duckboards to aid travel and drainage of water.

Some trenches were at least partially covered with material to afford some protection from descending shrapnel and shell fragments, as well as the worst of the weather. The cover also made the trench more difficult to spot from the air. They were not popular however and most trenches – including all front-line trenches – were totally exposed to the elements. This of course risked death or harm from exposure. Outside the trench, earth was built up at both the front and rear. Often carefully but unevenly laid sandbags were used for this purpose. Dummy trenches were also dug to confuse and entrap any invading enemy.

In Belgium and the northern parts of France the water table is very high – often only one or two feet below the surface. In these conditions it was not

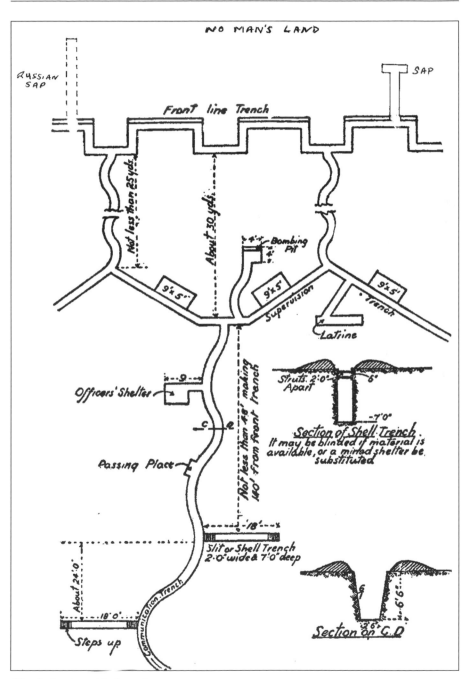

Sketch showing typical trench system.

practical to dig deep trenches. Instead a shallow trench was dug and then earth built up in front of the trench to form high breastworks and thus give as much protection as possible. Most trenches were a compromise between the two main types.

Trenches were initially dug by infantry soldiers, mostly under cover of darkness. Later in the war planned trench lines – as opposed to the majority that evolved due to prevailing circumstances – were often dug by labour battalions or even members of the Labour Corps. Whenever possible the trenches were profiled to afford maximum concealment. From the diagram it will be seen that the trench system was comprised of several elements, some of which are briefly described below. Despite seeming haphazard, trenches were very carefully thought out to give the best possible protection to their occupants, whilst affording a good field of fire with which to engage the enemy. Their mutual support capacity with nearby emplacements was vital and consideration was also paid to their drainage potential. It was not desirable that soldiers should stand in waterlogged trenches if it could be avoided. Some trenches were on the reverse slope of a prominence to improve their defensive capabilities. These required forward saps for observation and to act as fire-bays. Dead ground, that is, an area which cannot be covered by fire, was avoided at all costs. It could provide cover for an attacking force. Small excavations were frequently dug into the rear wall of the trench to contain a small fireplace for heating water and cooking breakfast. The schematic diagram of a trench system includes many of these terms.

Defence in Depth

As the war progressed, more and more lines of trenches were dug as the technique of 'defence in depth' evolved. The Germans were the first to use this system. Some trenches were many hundreds of yards behind the front, which was only lightly defended. An invader would be gradually drawn into progressively more heavily defended zones. Each layer would give way in turn, inflicting casualties before its garrison retreated. The attacking forces would additionally be subjected to enfilading fire from the flanks and would be continually expending its limited ammunition supplies. Meanwhile the defender fell back behind new fortified lines upon fresh and unlimited supplies. As the layers of trenches could stretch back miles in some cases, the attacker may well have been unaware of their existence and run out of fighting capacity before breaching the final line. With the old system, once the front and support trenches were broken through, there was little to stop the invader.

Elements of a Trench or Trench System

Barbed Wire

Inescapably linked to the maze of trench systems, and defending them from easy infiltration, were huge swathes of barbed wire. By 1915 these were not simple strands such as found surrounding fields at home but vast entanglements designed to be impenetrable. Belts of barbed wire stretched along much of the Western Front on both sides of No Man's Land and it was regarded as both a blessing to be behind and a barrier to try to penetrate – depending upon whose wire one was contemplating.

The wire was fixed in position by vast quantities of stakes driven into the ground or suspended from specially designed screw-pickets. Coils of wire were expanded and fixed to the stakes. Another method, when rapid wiring was required, was the use of chevaux-de-frise – a preconstructed obstacle of posts and barbed wire that could be carried into position, dumped and staked there.

The belts of wire varied enormously in height and depth but ideally were about 3 feet high and over 30 feet in depth (10m). Usually, a second band of similar dimensions was laid parallel to and further out from the first to keep enemy bombers at bay. Very often there was yet a third entanglement with a gap between it and the preceding one. A distance of around twenty yards from the front-line was generally left free of wire. These bands of intermeshed wire were so dense that they clearly show on aerial photographs taken from several thousand feet altitude. Single strands of wire, with tin cans containing stones suspended from them, were often set a few inches from the ground some distance from the front-line trench. It was designed to catch an intruder attempting infiltration by night and attract the attention of sentries.

At night parties would frequently go out to try to penetrate the enemy's wire and gather intelligence. Samples of the enemy wire were taken for analysis. Again, each night men would be sent out to repair and strengthen their own wire. Sometimes this led to confusion. In one instance, the then Lieutenant Philip Neame (15 Field Company Royal Engineers) sent a verbal message to supporting infantry, 'The R.E. are going out to wire. Don't fire.'

The message that finally reached the machine guns was: 'Enemy in the wire. Open fire.' The resulting mêlée, with both sides soon shooting at the unfortunate sappers, can well be imagined.

Before a major assault, gaps were made in one's own entanglements to allow the troops through. The gaps were zigzagged in such a way as to be invisible from the enemy positions and marked out with tapes. Various methods were tried to destroy enemy wire defences but none were entirely successful. At best the wire was partially cut but still represented a considerable obstacle for the soldiers trying to get through it. High explosive shells usually lifted the wire into the air and dumped it back on the ground in a jumbled heap, making it more difficult to cut and cross through than the original. Developments in fuse design made the shattering of areas of barbed wire possible with certain mortar bombs, but that depended upon great accuracy and the opposing wire being relatively close. Another method used was to fire shrapnel shells set to burst just over the wire to attempt to cut it with the shrapnel balls ejected. None of these techniques worked well in action and they consumed vast quantities of shells and bombs in the process. Time after time advancing soldiers reported the supposedly well-cut wire to still be a major obstacle that had to be cut manually with wire cutters of varying descriptions. The eventual use of tanks to drag the wire away was probably the best method discovered in the war.

Trench constructed almost entirely with sand bags.

Berm

This was a small flat space left between the rising parapet and the drop of the forward trench wall. It helped stop the parapet collapsing into the trench and also served as a place to keep spare ammunition, etc.

Bombing Pit/Trench

A short sap, often from the command trench, ending in a small pit a few feet square. It was located within grenade-throwing distance of the front-line in order that our bombers could attack any enemy who had occupied our front-line. It was well stocked with grenades for that purpose in a reinforced bomb store.

Bomb Store

Besides those in bombing pits, supplies of grenades (bombs) were kept nearby in communication trenches for the use of raiding parties and specially trained bombers. More were stored at the front to repel boarders.

Breastworks

Similar to parapets but built up higher above ground to protect soldiers standing in a shallow trench that could not be dug deeper.

Communication Trenches

These were dug to link the various trench systems running parallel with the front-line. They enabled troops from rear areas to reinforce the front-line garrison without exposing themselves to enemy fire. To defend against enfilade fire and the effect of shells bursting in them they were usually zigzagged or undulating throughout their length. They were often congested and at times soldiers climbed out and proceeded on the surface. Whilst this practice was reasonably safe at night it was very dangerous during daylight hours. Communication trenches were also used to bring up rations and replacement battalions.

Duckboards

Joined slats of wood laid on the floor of trenches to keep the soldiers' feet out of the worst of the mud and water. Beneath them there was usually a channel cut to carry away water to a sump from where it could (sometimes) be pumped away.

Dugouts

There were several types of 'dugout' depending upon its purpose. As a general principle, the British did not construct substantial subterranean bunkers, as they considered that any shelters were purely for very temporary accommodation. After defeating the enemy they would no longer be required. That is the exact opposite philosophy to the Germans who planned to stay in situ and consequently built very strong and comparatively comfortable fortifications. Theirs were often equipped with electric light and furniture taken from nearby houses.

Officers' shelters were constructed underground so that they would have a place for administrative work and a centre for local communications. It was essential that protection be afforded from the weather and light artillery fire.

Most dugouts were of a similar construction. Often curved corrugated iron sheets, known as elephant iron, were used to form the basis of the shelter. The roof was next usually reinforced with logs, railway lines or other such material that might be found locally. It was then covered with earth and then rubble to burst incoming shells, followed by as much compacted earth as possible to give greater security and to disguise its existence from aerial observation. Great care was taken that buried telephone lines and approach routes radiating towards it did not betray its presence. The doorways (usually at least two) would be protected from gas ingress by heavy and wet curtains made from blankets, etc. These also served to stop any glimmer of light escaping.

Shelters were also constructed as aid posts and to disguise emplacements for weapons such as machine guns, mortars and artillery pieces. These varied enormously in design and many were simply pure camouflage whereas others were fairly deep. Few British shelters offered more than scant protection from a direct hit from anything heavier than medium shells.

Soldiers generally got by in the fire-trenches with little or no shelter. The front faces of trenches were sometimes excavated, to make a small recess that a man might squeeze into when not on duty. Care had to be taken that the hollowing out did not weaken the trench and cause a collapse that might bury the recumbent soldier. In general the practice was discouraged. Support and reserve lines back from the front and artillery positions, etc., were often equipped with deeper shelters for men off-duty to afford protection from shelling. Whatever form of dugout was constructed it was common practice to hang any uneaten food from the roof in sandbags to deter rats. Rodents were a constant menace for besides stealing food they feasted upon rotting corpses, both animal and human. Their droppings were everywhere and they were a major cause of the spread of diseases. Because of the plentiful supply of food they bred at prodigious rates and the size they grew to is the stuff of legends.

Enfilade

Trenches were designed to avoid, if at all possible, enfilade fire. The word comes the French 'enfiler', meaning to skewer. It is slightly complex but generally means fire directed along the longest axis of the target. It could be shots fired along the length of a trench from one end to the other; or along the length of a body of advancing soldiers; or raking fire against the flank of a column of men crossing in front. Because it offers such an opportunity to inflict maximum damage it is to be strictly avoided. Trenches were zigzagged to prevent more than a short length being vulnerable to enfilade fire.

Fire-Step

An earth shelf forming part of the wall of the trench, on the side facing the enemy, for the sentry to stand on at night and see out across No Man's Land. During daylight hours men sat or lay upon it to rest and thus not obstruct the narrow trench floor. If an enemy trench was taken over it had to be modified with a new fire-step cut into the opposite wall. For this purpose several soldiers carried rather large and heavy army spades and picks when attacking the enemy in battle. Even more were similarly equipped to create extra trenches in captured ground.

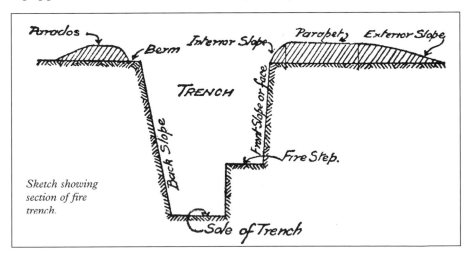

Sketch showing section of fire trench.

Front-Line

This was in two elements. The very front-line, which was called the fire-trench, could be continuous or made up of 'linked' shell holes or saps forming fire-bays. Where it was continuous, although never straight, the line was revetted for strength and often castellated to form traverses. A reserve of ammunition was readily available. Machine guns were usually strategically hidden there to be able to sweep the whole of No Man's Land. No shelters or overhead cover were permitted in the front-line.

The second element was the command or supervision trench. It was around thirty yards behind the fire-trench, and regularly linked to it. From there immediate help was available in the shape of additional concealed machine guns and bomb throwers sited in pits.

Keep

A strongpoint offering all-round defence and shelter to its garrison. Some parts of the front relied upon this method of accommodating troops rather than locating large bodies of men in the front-line. When necessary, the men streamed out along a web of communication trenches towards the front or other areas in need of reinforcement.

Latrines

One of the quickest ways to get infectious diseases was by contamination from untreated excreta. The British Army was very keen on trench hygiene. Latrines or field toilets were constructed to carefully considered designs at the end of short saps near to many of the lines. They were pits, often dug over five or six feet deep, and the faeces deposited were rapidly covered with a little earth, cresol solution or quicklime. Sometimes buckets, emptied each night, were used instead. A more biologically efficient type of latrine required that a short trench be dug to no more than one foot deep and filled as soon as possible. It may have been efficient but was more exposed and not greatly appreciated by men requiring a toilet close to enemy fire.

Each infantry company appointed two of its number to act as sanitary personnel who were excused normal duties in exchange for keeping the latrines in good condition and emptying urine buckets properly. The job of 'shit-wallah', as the sanitary men were affectionately known, was actually a sought-after appointment as it kept them away from the dangers of the front-lines for much of the time.

As for toilet paper – there was none. Some officers may have had a private supply but there was no official issue. Letters from home were never wasted but recycled! That is the reason why, whilst literally thousands of letters *from* soldiers to home survive in archives, there are almost none sent *to* soldiers abroad and subsequently brought back. As a veteran once said to me, 'we were country boys – maybe a tuft of grass; maybe nothing'. I doubt much grass was available in the trenches!

Loopholes

The parapets of traverses were periodically pierced obliquely at irregular intervals with loopholes gouged or built into them. These holes were disguised and camouflaged to avoid detection by the enemy. Their purpose was for observation, sighting of machine guns and sniping during the day. The observer was often partially protected from enemy sniper fire by bullet-proof (one centimetre thick) steel plates covering the gap. These plates, in turn, had a loophole in them that could be covered by a metal flap. It was vital also that the observer was shielded from behind so that no light came past him to be seen through the loophole. This would easily be seen from the enemy trenches and give away his location.

No Man's Land

The area between the opposing forces. It evolved rather than was planned and the distances between the two front-lines ranged from a few yards to half a mile or more in places. Sometimes it was so narrow that bombs could be thrown into opposing trenches and conversations easily overheard. It was frequently explored at night by each side's patrols seeking intelligence or enemy prisoners. The attitude of at least one senior officer, who maintained that there was no such thing as No Man's Land and that the front-line was the German wire, did not help. Whilst perhaps it was understandable, to keep up pressure on the enemy, it no doubt contributed considerably to the growing nightly casualty list in an attempt to fulfil that approach.

Parados

The build-up of earth above the rear of the trench was called the parados. Its purpose was twofold. It protected the trench from the blast of shells exploding at its rear. Additionally, it prevented soldiers on sentry duty standing on the fire-step from forming silhouettes against the skyline and thus presenting easy targets. In general terms the front-lines ran north–south. Each morning the sun rose behind the German lines and each evening it set behind the British lines. Each side therefore would have been exposed on the skyline in turn if a parados was not constructed.

Parapet
Earth was built up above the ground in front of the trench facing the enemy. It was called the parapet. It would be about one foot high and several feet broad before sloping towards the ground at around a 45-degree angle. The slope was designed to help deflect bullets and the blast of shells upward. The purpose of the parapet was to shield the sentry standing on his fire-step and generally add strength to the trench. For it to stop a bullet from a rifle or machine gun the parapet needed to be five feet thick if made from clay. Other soil types offered greater protection, especially if they were very stony or made from compacted sand. The height of the parapet depended largely upon the depth of the trench, which could vary considerably.

Periscopes
These were a vital trench tool used to see over the parapet during daylight hours and survive. Some were professionally manufactured whilst others were improvised by using pieces of salvaged mirror fixed in a wooded frame. Snipers shot at periscopes, as well as imprudent heads. Dummy periscopes were made so that the path of the bullet could be traced and perhaps the position of the sniper revealed.

Pill Boxes and Bunkers
These were strong steel-reinforced concrete constructions to supplement trench systems, especially where continuous lines were not possible. Their existence enabled fewer men to be employed guarding a section of front for they usually had great firepower from machine guns and were difficult and dangerous to neutralize.

Reserve Line
This was perhaps 500 yards behind the front and consisted of conventional trenches, linked redoubts or dugouts, holding reserve soldiers available to form a counter-attack if the front was over-run.

Reserve Trench System
These were successive lines of trenches similar in design to the front-line and linked to it and each other by communication trenches. There were often several lines of trenches some distance behind the front. They were not however so far apart that each line could not support its neighbour.

Sap

Usually a short cul-de-sac trench dug out from a main position – generally, but not always, from the front-line and into No Man's Land – for the purposes of observation and as a listening post. They were originally devised as a method of approaching a fortified position within the relative safety of a trench that was progressed towards the enemy. The man who dug saps was known as a 'sapper'.

A 'Russian sap' was similar to a sap but dug below ground level in the form of a shallow tunnel. When close enough for its purpose it would break through to the surface.

Shell Trench or Slit Trench

Short, narrow and deep trenches coming off communication trenches parallel to the front to afford protection during an artillery barrage. The men usually remained standing, with an NCO in charge, ready for action as soon as the shelling ceased.

Special Purpose Trenches

Telephone lines for general contact between the front and rear areas were laid in trenches and were often fixed to the trench walls. Unfortunately they were very exposed and easily broken by both enemy fire and careless soldiers. Important telephone lines were buried, often in triplicate, in 'trenches' six feet deep, which were then backfilled to bury and hopefully safeguard the lines. See Chapter 8 for more on this subject.

Strongpoints

See Keep.

Sump

A pit dug below duckboards to collect excessive rainwater so that it could be drained or pumped away.

Support Trenches

Similar in design and strength to the front-line trenches, to which they were linked by numerous communication trenches, to facilitate rapid reinforcement. They were sited around 100 yards behind the front and often incorporated some dugouts to offer shelter to soldiers during an artillery bombardment.

Traverse

A traverse was an integral part of the trench that gave it that castellated appearance when seen from above. They were designed to protect against enfilade fire sweeping the length of the trench and to minimize the blast damage from a shell exploding in it. They also gave protection and afforded some ability to recapture a section of trench that might be occupied by the enemy. For this reason loopholes were often cut into the sides of traverses. The distance between traverses ranged from 13 to 20 feet – centre to centre. The techniques for regaining a partially captured trench demanded that the distance must be close enough to throw a grenade into the next traverse but one.

Trench Block

Sometimes the same line of trench was occupied by both sides. This usually occurred during an attack. To stop infiltration along the trench it was blocked, by defender or attacker, with whatever was to hand. If there was a predictable risk of invasion preconstructed barriers of barbed wire in frames were set ready for rapid deployment. Often two blocks, several yards apart, were deployed for better defence.

Chapter 5

A SOLDIER'S LIFE: WHAT IT WAS LIKE

A Summary

Soldiers of the Great War suffered immense hardships with considerable fortitude and yet life was not intolerable all the time. They shared considerable 'black' humour. And the camaraderie was inescapable. It has often been said that men fought for the honour of their regiment. Whilst that is true, I suggest the soldiers' greatest loyalty was to their chums. One must also realize that they were certainly not in battle all or even most of the time. Anywhere in the fighting zones was risky but the most dangerous areas at the front were occupied in rotation. Life was a mixture of hard work, discomfort, boredom – and at times sheer terror. But there were many lighter moments when the soldiers, out of the line, were able to relax to a certain degree. There was always kit to be cleaned, heavy loads to be manhandled, trenches to be dug, rations carried to the front and many other hard jobs that required seemingly limitless manpower. And when all that was done route marches were devised to keep the men fit, occupied and out of mischief. But there was still some time left. Often this was occupied with sleeping. All soldiers quickly learn the knack of being able to sleep anywhere and at anytime – even if only for a very few minutes. Football matches were played. Improvised and infrequent baths were taken. Uniforms were disinfected in a vain attempt to kill the lice infesting them. When freed from duties remaining precious moments were often occupied reading those, so very important, letters from home and sharing with their mates the contents of parcels.

Gambling, in the form of the banned, but still practised, dice game of Crown & Anchor happened surreptitiously. Items that we now treasure in the shape of trench art were crafted. And millions of cigarettes were smoked. The war was not particularly discussed, for the average soldier knew little of what was happening, except in his current area. There was little point in talking about the dangers and discomforts, for his chums had exactly the same experiences. When he went home he did not discuss it there either for his folks could not really appreciate all he went through and the horrors he saw. Consequently the soldier of the Great War grew used to keeping his true feelings to himself. That is the main reason most veterans never really talked to others about the reality of war. They were generally happy to chat about the lighter moments – especially when humour was involved – but one really had to get to know them very well for the truth to gradually emerge about the darker moments. Post-traumatic stress disorder had not been recognized and counselling was non-existent. Soldiers either bottled up their feelings and coped with life or, in the worst cases, committed suicide. Some were eventually incarcerated in mental institutions, perhaps for the rest of their lives. The overall morale of the British forces was however very good, unlike the French and Russians in 1917 and the Germans in 1918.

Infantry and its Specialists

By far the greatest number of men served in the infantry. They were the foot soldiers and the backbone of the army. Their role was to fight the war by denying the enemy access to any more territory than he had already conquered and to seize that back at the first opportunity. In this, artillery, engineers, tanks, machine guns, supply units and other specialists assisted them. But none of these could fulfil the role of the infantry. It required armed men on the ground to take and hold on to territory.

Besides manning the trenches, whilst largely armed with rifles, the infantry gradually developed many other skills. Some became snipers; others light machine gunners. Many operated trench mortars or learnt the expertise of the bomber or grenadier. Their roles were far-reaching and vital. It was men of the infantry who dug most of the trenches and laboured for the tunnellers, road builders, etc. They conveyed their own messages, cooked their own food and buried their own dead. They were truly multi-functional.

There were many elements to life in the trenches and some are examined here.

Getting to the Front

As we have seen, soldiers of the Great War were largely pedestrians. British battalions, moving long distances on the Western Front, were sometimes loaded into French railway boxcars for expediency – although they did travel rather slowly. The carriage was hardly luxurious, being originally designed mainly for horse transport. Indeed the wagons were prominently labelled *Homme 40. Chevaux 8* (Men 40. Horses 8). For added comfort the bare wooden floors were thinly covered in straw. Upon reaching the railhead, they detrained and marched into action. The same principle applied to most armies. There are instances of German soldiers marching 1,000 kilometres in thirty days in 1914! In an attempt to avoid serious blistering of the feet men smeared them with wet soap. The hard pavé (cobbled) roads were especially punishing and most uncomfortable to march on. Many roads were unsurfaced and either very dusty or very muddy, depending upon the weather, after the tramp of many hundreds of boots.

At times of need, buses or lorries might be pressed into service, but that was a rare event. For those interested, a famously preserved London bus 'Ole Bill' can be seen in the Imperial War Museum.

The alternative transport to marching. A French boxcar designed to accommodate 40 soldiers or 8 horses.

Kit

When in action it was common for certain items such as the greatcoat to be left in the large pack with the transport. The downside was that additional ammunition, grenades and trench paraphernalia – such as picks, shovels, sandbags, duckboards, etc. more than made up for the weight of kit left behind. The soldier went into the line, in uniform, with a waterproof cape and such extra items of clothing as could be found to keep him warm. Steel helmets were worn in the fighting areas once they became plentiful in early 1916 and the respirator, once introduced, was always carried.

Besides their weapons to fight with, the British soldiers used over 10 million spades and 5 million pickaxes to dig up much of Northern France. To keep them fed and watered over 17 million mess tins and 12 million water bottles were issued. And to keep warm they were supplied with over 41 million blankets and 15 million ground sheets. Any losses of official kit had to be accounted for and, if it was judged the man had been careless, a stoppage of pay was made. Whilst in the trenches it was almost impossible to keep body and clothing clean. For obvious reasons weapons received the first priority when it came to cleaning. Once out of the line the kit was soon spruced up.

Battles and Trench Raids

Aggression was British policy and is typically illustrated by the Scots Guards history:

> A mere passive defence of these lines was never contemplated. The Germans were to be perpetually harassed, their men killed and their nerves kept on edge by local raids. To facilitate these, lanes were cut in the enemy's wire at intervals by the artillery, and once cut were kept open and unrepaired by regular artillery and machine-gun fire. Into which of these open sores and on what day or what hour, the poison might be injected in the form of a British raid, the Germans could never tell. (Petre et al., *Scots Guards in the Great War* (1925), p. 129)

By this aggressive stance it might appear that soldiers were always fighting. In reality there were far more periods of inaction than action. It is true there was hostility but it was not everywhere nor for every soldier. There were several 'quiet' sectors on the Western Front. And some units were more belligerent than others. The more successful divisions were sent into the fray more often than those judged inefficient, which is why some battalions saw more than their fair share of fighting.

Action was infinitely variable in its nature. It could be by day or night; in large formations or small patrols. Despite discarding certain items, the soldier usually carried over 46lbs of basic kit into action. To this was added extra ammunition and tools. He was truly a human packhorse expected to fight for his life on reaching his destination. No wonder men walked, rather than ran, into action. They had to climb from their own trench; traverse gaps cut in their own barbed wire; cross No Man's Land strewn with the detritus of war; hack through the enemy's forests of barbed wire and get into the enemy trench systems. All this time they were being shelled, shot at, bombed, burnt or gassed. The stench, crescendo and horrors of battle are indescribable. On arrival they then had to kill or be killed, using any means and any weapons available. Reality was often not as clear-cut as the battle plans, maps and orders envisaged and confusion often reigned. Direction was sometimes lost and Allied units occasionally fought and killed each other in error. And all this for perhaps as little as one shilling and one (old) pence war zone pay a day (less than 6 pence). He could however buy quite a lot with this and he had no real living costs, for the army provided his food, clothing and accommodation.

A veteran gave a most descriptive account of going into action:

> And over the top we'd go. As soon as you got over the top the fear left you; now it's terror. You don't look; you see. You don't hear; you listen. Your nose is filled with fumes and death. You taste the top of your mouth. Your weapon and you are one.

Artillery Formation

This method of deploying soldiers is often used but rarely explained. It evolved for use in offensives. The idea was that the men would not be bunched together in large formations and vulnerable to artillery or machine-gun fire. Essentially it was a number of small columns at varying intervals and distances scattered over the front across which the advance was to be made. The battalion would attack with two companies split across its front of around 400 yards. The other two companies were usually held in support or reserve. The leading companies were divided into half platoons of thirty men at most and arranged unevenly in depth, with perhaps 250 yards between the leading and supporting half platoon.

Rotation from Front to Rear

The amount of time spent in the trenches varied enormously and depended upon the part of the line occupied, the weather, the quality of the unit, the casualties sustained and whether or not relief was possible for one reason or other. In theory the average was about four days in the front-line, followed by another four days in close support. The men then went into reserve – not too far away. Often this was followed by a period in rear areas but sometimes the whole rotation process was repeated with more spells in the trenches. When relief was not possible, much longer periods could be spent at the front. Overall the average infantryman would have spent about half his life in one of the various trench lines – most often back from the front.

A division was assigned a section of the front ranging, on average, from 2,000 to 4,000 yards. Its time spent on duty varied enormously from a few weeks to over one year! It was frequently moved from one area to another. That did not mean however that the men were continuously in the front-line, for there were many to share those duties. The three brigades within a divisional front regularly exchanged from front-lines, to reserve lines, to the rear. Within each brigade of four battalions, two were at or near the front and two in reserve. The four companies of each battalion rotated between the front and support lines. Thus, at any one time, it could be that the actual front-line of the entire division was being held by two companies of less than 500 men. Naturally they could be rapidly reinforced by other units in close support and reserve.

When a new unit took over the line, great care was taken that the enemy should not realize it, otherwise extra shelling and perhaps trench raids might occur to catch them out. It was an ideal time, for the departing troops might relax their guard and the newcomers were not yet aware of all the pitfalls that awaited them. Noise was kept to a minimum and extra sentries were posted. Before the handover, reconnaissance parties consisting of officers and NCOs would examine the trenches and check on trench stores. Junior officers in particular had to keep detailed inventories of many items deposited at the front and report losses and ensure replacement equipment was ordered. The paperwork and questions about missing paraphernalia by brigade staff officers was legion and irksome.

Trench Life

This assumed a rather dull routine, assuming no excessive enemy activity.

It was a troglodyte existence with major activities always taking place at night. The ever-present sniper sought any target and anything appearing above, or in gaps, in the parapet could expect to be shot. Shortly before dawn each day 'Stand-To [your Arms]' was called and all men were ready for immediate action, with bayonets fixed, whilst the enemy lines were examined (by periscopes) for signs of aggression. Snipers crawled into their concealed positions ready for another day's 'bag'. After full daylight, and assuming all was quiet, the order 'Stand-Down' signalled the start of another supposedly normal day. Sentries were posted to peer through their periscopes and immediately sound the alarm if there was any enemy activity.

During daylight hours weapons were cleaned, meals eaten and, after clearing up as much as possible and passing various inspections, most tried to sleep anywhere they could. Breakfast was cooked and tea made in a small trench fireplace. Smoke was kept to a minimum for fear of attracting the attention of the enemy. However aggression was often kept to a minimum at this time of day, for both sides wanted their breakfast in peace and not blown apart. Washing and shaving, if attempted, was done with a little tea kept back for the purpose.

Whether asleep or awake men had to be fully dressed with their equipment on and rifles loaded and immediately to hand. Officers and NCOs regularly visited to ensure procedures and orders were followed. Sentries were posted to listen and watch for signs of enemy activity – including the approach of gas, for which a warning gong (often a hanging shell case) was available. Officers would censor the men's letters home and request any trench stores for delivery that night. Movement of any kind was kept to a minimum. Men wrote letters home, gambled and some made trench art. They also 'chatted' – that is, inspected their uniforms for lice. A candle flame was passed carefully along seams in clothing to expel the insects, which were then crushed between thumbnails. Unfortunately many of these creatures escaped detection to lay more eggs and start a new generation of irritation. Even freshly laundered uniforms quickly became reinfested with lice, which besides causing intense itching, sometimes started sores that easily infected in the unsanitary conditions of trench life. Flies too were a menace. With so much decaying matter in abundance they bred prolifically and contributed to the general unpleasantness. However, by far the most overwhelming condition to be endured in the trench was boredom.

Typical trench scene during daylight hours. Sentry on duty whilst chums sleep. Border Regt in front-line Thiepval Wood, Aug. 1916.

Before dusk 'Stand-To' was again called with similar precautions as at daybreak, before nocturnal activities commenced. Sentries in the fire-bays were posted but this time they stood on the fire-step with head and shoulders exposed above the parapet. A chum was immediately at hand to help if needed, whilst typically the third man in the bay rested. They exchanged tasks regularly. It would not have been possible to observe adequately at night with the periscopes available. By exposing the upper torso there was a chance at least that, if the parapet was swept by predetermined machine-gun fire, a hit might be to the shoulders (at parapet level) rather than in the head!

Nightly activities included: repairs of, or additions to, the wire or parapet; digging of new trenches or saps; reconnaissance or offensive expeditions into No Man's Land; ration parties to and from the rear; the burial of bodies in nearby cemeteries or convenient shell holes; emptying urine pails, digging, refilling or cleaning of latrines; evacuation of wounded; and exchange of front-line units. Padres, medical officers and senior officers made their visits and inspections to offer respectively: comfort, aid, unwanted advice and orders. They could offer little of value that an experienced NCO did not already know. Throughout the night there was much to be done and little time for rest or boredom.

Letters and Parcels

The Army Postal Service, part of the Royal Engineers, was extremely efficient and each day vast numbers of letters and parcels were delivered to and from the Front. Indeed it is estimated that the Home Depot of the service handled two billion letters and 114 million parcels. It was correctly judged that communication with friends and family at home greatly improved the morale of serving soldiers, sailors and airmen. Parcels often contained foodstuffs, such as homemade cakes, not available to the men in France. Other treasured items were warm items of clothing. Whereas letters addressed to a deceased soldier were returned, that did not apply to parcels, which were shared by his chums. Letters were censored for the men, whilst officers were privileged to 'censor' their own mail. Early in the war even place names on picture postcards were obliterated, although what that achieved is difficult to tell. Ordinary soldiers rarely knew anything of military significance and it was largely a pointless task for the junior officers involved. The infrequently distributed 'green envelope' was much sought after by soldiers, for letters enclosed in it were only subjected to censorship at the base and not locally. The owner, however, had to certify that the contents 'refer to nothing but private and family matters'.

For Christmas 1914 Princess Mary, the King's only daughter, organized a fund to supply comforts to everyone in the armed forces. It consisted of a brass box bearing her royal cipher, the names of several countries and the

Princess Mary tin with typical contents.

words 'Christmas 1914'. Besides a Christmas card and picture of the Princess it usually contained a combination of cigarettes and tobacco plus a tinder-lighter. Sometimes a pipe was sent as well. For non-smokers and Indian soldiers sweets, spices or writing material was provided. After consuming the contents many tins were sent home as souvenirs and are quite commonly found today.

Rations

Food was a very important part of a soldier's life. The British soldier was adequately if not extravagantly fed. At least he was most of the time, but there were many occasions in the line when it was not possible for food to be brought to him. To guard against this very real possibility two days rations were taken into the line at each changeover.

When possible hot food was provided from field cookers – a small cart that could prepare enough hot meals for 250 men. At least the food was hot once. But by the time it had been carried, maybe a mile or more, over rough ground at night, I suspect the stew or whatever was at best tepid. As an alternative, basic foodstuffs were often brought to the front-line during the night by ration parties. This would generally consist of loaves of bread, jam, cheese and bacon. It was usually carried to the front in sandbags. The food was not wrapped and in consequence the cheese and bacon was usually quite hairy from the sacking and the bread rather resembled the mud it was frequently dropped in en route. Soldiers were used to this and after grumbling – more about any delay in supply, rather than extra texturing to the food – proceeded to eat it. Improvisation was the order of the day. The bacon was cooked on tiny stoves fuelled by special solid pellets or charcoal, or candle wax or any wood or other fuel scrounged locally. For example, in 1916 around 100,000 Ayrton fans were supplied in the fond hope that by wafting them they could dispel approaching gas clouds. They were useless for the intended purpose but, as the handles were wooden, they provided much needed fuel! Corned beef and army biscuits were also available but not much relished. The canned beef was monotonous and the biscuits extremely hard. A slightly more palatable alternative was Maconachie's tinned ration of meat and vegetables, commonly called 'M and V'. The Ticklers jam supplied was most often made from plums and apples – both plentiful in besieged Britain.

Water carts with heavy galvanized mugs chained to them were located in

Field kitchen 1914.

strategic places in rear areas for thirsty soldiers to grab a quick drink as they passed by. Water for the front-line was usually carried up in former petrol tins. They were washed out prior to use as water carriers but nevertheless petrol had already seeped into the cans' seams and forever tainted the water. In addition to its unpleasant taste it could have a detrimental effect upon the bowels!

The prescribed daily ration initially was:

1¼lb (later reduced to 1lb) fresh meat or 1lb processed meat (corned or bully beef)

1¼lb bread or 1lb biscuit (army biscuits) or 1lb flour
4 oz bacon
3 oz cheese
2 oz peas or beans or dried potatoes
Small measures of jam, sugar, salt, mustard, pepper and lime juice
Up to 2oz tobacco and ½ gill (71ml) rum could be discretionally supplied

A brief comparison of just three items of field rations between British, German and American troops is rather interesting, if not surprising (see Table 4). Each number is the daily ration in ounces. Those at home and on lines of communication (except Americans) received less, especially meat and bread. They were the official figures. Frequently because of enemy action, or theft in the supply chain, the men at the front received far less than their full ration.

Table 4. Comparison of three items of field rations			
Item	**Britain**	**America**	**Germany**
Bread	16 oz	16 oz	26.4 oz
Meat	16 oz	20 oz	10.5 oz
Vegetables	10 oz	20 oz	18 oz
Calories per day	4,193	4,714	4,038

Many civilians received an average of not much more than 3,000 calories a day. That may sound good but one must remember that most were working long hours of hard manual labour. The composition of the food at home was filling but not particularly nutritious.

Weight Guide
16 oz (ounce) = 1lb (one pound)
1lb (pound) = .453 kilo or about ½ kilo.
Thus one kilo equals 2.2lbs and 1 ounce equals 28.34 grams.

Iron rations were defined in 1914 as consisting of: one pound of preserved meat (bully beef); three-quarters of a pound of (army) biscuit, approximately quarter pound cheese and half an ounce of tea, plus sugar, salt and meat extract (Bovril). The army biscuit was constructed to confound human teeth and only breakable by force; often an entrenching tool handle was used to knock pieces off. (Perhaps that is why they were called 'iron rations'!) Some were made by Huntley Palmer and endorsed 'Army No. 4'. Others were manufactured by the Delhi Biscuit Company. No doubt other contractors baked the unpalatable item as well. I understand the recipe for army biscuits is the same as that currently used by a well-known manufacturer of dog biscuits. An officer's permission was normally required before the iron rations could be consumed.

Pay

The men were paid in the local currency (French or Belgian francs on the Western Front) at irregular pay parades when out of the line. Indeed, the instructions stated that issues of pay 'will not be made more often than is necessary'. Soldiers had to formally and smartly queue up in front of an officer, salute, produce their pay book for it to be endorsed by the officer with the amount paid and then be dismissed in true military fashion. All payments made were recorded on the acquittance rolls, which had to be promptly forwarded to the regimental paymaster at the base. The paying officer was personally held responsible for any discrepancies. The exchange rate was about 28 French Francs to the British Pound throughout the war.

Battle Hardening

It really is amazing how quickly the men became accustomed to the most frightful sights, sounds and smells imaginable. The overpowering stench of death from unburied human and animal bodies surely pervaded the entire war zone. The noise of explosions not only shattered eardrums but rocked brains within their skulls, inflicting untold damage. And as for the sights of mangled bodies on an almost daily basis, it really does make one wonder how men coped and remained sane. It took just two weeks for the novice soldier to become so accustomed to death that he scarcely gave it another thought. Even the death of a best mate was seen as inevitable and to be avenged if possible, rather than mourned. There was so much carnage there was no time for pity. It is no wonder the men smoked so much. The only concern was availability (cigarettes were often supplied and additional ones were quite cheap – Woodbines 3d for twenty) and how to light them. Matches were hard to find and keep dry so lighters or tinder-lighters prevailed. The rum ration – if approved by the officer commanding, and not stolen en route – was eagerly awaited. The letters SRD stamped on rum jars officially stood for 'Special Ration Department', but the cynical soldiers soon dubbed the letters 'Seldom Reaches Destination'.

Despite the huge casualty lists few veterans ever admitted to deliberately killing enemy soldiers. Of course there are plentiful such accounts in literature but when critically examined, and the numbers totalled up, they really do not amount to very many deaths. This is partly because by far the greatest number of deaths occurred at a distance from the effects of shellfire. Most infantrymen fired their rifles in the general direction of the enemy at times but few, apart from snipers, took deliberate aim at a single man and then killed him. Machine gunners probably took the greatest toll with bullets, at the relatively short range of say 1,000 yards. But at that distance human features cannot really be recognized. Hand-to-hand fighting with bayonets, guns, coshes, etc., certainly occurred, however the resulting deaths were comparatively few compared to the overall carnage. There are nevertheless several accounts of aggression where retribution was the driving force. Men who had suffered at the hands of a particular unit or category of the enemy, such as a sniper, machine-gunner or mortar-man, showed little mercy if they encountered one. Surrender, if offered, was frequently refused and the unfortunate victim summarily despatched – usually by being run through with a bayonet.

As well as being hardened to the elements of battle, the other element soldiers had to endure was the weather. Their uniforms were not waterproof and were not adequately warm in the extremes of winters such as 1916/17. A rather smelly goatskin fleece or leather jerkin was issued for cold weather but it was scarcely adequate. Other garments were sent from home or improvised and at times the nationality of the soldier was difficult to determine from his garb. An issue cape was waterproof but only kept the worst off. Water still dripped down the neck. It also seeped through or over the leather boots. In summer the heat of the woollen uniform made it rather uncomfortable. The soldier of the Great War was certainly a tough individual.

Discipline

This was strictly enforced throughout the war and backed up by the severest penalties for transgressions. Whilst soldiers did not salute officers in the trenches there was no fraternization either. Once away from the front, the full pomp of military life resumed and differed little from that in barracks and parade squares back home. Altogether 304,262 officers and men appeared before a court martial during the war. When one considers that represents just over 3 per cent of the total mobilized from Britain and the Commonwealth, the discipline record of the army is extremely good. Not all those charged were found guilty of course. Whereas imprisonment, usually with hard labour, was an option for courts martial, it was more usual for fines to be imposed for minor offences and Field Punishments No. 1 or 2 for more serious matters. These involved, for No. 2, being physically restricted in shackles and, for No. 1, additionally chained uncomfortably to a fixed object, such as a wagon wheel, for two hours a day. This could continue for three out of every four days – maybe for between three weeks and three months. When not restricted the man was subjected to hard labour and loss of pay and privileges. In total 80,969 sentences to Field Punishment No. 1 or 2 were passed.

The most severe crimes were subject to the death penalty and this is discussed elsewhere. Officers were subject to the same discipline but it seems to have been applied less vigorously. Some 1,085 officers were dismissed from the Army. That is not altogether a soft option for they could then be conscripted as private soldiers.

Desertion

Despite the potentially severe punishments, including execution, that could be handed down there were 114,670 instances of desertion from the Army. Many rejoined; some deserted more than once; 266 paid the ultimate penalty. No doubt some got completely away to lead a secret life as a fugitive.

Billets

When away from the trenches, soldiers were housed in whatever accommodation could be found. Often barns and other farm buildings were commandeered (and paid for) by the Army and the men bedded down on straw if they were lucky. Occasionally better quarters were available. Officers generally found houses to requisition and sleep in. When away from the front the food improved considerably with the availability of the company cookers. More elaborate cleaning of the body, weapons, ammunition and kit was undertaken. A favourite place for soldiers' baths was the local brewery where old vats were commandeered. Water was heated (if they were lucky) and as many men as possible piled in at once. Despite the gradual solidification of the water, the grubby soldiers genuinely relished the opportunity to bathe. Whilst they were naked, sometimes to the glee of the local girls, their uniforms were disinfected and fresh underclothes were issued – very often of a totally different size to the ones removed. And finally, when all this was done, new tasks were found to keep the soldier busy.

Estaminets

These were usually small cafes or bars in rear areas still being run by local French and Belgian families. The usual bill of fare was coffee, cheap beer or the famous 'van blank' (*vin blanc*). The most popular food seems to have been 'oof and frits' (*œuf et frites* – egg and chips). And occasionally the proprietor's daughter became very friendly with visiting soldiers. Whenever possible off-duty soldiers tried to get to the nearest estaminet for some light relief.

Writing paper, cigarettes, tobacco, chocolate and other sundries were often purchased from huts run by organizations such as the Salvation Army, YMCA and similar bodies.

Religious Services and Padres

Services were held if possible in rear areas away from the fighting by Church of England, Roman Catholic, Jewish, Presbyterian, Baptist, Methodist and other ministers of religious faiths. Drumhead services were sometimes held on the eve of battle close to the front. Chaplains to the forces, within the Royal Army Chaplain's Department, were appointed in various classes from I to IV, which ranked from colonel to captain. They visited sick and wounded soldiers and conducted burial services if possible. Many visited the soldiers in the trenches, although soldiers usually complained that chaplains rarely if ever came to dangerous areas. That does not quite tally with the fact that three were awarded the Victoria Cross and 163 died, or were killed, in the course of their ministry during the Great War.

Prisoners of War

Aside from the very real risk of being killed or wounded there was a possibility of being captured by the enemy and made a prisoner for the duration of the war. It was often difficult to surrender alive but once the surrender had been recognized most prisoners were well treated. Many were malnourished but that was mainly because of the scarcity of food in Germany. Some severely wounded men were repatriated home via the Red Cross in Switzerland, but for the others the length of their confinement was unknown. Officers were required, upon repatriation, to justify their capture. In total some 6,949 British officers and 166,626 other ranks (this includes officers and men from the Royal Navy) were reported as having been prisoners of war or interned in neutral countries. Altogether 196,318 Commonwealth officers and men were captured and of these 16,402 died in captivity.

Leaving the Army – Honourably and Alive!

Although men in Kitchener's Armies were technically regular soldiers, their duration of service was effectively for the duration of the war. Because of the requirements of the Army of Occupation of the Rhine, regarrisoning the Empire with regular soldiers and fighting in Russia, etc., some men were retained. Additionally it was not possible for literally millions of men to leave simultaneously. Some men had already left to return to vital war work. Those with jobs waiting got some priority and there was a programme of release for the others. It was not however perceived as entirely fair and a certain amount of unrest occurred from soldiers awaiting release long after the end of the war. Regular soldiers naturally remained in the army. Territorial Force men, once released from active service, resumed their civilian roles, interspersed with military training and camps.

Various procedures, including the following, were carried out at Dispersal Stations:

- A medical examination recorded any injuries that might result in compensation.
- An inventory of equipment was taken. Deficiencies usually had to be paid for.
- Any remaining foreign currency was exchanged for sterling.
- Final pay and war gratuity was calculated and eventually paid.

Many Army Forms (AF) were completed, and some given to the soldier. Only a few can be described here.

• AF Z.11 was a protection certificate: a form identifying the soldier, authorizing an advance of £2 against monies due, and providing for more pay in instalments whilst on the 28 days furlough (leave).
• AF B.108E was a character certificate and vital for his next employment: with so many men looking for work, employers could afford to be choosy. It also certified the length of service in the Army.
• AF Z.21, perhaps the most important form, was the one that authorized his immediate future on leaving the Army.

There were four categories of release.

• Discharge (final release from the Army)
• Transfer to various classes of reserve.
• Disembodiment: the terminology used when a member of the Territorial Force is released from full-time active service.
• Demobilization: date physically left the army, but not necessarily without conditions, such as reserve service.

It also gave some medal entitlement details and of where to rejoin if recalled. Reserve classes were:

Classes P, T and W	Authority to leave the forces and return to civilian duties. It mostly applied to vital war work. Each class varies slightly in the conditions attached to the soldier's release.
Class Z	The most common. Most soldiers were not finally discharged at the end of 1918 but transferred to Class Z Reserve. This was in case Germany rejected the peace conditions and resumed hostilities. By March 1920 most men were finally released from the army.

Some received slips certifying such matters as that they were 'free from vermin, scabies and venereal disease'; and 'that clothing, boots etc are in a clean and serviceable condition'. The soldier could keep his steel helmet, boots and uniform but was not supposed to wear it with any badges or insignia after twenty-eight days. His greatcoat could be kept or exchanged for one pound. He was additionally given a ration book, an unemployment insurance policy, a railway warrant for travel home and civilian clothing.

Sailors who were killed or died in service were recorded as 'discharged dead'.

Chapter 6

WEAPONS OF WAR

Introduction

All 'guns', using the word generically, and no matter whether pistol, rifle, machine gun, mortar or artillery piece, have similar methods of operation and fulfil similar roles to a greater or lesser degree. Each normally uses a chemical propellant, effectively a relatively slow-burning explosive, to drive a projectile towards its target.

18-pounder field gun in action

Originally, guns fired mostly spherical objects through a smooth-bored barrel. The accuracy was greatly enhanced by rifling – a series of spiral groves cut into the inside (the bore) of a gun barrel – which caused the bullet or shell to spin. The gyroscopic effect created improved range and accuracy considerably, as the projectile remained point first and thus streamlined. Many rifling groves have a right-hand twist but the British SMLE rifles and Vickers machine guns, along with some French weapons, have a left-hand twist. This can easily be seen impressed on fired bullets. The copper (driving) bands on fired artillery shells will be seen to have been scored by the rifling as well. If a bullet or shell does not bear indications of rifling then it probably has never been fired. If the driving band on a shell has been removed, then it is often difficult to tell whether or not it has been fired.

In this section a brief description of the most important guns and types of guns will give an idea of the basic operation of the many hundreds of variations employed by the belligerent nations.

All small arms, machine guns and the lighter artillery pieces use a self-contained 'round of ammunition'. This usually consists of a brass (or alternative material) cartridge case, containing in its base a primer that, on being struck by a firing pin, explodes and sends a jet of flame into the cartridge case. Inside the cartridge case is a compound of propellant such as cordite or nitrocellulose that is lit by the primer. Pressure builds up and forces the bullet or shell out of the neck of the case into the barrel of the gun and onwards towards its target. The bullet or shell may be solid or may contain various materials depending on the space available and its purpose. The round of ammunition is initially placed, ready for firing, into the base or 'breech' of the barrel. That is a slightly wider and stronger area built to contain the complete cartridge case. In small arms the term used is 'chamber'.

The term 'small arms' applies to the weapons usually carried by a soldier, such as a pistol, rifle or light machine gun. They were cleaned regularly to try to ensure they would fire when required. Oil was kept in a small brass tube in a hollow in the butt of the rifle along with a cord, weighted at one end and known as a 'pull-through'. A small piece of flannelette, measuring four by two inches, was inserted in a loop in the cord, lubricated with oil, and pulled through the bore of the gun to remove fouling that could cause rust. The flannelette was supplied in rolls and strips torn off it as required. During the war enough length of flannelette was supplied to more than circle the earth at the equator. There are numerous excellent specialist books detailing specific guns, from pistols to the largest artillery pieces, which may be consulted if required.

Rifles and Bayonets

The rifle was the personal weapon, and most important piece of kit, of most soldiers in the First World War. It was cherished or hated but nevertheless cleaned and inspected regularly. Many different rifles or pattern of rifles were in use by the belligerent nations throughout the 1914–18 war. Shorter rifles, some intended for use by the cavalry, were called carbines. Here we only briefly consider two of the most famous rifles.

British Rifle

The standard service rifle of the Great War was the Short, Magazine, Lee-Enfield or 'SMLE' as it was known. The name came about because the rifle was shorter than earlier versions and it had a magazine for cartridges; James Lee invented the rear-locking bolt system; and it was initially made at the Royal Small Arms Factory at Enfield, Middlesex. Later, several wartime contractors, both at home and abroad, manufactured it. Various marks of the rifle evolved but the most common during the Great War were the Mark III and Mark III* which simplified the earlier version. The weight of the SMLE was 8lbs 10oz (4kg), unloaded and without a bayonet.

The rifle's magazine held ten cartridges, otherwise known as 'rounds'. They were loaded into it from above, using disposable clips which each held five cartridges. The rifle used a bolt-action system. To shoot, each round had to be fed into the part of the barrel, known as the chamber, by using the bolt. It was opened and closed in a somewhat similar fashion to a common door bolt. As the bolt was lifted, thus unlocking it and then pulled to the rear, any previously fired cartridge was ejected. Simultaneously a fresh cartridge was pushed up by a spring from the magazine beneath it. The bolt was then pushed forward, feeding that cartridge into the chamber. Finally, and before the rifle could be fired, the bolt was pushed down to lock it safely into place. The rifle was aimed and its trigger squeezed. After each shot was fired the above procedure had to be repeated. The pre-war British infantry soldier was trained to fire his rifle at the rate of fifteen accurate shots per minute. This endeavour entailed reloading the magazine that only held ten rounds. Such a sustained high rate of rifle fire gave rise to the German belief that we had far more machine guns than was the case in the early days of the war. Unfortunately the high standard of marksmanship was unable to be maintained during accelerated wartime training. An average of perhaps eight rounds per minute for rapid fire would be more realistic.

The standard British rifle cartridge of the time was of .303 calibre and had evolved into the Mark VII. The 174-grain spitzer (i.e. pointed, as opposed to round-nosed) bullet had a muzzle velocity of 2,440ft/sec. that delivered 2,408ft/lb energy at the muzzle. For its time it was a highly efficient cartridge in all aspects. And, according to Ordnance Committee calculations, should the rifle be elevated to nearly 35 degrees, the bullet was theoretically capable of travelling 4,457 yards (4,075m) before it would fall to the ground some 31 seconds later. They said that, even at that distance, it would be travelling at 416ft/sec and capable of inflicting serious injury. In fact it took just one second to travel the first 600 yards (548m) – the velocity decaying rapidly the further it travelled. For practical purposes 1,000 yards was considered its reasonable maximum range, although in reality most aimed shots were at considerably less distance than that. After all, if one cannot see the target one can hardly be expected to hit it! That said, the SMLE was sighted to 2,000 yards and the Vickers machine gun to 2,900 yards, so very long-range shooting had at least been contemplated when these weapons were designed. Hundreds of millions of rounds were fired during the war but we still had over 325 million .303 cartridges left by November 1918.

Incendiary ammunition was developed for use against Zeppelins and other specialist ammunition was introduced to fill particular requirements.

British Bayonet
The SMLE accepts a sword bayonet Pattern 1907 that has a blade length of seventeen inches, wooden grips and weighs, with scabbard, over one and a half pounds (750g). It was attached to a circular protuberance just below the muzzle of the rifle and clipped into place on a lug beneath the barrel. The scabbard in particular was simplified to meet wartime production quotas and the bayonet itself was soon made without an upturned hook to its quillon (cross-guard) that was regarded as unnecessary.

German Rifle
The standard rifle of the Great War was the Mauser Gewehr (rifle) 98. It had a calibre of 7.92mm and overall its operation, size and performance was roughly similar to the British SMLE. It did however have two major

differences. The bolt design, and especially the method of locking it, gave the rifle greater strength and accuracy. The drawback was that its rate of fire and reloading was far slower than the SMLE. Additionally, the magazine of the Mauser G.98 held only five rounds. It was however an extremely good rifle and served not only the German Army but also many others throughout the world.

German Bayonet

The G.98 accepted many different bayonets, some of which were Ersatz models, made wholly from steel to economize on other materials and simplify production. The most famous German bayonet was by far the so-called 'butcher's knife', for that is what it closely resembled. Here again there were several variations but the one that caused most concern and adverse propaganda was the saw-backed version. It was portrayed as barbaric but in reality was used as a dual-purpose item by pioneers and artillerymen. The saw back was intended for cutting wood and not to inflict a jagged wound – although it could no doubt do so if thrust in too deeply.

Pistols

The pistol or handgun was initially almost a badge of office for officers and very few others carried one. Officers had to purchase their own pistol, which could be any make or model but had to accept government ammunition of .455 calibre. Most initially chose the Webley Mk IV revolver but the Webley Mk VI revolver, slowly introduced from mid-1915, gradually became the firm favourite. It held six rounds and, with practice, was capable of accurate shooting to fifty yards or more. Later it was issued to other ranks, at government expense, where deemed necessary – for example, to machine gunners, despatch riders, tank crews, etc., where a rifle would have been unnecessarily cumbersome.

The popular German pistol, seen in films and indeed used extensively throughout the war, was the P'08 Luger in 9mm (parabellum) calibre. That is essentially the same cartridge still used throughout the world in hundreds of different firearms. The P'08 Luger is a semi-automatic pistol holding eight rounds in a detachable magazine that fits inside the grips (handle). As each shot was fired, the empty case was automatically ejected and a fresh round loaded ready to be fired next time the trigger was depressed. The magazine was removed to reload, or it could be replaced by a spare magazine that was already filled. This enabled a faster rate of fire than a revolver that had to be opened by the shooter and the fired cases manually ejected before fresh cartridges were inserted, then the weapon had to be closed ready to resume firing.

Machine Guns

Unlike a rifle or pistol, a machine gun is a firearm capable of continuous fire for as long as the trigger is depressed and the ammunition supply remains available – subject to mechanical failure. Britain and Germany used similar medium machine guns, both based upon the original design of Sir Hiram Maxim, but modified to suit requirements. The two guns performed in a very comparable way. The British version was the Vickers Machine Gun Mk 1 in .303 calibre. When complete, with its essential water for cooling, it weighed over 40lbs. The necessary tripod weighed an additional 52lbs. In total, but without ammunition, 92lbs (42kg) – not easily portable! Medium machine guns were usually sited in very well concealed positions slightly back from, or actually at, the front.

The German gun was the MG '08 in 7.92mm calibre and was usually mounted on a sledge rather than a tripod. Altogether it weighed 137lbs

Vickers machine gun being fired during a gas attack on 2 May 1915 by John Lynn VC, DCM. He died the same day from gas poisoning.

(62kg). Both countries' guns fired at the rate of around 400–500 rounds per minute with the ammunition contained in fabric belts that each held 250 rounds. A team member fed the belts of ammunition into the gun. They were heavy (a box of 250 rounds and belt weighed 22lbs) and did not last long on continuous fire. Most often the guns were fired in short bursts of a few rounds to conserve ammunition stocks and avoid the gun overheating. Instances of 10,000 rounds per hour, sustained fire, are however well documented. In 1915 a lighter version of the German MG '08 was introduced for certain tasks.

The .303 Lewis Machine Gun was introduced into British service in 1915. Of American design, this 'lightweight' gun, at 28lbs (13kg), revolutionized warfare. For the first time it was possible for a single infantryman to carry into action a fully automatic weapon. It was air-cooled, fired at a rate of up to 550 rounds per minute and used a circular magazine holding 47 rounds of ammunition. A full magazine would only last five seconds on continuous fire but firing in short bursts was always more efficient. Naturally the machine gunner had assistants carrying spare magazines of ammunition, but it was no longer necessary to have a large support team for every machine gun. A stripped-down version was made for use in aircraft and the magazine for that held 97 rounds.

Hand Grenades

The use of hand grenades or 'bombs' was well known prior to the First World War. Indeed the Grenadier Guards history dates back to 1656. As the name implies, grenadiers originally specialized in throwing bombs at the enemy. It was not however until the Great War that 'safe' yet easily ignited bombs were developed. And the throwers were by then usually referred to as 'bombers'. Germany started the war better equipped with safer and more reliable bombs than the British. Indeed in the early months of the war, British engineers and troops frequently improvised grenades as existing manufactured stocks became exhausted. Some, known as 'jam-tin bombs', were simply old tins refilled with explosives and scrap iron, then fused ready to be lit and thrown when the opportunity presented itself. Despite many millions of grenades being thrown, the residual British stock in France at the Armistice was over seven million.

Although a multitude of grenades appeared between 1914 and 1918 I will only consider here the two most commonly encountered: one British and one German, and both coming into use in 1915. From very small stockpiles in 1914 all belligerents manufactured very many millions of grenades during the next four years. It became one of the most effective offensive infantry weapons of the war.

British: The Mills Bomb

Introduced as the No. 5 Mk I, it was an egg-shaped device made from thick, segmented cast iron that shattered into fragments when it exploded. The base was sealed with a screw plug that was opened to insert the detonator. The top was shaped to accommodate a striker lever and retaining split pin. It weighed nearly one and a half pounds when filled with explosives and was just under four inches in length. A well-trained man could accurately pitch a Mills Bomb about thirty-five yards. To operate, the bomb was grasped firmly, so as to restrain the striker safety lever, whilst the safety pin was withdrawn. All the time the lever was held against the body of the bomb it would not explode. When thrown (or more properly pitched, rather like a cricket ball) a powerful spring would cause the lever to fly off and simultaneously propel the internal striker into a cap thus starting a timed safety fuse of usually five seconds. When the fuse burned into the main detonator it would explode the bomb. A specialized bomber would carry, in addition to his rifle and other equipment, eighteen Mills bombs in a canvas bucket.

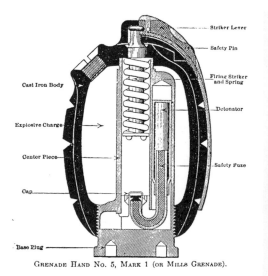

GRENADE HAND No. 5, MARK 1 (OR MILLS GRENADE).

Section of Mills bomb showing components.

Hand grenade No. 5 Mk 1 (Mills bomb). Terry Whippy Collection.

German: The Stick Grenade

Evolved from the 1915 model, the 1917 version is the one most frequently portrayed in books and films. At nearly double the weight and over three times the length of a British Mills Bomb the German stick grenade was more cumbersome but its very length permitted it to be thrown further than the Mills. The four-inch long cylindrical body of the grenade had a hollow wooden handle screwed to its base. Its popular name of 'potato masher' accurately described the weapon that, with its thin sheet steel body, relied upon explosive force rather than fragmentation for effect. To use, a screw cap was removed from the bottom of the hollow handle thus releasing a ceramic pull ring with a thin cord attached. The other end of the cord was attached to a friction ignition system that, upon pulling, started a time fuse of about six seconds. There was no going back – once the fuse was activated the bomb had to be thrown. Other versions were introduced that automatically 'lit' upon being thrown.

German stick genade. Terry Whippy Collection.

Like most other munitions of war there are many variations of grenades. Their exact measurements, methods of fusing and use differed considerably but the basic principles remained. Each was a small explosive bomb that could be carried relatively safely by a soldier until required. It was then activated and lobbed towards the enemy with varying degrees of success. Some grenades were designed or modified to be fired using rifles or other launchers in order to achieve a greater range. Those interested should refer to specialist publications for precise information.

Artillery

The responsibility of the Royal Artillery in the First World War is discussed in Chapter 8. Here, we are only concerned with the weapons and their projectiles. All artillery pieces fired a projectile, at high speed and with considerable accuracy over a relatively long range. That range far exceeded the capabilities of any small arms, machine guns or mortars. The projectile was a canister capable of containing different contents, the use of which depended upon the job the projectile, normally a shell, was required to do.

The guns themselves, besides differing considerably in size, portability and method of loading, were divided into two main groups. There were guns and there were howitzers. Both guns and howitzers could be large or small. The difference was their design and purpose. The smaller guns were called field guns. A gun was intended for direct fire. That is, the target, even if a long way away, was preferably visible to the gunner or forward observation officer. A howitzer, using variable propellant charges, was intended to fire at a high angle, over an obstacle obscuring the view of the gunner. It will be appreciated there was considerable crossover of use. The above definitions were, in reality, largely theoretical. Often a faraway target had to be fired at by prediction rather than direct observation. Howitzers, when fired at a much lower angle than their maximum capability, behaved in a similar way to guns.

The way the main part of each gun or howitzer (i.e. barrel and breech) was supported varied in two main ways. It could be on wheels or a fixed mounting. Some were so heavy they had to be dismantled to transport over even short distances. After firing a certain number of rounds, the barrel of an artillery piece suffered considerably from erosion and corrosion. It began to wear out. Each shot produced considerable friction between the driving bands of the shell and the rifled barrel. If it and other parts were not replaced regularly, accuracy suffered considerably.

Guns are classified according to their size. The 18-pounder field gun was so named because the shell it fired weighed (notionally) 18lbs. The 9.2" howitzer conversely was so named because that was the diameter of its shell. Great War artillery ranged from 1-pounder, where the shell weighed one pound, to the huge 15" howitzer firing a shell weighing over half a ton. Some German and Austrian shells were far larger still. Despite huge losses of artillery pieces by the war's end, there remained 7,578 British guns and howitzers in France and Belgium, plus nearly sixteen million shells.

The shells for the field guns of the Royal Horse and Royal Field Artillery were self-contained – that is, the propellant charge was contained in a shell case that also held in its neck the projectile (shell). It looked rather like a very large rifle cartridge. The advantage of this system is that the entire round of ammunition was loaded as one unit into the gun. It was fired and the empty case subsequently ejected. With a heavier shell it was not practical to use this method. The shell was first loaded into the breech of the gun and then the propellant, in combustible bags, was inserted behind it.

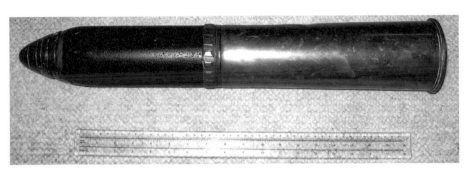

Assembled 18-pounder shell.

After the gun had fired there was no empty case to eject. Each system, together with the finer points of the guns and ammunition, had advantages and disadvantages, the technical details of which are the subject of specialist publications.

Shells came in two main groupings: high explosive and carrier shells. High explosive shells were used against most targets once trench warfare was established. Depending upon their size and fusing they were capable of damaging or destroying trenches and fortifications. Casualties were caused by the blast effect of the high explosives, collapsing trenches, etc. or simply by

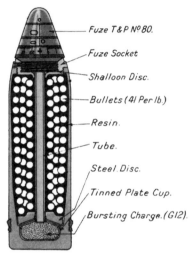

Fuze T&P Nº 80.
Fuze Socket
Shalloon Disc.
Bullets (41 Per lb.)
Resin.
Tube.
Steel Disc.
Tinned Plate Cup.
Bursting Charge. (G12).

18-pounder shrapnel shell, sectioned to show workings.

being struck by high velocity jagged pieces of shattered shell casing (not to be confused with shrapnel). High explosive rounds were usually fitted with a fuse that detonated the shell on impact.

The carrier shells could contain many things. In the early months of the war it was invariably shrapnel. Shrapnel is strictly small balls of lead blown from a special shell, after a time interval, whilst the shell is still in the air. They were designed originally to burst over the heads of troops in the open. Later they were used to cut barbed wire with varying degrees of success. The shrapnel balls (often called 'shrapnel bullets') were typically one half-inch diameter, although some were much larger. The 18-pounder shell held 375 such shrapnel balls. Larger calibre shrapnel shells naturally held considerably more balls. Other fillings for carrier shells included incendiary compounds, smoke, illuminating materials and irritant or poison gas. Carrier shells were usually fitted with fuses that caused the shell to discharge its contents after a time interval. The fuse was set to activate the shell by deciding the distance to the target and then calculating the time it would take to go that far.

Table 5. Some of the British Artillery Pieces of the War		
Equipment and its weight	Shell weight	Maximum range
18-pdr (Mk 1) 1.25 tons	18lbs	6,525 yards
4.5" howitzer 1.45 tons	35lbs	7,300 yards
4.7" field gun 3.75 tons	45lbs	10,000 yards
60-pdr (Mk 1) 4.5 tons	60lbs	12,300 yards
6" (26cwt) howitzer 3.63 tons	100lbs	11,400 yards
6" (Mk 19) field gun 10.2 tons	100lbs	18,750 yards
9.2" (Mk 1) howitzer 13.3 tons*	290lbs	10,060 yards
14" rail gun (Mk 3) 248 tons	1,400lbs	34,600 yards
15" howitzer 10.7 tons	1,400lbs	10,795 yards

* A ballast box filled with 9 tons of earth was also required for this howitzer.

Because most shells were supersonic at the muzzle of the gun (speed of sound notionally 1130ft/sec (344m/sec) at sea level), it was common for close-range shots to arrive before the report of the gun that fired them. British soldiers gave the name 'whiz-bang' to this type of German shell. The names 'coal-box' or 'Jack Johnson's' (the latter after a famous American boxer) were attributed to German heavy shells giving off clouds of dense black smoke when bursting.

Mortars

One of the main differences between a gun and a mortar is the cost and simplicity of production of the latter. Fulfilling a similar role to a howitzer, the mortar was designed to 'lob' an explosive projectile over a relatively short range but in a high arc or trajectory so as to clear intervening obstacles. They are primarily muzzle-loading weapons and, in smaller calibres, relatively light and portable. Many, but not all mortars were smooth-bored, again for simplicity. Being relatively small many mortars could be concealed in and fired from trenches whereas this would have been all but impossible for an artillery piece.

In the conditions of the Western Front the mortar was an ideal weapon. Generally the opposing trenches were less than 800 yards apart – most far less than that. With the high arc of the bomb it descended almost vertically and in consequence it was possible to lob a mortar bomb directly into an enemy trench. As long range was not required, the mortar bomb was propelled by a relatively small charge that developed low pressures. In consequence very strong and heavy barrels were not necessary, which all added to the portability of the mortar. With a much smaller propellant charge the pressures on the bomb were also less than on a shell fired by a gun or howitzer. Again, because of this, it was possible to reduce the amount of protective steel surrounding the high explosive bursting charge in the bomb. Overall the ratio of charge to total weight was extremely efficient at up to 40 per cent, as opposed to around 12 per cent, or sometimes much less, explosive in a typical shell fired from an artillery gun or howitzer.

Mortars were much feared by soldiers because of the devastation they caused. However, because of their operation – low velocity and high angle of fire – experienced troops learnt to listen out for the distinctive 'plop' of their being fired. They then scoured the skies for sight of the mortar bomb coming their way and rapidly took evasive action! Infantry soldiers not only disliked enemy mortars, they were not too impressed by our own mortar companies which had a habit of turning up in a trench unannounced, firing off a few bombs and then retreating rapidly from whence they came. The enemy was soon able to calculate the area the assault originated and retaliate in kind, leaving the poor infantry to reap the whirlwind occasioned by the mortar teams.

At the beginning of the war the German (and Austro-Hungarian) Armies had a variety of huge mortars (known in Germany as *Minenwerfer* – literally 'mine-launcher'). The enormous 42cm Mörser, along with the 25cm model and others, was used to destroy the forts in Liège, Namur and Mauberge. Later on came many more designs, notably the light 7.58cm model. All these weapons were highly efficient and yet the French and British really had next

German Minenwerfer *in the act of firing.* Julian Sykes archives.

to nothing to counter them to start with. Even large catapults were tried in desperation.

Experiments with French museum exhibits, relics from earlier conflicts, convinced the British that mortars had a lot to offer. Two models evolved in 1915 after many failed or inefficient prototypes. Officially named Bomb HE 2" Trench Mortar, our first example was a spherical bomb mounted on a two inch steel tubular stave. It was affectionately called either a 'plum pudding' or a 'toffee-apple' by the troops. The bomb weighed altogether 60lbs (27kg) of which 10lbs was the weight of the two inch stave which occasionally, rather alarmingly, came straight back towards the firer! A plum pudding was capable of being fired 500 yards. The large explosive charge of 20lbs of ammonal, lyddite or amatol was quite effective in destroying wire entanglements if the bomb exploded in the correct place. There were however teething problems. The early bombs, with a slow-to-react fuse created a large crater, which gave a false sense of security. It often appeared from a distance that the wire had been cleared when in fact it was hidden, perhaps under water, in the crater. This problem was solved by the introduction of a fuse (no. 107) that detonated the bomb instantaneously, shattered the wire into fragments and formed little or no crater. One of the drawbacks to this weapon was its weight. The bombs were not exactly light at 60lbs, including the stave, and the mortar itself weighed in at 285lbs (130kg), which did not lend itself to rapid portability.

The other stalwart British mortar was the three-inch Stokes. Weighing almost 10lbs (4.5kg) that bomb could travel nearly 1,200 yards (1,100m). It was initially fitted with a modified grenade fuse before an 'always' impact fuse was developed. (It would explode the bomb no matter which way up it landed.) The mortar, from which it was fired, was very simple and reasonably portable, consisting of a metal tube on a base-plate supported by a bi-pod mount. Sights were added for aiming purposes. Bombs could be fired rapidly by simply dropping each one, base first, down the barrel after removing the safety pin. On reaching the bottom of the barrel a striker automatically fired a propellant charge contained within the bomb. Because of its simplicity a rate of fire of twenty-two bombs per minute has been known, with often seven or more being in the air at once from the same mortar!

After initial confusion as to who exactly was responsible for these new weapons a system evolved whereby Infantry Brigades were in charge of light mortars such as the Stokes, and Division Artillery took charge of the heavier equipment. Dedicated trench mortar officers were appointed and personnel had their own identifying badge.

Landmines

Landmines must not be confused with large charges placed at the end of tunnels dug under enemy positions and detonated by the minelayer at a time of his choosing. There is a separate section on that subject in Chapter 8.

A landmine is triggered, usually unintentionally, by its victim. The modern concept of a landmine or anti-tank mine is a device designed and manufactured to be hidden and detonate when trodden on or run over. It is far removed from those deployed in the Great War. Those mines were generally improvised from surplus shells or mortar bombs rather than being purpose-built.

Many buildings and apparently abandoned equipment were referred to as 'mined' (but more properly 'booby-trapped') by retreating German forces using rigged grenades or demolition charges with rather sophisticated fuses. Sometimes those mines exploded after a time delay, occasionally as long as three days, but more often unwary soldiers fell foul of the devices.

Explosives

During the First World War vast quantities of different explosives were used for a multitude of purposes, ranging from the propellants in small-arms cartridges, to the bursting charges of the millions of shells and bombs.

There were further specialized explosives employed by engineers in cutting railway lines or blowing up bridges for their retreating armies. The signal rockets and flares used by the million were a form of explosives. So, too, were the enormous underground mines detonated with such dramatic effect.

Most explosives are substances that undergo violent decomposition accompanied by the formation of large quantities of heat-expanded gas and sudden high pressures. For military purposes, an explosive must be capable of retaining its original stable form until it is required to be detonated – an explosive is by its very nature unstable. The degree of instability has to be precise otherwise it would either be a danger to transport and use or would fail to 'go off' when required.

The many explosives available either detonate or burn at varying rates and each has specific physical characteristics and purpose. Gunpowder, an old general-purpose 'low' explosive, will decompose or burn at around 1,200ft/sec (365m/sec.); whereas for example, TNT, a 'high' explosive will similarly 'decompose' (detonate) at 22,800ft/sec (6,850m/sec) or, to put it another way, at over 4¼ miles per second. Just a slight difference!

For mining purposes the requirement is for an explosive with great lifting potential rather than one that gives a sudden shattering effect. This is achieved by employing a substance with a lower velocity of detonation, rather than a high-speed blast. The aim is to push the material out to create a large crater and not just blast a small hole through it. Indeed some underground mines never broke through to the surface at all. They resulted in an underground cavity, which is called a camouflet. These were often used to destroy the opposition's mining activities using relatively small charges.

Probably the best explosive of all for lifting great masses of earth in mining is gunpowder. It was used initially but its drawbacks over more modern explosives rendered it impractical. It is bulky, very flammable and requires to be tamped (packed in with clay, etc.) for maximum effect. Far more practical is ammonal, which does not suffer the same drawbacks but, being very hygroscopic, must be sealed from damp. As ammonal is several times more powerful than gunpowder (but not too powerful), a considerably smaller mine chamber is required, thereby reducing the attendant risks of digging and shoring a large orifice for the installation of the charge.

Further details on the precise composition of explosives or the methods of initiating an explosion are not appropriate for this book.

Chemical Weapons – Gas

There were many types of gas used in the Great War. Some, such as chlorine, phosgene and mustard were potentially, if not immediately, lethal. Others such as types of teargas were designed to incapacitate rather than kill.

The first known use of chemical weapons in the Great War, in any form, was on 27 October 1914, when 3,000 shells containing *Niespulver* (a form of sneezing agent) mixed with shrapnel, were fired at British and Indian troops. No one seemed to notice the irritant and its use was only discovered after the Armistice. Other inconsequential uses of gas followed but the first significant deployment was by the Germans on 22 April 1915 when clouds of chlorine gas were released from thousands of cylinders dug in near Langemarck and blown by the wind towards St Julien in the Ypres Salient. The British retaliated in kind at Loos in September 1915, but with limited success, as the chlorine gas released from their cylinders drifted back when the wind changed, onto British soldiers.

Most belligerents soon adopted the use of gas and many different types were produced with varying results. The first lethal gas, chlorine, was not particularly efficient once the initial element of surprise was overcome. It was visible, had a strong smell and even simple masks prevented heavy casualties. Phosgene was far more deadly. It was not so easy to detect and often had a delayed action. Perhaps the most unpleasant gas of all was mustard, which was a blistering agent. If inhaled in quantity it slowly destroyed the lungs. If it got on the skin it produced painful burns that were not easy to treat. It was not specifically intended to kill – although it did

Early primitive British gas masks.

produce many fatalities. There were several other gases of varying deadliness tried by both sides.

Gas was initially dispersed from cylinders but soon shells and bombs were developed which could send large quantities of gas into enemy lines regardless of wind direction. One of the most efficient devices was the Livens Projector – a type of mortar that discharged a cylindrical bomb filled with 30lbs of poison gas to a distance of 1,500 yards.

Throughout the summer of 1915 desperate measures were taken to find protection from poison gas. Makeshift pads from cotton waste and even sanitary towels to be soaked by the soldiers in bicarbonate of soda or even urine were sent to the front. Soon the first gas helmets, albeit of limited value, were issued in time for the Battle of Loos. Better protection evolved and eventually the small box respirator, proof against most gases, became standard issue. They were not however the full answer to mustard gas as that could be absorbed through the skin as well as inhaled. They had the additional drawback of limiting a soldier's fighting efficiency because the eyepieces quickly steamed up. Officers in headquarters in the affected zone were not immune. They too had to wear masks as the gases were heavier than air and could penetrate their dugouts.

Warnings of the presence of gas were usually sounded by banging on suspended shell cases that formed quite efficient gongs. A keen eye was also kept on the wind direction, especially in the early days, when gas was dispersed from fixed cylinders.

Although dreaded by soldiers in the war poison gas was not as lethal to British forces as imagined. Russian soldiers are believed to have suffered considerably more from gas poisoning as they were inadequately protected from its effect. British casualties are discussed in Chapter 9.

Miscellaneous Weapons

Flamethrowers

These were mostly portable mechanical devices designed to propel a jet of flammable liquid into the enemy or his positions. The liquid, a thickened form of petrol, was lit, before or after discharge, to burn the victim or set fire to his emplacement. Its first notable use was by the Germans at Hooge on 30 July 1915 but that was not its first outing. The British and French also used flamethrowers but with limited success.

Kukri

This was the weapon of choice of the Gurkha soldier. It is an awesome, exceedingly sharp, curve-bladed knife, used primarily as a chopping rather than stabbing instrument. It is an ideal weapon for fighting in the close confines of a trench, or on a raid to kill sentries or to threaten captured prisoners. The reputation of the much-feared Gurkhas beheading enemy soldiers silently with a kukri, or collecting ears as a count of their tally, always reached their adversaries. They made sure of that. The weapon was used with deadly effect at Neuve Chapelle. No one wanted to meet a Gurkha on a dark night!

Caltrop

This was a rather unpleasant spiked instrument that was scattered by the hundred wherever enemy horses might be present. It was deliberately designed so that no matter which way up it landed, a sharp point would always be uppermost. Its sole purpose was to maim the animal. War is never a pleasant business.

Fléchettes

The First World War fléchette was essentially a mass-produced steel dart, a few inches in length. In the early days of the war, when aircraft began to be used for offensive purposes but aerial bombs were still primitive, quantities of fléchettes were sometimes thrown out of aeroplanes over enemy positions. Both sides used them. Because they were very aerodynamic, by the time they reached earth, they would be travelling at quite a high speed and were quite capable of piercing the body of a soldier on the ground.

Improvised Weapons

Although soldiers were armed at government expense, there were many occasions when the weapons provided did not meet all the requirements of warfare. One such example is close-quarters combat in trenches. The rifle and fitted bayonet were unwieldy items at 5'1" (1.55m) overall length in a trench measuring perhaps three feet wide. The men, on both sides, found that short heavy or sharp items served them better in trench fighting than those provided. It was usual therefore for fighting knives, clubs, etc. to be fashioned from whatever was to hand, and carried into the fray. Whereas France and Germany provided fighting knives in the Great War, the British government did not. Broken bayonets were reshaped and sharpened into very effective weapons by soldiers. Some commercially made knives were available for private purchase. And both sides used their entrenching tools (small spades) to great lethal effect.

Chapter 7

DEATH IN ITS MANY FORMS

The precise medical cause of death was rarely established during the Great War. There was not time, nor was it considered necessary when the obvious overriding cause was by enemy action or, as officially defined, 'battle casualty'. Small statistical samples of wounds of men in hospital were analysed, but the dead were usually classed as 'killed in action' unless certain situations, such as suspected murder, demanded special attention. The medical records of wounded men naturally did show the nature of the injury or disease. Unfortunately virtually all those records were deliberately destroyed a few decades ago. With two-thirds of all British and Dominion fatalities classed as 'killed in action' it is no wonder that our knowledge of how they were killed is incomplete.

For an analysis of those who died see Chapter 10.

Casualty

The term 'casualty' is used in most official publications to include not only those killed but also those wounded, missing or taken prisoner of war. The reason is that, for military purposes, the person, whatever his condition, was not available for battle. To avoid confusion, and where it is not obvious, I have used the terms 'casualty' to include dead and injured, etc., 'fatal casualty' to indicate loss of life and 'wounded' to refer those requiring medical attention.

Categories of Death

In the official casualty lists, *Soldiers (and Officers) Died in the Great War*, there are three main causes of death. They are:

Killed in action	Those who perished as direct result of the war.
Died of wounds	Those who perished as a direct result of war after being first received alive at a medical unit.
Died	Those who died anywhere from non-military causes such as disease or accident.

During the war many men went missing in the heat of battle. Some were captured, some were blown into unidentifiable pieces, some absconded, others simply vanished. Dead bodies were buried as quickly as possible, no matter whether friend or foe. It was simply a matter of hygiene and besides the stench of putrefying flesh was most unpleasant. Such bodies were often unidentified perhaps because the official tags were missing or because there was not time to search properly for one. In consequence that man's identity could never be linked to his resting place. After a period of time – usually one year – the missing man was officially 'presumed dead' if nothing more had been heard. Both sides notified the Swiss Red Cross of prisoners of war as soon as possible but there were lapses in this respect on occasions, perhaps through human error or the inability to identify the prisoner.

The distinction between 'killed in action' and 'died of wounds' does not seem to be officially defined and there is some inconsistency. However, from the detailed examination of many contemporary military documents, it would appear that if a man died from enemy action, or was killed in error by our own forces, *and* before reaching at least the first echelon of organized medical aid, then the category of death was 'killed in action'.

That definition did not take into account how long the man took to die. It could have been immediate or he may have lingered for many hours away from medical aid and recording facilities. If a man died having been registered as 'wounded' by the medical authorities then the cause of death would be noted as 'died of wounds'. Men who died from any form of sickness or accident – perhaps in training – were usually recorded as having 'died'. *Soldiers Died in the Great War*, unfortunately, contains many errors and omissions made at the time. It does however show that a staggering 146,443 men died of wounds during the Great War.

Other causes of death are occasionally listed such as 'drowned', 'died (gas poisoning)', 'killed (air raid)' – there are however only a few of these. The Commonwealth War Graves records occasionally give more elaborate details as to the cause of death, especially where a Victoria Cross or Albert Medal has been awarded posthumously. For most of their records, however, there is no indication as to how the serviceman died. A few examples where more information is given about the cause of death are:

Died of diabetic coma contracted in France.
Died of frostbite.
Died of injuries sustained from falling from an aeroplane.
Died of septic poisoning following wounds received in action.
Died of wounds (gas), received at Ypres.
Died of wounds received at the Battle of the Somme 1 July.
Died of wounds while a prisoner of war in a Turkish hospital at Tekrit.
Drowned at sea, while flying off Torquay.
Killed by lightning.
Killed in action at Messines in a gallant attempt to rescue a wounded
    Belgian peasant.
Killed in saving the life of a French boy on the railway lines at Barentin.
Shot by sentence of a German court martial at Bruges.
Shot whilst escaping from German prisoners of war camp.

Compassionately, they do not identify the many tragic instances of suicide committed during the war.

Those deemed to have suffered a 'disgraceful death' – for example by execution – are not usually mentioned in *Soldiers Died in the Great War*. The Commonwealth War Graves Commission records them but the cause of death is not shown. For the differences between these sources of information see Chapter 12.

Instantaneously

Officers and chums of those killed often wrote letters of condolence to the next of kin. Many of these letters survive in national, regimental and private collections. It is amazing how often the word 'instantaneously' occurs, even when it is obvious from the text that the man died some long while after being wounded. Done to console the bereaved that their loved one did not suffer, these letters nevertheless often contain quite graphic accounts of the action and the mortal, but not instantaneously fatal, injuries.

Causes of Death

Friendly Fire

The term 'friendly fire' is only used in this section for index purposes. It is not very friendly to fire on and kill your comrades. The term fratricide (killing one's brother) is also sometimes used. I consider however that, in connection with First World War accidents of this nature, no special phrase is necessary. None appear to have been coined at the time and such incidents were accepted with stoicism. It happened, it was probably unavoidable under the circumstances of the time and it was most unfortunate, but alas accidents will occur during the 'fog of war'.

No one knows how many soldiers on either side were killed or wounded by their friends. It was sufficiently common that separate accounts were not kept. There are a great many official and anecdotal descriptions of incidents where men were accidentally killed by their own side. The numbers of deaths may well run into the tens of thousands during the Great War. The French General Alexandre Percin, a gunnery specialist, estimated that their own artillery accidentally killed around 75,000 Frenchmen.

The causes of death or injury inflicted by one's own side were many but the most common are noted here.

Faulty artillery pieces

The artillery was generally stationed quite a way behind the front-lines and fired over the heads of soldiers into enemy positions. As the war progressed old guns wore out and could not be replaced or totally overhauled in sufficient numbers by the arsenals. After firing a certain number of rounds any artillery piece begins to wear beyond the remedy of field workshops. The gun became considerably less accurate than when it was new, with the result that the shell might fall hundreds of yards short of the intended target onto one's own troops. The 4.7" field gun, originally a naval piece, was notorious for its inaccuracy as it wore out and earned itself the unfortunate nickname 'strict neutrality'. All artillery pieces had the same problem: too much demand and insufficient replacements.

Faulty artillery ammunition

This was equally dangerous and caused a great number of deaths and injury but in different ways. First, if the propellant charge, which fired the shells, was not of sufficient uniformity and quality, those shells would not all arrive at the correct point of aim. They could go over or under. If under, our own soldiers suffered by being hit. If over, the shell would not strike the intended enemy position and in consequence it would not be neutralized. Again our men would suffer. Many shells failed to explode at all and consequently did not do the damage intended to enemy positions or troop concentrations. Sometimes our men were exposed to fire, perhaps as a result of uncut barbed wire that might otherwise have been destroyed. Another situation that caused a great many deaths was the faulty ammunition that prematurely exploded in the barrel of the gun firing it. This was a constant nightmare for the gunners and killed many of them.

Faulty identification of target
This always happens in war. It is tragic but so far no one has found a fail-safe solution. Soldiers are often in a different place to that expected, incorrectly identified as the enemy and fired upon – not only by the artillery but also by the infantry using rifles or machine guns. It is often not possible to positively identify, especially in poor conditions, dirty uniforms that were designed to be inconspicuous. And our lack of up-to-date communications did nothing to relieve the situation.

Calculated risks
In a creeping barrage, shells were exploded ahead of advancing infantry with the intention of killing the enemy and denying access to the ground prior to our infantry taking over. If our soldiers were too far behind the line of moving explosions, any surviving enemy would rise out of dugouts when the barrage had passed over their position and fight our men. To minimize the time the enemy could exploit that situation our men were ordered to keep close to the barrage of shells sweeping ahead of them. If they got too close or if the barrage lacked perfect accuracy some soldiers were killed or wounded. This was accepted as a justified risk at the time.

Similarly, when an underground mine was exploded, it was usual for infantry to rush forward in the race to seize the mine crater – often whilst the debris was still in the air! What goes up will come down. And several hundred tons of rock landing on you is not exactly healthy. Again this was an accepted risk.

Sometimes death came from a very unexpected quarter. There are recorded instances of aircraft, employed observing the fall of shot for the artillery, being hit by a shell from their own side. Captain Cecil Lewis, a fighter pilot with six (plus two shared) victories, wrote a classic account entitled *Sagittarius Rising* in which he describes seeing shells 'hover at [their] peak point' and others whose 'eddies made by their motion flung the machine up and down as if in a gale. Each bump meant that a passing shell had missed the machine by four or five feet.' These shells would have been fired at targets on the ground several miles away. A shell often rose thousands of feet into the air along its trajectory before it commenced its downward plunge. In the case of a 9.2" howitzer that apex could reach 8,000 feet – a typical observation altitude. And a collision is precisely what happened in the example of a Be2a of 2 Squadron Royal Flying Corps. It was brought down by British artillery fire on 10 March 1915 killing the crew. The height here is by no means unique. Many anti-aircraft shells rose to over 28,000 feet. The exceptionally long-range Paris guns, with which the Germans shelled the French capital in 1918 from a range of 115km, sent their shells a staggering 42.3km into the sky on their trajectory. That weapon was in every way incomparable, of course, and employed principles that would not be used again for another fifty years.

Artist's impression of the Paris gun.

Shell-Fire

Artillery was, by a very substantial margin, the greatest cause of death and mutilation during the Great War. Those killed or injured were 'in the wrong place at the wrong time'. The effect on the human body of the blast from explosions capable of destroying heavy masonry, excavating sizeable craters in the earth or ripping apart steel is dramatic. Human bodies often ceased to be recognizable as such.

Shrapnel

One constantly heard the old tale, 'Grand-dad still had lots of shrapnel in him when he died. At one time they used magnets to try and pull it from his body.' This cliché is strictly wrong. True shrapnel consisted of spherical lead balls, as described in Chapter 6, and lead is not attracted by magnets. The effect of being hit by one or more was roughly similar to being hit by rifle or machine gun bullets. Conversely shell splinter, jagged pieces of casing from disintegrating high explosive shells, could come in any shape or size. Some were minute whilst others were large razor-sharp chunks of high velocity steel that could sever a limb, or cause other horrific injuries instantly. And indeed magnets were tried in an attempt to remove them.

Bullet Wounds

The following extract from an account written in December 1914 by Captain Noel Chavasse VC and Bar, RAMC, gives some idea of gunshot wounds.

> The wounds one had to dress were not the clean punctures I had imagined gunshot wounds to be, but because of the near range they at first made one think they had been made by explosive bullets . . . to take an instance of a wound in the fleshy part of the thigh, the entrance wound was neat and punctured, but the exit was a gaping burst, a big hole that I could put my fist into, with broken muscles hanging out. As a matter of fact, I believe that at such near range, the bullet turns over and over, and practically bursts its way out.

As a British doctor, Captain Chavasse was probably examining British soldiers wounded by German bullets. The hydraulic pressures set up by the very high velocity of close-range bullets, inflicting permanent cavitations, most likely caused the traumatic wounds he examined. That applied to military bullets of any nationality. They usually had a heavy core, generally lead, surrounded by a jacket of copper, nickel or steel. However his conclusion may well have been correct if he was examining any wounds caused by British bullets. They were designed with a built-in instability. It was accomplished by filling the front section with aluminium or wood, before the remainder of the jacketed case was filled with lead. This moved the centre of gravity back and caused yawing or tumbling, and hence greater injury, on striking a body.

Conversely, German bullets were solid lead beneath a covering jacket of copper or steel. French bullets, unusually, were not jacketed but made of solid brass. The British practice was not specifically secret but nevertheless not widely advertised. It was perfectly legal, if unconventional, under the various conventions of the time governing war. On the contrary, bullets that were designed to expand upon hitting flesh – so-called 'Dum-Dum' bullets – were banned and anyone caught in possession of them upon capture, by either side, was very harshly dealt with. For practical purposes it makes no difference which bullet hits you, be it from a rifle or machine gun. It was quite likely however that a burst from a machine gun would result in more than one wound.

Bayonet Wounds
The numbers killed in hand-to-hand fighting on either side is unknown. This is because so many statistics were derived by hospitals analysing the types of injuries received by the wounded. The very nature of a fight at extremely close quarters usually involved a duel to the death. Surviving much more than a misplaced flesh wound was unlikely and so relatively few got to hospital to be categorized. Dead bodies were not studied and their cause of death recorded. It must therefore be presumed that far more than the 684 instances recorded in the *Medical History of the War* died from bayonet wounds. It should not however be presumed that vast numbers were killed that way, as most deaths were 'at a distance'.

Snipers
The practice of sniping was not new in 1914. The Germans were exceedingly adept at it and dominated the activity for the first year of the war. Balance was not struck until Major Hesketh-Pritchard, a former big-game hunter, gradually introduced the art and the telescopic-sighted rifles necessary to accomplish it. It was not just the weapon that was important. New skills in long-range shooting and camouflage had to be learnt and practised. A skilful enemy sniper not only causes casualties, he also lowers morale considerably in his area of operations. The slightest exposure would invite a bullet, which invariably struck without warning or the chance to avoid it. Several snipers were credited with well over 100 'kills'. As prime targets themselves, many were in turn sought out and killed by enemy snipers.

Gas
The effects of gas poisoning are always emotive and some of the most

dramatic pictures emanating from the war portray soldiers apparently blinded by gas. In reality the number of gas casualties was relatively low. It was not the big killer portrayed by propaganda. The official figures show that 5,899 died from it, which is less than 1 per cent of all fatal casualties. See Chapter 9 for more information.

Daily Attrition and Truces

There were many battles and engagements throughout the war but there were far more days when no formal set-piece battle took place. That does not mean that peace broke out – indeed, far from it. The British policy was one of aggression designed to demoralize the invaders and instil a sense of purpose in our troops. It frequently took the form of trench raids, some of which involved hundreds of soldiers. The latter were not small skirmishes but pitched battles in the area they occurred. They did not happen every day but were nevertheless quite frequent. Even with small-scale raids involving only a few men, it was inevitable that casualties would occur. When there was no actual fighting at all, casualties still mounted up. Trenches were routinely shelled; sniping and random shots were fired. Accidents occurred and disease was always present. There were no days between 5 August 1914 and 11 November 1918 when men in the King's uniform did not die from one cause or other. And that included 25 December 1914 – the day of the Christmas Truce – when forty-one men were reported as killed in action on the Western Front.

The Truce, when large bodies of troops fraternized quite openly on No Man's Land on the Western Front, caused considerable embarrassment to the authorities. To try and ensure it did not happen again, the following uncompromising message from the General Officer Commanding 47 (London) Division was circulated. It was typical of many.

> The GOC directs me to remind you of the unauthorised truce which occurred on Christmas Day in one or two places in the line last year, and to impress upon you that nothing of the kind is to be allowed on the Divisional Front this year.
>
> The Artillery will maintain a slow gunfire on the enemy's trenches commencing at dawn, and every opportunity will as usual be taken to inflict casualties upon any of the enemy exposing themselves.

There were very few transgressions of this order at Christmas 1915 and then it was usually only a short ceasefire for the burial of the dead. Despite this seemingly sensible stance the authorities sought to court-martial those responsible. The British Christmas spirit had drained away.

Live and Let Live

By December 1916 the overall animosity was such that there was no further contemplation of a Christmas Truce. That did not however prevent the situation known as 'live and let live' from occurring on a daily basis throughout the war in some sectors. Very much more subtle than a truce it consisted of, almost invariably, unspoken agreements between the opposing sides. In areas where it occurred, at breakfast time for example, shots were rarely exchanged. This even extended to situations where the local commander, suspecting an informal agreement, ordered fire to be commenced upon the enemy front-line. It has been known for such fire to be aimed high to preserve the status quo. Strangely, considering that the Germans occupied part of France, the French soldiers were especially keen on 'live and let live' agreements. It also occurred in parts of the British front but many units were expressly opposed to it and maintained belligerence at all times.

Accidents and Disease

Many succumbed to illness of one form or other and examples of diseases are discussed in Chapter 9. Altogether over 91,000 officers and men in the army died from non-military causes in the Great War. Accidents and diseases were always present on the battlefields and indeed behind the lines. On average, fifty-eight men died of disease or accident every day.

Death from accidents came in abrupt forms. Many died in training both at home and overseas, from such causes as falling from horses, being run over by wagons and in bayonet exercises. Training large numbers of men in the art of killing, in as short a time as possible, whilst using lethal weapons and live munitions, was fraught with danger. Hand grenades alone resulted in many deaths. Recruits were instructed in the use of live grenades but, until proficient, were a danger to themselves and others. 'Lit' bombs were dropped in the grenade pits rather than thrown down range. Others struck the parapet and rolled back in. In the confined space, carnage resulted from the explosions, and many were killed.

Instructors as well as their trainees were often seriously injured or perished. The Roll of the Albert Medal contains many such instances outlining the courage displayed, as the following example (*London Gazette*, 30457) illustrates:

> The KING has been graciously pleased to award the Decoration of the Albert Medal in recognition of the gallant action of Sergeant Michael Healy, Royal Munster Fusiliers, in saving life in France, in March last, at the cost of his own life. The circumstances are as follows: —
>
> Sergeant Michael Healy, Royal Munster Fusiliers. In France, on the 1st March, 1917, during bombing practice, a live bomb failed to clear the parapet, and rolled back into the trench, which, was occupied by the thrower, an officer, and Sergeant Healy. All three ran for shelter, but Sergeant Healy, fearing that the others would not reach shelter in time, ran back and picked up the bomb, which exploded, and mortally wounded him. Sergeant Healy had previously performed other acts of distinguished gallantry, for which he had been awarded the Distinguished Conduct Medal, the Military Medal, and a bar to the Military Medal. Whitehall, January 1, 1918.

On the same page of that *Gazette* there are three other awards in connection with grenade accidents. And fatal accidents occurred in just about every possible way.

Drowning seems to have been fairly common, with off-duty soldiers jumping blithely into rivers before learning to swim! Others fell into docks, lakes and canals with often fatal results. And that does not include the many poor unfortunates who slipped into mud or deep shell holes on the battlefields and sank from sight before they could be rescued. Not that rescue was often an option in the heat of battle. Most naval deaths were the result of drowning. These of course were not usually accidents but the result of enemy action. Nevertheless a great many sailors were drowned accidentally – often through falling overboard. The ability to swim was not very widespread in 1914.

It was not only on, or on the way to, battlefields that accidents occurred. Early on 19 January 1917 Summertown, London, was rudely awoken by 50 tons of TNT exploding in a purification factory. Around 70,000 properties were damaged and sadly seventy-three people died. Then there was the dreadful accident involving a troop train, a local train and an express on 22 May 1915 at Quintinshill, near Gretna Green, Scotland. Some 214 officers and other ranks died in the crash, plus several civilians.

Executions

Records indicate that, for a variety of offences committed during and shortly after the war, courts-martial pronounced the death penalty on at least 3,118 British, Dominion and Colonial soldiers. And a further 224 death sentences were passed on civilians and prisoners of war for various crimes in areas where military law prevailed. The authority was enshrined in the *Manual of Military Law 1914*, which gave substance to the annually renewable Army Act. Because various records no longer exist, and others are difficult to interpret, it is difficult to be precise about the numbers involved. The figures quoted are the best obtainable.

Although most were sentenced for military offences, other capital crimes such as murder were in evidence. All death sentences had to be individually confirmed by the commander-in-chief of the expeditionary force involved and about 87 per cent were commuted. Altogether 113 Australian soldiers were sentenced to death but none were actually executed, as their government expressly prohibited the death penalty.

A total of 438 executions by the military authorities are believed to have occurred between 4 August 1914 and 31 March 1920. It is calculated that at least 327 of these were of armed service personnel, including three officers, of British, Dominion and Colonial Armies. Others who faced the firing squad were mostly civilians or non-combatants such as coolies or labourers in the Chinese and other Labour Corps. Altogether there were 322 executions in France and Flanders during the war.

Table 6. Figures for Military Executions in the Great War	
Offence	**No. of men executed**
Desertion	266
Sleeping at post	2
Cowardice	18
Disobedience	5
Striking or threatening a senior officer	5
Quitting post	7
Shamefully casting away arms	2
Mutiny	3
Murder	19

At least forty of those shot had been reprieved on earlier occasions for similar crimes and had then gone on to reoffend. One soldier who was shot had been sentenced to death on two previous occasions and each time had his sentences commuted. Recent research shows slight variance on the numbers but the figures in Table 6 are those officially published in 1920 for military executions.

The method of execution was by a firing squad, sometimes comprised of soldiers from the condemned man's own unit. There were usually twelve men in the firing party but this number varied. Sometimes, but not always, one or more rifles was unloaded or reloaded with a blank cartridge, prior to the execution. The firing party were not told which rifles were loaded with live ammunition. (Any experienced soldier would however immediately realize the difference because a blank cartridge has almost no recoil.) On command, a volley was fired into the aiming mark pinned over the heart of the pinioned prisoner. Many shots, intentional or otherwise, missed the intended target. If the man did not die immediately then the officer in charge of the firing party stepped forward and administered the coup de grâce to the head of the condemned man with his pistol.

Morale and Courage

Whatever the cause of death – and a premature and violent demise was highly likely – what was rarely in dispute was the sheer courage and fortitude of the soldiers, sailors and airmen in our armed forces.

An account by Lieutenant Malcolm Kennedy of B Company 2/Scottish Rifles just before the Battle of Neuve Chapelle on 10 March 1915 illustrates this point. An obvious failure by the artillery had resulted in the battalion having to advance against undamaged German defences and barbed wire entanglements. The men were fully aware of the maelstrom of lead and steel that awaited them and that there was a high probability of an unpleasant death.

> The men were in great form, cracking jokes with one another and singing as though they were on a picnic. I went round from time to time to see how they were getting on. Some of them laughingly held out their hands for me to shake, in case either they or I got 'blotted out'. The prospect seemed to amuse rather than upset them, and one realised then, as never before, what a wonderful bunch of fellows

they were, and how damned lucky one was have such men to command. The tragedy of the whole thing is that most of them are now gone. (Papers of Captain M D Kennedy, IWM and Sheffield University)

Their high morale was self-evident and their prophecy was correct, for sadly 162 of them were to be killed within minutes of the battle starting.

Chapter 8

ARMY CORPS

Confusingly, in the army the word 'corps' has two definitions. Here it refers to units, somewhat similar to regiments, whose role was to support the infantry. See Chapter 2 for a definition of 'corps' meaning a subdivision of an army.

The Royal Army Medical Corps (RAMC)

This famous corps had overall responsibility for the general health of the army and the treatment of wounded or sick soldiers. Whether treated at a regimental aid post, field ambulance, casualty clearing station, base hospital or any medical centre, the wounded or sick soldier was the responsibility of the RAMC. They were nobly assisted by the qualified nurses of Queen Alexandra's Imperial Nursing Service. In addition Voluntary Aid Detachments and Red Cross detachments also helped with the sick and injured. See Chapter 9 for further details.

Royal Flying Corps (RFC)

A brief summary is given in Chapter 1.

Royal Regiment of Artillery (RHA, RFA, RGA)

The Royal Regiment of Artillery dates back to 1722 and has a splendid history. In 1899 the regiment split into two groups: the Royal Horse and

Royal Field Artillery in one group and the coastal defence and heavy guns in another, which was named the Royal Garrison Artillery. They did not reamalgamate until 1924.

The First World War was most definitely dominated by the artillery of all belligerents. And, to reiterate, by far the greatest loss of life and greatest number of appalling injuries were caused by artillery fire. The effect of explosions and high velocity jagged pieces of splintered shell on the human body is catastrophic.

Artillery played many roles. The Royal Horse and Field Artillery batteries supported the cavalry and infantry by firing shrapnel at enemy formations and scything down men in the open, attacking – or retreating. Indeed, when the war started, the British only had shrapnel shells for the horse and field artillery guns. The guns used were relatively light and mobile. The Germans did use high explosive shells but they too placed great reliance upon shrapnel. When trench warfare evolved, shrapnel was of no further use for its designed purpose and so the emergence of high explosive and other types of shell resulted. These too were fired by the lighter guns of the Royal Horse or Royal Field Artillery, which were much more manoeuvrable when rapid change of targets was desired. They could not however fire the large shells that were sometimes required.

High explosive shells were fired against various targets within trench systems or against known positions in rear areas. Massive bombardments designed to destroy enemy trench positions and fortifications prior to an attack became the symbol of the artillery. Shells were also used to deny areas of ground to opposing forces and hinder reinforcements. Enemy gun batteries were always a prime objective and most of the 46,605 gunners who died did so in this type of activity. Targets of opportunity, such as vehicles observed moving in the distance, were fired upon. This had the effect of destroying enemy material and also inhibited movement in daylight. Aeroplanes were engaged, with limited success, by specially developed anti-aircraft guns. Likewise tanks were susceptible to artillery fire. In common with all other units, the guns rapidly disappeared from the surface to disguised positions in order to avoid aerial detection and hostile artillery fire. The guns and shells are explained in Chapter 6.

Communication between the front-line infantry and the guns was via the artillery forward observation officers (FOO) and was vital. The infantry needed artillery support and the guns were some distance back. As his title implies, the FOO was the eyes for his guns and, by observing the fall of shot, could direct them onto their objective. He worked alongside the

Artillery forward observation officer with team of Royal Engineer signallers.

infantry in forward and often exposed positions. When telephone contact between him and his battery was lost, the guns could not respond rapidly to any change of target.

Regular and territorial units were similarly armed but the Territorial Force at the beginning of the war often had older guns. The Royal Horse Artillery (RHA) was armed with light guns for the greatest mobility but the 'equipment' (the technical term for a complete gun, carriage and limber) of the Royal Field Artillery (RFA) was also mounted on wheels and transportable. They both fired relatively light shells and had a high rate of fire.

The Royal Garrison Artillery (RGA) was responsible for the big guns. These usually ranged upwards from 6" calibre, were heavy and often not so manoeuvrable. Indeed, many guns were so heavy they had to be dismantled to move them and were often without wheels at all. Some huge guns were mounted on railway carriages.

Guns were laid on their targets. In simple terms that means they were restrained on a stable platform so that the barrels returned to the same position after recoiling from firing each shell. The platform could be purpose-built or just solid ground. Invariably the guns were hidden in pits or elsewhere and direct observation from the gun to target became less frequent as the war progressed. The gun was levelled, precisely aligned on its properly identified target, and increasingly complex indirect fire techniques were used. This is where the skills of the gunnery officers, and the training of the men came into play. With guns commonly shooting from 6,000 to 10,000 and some to over 30,000 yards that skill was paramount.

Bombardments from hundreds of guns firing simultaneously occurred at times during the First World War. For example, in excess of 1¾ million shells of all types were fired by over 1,500 guns during the week preceding and on 1 July 1916, the opening day of the Battle of the Somme. Those figure were well surpassed for the Battle of Messines in June 1917 when, over a similar period of time, 3¼ million shells were fired by more than 2,500 guns. Hundreds of trench mortars added to the maelstrom. Of course most bombardments were not of that intensity but, nevertheless, perhaps as many as one billion shells and mortar bombs were fired altogether on the Western Front during the Great War. The horrendous noise they made permanently ruined the hearing of hundreds of thousands of soldiers and can scarce be imagined by those who did not experience it.

Various terms are used to describe the types of artillery fire used during the war. For example, shrapnel was used to scythe down soldiers caught in the open. Along with high explosive shells, it was also used against aircraft or to cut barbed wire. Counter-battery fire was that specifically targeted against the enemy's artillery emplacements.

Bombardments were munitions aimed at specific enemy positions or areas, such as front-line trenches, defended zones or fortifications, with the purpose of destroying them. Barrages were intended to form an impenetrable barrier – an example being cut-off fire when shells were fired into the area behind enemy positions to prevent reinforcements being rushed forward. Conversely, creeping barrages were fired ahead of advancing formations of soldiers to form a wall of explosions between them and the enemy.

Hurricane fire and drumfire are essentially interchangeable terminology. It was rapid gunfire, at far greater intensities, and usually occurred just before the infantry attacked. Most gunners were quite deaf from the concussion of the guns being fired, despite stuffing cotton waste into their ears.

Various techniques evolved during the war that permitted ever-more-accurate artillery fire without preliminary, ranging shots being fired that betrayed one's intentions. Some such techniques were precise surveying of the ground to improve mapping, accurate interpretation of aerial photographs and meteorological conditions, sound ranging and flash spotting.

Machine Gun Corps (MGC)

The Machine Gun Corps did not come into being until late 1915. Prior to that each infantry battalion was responsible for its own two .303 machine guns – either the Vickers Mk 1 or the older Maxim Machine Gun. In the battalion, a junior officer commanded the machine guns in two sections of six men, each led by a sergeant or corporal. Transport was provided by one cart for the guns and another for the ammunition. By February 1915 the number of machine guns per battalion was increased from two to four when they became available. The use of those guns was however still dictated by the battalion.

Early in 1915 it was decided that the use of machine guns required greater specialization and training than hitherto and an embryonic Machine Gun Corps began to take shape. Specialist training schools were formed and the machine guns were to be withdrawn from battalions to become the responsibility of each brigade. There they formed Machine Gun Companies, each taking as its identity the number of the parent brigade. In order that infantry battalions were not left without any machine guns, those taken away were replaced by light Lewis machine guns – also in .303 calibre – as they became available. This all followed the formation of the Corps on 22 October 1915. A fourth Machine Gun Company, under the control of each division, was desired but could not be completely implemented until April 1917, by which time sufficient guns had became available.

In mid-1918 it was decided further reorganization was necessary. The four machine gun companies within each division were amalgamated into a single machine gun battalion, under the command of a lieutenant-colonel. It took its identity from the parent division. By now the Corps comprised some seventy battalions, each with sixty-four machine guns, and it had a total strength of over 124,000 officers and men. Whereas most of the Corps was with the infantry, other units served with the cavalry. The Motor Machine Gun Branch was mobile, with its guns mounted on sidecars or armoured vehicles. The Heavy Branch went on to become the Tank Corps in July 1917.

Machine guns firing long bursts were deadly to an enemy and became a prime target to be sought out and destroyed. As they were often in static positions they were not too difficult to locate, no matter how well disguised. This resulted in the death of nearly 14,000 of the men from the Machine Gun Corps. From being a comparative rarity in 1914, the number of machine guns available to the British Army on the Western Front rose to 52,358 by November 1918.

Royal Engineers [RE]

The Royal Engineers were arguably the most versatile unit of the army in the Great War. They fulfilled many roles, ranging from infantry, when required, to specialist artisans. The basic rank of a Royal Engineer is a sapper. By definition, a sapper originally specialized in digging saps, that is, tunnels towards enemy positions. A sapper was however trained in many other skills. He was also expected to fight if need be and in consequence was armed accordingly. Such was the demand for their expertise that their numbers grew from around 25,000 in 1914 to well over 300,000 by the Armistice. These figures include the transportation sections. Most sappers belonged to field companies that were distributed throughout the army. Each company consisted of around 220 officers and men at full strength and initially two, soon to be three, such companies was attached to every division. Others were attached to higher echelons of command.

Among their jobs was the design and construction of fortifications, a traditional role for the corps. They were instrumental in building the vast network of trenches on the Western Front. That is not to say they did all the spadework – the infantry did much of the actual digging, but under guidance from the engineers.

They were also responsible for the construction and maintenance of countless miles of road and railway track to bring up vital war supplies. Likewise the canals were in their charge. They were proficient in building bridges, road and railway tunnels and maintaining an efficient water supply for men, horses and machines. Most horses were shod by their farriers. Pigeons too were their responsibility. Engineers repaired almost anything, ranging from weapons to wells, and they made most of the early improvised hand grenades. They were also adept in the art of demolition.

The storage and discharge of poison gas was the responsibility of special companies. Other companies surveyed the land and made maps. A description of all their tasks could fill a book. But perhaps one task for which they were justly famous was tunnelling under enemy lines. After all, they were sappers!

Tunnelling

Early tunnelling was rather haphazard. It started mainly out of necessity to counter enemy mining and employed previous miners taken from the ranks. Formed into brigade mining sections they went underground with whatever materials were available. Major John Norton Griffiths had been a civil engineer with considerable experience of tunnelling for sewers in London and Manchester. He suggested that specialist miners be recruited and sent immediately to France to commence burrowing, or 'moling', beneath the German lines and then explode mines to destroy the enemy defences. After considerable bureaucratic delay the idea was finally approved, but only after several German mines had exploded beneath British trenches.

Miners were hastily 'volunteered', convinced by a prospective huge pay rise, given uniforms and sent directly to France. The backbone of the new force were 'clay-kickers'. They employed a technique using specially adapted spades and a wooden frame to lie on underground. This enabled spits of clay to be cut from the tunnel face with minimum effort where there was insufficient room to use traditional picks and shovels. At the end of each tunnel a chamber was excavated and packed with explosives. The tunnel was sealed and the mine exploded when required.

The new force rapidly grew in strength and successful operations commenced from mid-1915. The burrows they dug turned the Western Front into a two-tier system with moles eventually creating a subterranean world beneath much of the front. Mines were exploded regularly, which caused trepidation among soldiers not knowing if they were going to be

Clay-kicker with grafting tool and cross.

The famous explosion of the Hawthorne Ridge Redoubt Mine which, at 07.20 on 1 July 1916, signalled the start of the Battle of the Somme.

blown sky high without warning. They could sometimes avoid approaching shells or mortar bombs – they could not avoid a mine. Hundreds of mines were exploded in France and Belgium but surely the most famous was at Beaumont Hamel. Anticipated to be 65ft beneath a German redoubt, 40,600lbs (18,500kg) of explosives were detonated at 07.20 on 1 July 1916. This finally launched the Battle of the Somme. It was filmed erupting by Geoffrey Malins and this has frequently been shown on television. Another huge crater at La Boisselle is still evidence of the destructive power of a mine. The debris from that explosion rose over 4,000ft into the air. The most ambitious undertaking must surely be the mining in advance of the Battle of Messines. With galleries up to 2,160ft (980m) in length, at least twenty-two mines were excavated. Eventually, on 7 June 1917, nineteen of them, packed with almost one million pounds of explosives, erupted beneath the German lines and enabled a breakthrough in that sector.

Listening posts utilizing sensitive geophones, devices for amplifying underground movement, were established to try and detect enemy mining activities. Each side regularly attempted to disrupt the opposition's tunnelling achievements by counter-mining and exploding small charges underground to collapse their workings. It was not unknown for the two sides to meet as a result of merging tunnels and then fierce fighting in the darkness often ensued. Mine rescue stations containing primitive breathing apparatus were established to attempt the rescue of men trapped or overcome by fumes underground.

Communication

The Signal Service was formed in 1908 as a separate branch of the Royal Engineers and signal companies were attached to most army formations. They were responsible for maintaining the system from the various headquarters to the front-lines. Despite many heroic deeds repairing broken wires, they and infantry soldiers assisting them were fighting an uphill struggle. Around 2,000 men in the Signal Service alone, plus many hundreds of signallers in the infantry, were to die during the Great War.

Communication, or rather lack of it, was arguably the biggest problem of the First World War. It was mostly by telephonic means, connected by a network of very vulnerable cables, run along trenches or buried in the ground. These cables enabled conversation between front and rear areas. In an offensive operation, cables could rarely be laid quickly enough to keep pace with the advance. And none could be laid to connect units on either side that were also moving forward. There was no effective way, therefore, for two advancing battalions to speak to each other.

Alternative methods of conveying messages were of limited value. Visual signalling was not usually practical. Pigeons could take messages but naturally not return with any reply! Dogs were used occasionally. Radio transmitting and receiving equipment was bulky and heavy and required large accumulators for power. It was not available to forward troops for most of the war. The early aerials were large, probably exposed and vulnerable. Signals were easily intercepted by direction-finding equipment, with potentially dire consequences. In addition, such radios as existed were relatively short-range and few in number. Some had notable success but most wireless communication available was retained for use between higher echelons of command at rear bases. It was used at times to send signals in Morse code from aircraft to the ground to indicate targets, the primitive transmitters being powered from the aircraft's generator. Semi-portable sets, which could utilize much smaller aerials, became available in limited numbers from late 1917 but were not widely used.

Where telephones were impossible or failed, by far the most commonly employed alternative was the human message carrier or 'runner'. It was a most dangerous job. A man, probably an infantryman, would be despatched to go to another unit or higher command with a written message. He, or another, then had to retraverse the broken battlefield, often under fire, with the response. If the runner(s) survived, the time taken between request and reply could be several hours. And by that time the question, in the heat of battle, may no longer have been relevant.

Tank Corps

Code-named a 'tank', to disguise its true purpose, the weapon along with its corps slowly lurched into being. Conceived by Lieutenant-Colonel Ernest Swinton as early as 1914, it took the intercession of Winston Churchill to get the beast into service. It first saw action at the Battle of Flers-Courcelette on 15 September 1916 under the command of the Heavy Branch of the Machine Corps. In that action thirty-two Mark 1 tanks, each weighing 28 tons, were deployed. They were mechanically unreliable and unfortunately fourteen either broke down or became ditched. There were two variations of heavy tank, each having a crew of eight. The male was

Tanks excelled at crushing barbed wire entanglements.

armed with two 6-pounder guns, one in the purpose-built sponson attached to each side. The female version was equipped with five Vickers machine guns. Their top speed was less than four miles per hour. Many models succeeded the Mark 1 but were all somewhat similar in appearance and firepower. Lighter and much faster tanks, such as the Whippet, were introduced in early 1918. The Tank Corps itself was formed on 27 July 1917.

Notable successes for tanks were at the Battle of Cambrai in November 1917, at Amiens in August 1918 and in the final advance. In those actions tanks were deployed in their hundreds, better tactics had been evolved and they were more mechanically reliable. Some had wireless sets and could receive messages but were not able to transmit from within the hull. No wireless inter-tank communication was possible during the war. Sadly, all First World War tanks were relatively lightly armoured and vulnerable to even light artillery fire. Perhaps one of their best uses was in crushing and dragging away barbed wire entanglements to enable the infantry to advance.

Army Service Corps (ASC)

Unless fighting soldiers are continually resupplied with materials of war no battles could ever be won. And the organization that supplied it was the Army Service Corps. They not only carried the materials of war – which could be anything from bullets to biscuits – they also frequently processed that material. For example, the flour that they carried was frequently baked into bread by Army Service Corps bakers.

Fielding only a tiny force in 1914, the Corps grew to number to over 325,000 men. Their role changed to suit requirements and many men were transferred to infantry battalions to fight when required. The rather unkind nickname of 'Ally Sloper's Cavalry' does not take into account the fact that around 8,500 officers and men died of various causes with the corps. It is not well-known, for example, that in the first tank action at Flers-Courcelette most of the drivers were members of the Army Service Corps. The drivers of ambulances, both horse and mechanical, were ASC men.

The subunit of the Army Service Corps was the company and there were over 1,200 companies. Most were numbered (e.g. 136 or 1082), but some had names such as Auxiliary Water Company or No. 3 Donkey Company. They had many specific roles and were allocated throughout all the armies as required. Many formed part of the divisional train that supplied goods to fighting units. Others were higher up the resupply chain, moving material from England to base depots, railheads, etc. Stores were maintained throughout the war zones. Remount companies and squadrons were involved in breaking and training horses ready for the army. The jobs of the ASC are too numerous to be listed here. One group does however deserve special mention. The Wolds Wagonars (sic) were a group of qualified civilian wagon drivers formed into a special reserve in 1912. Volunteers from the Yorkshire Wolds were enrolled with a small retainer and in 1914, when their services were required, were mobilized and were sent with virtually no military training to France, where they served with distinction. It was their skill at driving the heavy general service (GS) wagons that was required, not their saluting abilities.

In 1914 most stores were moved by horse-drawn transport and overall the animals required a total of over 2,500,000 tons of hay and 3,250,000 tons of oats to keep them provisioned during the war. Horses were widely used, not just for transport. The Royal Horse and Field Artillery guns were horse-drawn and officers and many men were mounted. Horses, mules or donkeys pulled many items of equipment, such as general service wagons and ammunition carts. Lots of shells were carried into action by pack animals where it was impossible for vehicles to travel. Hundreds of thousands of horses were purchased from overseas and the army in Britain commandeered many others. Sadly, at the end of the war, relatively few of

Army Service Corps 3-ton lorry (American Pierce Arrow).

those seized were returned to their former owners. Most remained abroad. Of the 828,360 transport animals supplied, it is thought around 500,000 horses and 250,000 mules perished as a result of the war; many were sold for meat when it was over.

The Army Service Corps was certainly not slow to accept mechanical transport and its first vehicles arrived in 1903. By August 1914 there were 507 vehicles already in service, ranging from cars and lorries to ambulances and steam tractors. Vehicles purchased and requisitioned on mobilization increased this figure to well over 1,300. By the Armistice that number had risen to about 120,000 vehicles of all descriptions and more and more items, formerly transported by horse, were hauled by lorries. The Army Service Corps supplied the lifeblood of the Army, with men working continuously and mostly thanklessly in their tasks. I have never ceased to be amazed, for example, how drivers were able to locate, at night and with no lights on their vehicles, isolated gun batteries to resupply them with shells.

In recognition of the vital role played by the Army Service Corps during the war it was granted the title of 'Royal' on 27 November 1918.

Labour Corps and Similar Units

Given the nature of the Western Front, accommodation had to be constructed, fortifications built, and thousands of miles of trenches dug. Lines of communication in the shape of roads, railways and canals had to be built and maintained. Ships had to be loaded and unloaded – likewise trains, supply dumps and distribution points. This all took up huge amounts of manpower – manpower the Army could ill afford to take from the combat forces. And yet somehow those vital jobs had to be done. Army Service Corps and Royal Engineer soldiers performed many of the skilled jobs but there was still a vast amount of semi-unskilled work to do – much of it digging or carrying. The partial answer was to recruit labourers from wherever they could be found.

Initially labourers sent from Britain were grouped into Labour Companies of the Army Service Corps and the Labour Battalions of the Royal Engineers. Most were eventually absorbed into the Labour Corps when it was created in February 1917.

With the chronic shortage of labour, desperate measures were taken. Men were brought in from all parts of the Empire and places such as China and Egypt to help. Pioneer Battalions were created from ordinary infantry battalions – often from the Territorial Force, where their mix of civilian trade skills was invaluable. They were trained soldiers but normally engaged on labouring or construction work unless called upon to fight.

The Labour Corps grew to huge proportions and eventually numbered in excess of 389,000. On occasions of crisis men from the Labour Corps were armed and fought as infantry. Of over 5,000 men from the Corps who died in the war, 2,309 are recorded as being killed in action or dying from wounds.

Other sources of labour came from infantry labour battalions composed of men medically graded as unsuitable to fight. Conscientious objectors were formed into Non-Combatant Companies. Even enemy prisoners of war were put to work. And women contributed to the war effort. The Women's Auxiliary Army Corps was formed in March 1917, later to become the Queen Mary's Army Auxiliary Corps. They were engaged in basic tasks that officially did not require too much heavy labour. That said, having seen pictures of women working with large munitions, I rather suspect they took their fair share of hard work along with their men-folk.

Royal Defence Corps (RDC)

This corps consisted of mostly older men and others unfit for front-line duties. Many were already serving in various home service garrison battalions and were, from August 1917, amalgamated with others in reserve battalions. Their duties, none of which were overseas, were guarding various establishments and prisoners of war and helping with anti-aircraft observation.

Other Corps

There were several other corps whose names, listed below, largely indicates the responsibilities they undertook. Each was essential and played a vital role in the overall smooth running of the army and the conduct of the war. Unfortunately space does not permit further amplification here.

Corps of Military Police
Military Provost Staff Corps
Intelligence Corps
Army Veterinary Corps
Army Ordnance Corps
Army Pay Corps
Army Chaplain's Department

Chapter 9

MEDICAL MATTERS

The Royal Army Medical Corps (RAMC) had overall charge of the general health of the army and the treatment of wounded or sick soldiers. Whether treated at a regimental aid post, field ambulance, casualty clearing station, base hospital or any medical centre, the wounded or sick soldier was the responsibility of the RAMC. Stretcher-bearers were often taken from infantry units and attached to, rather than transferred to, the RAMC.

Wounds

The causes of wounds are often the same as those where the injury resulted in death. Not all wounds were initially life-threatening but could prove to be so if not treated promptly and properly. Despite the lack of certain techniques we presently take for granted, the medical services were highly efficient where the patient could be treated in time. And they continued to improve greatly as the war progressed. In war conditions it was unfortunately simply not possible to rescue injured men speedily. Operational matters often took priority over the evacuation of the wounded. Men and transport required for fighting could not be spared to help.

When we consider the type of wounds soldiers received in the Great War, we also have to consider the possible treatments available at the time. And what was not yet available.

Wounds to the body, however caused, result in blood loss. The loss of large quantities of blood, which is not rapidly replaced, will result in death. Blood transfusion was not properly developed during the war. Prior to 1910

The popular concept of the wounded soldier. Sadly the reality was often horrendously different.

any transfusions had to be direct between donor and recipient, because of the problems of coagulation. The science of refrigeration and storage of blood was in its infancy and blood type incompatibility was not fully understood. Transfusions would not have been possible on the battlefield – the one place where they would have had the most dramatic effect – to save lives after traumatic injuries. Any transfusions at base hospitals, rare before 1917, would have been risky. In short, a great number of wounded soldiers, sailors and airmen simply bled to death on the battlefields from often relatively simple wounds. A tourniquet is a mechanical device to totally block the flow of arterial blood by means of compression. If available, they were used to staunch the flow of blood, but they were no use if too much had already flooded away. Nor was the detrimental effect of keeping a tourniquet on too long fully appreciated. The treatment of many conditions prescribed by Royal Army Medical Corps wartime training manuals often differs radically from twenty-first-century medical practice.

Another great saviour of human life – antibiotics – would not become available until the Second World War. It was, and still is, rare for any penetrating injury caused by a foreign body such as a bullet, shell fragment or bayonet to be clean. The foreign body would usually carry particles of dirty uniform or other matter into the wound and an infection would result and spread. Infections often developed into septicaemia or, even worse, gas gangrene, which had its origins in the soil. The management of these complications would have been much easier if antibiotics had been available. As it was, the only treatment was prevention by the use of antiseptics. Many were employed; indeed within the larger wound dressings was an ampoule of iodine. Sphagnum moss dressings, impregnated with garlic, were also tried, as they had antibacterial and water (body fluid) absorbing qualities.

Others in use included carbolic acid, boric acid, potassium permanganate and many mercury compounds that often had rather nasty side effects. Once a major infection had set in, amputation of the offending limb was often the only course of action possible. If the infection was to a wound in the trunk of the body, death was highly likely.

X-ray examination, anaesthesia and morphine-based drugs for pain relief were available during the war. Surgical techniques, to remove bullets, shell fragments and to repair injuries, improved throughout the war as more and more patients were operated upon. Just as important was the dedication and care of most surgeons, doctors and nurses. Following surgery to remove foreign bodies, clean and drain wounds, repair or amputate shattered limbs, etc., much depended upon the nursing care available. Over 41,000 men had limbs amputated and sadly, on average, 10 per cent died. This number rose to 28 per cent if gangrene set in. Despite the difficulties, by far the greatest number of wounded men returned to duty after treatment.

Plastic surgery, although experimented with in earlier years, was not normally available. However between 1920 and 1925 some 2,944 facial repair operations were performed at Queen Mary's Hospital, Sidcup. More usually, facial masks were cast and painted, to cover the worst disfigurements. Artificial limbs

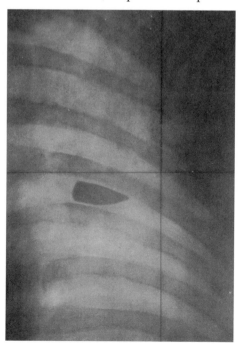

1915 X-ray showing a bullet lodged in the right lung of a soldier.

were produced and supplied to those who had lost limbs but they were primitive by today's standards of prostheses.

Initial Treatment

Unless able to walk to get help, many wounded soldiers had to treat themselves initially until a stretcher-bearer could reach them. It was forbidden for a soldier advancing into battle to stop and assist a wounded comrade. In basic training the subject of first aid was not given much prominence and so common sense had to take over. Inside each soldier's tunic was sewn a first field dressing. This was a sterile bandage with a gauze pad attached. This basic item of kit was often all that was available. Assuming rescue from the field of battle, the man would be assisted perhaps on a stretcher, to the nearest 'regimental aid post' (RAP), sometimes called the 'battalion aid post'. That would consist of an improvised shelter close to the fighting zone. It was generally staffed by a medical officer (doctor) and several men of the Royal Army Medical Corps, plus others allocated by battalions to act as stretcher-bearers and carry out other basic tasks. The job of the doctor was to stabilize the wounded man to try and prevent him from dying before the next stage of treatment. There was neither time nor facilities to do much more than bandage up wounds, administer morphine and record the dosage on the patient. The wounded soldier then commenced a journey via several establishments, each of which performed vital medical and filtering processes. The number of stretcher-bearers available increased as the war progressed.

Evacuation

Field Ambulance

The next stage was to a 'field ambulance' that served many functions. Elements of it were often located miles apart. Doctors and medical orderlies staffed the various elements. Often the journey there would be hazardous and difficult for the stretcher-bearers trying to negotiate narrow, muddy, trenches and even narrower traverses whilst carrying a heavy human burden. They were the first place a man might realistically expect more than cursory treatment. Field ambulances were not off-road vehicles equipped with sirens and flashing lights!

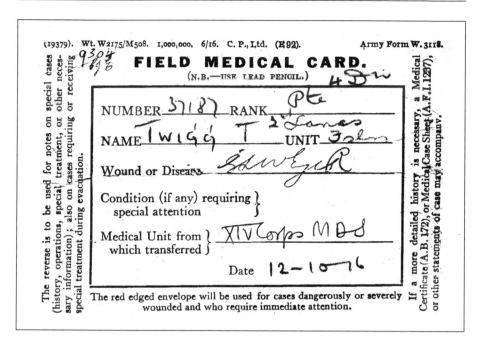

Field Medical Card (Army form W. 3118). NB 'gsweyeR' = gunshot wound right eye. The cards were enclosed in a waxed envelope and attached to the patient.

One aspect of their duties was to establish an advanced dressing station (ADS) close to the front. It would serve perhaps four regimental aid posts. On arrival, bandages and splints could be checked, the patient given drinks, if appropriate, and made a little more comfortable. And forms were filled in. The Field Medical Card, completed for casualties, recorded the progress in treatment. It is interesting to note that in June 1917 the War Office ordered a new batch of 1,750,000 such cards. The war was far from over!

The casualty was then despatched, perhaps by horse or motor ambulance, to the next echelon – the main dressing station of the field ambulance. Here his condition was reviewed. In the case of relatively minor injuries, the soldier would be patched up and, after a period of rest, returned to his battalion to continue his duties. If he had more serious injuries they would be examined, cleaned and treated. Sometimes this involved life-saving surgery at a nearby advanced operating station.

Each division had three field ambulances attached to it. Field ambulances had many other responsibilities but the main one relevant here was to be responsible for transportation of the casualty between its various units.

Casualty Clearing Station (CCS)

Motor ambulance convoys, sometimes assisted by the field ambulance, would then take the man to the next link in the medical chain – the 'casualty clearing station'. A casualty clearing station was generally a large, fully equipped, often tented hospital set up around ten miles behind the front. It rarely kept patients for more than a few days. Their primary job was collection of casualties from allocated field ambulances, to tackle more complex conditions and prepare the patient for dispersal to the next level. They were able to X-ray and perform major operations on a lot of men, under far more favourable conditions than those at a field ambulance. Often, after a battle, a great many casualties required expert medical attention simultaneously. The CCS was better equipped and staffed to deal with that situation, although inevitably delays in receiving aid occurred. In addition to surgery they gave much needed comfort and stabilized the patient ready for his onward journey. The patient could be returned to his unit if sufficiently recovered. Or he could be placed upon an ambulance train, hospital barge or other conveyance and taken onwards.

Any echelon could be by-passed if circumstances warranted it. Thus, for example, casualties deemed by the doctors to have no realistic chance of survival were retained at the place they were so assessed and placed in the local moribund tent or ward. There they would be given every possible comfort, nursing care and painkillers, but effectively left to die. Unfortunately patients with severe abdominal or head wounds were often untreatable, given the conditions at the time. Over 43 per cent of those wounded in the abdomen subsequently died. With the huge numbers of more lightly

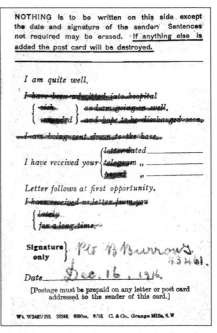

Field Service Post Card that broke the rules! Pte B Burrows was subsequently killed in action, 23 Aug. 1918.

wounded men flooding in who stood a greater likelihood of survival, available resources were allocated to them in preference to those most likely to die anyway. It was harsh, but it was during a war nearly a century ago.

Further treatment and long-term care would be undertaken at huge, fully equipped general, stationary or base hospitals often located near the large costal towns such as Boulogne, Calais and Etaples. These hospitals specialized in certain injuries and in consequence the patient would, hopefully, be sent to the appropriate one for his condition. The main remaining type of hospital was the home hospital. And to be sent there was the wounded soldier's greatest desire – back home to Blighty! (Blighty derives from the old army in India where *belati* was Hindi for 'far away' (home).) Field Service Post Cards were provided for the wounded but strict rules applied. Note the patient could only say how well he was! Sadly death sometimes preceded that letter 'to follow at first opportunity'.

Ailments

Service personnel are no different from civilians when it comes to catching a cold or flu or any other ailment prevalent among the human race. What was different was the treatment. Many poorer people at the time of the Great War never or rarely saw a doctor, as he had to be paid. There was no National Health Service. Illnesses were often left to run their course. The patient recovered or the patient died – and all without medical intervention. The better off could afford medical attention but there was, in reality, not that much that was beneficial for bacterial or viral infections.

In the armed forces medical aid was available free and doctors were on hand to prescribe appropriate treatment. What was lacking was the equivalent of 'bedside manner'. Men had to parade to see the doctor who, from many accounts, rarely had much sympathy with the presumed malingerer who stood in front of him. After all, the serviceman, on attestation, had once been certified as fit for military service. Commonly, the prescribed remedy was M & D – that is, medicine and (return to) duties. More often that not the medicine prescribed was a 'Number 9' pill. Laxatives were the favourite antidote for most illnesses at the time. I know of one instance where the patient, seriously ill with Spanish Flu in 1918 was prescribed castor oil. He was not best pleased but eventually recovered to tell the tale. Perhaps castor oil was all that the overworked doctor had. Even today there is no cure for the common cold or the flu virus.

The Army was well aware from previous campaigns that certain diseases killed more men than bullets. Those diseases were typhoid, dysentery, cholera and diarrhoea. Officers were trained to pay particularly attention to hygiene, as prevention was always better than cure. Because of this care, deaths from those diseases were comparatively rare on the Western Front.

Life in the trenches or behind the lines was not particularly healthy and often the strength of a unit was deficient through sickness. It is impossible to cover them all but a few notes may illustrate the typical health problems that prevailed. Soldiers suffered from, and a ratio died from, just about every disease known. The incidence obviously depended to a great extent upon the theatre of war he was assigned to.

Dentistry

Dental hygiene was not uppermost in the minds of either servicemen or the army council, despite the official issue of toothbrushes. With more and more sugar in the diet, dental decay and toothache was common. And the easiest treatment was extraction of the offending tooth. The local anaesthetic Novocain was in existence but rarely used in war zones. Although teeth were being filled by the time of the Great War, the dentists' drill was foot operated, bulky and only available overseas in base hospitals. The manufacture of false teeth was however well established and no longer relied upon 'Waterloo Teeth' – which were those formerly gathered from dead soldiers after a battle. The actual teeth were totally false, made of porcelain and were set in vulcanite. Many officers had high-quality false teeth made and fitted whilst on leave. For others, the Army Dental Service made tens of thousands of new dentures to aid the toothless. Extractions always exceeded repairs and fillings.

Drunkenness

Alcohol and its consumption in excess was a condition well-known to the Army and did not pose any real problem. The possible long-term degeneration of the men's livers was not their concern. Minor punishments for drunkenness were liberally handed out to offenders who, when sober again, continued their tasks as if nothing had happened. Hangovers were not accepted as an excuse for sick leave.

Dysentery

Dysentery was another great cause of losses to the Army. Insanitary conditions, common in warfare, were the prime cause – a factor well recognized by the authorities who fought hard to control it. Contact with faeces, whether alone, in soiled ground, in enemy positions or combined with rotting bodies, was the chief culprit. Once an area is contaminated it is very difficult under war conditions to clean it. Personal hygiene was generally not possible in the trenches. Of all the signs I have seen in museums, and in photographs associated with trench life, the one I have never noticed is 'and now wash your hands'. Thirsty men crave water to such a degree that even obviously polluted water is better than no water. The sanitary arrangements improved as the war progressed, with great emphasis being placed on latrines and the proper disposal of their contents. Nevertheless some 203,421 men were admitted to hospital during the war with dysentery and hundreds died of it.

Gas Poisoning

Gas was a much-feared weapon of war but the number of related casualties was relatively low. It is estimated about 186,000 British soldiers suffered from gas poisoning. By far the majority recovered – at least in the short term, but more than 5,899 are officially known to have died. That figure does not include many Canadian soldiers who were in the forefront of the first poison gas attack on the Western Front on 22 April 1915. It could also be an underestimate as many men were simply recorded as 'killed in action' in the pandemonium that day. However, as most poison gases used in the Great War were not immediately lethal, the numbers are unlikely to be much higher. The majority of victims reached medical aid and were then accurately categorized as gas casualties. Rather less than 10 per cent of all admissions were the result of gas.

Of those who seemed to recover, many were to die young from the detrimental effects of poisonous gas on their lungs. The number of these is totally unknown, as they would have already been discharged from the Army. Those premature deaths would no doubt have contributed significantly to the total number of war-related deaths, had records been kept.

All forms of gas, whether potentially lethal or not, were primarily intended to create fear and confusion and then incapacitate and demoralize the victims. An injured soldier with a difficult incapacity requires far more manpower, equipment, expertise and expense than one who is killed outright.

Influenza

Flu, along with the common cold, was quite common during the Great War and not normally life-threatening. Here though, we are briefly considering the much more deadly virus that was popularly called 'Spanish Flu'. The name seems to have originated after widespread reporting of many cases in the uncensored Spanish press. Scientists still debate its exact origins and the precise type of flu strain involved, neither of which is relevant here. The flu seems to have come in several waves, starting in March 1918, with the main pandemic gathering pace from August that year. The disease continued into 1919 but finally came to an end almost as abruptly as it started, leaving whole communities devastated. Both sides in the war were equally affected. Various sources suggest it originated in the United States, but again there are many contenders for this dubious honour. The numbers of people worldwide who caught the flu is unknown but estimates of 50 to 100 million deaths from it are probably accurate. Strangely, it seems to have been deadliest to the young, fit and healthy members of the community rather than the old, weak and malnourished. Robust American soldiers suffered rather badly – indeed proportionally worse than seasoned troops from Britain, who had already endured several years of trench privations. It was a most virulent outbreak and often resulted in massive haemorrhaging in the lungs resulting in the victims literally drowning in their own blood.

Malaria

Almost half a million British troops were treated for malaria during the Great War and about 3,000 died from it. Incidence was highest in Macedonia, East Africa, Mesopotamia, Egypt and Palestine. But there were also some 9,022 cases in France and Flanders – with at least fourteen resultant deaths. To give some idea of the severity of the disease, in Macedonia battle casualties totalled 23,762; that is men no longer able to fight because they were dead, wounded, missing or prisoners of war. In the same theatre of war 162,517 men were incapacitated by malaria. The only effective treatment for malaria was quinine, which can cause undesirable side effects.

Self-Inflicted Injuries

From their very nature this condition was disguised from the medical authorities and attributed by the injured man as either caused by enemy action or an accident. The penalties for deliberately wounding oneself were very severe. As the culprit obviously planned to survive the incident, the relatively minor injury was almost invariably to an extremity such as a hand or foot. Occasionally the fleshy parts of an arm or leg might be injured but at risk of serious long-term damage. Indian soldiers in France were under the unfortunate illusion that if they were wounded in action in any way they would be sent home to India to recover. Some did not want to be in France at all but others genuinely believed that an injury was most honourable and that, as a result, they had entirely fulfilled their duty. In consequence of this false belief it became a practice to try to sustain a minor injury. Several instances are recorded of men, not only Indian soldiers, raising a hand above the parapet as an invitation to German sharpshooters who naturally were happy to oblige. A shot-off finger seemed a small price to pay to get out of the war. Because of this, instances of hand wounds where no other injuries were present were viewed with great suspicion. Sometimes drugs or chemicals were consumed to fake serious illness, but again the medical authorities were generally well aware of this and retained the man, under close observation, to await natural recovery. In practice, especially early in the war, only severely wounded men from India were repatriated back home. The total number of instances is obviously unknown but 3,904 officers and men were convicted of self-inflicting a wound to escape military service.

Shell-Shock

This is the common name given to the condition of patients suffering from nervous disorders or mental illnesses caused by the stress of war. It was officially, if recognized at all, called neurasthenia during the Great War. Sometimes men, obviously incapable of reason, were classified as 'not yet diagnosed (neurological)'. Others were simply said to be suffering from 'lack of moral fibre'. If the man ran away in his distressed condition, he might well, upon capture, be charged by the military authorities with desertion. The term 'post-traumatic stress disorder' would not be applied until 1980. Shell-shock, in whatever guise, was simply not generally understood, or accepted, as a reason not to fight. Treatment was mostly primitive or even brutal in spartan mental institutions unless the patient was lucky enough to be sent to one of the few specialist hospitals such as Craiglockhart War Hospital. There, a psychiatrist, William H Rivers, used several clever and revolutionary techniques to help cure those in his charge. Hypnotism, drugs and electric shocks were used, along with much kindness and understanding. For example, he reversed the old practice of banning the patient from actively thinking of the grisly situations that had caused the breakdown – only for the deranged soldier to have vivid and uncontrollable nightmares on sleeping. Instead, Rivers encouraged the man to modify the memories to either get some solace or perhaps black humour from what had happened. His treatment helped many. Among his famous patients were Siegfried Sassoon and Wilfred Owen. Unfortunately few records were kept of the condition and so we do not know how many cases were involved. It did however run into several tens of thousands.

Trench Foot

Sometimes called immersion foot and loosely linked with frostbite, this debilitating condition was especially bad during the first part of the war. The British Expeditionary Force had moved to the Ypres Salient, which has a very high water table. The trenches were invariable wet, and more often than not flooded. Men were obliged to stand for long periods in cold water with inadequate protection. The standard army boots did not keep out water that was deeper than the boot and even shallower water soon seeped through the leather. Indeed, the boots may well have been restrictive and, together with tightly wrapped puttees, exacerbated the problem. (Puttees are long strips of wool serge wound spirally around the lower leg, over the top of the boot, to below the knee. They were intended to offer protection and support as well as keeping dirt and small creatures from entering the boot. The origin of the name is the Hindi *patti* (bandage). The illustration of a British Tommy 4/Middlesex 1914 shows them being worn.) Trench foot, unlike frostbite, does not require freezing temperatures and can break out after as little as half a day's exposure. Initially the feet go numb and then turn blue or red and blister. Unfortunately the soldier would probably have had more pressing matters to deal with during the fighting around Ypres than to examine the colour of his insensitive feet. By the winter of 1915/16 the authorities realized the gravity of the situation and introduced preventative measures. These included the use of duckboards, sumps and pumps to ease the water problem. Additionally there was frequent inspection of the men's feet, whale oil was liberally applied to them and socks were regularly changed. Gradually trench waders were provided for the wettest areas. Unfortunately, before the condition was fully recognized and treated, many men suffered the loss of toes or even feet caused by fungal infections that turned gangrenous. The problem did not entirely go away and was rather bad in Gallipoli but it was never again as severe as at the beginning of the war.

Venereal Diseases

Life in the trenches was most unpleasant and totally devoid of any sexual excitement. On returning to areas away from the war, in the little free time available, men's thoughts often returned to the normal pleasures of life. Who could blame them? They were living with the very real prospect of a violent death any day. Sex was often available for purchase from local ladies at a price. The financial price was not high perhaps because, with the number of men visiting each prostitute, and the very limited time given to each customer, the costs were kept down. There was often however another price to pay. Cleanliness was not a first priority of either party and venereal disease was quite common. Contraception in the form of condoms (known at the time as 'preventative outfits') was rare. Although some were issued to troops they were not popular. They were mostly heavy, hand-dipped items made from rubber cement. They were as thick as bicycle tyre inner tubes, uncomfortable to use and not very reliable. Brothels, official and otherwise, certainly existed, mostly in back areas and controlled to a degree by the French civilian authorities. French and German troops were permitted brothels whereas the British authorities did not officially organize them but generally adopted a pragmatic view of their existence. This periodically extended to the girls being inspected for disease by medical officers and for military police to control any queues that formed outside.

Table 7. Admissions for treatment for venereal disease	
Theatre of war	**Admissions**
France and Flanders	153,531
Other theatres of war	63,248
United Kingdom	199,719
Total	416,498

The figures in Table 7 for admissions for treatment for venereal disease generally include both British and Dominion soldiers and their officers. Some of the figures relate to relapses. The lower numbers from theatres of war other than the Western Front reflect the fewer troops posted there and also the relative lack of opportunity or prostitutes. The high incidence in the United Kingdom probably reflects the numbers of troops under training and away from the confines of their families for the first time. Additionally, soldiers home on leave may well have brought the previously undiagnosed disease back with them.

The figures combine gonorrhoea, syphilis and the various other venereal diseases. Overall, approximately four times as many cases of gonorrhoea were treated than syphilis. Without antibiotics, treatment was rather painful and, before 1910, fraught with dangers. It was discovered that syphilis could be treated with Salvarsan, an arsenical compound, otherwise known as '606'. The latter name was given as it was the 606th such compound to be tested. One famous Wimpole Street venereologist was even known among many officers as 'Dr 6-0-6' and, as a pragmatist, he gave his young nephew a small packet of it to take to France lest he should catch syphilis. Although gonorrhoea was perhaps less serious than syphilis, there was no effective treatment for it during the First World War. Attempts to cure it were however made by using quite toxic injections of silver nitrate or mercury. All treatments were very painful and had potentially dangerous side effects.

Various Notes and Medical Statistics

Whereas the precise cause of death was rarely investigated and recorded – beyond the term 'killed in action' – records were kept of the causes of injuries, including those that resulted in death. Statistics exist to show the ratio of battle to non-battle wounded. Battle was the result of enemy action. Non-battle was from all other causes such as sickness and accidents. The ratio of the latter varies considerably depending upon the theatre of war.

Table 8. British Expeditionary Forces: official statistics for admissions to hospitals		
France and Flanders	Battle	1,988,969
France and Flanders	Non-battle	3,528,486
All theatres of war	Battle	2,169,072
All theatres of war	Non-battle	6,186,767

However, more men were out of action through non-battle incidents than as a result of enemy action during the Great War.

The figures quoted in this book differentiate as far as possible between those already dead and those who reached medical aid still alive. That is not always easy, for the published figures are often blurred.

It will be seen from Table 8 that more were unavailable for duty through sickness or accidental injury than from enemy action. It must also be realized that the figures relate to occurrences of injury or sickness and not people. Some soldiers were wounded or sick several times. Indeed, nearly 11,000 men serving on 25 October 1917 had already been wounded three times or more. A good number of 'sick' were undoubtedly suffering from 'Spanish Flu'. All official figures seem to imply that all the casualties were men. That is not true. We must remember that women also served in theatres of war and many were killed or wounded.

Table 9 shows causes of wounds analysed at a casualty clearing station for the Director-General, Army Medical Services. The sample, at 212,659 cases, is relatively small but probably representative. It does not analyse those killed outright and it is possible that certain machines of war were more lethal than others. It clearly shows that the greatest killer was artillery fire.

Table 9. Analysis of causes of wounds seen at a casualty clearing station		
Wounding agent	**Number**	**%**
Bullet: rifle or machine gun	82,901	38.98
Shells, trench mortars, etc.	124,425	58.51
Bombs and grenades	4,649	2.19
Bayonet	684	0.32

The Germans recorded that 12 per cent of leg wounds and 23 per cent of arm wounds resulted in death, mainly through infection. The Americans recorded that 44 per cent of casualties that developed gangrene and half of those who were wounded in the head died.

Overall approximately 58 per cent of British wounded were treated and returned to duty in the theatre of war where the injury occurred. Around 38 per cent were evacuated overseas to recover. It is thought 82 per cent of injured or sick soldiers eventually returned to serve in the Army, even if in a less demanding unit than their original one.

War Pensions

Depending upon the severity of the injury, pensions were paid to wounded officers, men and nurses. By 31 March 1920 the number of awards had reached 1,182,368 but many pensions were only paid for a limited duration. The wives of severely disabled pensioners received a supplementary sum. In addition, nearly two million dependants, mostly comprising 232,254 widows and the children of the war dead, received a small pension. The majority of the dead were young unmarried men and it was extremely rare for their parents to receive any compensation from the state.

Chapter 10

INTERESTING FACTS, DEFINITIONS AND STATISTICS

First Casualties

In all probability the first British casualties from enemy action in the Great War occurred on 6 August 1914, less than thirty-two hours after the war started. HMS *Amphion* was engaged in action with the German minelayer *Königin Luise* in the North Sea. The enemy ship was sunk but the *Amphion*, having rescued some of her crew, ran over two of the mines laid by the *Königin Luise*. Some 150 British sailors were lost, together with several German prisoners.

First British Rifle Shots in Anger

On 22 August 1914, Corporal Ernest Thomas, 4th Irish Dragoon Guards, was on patrol on the Mons-Charlois Road in Belgium when a German cavalry patrol approached. Corporal Thomas, who came from Brighton in Sussex, fired upon the patrol at 400 yards range and hit a German officer.

First Royal Flying Corps Aircraft Shot Down

This occurred just after 10.16am on 22 August 1914 when an Avro 504 of 5 Squadron flown by Second Lieutenant Vincent Waterfall, with Lieutenant Charles Bayly as his observer, were on reconnaissance above Enghien. The observer's report (later recovered) recorded extensive enemy formations below. This transpired to be the 12th Brandenburg Volunteers, which shot the aeroplane down with rifle fire.

Armistice Day Fatalities

Sadly this day, 11 November 1918, several hundred servicemen throughout the whole British 'Empire' died from all causes – many of them from influenza. Of those, eight soldiers in the British Army were actually killed in action that morning. Private George Price, 28 Battalion Canadian Infantry, was also killed. It is thought he was the last soldier to be killed in action when he was shot dead by a sniper at two minutes to eleven – the hour appointed for the ceasefire. He is buried at St Symphorien Military Cemetery near Mons.

Duration of the War

This was the term that was applied on enlistment for general service in the regular army. Soldiers signed up for a number of years – usually three – or 'the duration of the War'. Sometimes the phrase used was 'until the War is over'.

With the Great War commencing at 11pm on 4 August 1914 (midnight Berlin time) and the Armistice taking effect at 11am on 11 November 1918, it lasted, on the Western Front, for 1,560 days. That is true for the British. The French and Belgians were at war a few days earlier. Many countries joined in, at least notionally, as the war progressed and the likely outcome became more certain.

The USA declared war on Germany on 6 April 1917 and on Austria-Hungary on 7 December 1917. It busied itself under the command of General John Joseph 'Black Jack' Pershing, building up its embryonic army with men and machines. With a few exceptions it did not get heavily involved in fighting until July 1918. Their biggest period of engagement was from 26 September 1918 until the end of the war. They did however sell war materials to the Allies from a much earlier date. And they bankrolled much of the war. Their greatest accomplishment was in their potential to supply both men and materials in huge quantities. The Germans knew this threat and realized they could never win once the American steamroller got under way. They considered they had one last chance and thus launched the Spring 1918 Offensives to pre-empt the involvement of America.

Theatres of War

These are based upon Army Order 391 of 1922, which supersedes earlier orders and was the criteria used to determine whether or not the Victory Medal should be granted (see Chapter 2). Essentially the operational areas are divided into seven regions. These in turn are subdivided and numbered accordingly. The numbering system changed slightly from 1 January 1916.

Many soldiers in fact died in non-operational areas – sometimes, but by no means always, as the result of enemy action. The full text of Army Order 391 of 1922 is complex and most places listed have date qualifications added. These are omitted here for brevity. There were in addition other areas where deaths occurred. I have included these at the end of Table 10 and for uniformity I have continued with the run of numbers.

Table 10. Theatres of War	
1 Western European Theatre	France & Belgium and Italy.
2 Balkan Theatre	Greek Macedonia [Salonica], Serbia, Bulgaria, European Turkey, Gallipoli and islands of the Aegean Sea.
3 Russian Theatre	All operations.
4 Egyptian Theatre	Includes Palestine and Syria.
5 African Theatre	British East Africa, German East Africa, Portuguese East Africa, Rhodesia, Nyasaland and Uganda, German South West Africa, Cameroons, Nigeria, Togoland.
6 Asian Theatres	Hedjaz, Mesopotamia, Persia, South West Arabia, Aden, Frontier Regions [only] of India, Tsing-Tau (China).
7 Australasian Theatre	New Britain, New Ireland, Kaiser Wilhelm-Land, Admiralty Islands, Nauru, German Samoa.
8 Home	All those who died, from all causes, within the British Isles. Many were soldiers wounded overseas in an operational theatre who had been returned to Britain for treatment but succumbed to their injuries. Others died in Britain from illness or accident.
9 At sea	Mainly men on troop or hospital ships which sank. (Royal Navy rules differed from the Army.)
10 Other areas	Those who died in non-operational areas, including prisoners of war who died in captivity.

Strategy and Tactics

Strategic policy may be defined as the long-term objective of, for example, a war. The strategical policy of the Great War was to defeat the enemy and force him to leave occupied territory. How a strategic objective was achieved depended upon the tactics used. The decision to attempt a breakthrough on the Somme was a tactical move. By itself it could not realize the overriding strategical policy but was one of the many tactics used to achieve the goal.

Flak

Flieger Abwehr-Kanone (flak) was the German term for both anti-aircraft guns and the fire from guns designed or adapted for use against aircraft. The idea was not new. It began as early as 1846. By 1870 French balloons in the Franco-Prussian war were being shot down by flak. German anti-aircraft equipment was well developed and most formidable by 1915.

Britain also deployed large numbers of guns to defend important sites in Britain and on the Western Front but their overall success rate was very poor. Anti-aircraft guns were manned by the Royal Garrison Artillery from 1916. The accompanying searchlights were the responsibility of the Royal Engineers.

Calibre

This normally refers to the diameter of the hole (or bore) in the barrel of a gun. In military weapons it is usually measured in inches or millimetres or even in centimetres for large continental artillery pieces. As the bore had rifling groves cut in it, it is important to realize that there were two different measurements. This depends on whether one measures across the wider parts (grooves) or the narrower parts (lands). Unfortunately there is no 'industry standard' so it can be confusing. The British .303 is measured across the lands. If it were calculated across the grooves it would measure .311. In any event, the specified calibre is notional because manufacturing tolerances plus wear and tear result in varying gauge measurements. The differences and reasons are not of concern here.

Parachutes

It is true British aircrew were denied the 'luxury' of parachutes during the Great War. There does not seem to have been any official dictate that prohibited their use on the grounds that, if pilots had parachutes, they would not press home an attack but seek to bale out at the first opportunity. That story seems to be one of the many myths of war although there is some element of truth in it. The reality is a little more complicated.

By 1914 the development of parachutes was already progressing well. There were two main types. One was heavy and bulky and essentially consisted of an upturned container fixed to the side of a balloon basket. It contained a parachute that was attached by a primitive harness to the airman whilst aloft. All he had to do was jump and his weight pulled the parachute from the fixed container and deployed it. The other type was self-contained in a pack worn by the parachutist and opened with a pull or ripcord when required. The former were used during the Great War by observation balloon crews and saved many lives. They were totally unsuitable for aircraft use and the existence of these free-fall types was rapidly forgotten.

Attempts to interest high command in the self-contained parachute were made many times during the war by interested parties. It seems that each time the official on whose desk the letter landed had more pressing matters to consider. Generally he was a senior officer in the flying corps who had not personally seen combat and the effects of being shot down in flames. Besides, as was frequently pointed out, relatively few pilots and observers were in fact being killed. It was not judged of sufficient imperative to expend time and money on development of what was later realized was already quite a good parachute. And they were not prepared to sanction the purchase and issue of the existing model. It may not have been perfect but was certainly better than no parachute! Each approach was met with procrastination. The excuse sometimes given was that the pilots did not want them! Unfortunately I doubt if any combat pilots, as opposed to deskbound senior commanders, were ever asked. Various committees were eventually formed to consider parachutes for airmen but it took until September 1918 for an order for parachutes to be placed. In the event none were ever deployed in action by the Royal Air Force. German pilots were slightly more fortunate in that parachutes were made available to them by mid-1918. Besides the use by balloonists, the only British deployment of parachutes in the Great War was to drop a few spies behind enemy lines in 1917.

Pyrotechnics

Both sides fired vast numbers of flares and rockets to illuminate the battlefields at night and to signal their artillery that support was required. Flares were chemical illuminates generally fired from hand-held pistols and were in a variety of colours. White flares were mostly used to detect or deter approaching enemy patrols. Whenever sentries heard a strange noise the sky would rapidly be lit up. Complete stillness was the only way the intruder might escape detection.

Signalling by rockets was all very well but the observer could only respond to a prearranged code, depending upon which colour rocket was used. If the message was the usual SOS – meaning 'I need artillery support now' – that's fine, but what exactly does the artillery fire at? Like all communications in the First World War, signal rockets were of limited value.

France

France suffered many more war dead and wounded than Britain. The figures are analysed later. We must also remember it was land in France and Belgium where much of the fighting and destruction took place. See Table 11 for some recently published statistics for France.

Table 11. Destruction suffered in France	
Villages 100% destroyed	1,699
Villages 75% destroyed	707
Villages 50% destroyed	1,656
Houses completely destroyed	319,269
Houses partially destroyed	313,675
Factories destroyed	20,603
Railway track destroyed (kilometres)	7,985
Railway bridges destroyed	4,875
Railway tunnels destroyed	12
Roads destroyed (kilometres)	52,754
Non-cultivated land ruined (hectares)	2,060,000
Cultivated land ruined (hectares)	1,740,000

German Spies and their Fate

Prior to the war, Germany set up a spy network in Great Britain. This was discovered by the authorities and, when war started, most involved were arrested and interned. This effectively destroyed German espionage in Britain. Eleven further spies arrived after hostilities began but, because of their incompetence, were quickly discovered and arrested. All were tried and convicted and subsequently executed by firing squad at the Tower of London. The eleven men listed, with their dates of execution, were all buried in the East London cemetery at Plaistow.

Karl Hans Lody	6 November 1914
Karl T Muller	23 June 1915
Wilhelm Johannes Roos	30 July 1915
Haike Marius Petrus Janssen	30 July 1915
Ernst (or Emil) Waldermar Melin	10 September 1915
Agusto Alfredo Roggin	17 September 1915
Fernando Buschmann	19 October 1915
Georg T Breecknow	26 October 1915
Irving Guy Ries	27 October 1915
Albert Mayer	2 December 1915
Ludovico Zender y Hurwitz	11 April 1916

British Army Ranks 1914–1918

In the British Army, because of the peculiarities of the time some 'ranks', for example, lance-corporal, were classified as 'appointments'. Many of the lower ranks especially had traditional, comparable titles for men in non-infantry units. For example, both a sapper (Royal Engineers) and a gunner (Royal Artillery) were approximately equivalent in rank to a private. A bombardier in the Royal Artillery and a forewoman in Queen Mary's Army Auxiliary Corps were equivalent to a corporal.

At the non-commissioned officer (NCO)/warrant officer (WO) level there were many titles depending upon the branch of service and the job. Examples include: 'shoeing and carriage smith corporal', 'artificer lance-corporal', 'bandmaster', and 'armament quarter master sergeant'. Indeed, the supply and provision sections (the quartermasters of the army) had a whole plethora of ranks to themselves. The regimental sergeant-major was the senior warrant officer (first class) in a battalion responsible for discipline. Following the Royal Warrant of 28 January 1915 regimental quarter master sergeants adopted the rank of Warrant Officer, Class II.

Some units had interesting titles for various ranks. In the cavalry a corporal of the horse was equivalent to an infantry sergeant, a conductor in the Royal Army Ordnance Corps was a warrant officer (first class) and a nagsman was a private in the Army Service Corps. A list of ranks is given later.

Commissions during the war were most commonly temporary ones that would not continue much beyond the cessation of hostilities – hence the expression 'Temporary Gentlemen'. As a result of casualties, officers holding comparatively junior substantive ranks quite often held fairly senior posts temporarily, until regular army officers became available to fill those senior posts on a permanent basis. There were no temporary gentlemen appointed on a substantive basis to command brigades and above. For examples of the jobs held by different ranks see Chapter 2. Table 12 shows comparative ranks for officers with the Royal Navy. From its inception on 1 April 1918 until after the end of the Great War, the Royal Air Force used the same rank names as the army.

Table 12. Ranks of officers in the Army and Royal Navy	
Army	**Royal Navy**
Field Marshal	Admiral of the Fleet
General	Admiral
Lieutenant-General	Vice-Admiral
Major-General	Rear-Admiral
Brigadier-General	Commodore
Colonel	Captain
Lieutenant-Colonel	Commander
Major	Lieutenant-Commander
Captain	Lieutenant
Lieutenant	Sub Lieutenant
Second Lieutenant	

Using *Soldiers Died in the Great War* as a source, it is possible to identify well over 100 different army 'ranks' of men and women who perished in the conflict and these are listed below in their main groupings.

Warrant Officers

Armament Sergeant Major, Bandmaster, Battery Sergeant Major, Company Sergeant Major, Conductor, Corporal Major, Drill Sergeant, Farrier Sergeant Major, Machinist Sergeant Major, Master Gunner (WO I), Master Gunner 1st class, Master Gunner 2nd class, Orderly Room Quarter Master Sergeant, Regimental Quarter Master Sergeant, Regimental Sergeant Major, Sergeant Major, Squadron Corporal Major, Staff Sergeant Major, Sub-Conductor, Superintending Clerk Transport Sergeant Major, Warrant Officer, Warrant Officer Class I, Warrant Officer Class II, Wheeler Quarter Master Sergeant.

Sergeants

Armament Quarter Master Sergeant, Armourer Staff Sergeant, Band Sergeant, Battery Quarter Master Sergeant, Bugler Major, Bugler Sergeant, Colour Sergeant, Company Quarter Master Sergeant, Cook Sergeant, Corporal of Horse, Drummer Sergeant, Farrier Corporal of Horse, Farrier Quarter Master Sergeant, Farrier Sergeant, Farrier Staff Sergeant, Fitter Sergeant, Fitter Staff Sergeant, Flight Cadet, Lance Sergeant, Orderly Room Sergeant, Piper Sergeant, Quarter Master Sergeant, Saddler Quarter Master Sergeant, Saddler Sergeant, Saddler Staff Sergeant, Saddle-Tree Maker Sergeant, Sergeant, Shoeing Smith Sergeant, Signaller Sergeant, Squadron Quarter Master Corporal, Staff Sergeant, Trumpeter Sergeant, Wheeler Quarter Master Sergeant, Wheeler Sergeant, Wheeler Staff Sergeant, Wheelwright Sergeant.

Corporals

Artificer Corporal, Artificer Lance Corporal, Bombardier, Corporal, Farrier Corporal, Farrier Staff Corporal, Fitter Corporal, Forewoman, Lance Bombardier, Lance Corporal, Saddler Corporal, Shoeing and Carriage Smith Corporal, Shoeing Smith Corporal, Signaller Bombardier, Signaller Corporal, Signaller Lance Bombardier, Smith Corporal, Wheeler Corporal.

Privates

Armourer, Artificer, Band Boy, Bandsman, Boy, Bugler, Cadet, Cyclist, Driver, Farrier, Fitter, Guardsman, Gunner, Motor Cyclist, Musician, Nagsman, Piper, Private, Rifleman, Rough Rider, Saddler, Sapper, Shoeing & Carriage Smith, Shoeing Smith, Signaller, Strapper, Tailor, Trooper, Trumpeter, Waggoner, Wheeler, Wheelwright, Worker.

See Table 13 for ranks in the Indian Army and Table 14 for selected ranks in the German Army.

Table 13. Indian Army ranks 1914-1918 (Infantry)

Viceroy's Commissioned Officers

Subadar-Major	
Subadar	No British Army equivalents
Jemadar	

Other Ranks

Havildar-Major	Company Sergeant-Major
Havildar	Sergeant
Naik	Corporal
Lance-Naik	Lance-Corporal
Sepoy	Private

Table 14. Selected German Army Ranks 1914-1918

Armierungssoldat	Armourer
Fahrer	Driver
Feldwebel	Company Sergeant-Major
Füsilier	Rifleman
Gefreiter	Lance-Corporal
Grenadier	Bomber
Hauptmann	Captain
Infanterist	Infantry soldier
Jäger	Rifleman
Kanonier	Gunner

Table 14 - *continued*

Landsturmmann	Storm-trooper
Leutnant	Second Lieutenant
Major	Major
Musketier	Private
Oberleutnant	Lieutenant
Oberst	Colonel
Oberstleutnant	Lieutenant-Colonel
Pionier	Pioneer
Reservist	Reservist
Rittmeister	Captain (Cavalry)
Schütze	Sniper or Marksman
Sergeant	Senior Non Commissioned Officer
Soldat	Soldier/private
Telegraphist	Telegraphist
Ulan	Cavalryman
Unteroffizier	Non Commissioned Officer

Stores

War is a costly business and not just in respect of the human and animal lives lost or injured. The following few figures give us just a small picture of the logistical problem of supplying the 'men at the front'. Table 15 shows stores shipped to France, for use on the Western Front alone, during the war. There were many other items and altogether over 25 million tons were shipped.

To give some small idea of what all this represents, Table 16 shows some items purchased for the army in 1918 alone. This is but a small sample. There were many more items of equipment, etc. With cigarettes at the time of the Great War being much smaller than they are now, and without a filter tip, this represents rather a lot of cigarettes. No wonder so many pictures of soldiers show them with either a pipe or cigarette in their mouths.

Table 15. Stores shipped to France during the war	
Supply	**Weight in tons**
Food	3,240,948
Fodder (oats and hay)	5,438,602
Coal	3,922,391
Ammunition	9,438,614
Ordnance (artillery pieces)	1,761,777
Petrol and sundries	758,614
Royal Engineer stores (general)	1,369,894
Railway material	988,354

Note: The difference between approximate imperial and metric tons (tonnes) is negligible for the purposes of this table.

Table 16. Some items purchased for the Army in 1918	
Biscuits	129,204,000lbs (58,606,549kg)
Margarine	52,203,000lbs (23,679,125kg)
Sugar	167,234,000lbs (75,856,844 kg)
Meat and vegetable rations	38,262,000 tins
Preserved meat (Bully beef)	168,745,000 tins
Tobacco and cigarettes	14,409,000lbs (6,535879kg)

To help with the supply of meat, shortages of which were occurring due to losses in shipping caused by enemy submarines, rabbits were introduced as an occasional substitute early in 1917. During the remainder of the war 5,649,797 rabbit skins were sold to help with the costs. Many women of the time wore rabbit skin (marketed as coney) fur coats.

Women on the Western Front

In August 1918 the following numbers of women were recorded as being on the Western Front: Royal Army Medical Corps (all grades, British, Colonial and American) 7,123; British Red Cross Society (nursing sisters and other workers) 1,094; Queen Mary's Army Auxiliary Corps 7,808; YMCA, Church Army, Salvation Army, other institutions 1,056; General Service Voluntary Aid Detachments (VAD, drivers) 99. Of these, 302 were to die, including 45 as a direct result of enemy action.

Boring But Important Statistics

The figures shown below are derived, wherever possible, from official sources. These include: *Statistics of the Great War, Official Histories, Hansard* (5 May 1921), *Soldiers Died in the Great War* and the Commonwealth War Graves Commission.

Unfortunately there are many official sources, no two of which seem to agree. Indeed the official *Statistics of the Great War* sometimes shows different figures for apparently the same criteria on different pages! This is a compilation using the figures most likely to be accurate. We must realize that different sources use different criteria. Often they do not show clearly who is included or excluded or for what precise period. Again, whether or not all theatres of war are included is often shrouded in mystery. For many events, especially early in the war, few records were kept. Reasonably accurate statistics did not start until October 1916. Because of the very nature of war the record keeping was not precise. Sometimes records were lost or deliberately destroyed. Many men simply disappeared without trace. Unless otherwise specified, the figures relate solely to British personnel. Sometimes however they include British, Dominion, Commonwealth and Colonial Forces. In that case the term 'Commonwealth' is used as an indicator.

Please use all these statistics with the 'health warning' attributed to Benjamin Disraeli who once said, 'there are three kinds of lies: lies, damned lies, and statistics'! We must also remember that, although the Armistice took effect on 11 November 1918, that did not mean the end to all conflict. It was the cessation of hostilities on the Western Front. But it took a while for the message that it was over to reach far-flung operations. And fighting continued in Russia between the Allies and the Bolsheviks until the final withdrawal on 12 October 1919.

Additionally, men still died of wounds, disease or accidents after the Armistice and indeed sometimes long after the official casualty lists had closed. Variations will also occur as, for example, deaths were often not recorded until after the fateful event and in consequence the wrong date attributed. For the First World War the Commonwealth War Graves Commission's records run from 4 August 1914 to 31 August 1921.

Table 17. Overall mobilization and losses figures			
Country	**Mobilized**	**Military deaths**	**Wounded**[a]
British Forces[b]	9,496,170[c]	989,075	2,121,906[d]
France	8,410,000	1,385,300[e]	4,266,000
Italy	5,615,000	462,391	953,886
Russia	12,000,000	1,700,000	4,950,000
United States	4,355,000[f]	115,660[g]	205,690
Germany	11,000,000	1,808,545	4,247,143[h]
Austro-Hungary	7,800,000	1,200,000	3,620,000[i]
Turkey	2,850,000	325,000	400,000

Note: The figures are based upon War Office statistics and do not include civilian deaths during or after the war, regardless of cause.
[a] Number of times wounded, not necessarily the number of men. Many men were wounded more than once.
[b] All British and Commonwealth forces.
[c] Includes all arms, e.g. army, naval and air services, plus women's services. Not all saw active service and many remained at home. Of the total, 8,586,202 served in the army.
[d] An additional 196,318 Commonwealth all ranks were reported as prisoners of war or interned in neutral countries. Of these 16,402 died in captivity.
[e] It is thought around 400,000 French colonial troops also perished in the war.
[f] Of these, nearly 2 million had arrived in France before the Armistice.
[g] Of these around 51,000 relate to deaths in battle, i.e. killed in action or died of wounds.
[h] In addition about 1 million German officers and men were captured and became prisoners of war. During 6 Aug.–11 Nov. 1918 (the last '100' days) 186,684 enemy prisoners were captured on the Western Front.
[i] Another 2 million Austro-Hungarian servicemen became prisoners of war.

Table 17 shows the numbers of people mobilized and of losses. The total estimated population in the British Isles at July 1914 was 46,331,548. By the end of the war Germany had 3,403,000 men, both combat and otherwise, available on the Western Front with more in other theatres of war and at Home. To oppose them Britain mustered 1,731,578, France 2,562,000 and the

USA 1,924,000 men respectively on the Western Front. Not all of these were combatants.

The word 'strength' was officially defined as follows. Ration strength was the total number of men (excluding coloured labour and prisoners of war) who were being fed from Army stocks in France (and Belgium). Combatant strength was all fighting troops (infantry, cavalry, artillery, and engineer field units), together with the troops in divisional or base depots. Rifle strength was officers and men in infantry battalions alone. The following numbers, for 11 November 1918, are very different from those in Table 18 and we must remember only apply to France and Belgium: ration strength 1,731,578, combatant strength 1,164,790, rifle strength 461,748.

Table 18. Estimated strength of British Army (only) personnel (including Territorial Force, and regular reservists)		
Officers	4 August 1914	28,060
	11 November 1918	164,255
Other ranks	4 August 1914	708,618
	1 November 1918	3,595,216

Note: Included in the totals for Nov. 1918 were 1,514,933 officers and men in various medical categories retained in Britain.

Table 19 shows the estimated British air strength. There were, in addition, vast quantities of spares including 22,171 airframes and 37,702 engines! This, no doubt, is the reason for the often-quoted number of 20,000 aircraft available to the Royal Air Force in November 1918. Table 20 gives the figures for the Royal Navy.

Table 19. Estimated strength of British air services (all branches that served during the war)		
Officers	August 1914	276
	November 1918	27,333
Other ranks	August 1914	1,797
	November 1918	263,842
First-line strength in aircraft		
August 1914	50 aeroplanes and seaplanes, 6 airships	
November 1918	3,300 aeroplanes and seaplanes, 103 airships.	

Table 20. Estimated strength of the Royal Navy (all branches that served during the war)

Officers	15 July 1914	9,986
	Commissioned or entered service during the war	45,391
Other ranks	15 July 1914	136,061
	Mobilized or entered service during the war:	448,799

Major British warships[a]	4 Nov. 1914	Ships lost[b]	11 Nov. 1918
Battleships: Dreadnoughts	20	13[c]	33
Pre-Dreadnoughts	40		29
Battlecruisers	9	3	9
Cruisers and light cruisers	108	19	129
Torpedo boat destroyers	215	64	407
Aircraft carriers[d]	1	3	13
Submarines	76	54	137

[a] Details from *Official History (Naval Operations)*
[b] Includes not only ships sunk – some deliberately as blockships – but also others which were scrapped, assigned to other navies, or converted to depot ships etc. during the war.
[c] Battleship losses include pre-Dreadnoughts.
[d] The aircraft carriers might more properly be described as seaplane carriers.

Table 21 includes all causes of death (e.g. killed in action, died of wounds or otherwise died from causes which may or may not have involved enemy action, such as accident, disease or drowning). It must be realized that the vast majority of men in the Royal Navy who died were technically drowned, but this was usually as a result of enemy action.

For the figures listed for the air services, 43 per cent were killed in action or died of wounds; 32 per cent were killed or died as a result of flying accidents etc. and 25 per cent died from other causes. For full details of all British and Commonwealth air service casualties, and a lot more, see *Airmen Died in the Great War* by Chris Hobson.

The figures concerning the Army are an amalgam of causes approximately attributable to the three main groupings – killed in action, died of wounds (both attributable to enemy action) and died, which applies to non-battle casualties. For example, in the non-battle casualties are included over 283 army officers and men known to have drowned by misfortune. The fatal casualties also includes those who died, other than in

---

Table 21. Deaths in the British armed forces during the Great War

British Army (excluding Royal Flying Corps)

Cause of death	Officers	Other ranks	Totals
Killed in action	27,444 (70%)	437,872 (66%)	465,316 (66%)
Died of wounds	8,508 (22%)	137,935 (21%)	146,443 (21%)
Died	3,318 (8%)	86,153 (13%)	89,471 (13%)
Total	39,270	661,960	701,230

Royal Navy

Officers	3,279
Other ranks	36,533
Total	39,812

Royal Naval Division

Officers	463
Other ranks	8,127
Total	8,590

Air Services[a]

Officers	6,059
Other ranks	3,069
Total	9,128

Officers and men in the British Mercantile Marine	14,879
Officers and men of British Fishing Vessels	434

[a] Royal Flying Corps, Royal Naval Air Service and Royal Air Force.

action, in the United Kingdom and overseas, perhaps from accident or disease.

On average 634 British and Commonwealth service personnel were killed every day of the Great War. The British Army alone lost, on average, 450 each day. Overall, on all sides, one person perished about every ten seconds.

The Commonwealth War Graves Commission shows the following figures in its Annual Report for 2007. The figures are for Great War servicemen and women from the United Kingdom and Colonies, Undivided India, Canada, Australia, New Zealand and South Africa.

Identified war burials	587,684
Unidentified war burials	187,853
Total number of graves	775,537
Commemorated on memorials	526,974

Examination of these figures reveals the stark truth that, despite the best endeavours, vast numbers of British and Commonwealth bodies remain to this day where they fell – be it on land or sea. They are not alone, for there are also many hundreds of thousands of soldiers, sailors and airmen from other nations who fought and died in the Great War and who have no known grave. They are all still missing.

Table 22. British military deaths from all causes by year

	Officers	Other ranks	Totals
1914 (5 Aug.–31 Dec.)	1,465	25,421	26,886
1915	5,694	107,408	113,102
1916	9,125	161,057	170,182
1917	11,079	189,528	200,607
1918 (to 11 Nov.)	10,886	174,266	185,152
Other periods	1,021	4,280	5,301
Totals	39,270	661,960	701,230

Table 23. Miscellaneous statistics for the Army

Soldiers only	Killed in action	Died of wounds	Died
Western European theatre	404,255	120,890	34,284
United Kingdom	20	6,167	26,369
Other theatres	33,597	10,878	25,500
Total	437,872	137,935	86,153
Total of British other ranks who lost their lives in the Great War			661,960

Table 24. Deaths from all causes in various different branches of the army			
Corps etc	Officers	Other ranks	Totals
Cavalry (total)	1,047	8,727	9,774
Artillery (RFA)	2,511	30,451	32,962
Artillery (RGA)	894	12,749	13,643
(Total Artillery)	(3,405)	(43,200)	(46,605)
Medical Corps	709	5,538	6,247
Royal Engineers	1,165	16,125	17,290
Army Service Corps	410	8,050	8,462

Table 25. Deaths of Commonwealth service personnel	
Country	Total Service Deaths
Canada	64,962
Newfoundland	1,204
Australia	61,927
New Zealand	18,051
Undivided India	74,190
South Africa	9,474
Other colonies	507
Total	230,315

Attrition

When taking into account the casualties in all armed forces who died from any cause, plus those missing, wounded, or made prisoner of war, approximately 52.3 per cent of all Allied forces became casualties compared with 57.5 per cent of enemy forces. What none of these statistics reveal, however, is the immense suffering endured by the victim before oblivion intervened. I doubt many truly died instantaneously.

Chapter 11

A GUIDE TO VISITING THE WESTERN FRONT BATTLEFIELDS

Having read about the Great War and maybe seen pictures, films or videos, the next step surely is to visit some of the battlefields. It really is simple. You can use the services of a specialist travel company or go on your own. The principle is no different from taking any other kind of holiday.

This is not a conventional annual guidebook and so I am not recommending any particular places to stay or eat as they can easily go out of business or change in quality over the years. It is far better to consult a good travel agent or surf the internet to find somewhere to suit your taste. What I am offering are sensible travel tips and advice commensurate with travel on the Western Front. Please do not think that the First World War only concerned the Ypres Salient with Passchendaele or the Somme. There is so much more to see. Why not visit Neuve Chapelle, or the Loos battlefields, or Cambrai, or indeed any of the battlefields where British soldiers fought and died? A list of battles appears at the end of this chapter. The French battlefields and museums around Verdun are also well worth visiting and give some idea of the huge sacrifices made by our allies.

Getting There

The main areas of the Western Front are very easy to reach and your motoring organization can supply not only the best route but inform of any current disruptions likely to cause delay. The easiest ways to cross the English Channel are by ferry or the Channel Tunnel. Quite frankly, any time of year is good to visit the area for each season has its own attractions and disadvantages.

Suggested Kit List

The most important items are of course your passport, travel documents, euros and a credit card. You should also carry your EHIC (European Health Insurance Card) that offers limited medical cover in the European Community. It is additionally highly advisable to have a separate comprehensive holiday insurance policy.

If you are driving then be sure to take your driving licence, insurance certificate – endorsed for overseas use – and the vehicle's registration document. You are required to adjust your headlamp beams to suit driving on the right on the continent, even if you only intending to drive in daylight hours. Compulsory accessories include a breakdown warning triangle, a spare set of bulbs, a first aid kit and a high-visibility jacket for each occupant. I recommend a vehicle recovery insurance that will repatriate passengers and car and supply a loan car in event of breakdown. Motoring organizations have various policies on offer. It is always best to check the latest driving regulations, including essential car accessories, before starting out. Laws and regulations change and do not always mirror those in the United Kingdom.

Most personal items, left at home in error, can be purchased overseas. The amount and extent of luggage you take will depend upon the type of accommodation chosen and the amount of time you plan to spend there. There are however several extra items which may be useful and increase your enjoyment.

A good guidebook for the area you are visiting.

Overview and local maps.

Perhaps a GPS or similar device and a compass. (See separate section on trench maps.)

Suitable warm/cool weatherproof clothing and footwear depending on the season.

Notebook and pencil.

All-weather ballpoint pen (for signing cemetery registers).

Torch – always useful.

Camera, plus spare batteries and films or memory cards.

Binoculars.

Water bottle. It can be very thirsty work exploring the battlefields.

Useful Telephone Numbers

Throughout the European Union the general emergency number is 112. It works equally well in the United Kingdom. If you are using a mobile phone it is simplest and generally best to use this number for any emergency service within the European Union. Even if you have no credit or SIM card in your phone, it will work for the 112 designated emergency number. Most operators speak English.

In France the quickest response to a medical emergency is by dialling the fire brigade (Pompiers) who will despatch a competent medical team. Separate emergency numbers for France are: medical (Samu) 15, police 17, emergency medical aid or fire (Pompier) 18. In Belgium the numbers for fire or ambulance are 100 and for police 101.

The numbers for British Embassies etc. are:

Foreign and Commonwealth Office – London	++ 44 (0) 207 008 1500
British Embassy – Paris, France	++ 33 (0) 1 44 51 31 00
British Consul – Lille, France	++ 33 (0) 3 20 12 82 72
British Embassy – Brussels, Belgium	++ 32 (0) 2 287 62 11

The initial two digits in international dialling can vary in different parts of the world. Consequently the international codes are frequently shown as: ++ followed by the country code. Here we are only considering calls between the United Kingdom, France and Belgium. Within those countries the initial access codes are currently: 00. Therefore dial for:

United Kingdom	00 44 (followed by national number – but see below)
France	00 33 (followed by national number – but see below)
Belgium	00 32 (followed by national number – but see below)

When dialling the United Kingdom from France or Belgium enter 00 44 then dial the full UK number *but omit* the leading (0) (zero). Thus, if you wanted to call 01234 567899 from France or Belgium dial: 00 44 1234 567899. With mobile phones you can generally just dial the usual number and the system will sort out where you are calling. If that does not work treat your mobile as a landline and enter the full international access codes, then omit the leading (0) zero but enter the remainder of the national number.

For tourist information contact:

French Tourist Board, Lincoln House, 300 High Holborn, London WC1V 7JH (tel. 09068 244 123): http://uk.franceguide.com/
Belgian Tourist Office, Innovation Centre, 225 Marsh Wall, London E14 9FW (tel. 0800-954 5245): http://www.visitbelgium.com/

Language

There are many differences between Belgium and France and language is just one element. Belgium is a small but vibrant country that is anxious to be involved in international commerce and world affairs. In consequence most modern Belgians speak several languages, with English being the most frequent second language. That said, many farmers and others from rural areas near the Ypres Salient only speak and understand Flemish. Conversation can occasionally be complicated!

The French are very proud of their culture, traditions and language and in France English is not so widely spoken. One may be lucky and find a friendly soul to help out, but do not presume. Finding that the waiter in the hotel speaks English is one thing but trying to explain exactly what you are doing to an irate French farmer who does not speak English can be quite another. It is also rare to find a French gendarme or police officer conversant in English. A little French can go a long way and be very useful on the battlefields and in the towns.

If all else fails, smiling, whilst reaching for the phrase book, often helps. Always be polite and friendly, as a guest in another country.

Recommended Guidebooks

There are, in addition to the short general list below, many specialist books concentrating upon specific battles and areas of conflict. The Battleground Europe series of guides published by Pen & Sword Books Ltd covers many of the areas on the Western Front and are well worth reading. An up-to-date list can be obtained from the publishers of this book. Guidebooks are notorious for becoming rapidly out of date, especially regarding accommodation and popular tourist attractions. Always check you have a recent edition.

General Books

Coombs, Rose E. *Before Endeavours Fade* (London: Battle of Britain Prints international Ltd – many editions). This is still one of the best single-volume guidebooks available.

Holt, Major Tonie and Mrs Valmai. various battlefield guides, for example:
Battlefield Guide to the Somme (Pen & Sword, 1996)
Battlefield Guide, Ypres Salient (Pen & Sword, 1997)
Battlefield Guide to the Western Front – North (Pen & Sword, 2004)

Battlefield Guide to the Western Front – South (Pen & Sword, 2005)

Detailed maps are included within each book and in the Somme and Ypres Salient editions separate maps are included which give a good overview and much more besides.

Walking Guides

Reed, Paul. *Walking the Somme* (Pen & Sword, 1997)
Reed, Paul. *Walking the Salient* (Pen & Sword, 1999)
Reed, Paul. *Walking Arras* (Pen & Sword 2007)
These are essential companions when walking the areas covered.

Maps

It is worth noting that many place names we are familiar with are not spelt the same in their own country. For example Dunkirk is spelt Dunkerque and Ypres is now Ieper. A grid showing maps for both France and Belgium can be obtained from the Institut Geographique National (IGN) or Nationaal Geografisch Instituut (NGI) or viewed on the internet.

France

By far the best to take are the IGN series. For a good overview and general driving (includes parts of Belgium): 1:250,000 scale (1cm = 2.5km), IGN RO1 Nord-Pas-de-Calais, Picardie. For more local detail, in 1:100,000 scale (1cm = 1km) IGN maps numbered from 01 to 10 cover the main battlefields but these two are especially useful.

> Map 02 Lille – Dunkerque (Dunkirk to Arras and including the Ypres Salient)
> Map 04 Laon – Arras (includes the Somme, St Quentin and Amiens)

Much more detail can be seen on the IGN 1:25 000 series (1cm = 250m). There are many covering the battlefields and it is worth consulting the latest catalogue from IGN before purchasing the ones for your chosen area.

Belgium

I recommend similar maps by NGI. These maps have a different numbering sequence and, for the Salient, the area is covered by Sheet 28. The area is subdivided and sections may be purchased in 1:50,000 or 1:20,000 scales. At 1:20,000 scale, the sections within Sheet 28 (using current spellings of Belgian towns) are:

28: 1–2   Poperinge–Ieper
28: 3–4   Zonnebeke–Moorslede
28: 5–6   Heuvelland–Mesen
28: 7–8   Wervik–Menen

You may also require sections within other sheets for other parts of Belgium.

As an alternative to IGN/NGI maps, Michelin make excellent maps for France and Belgium in various scales.

First World War Trench Maps

These are the maps, prepared during the course of the war, usually at 1:10,000 or 1:20,000 scale, showing not only the usual features but also with the enemy trench systems superimposed. Some maps also show and name the British trenches. British trench lines are shown in blue and German ones in red. That is until mid-1918 when, to conform to the French system, the situation was reversed. Thereafter British and Allied trenches were in red and the enemy trenches in blue. Check with the map date and key to verify which identification is in use. The method of pinpointing a map reference on trench maps is different to that in use today. It is explained, usually with examples, on each trench map or digital version and a few minutes learning the principle used would be advantageous. War diaries often quote map references and it is very useful to be able to locate the positions quoted on a trench map. Original maps are collectors' items and rather expensive but there are alternatives. It is possible to purchase photocopies of the desired area from the Imperial War Museum or from the Western Front Association.

Digital Mapping

Perhaps better still are the CD or DVD versions available which contain a very good selection of maps that can be printed – and in case of the DVD, with so much more besides. Before buying any digital item check it is compatible with your computer system. One thing about paper trench maps is that they do not 'crash' or become out of date!

There is now a system called LinesMan that incorporates around 750 scanned trench maps at 1:10,000 scale, plus sections of current French IGN maps at 1:25,000 scale, along with aerial photographs that cover much of the Western Front. Modern Belgian NGI maps are now also incorporated. It is possible to view any desired area on a computer and, if required, see two different maps side by side. Additionally any map can be viewed in 3-D that enables one to see the exact lie of the land. The features it incorporates are truly amazing and it revolutionizes trench mapping. Perhaps its greatest attribute is the ability to download maps to a hand-held GPS device and then plot your precise position whilst on the battlefields. This can be seen superimposed on either the trench maps or modern maps. I have used it 'in action' and highly recommend it.

Visiting the Battlefields

The swathes of land taken over by the trench systems of the First World War were, and still are, valuable agricultural fields. As soon as the war finished the farmers returned to their land and attempted to restore it to a pre-war state. They were not interested in preserving the legacy of the war. Today, most of the land fought over remains in private ownership and the farmers do not take kindly to their crops being trampled by visitors – most especially without prior permission.

It does not mean however that little remains to be seen on the public parts of the Western Front. Far from it. And most can be accessed easily and legally. Apart from visible scars on the landscape there are many museums and preserved sights to visit. There are areas however that cannot be reached by road or public path and it is here that the use of binoculars may help you avoid trespassing. Using the extract from the Battles Nomenclature Committee report of 1921, shown at the end of this chapter, you will get some idea as to the extent of the fighting on the Western Front. It shows only the places and years involved. Many were fought over more than once and reference to the *Official History of the War: Military Operations: France and Belgium* or other good history books will flesh out the details of the battles. The list, together with maps, gazetteers and guidebooks, can be used as a pointer to places to study and visit. There are so many worthwhile places to see and a little research will make your journey so much more rewarding.

There are literally thousands of cemeteries on the Western Front where British and Commonwealth soldiers lie buried. No visit to the battlefields can be complete without visiting some to remember the brave men and women who perished in the Great War. There are also many French, Belgian, American and German cemeteries, as well as those dedicated to other nationalities. It was British policy that every man should either have an individually named grave or be commemorated by name near to where he fell on one of several memorials constructed on the battlefields. Many bodies were recovered but not identified and were buried alongside their comrades. Those graves bear the mark *Known Unto God* and show as much information as possible, but all too frequently they simply state, *A Soldier of the Great War*. I have deliberately not suggested any particular cemeteries. It is for you to choose. The smaller cemeteries and the areas set aside in communal cemeteries contain a Cross of Sacrifice. Larger cemeteries also have a large Stone of Remembrance. Aside from smaller burial sites the graves are arranged in plots and then usually in uniform rows. Reference to an individual grave is by plot (if

Grave of unknown British soldier.

more than one), then by row and finally by grave number from the beginning of the row. For example the grave reference for Lieutenant Henry Webber, who died of wounds aged 68 and is buried in Dartmoor Cemetery, Becordel-Becourt is: I.G.54 (Plot 1, Row G, Grave 54).

The British and Commonwealth graves are beautifully tended by gardeners of the Commonwealth War Graves Commission and are a credit to that wonderful organization. When visiting any cemetery please respect the dead and do not mark a gravestone in any way to try and improve photography. They can be photographed quite adequately by shading the camera from the sun and/or choosing a slightly angled shot. It may sometimes be necessary to return at a better time of day when the light is more appropriate. Flash does not usually work as it obliterates any contrast. It is perfectly acceptable to place a poppy cross or wreath in front of a grave and then sign the visitors book found in the unlocked safe at most larger cemeteries or memorials. That safe

Grave of unknown German soldier.

usually contains a copy of the cemetery register. It is for all to use and must not be taken away.

If in the Ypres Salient and time permits I suggest you go to the Menin Gate in good time for the Last Post ceremony that takes place every night of the year at 8pm. It is very moving and really brings home the great sacrifice made by so many. Please just stand silently, respectfully and observe. Despite their excellence, do not applaud the buglers from the town fire service – it is not appropriate

Guidebooks will show precise locations of sites and suggest tours within your chosen area but there are a few places one should really not miss and are well worth incorporating into your itinerary. We must also remember that there were other areas where British soldiers fought and died – for example on the Marne and the Aisne. In addition there are literally hundreds of miles of front where our brave allies, the Belgians and French were solely responsible. The Verdun battlefields alone took hundreds of thousands of lives and there is much to see there. Alas space permits only brief details of a few places. There are many more.

Belgium (Ypres Salient)

• Talbot House, Poperinghe: Its 'Everyman's Club' was started in 1915 by Reverend 'Tubby' Clayton as a rest home for soldiers going to and from the front. Famous for the 'Upper Room' – a tranquil chapel on the top floor, its hospitality and motto, 'abandon rank all ye who enter here'. (Visitor toilets available.)

• St Georges Memorial Church, Ypres: A very moving British church containing many memorials to the dead.

• Menin Gate: An imposing arched gateway to Ypres that commemorates by name nearly 55,000 soldiers with no known grave who died in the area before 15 August 1917. A further 35,000, who died after that date, are commemorated on the walls around Tyne Cot Cemetery.

• Hill 60: A preserved area where much tunnelling and fighting took place throughout most of the war. Many dead are still beneath it. Caterpillar mine crater is adjacent.

• Spanbroekmolen (Pool of Peace): The largest crater resulting from the mines blown on 7 June 1917 to open the Messines offensive.

• Sanctuary Wood: Preserved trenches now in private ownership. (Customer toilets available.)

France

• Thiepval Memorial: The largest memorial on the Western Front commemorating over 72,000 named soldiers with no known grave who died in the Somme region. There is a visitors' centre near to the memorial. (Visitor toilets available.)

Thiepval Memorial to the Missing of the Somme.

• Vimy Ridge and Canadian Memorial: An area of preserved trenches and tunnels. The outstanding memorial commemorates 11,000 Canadian soldiers with no known grave who died in the First World War. (Visitor toilets available.)

• La Boisselle Mine Crater: An enormous crater resulting from the mine exploded on 1 July 1916. Unlike the craters in Belgium this one is dry and the full extent of its size can be appreciated from its rim. It is in private ownership but can be freely visited.

• Ulster Tower: In the heart of the Somme it contains a small museum and is dedicated to the memory of the Ulstermen who died in the Great War. (Customer toilets available.)

• Newfoundland Park: An area of preserved trenches, which gives some idea of the systems in place for the Battle of the Somme. It especially commemorates the men from Newfoundland, which was not part of Canada at the time. (Visitor toilets available.)

• Arras: There is an important memorial here to the missing of the region. It is attached to the Faubourg d'Amiens Commonwealth War Graves Cemetery and includes a separate memorial to missing airmen. Also at Arras is a new underground tunnel system in the Wellington Quarry, dug largely by New Zealand tunnellers and intended to shelter thousands of soldiers prior to the Battle of Arras. (Visitor toilets available.)

Museums

There are many municipal and private museums and a visit to the local *mairie* (town hall) will often reveal their whereabouts. Before visiting it is advisable to check the opening hours and cost and indeed if it is still there, as museums come and go! All museums vary in content, specialization and presentation. Some may appeal to you more than others. A few of the larger, and excellent museums in Belgium are:

In Flanders Fields Museum. The Cloth Hall, Ieper [Ypres]. (Visitors toilets available.)
Hooge Crater Museum, Old Chapel, Meenseweg 467-8902 (Menin Road), Zillebeke. (Customer toilets available.)
Dugout Experience. Ieperstraat 5, B-8980 Zonnebeke. (Visitor toilets available.)

And in France:

Historial de la Grande Guerre, Péronne. (Visitor toilets available.)
Musée des Abris, outside Basilique, Albert. (Nearby toilets available.)
Notre Dame de Lorette.

Metal Detectors

Do not take a metal detector with you. It is against the law to use them in most of the First World War battlefields. It is now also an offence to remove artefacts, however found, from the battlefields without official sanction and this law can be rigorously enforced. A good policy is that suggested at many world heritage sights. 'Take only photographs. Leave only footprints' – and even then be careful neither to photograph any current military installations nor to trespass.

Munitions Seen on the Battlefields

The first and only rule is: leave them alone! During the Great War the belligerents fired many hundreds of millions of shells of varying calibres and types. The British alone fired over 170 million shells – many containing poison gas. There were also many more hundreds of millions of grenades, mortar bombs and other lethal devices used in the fighting. Many millions failed to explode at the time, for often quite simple reasons. They were designed, with great skill and expense, to explode and kill. And that is what they can and sometimes will still do, if interfered with. Barely a year goes by without someone being killed by unexploded First or Second World War munitions. Leave their disposal to the French or Belgian authorities.

Beware. Even items such as deactivated shells etc. bought at militaria fairs can cause you problems with the authorities. Not all are properly deactivated. Relic rifles, for example, can be deemed under the strict British Firearm Acts as not legally deactivated. Many rusty and bent remnant guns, with their bolts etc. firmly closed, are found upon closer inspection to be loaded. They were probably lost during fighting and it must be assumed that such weapons, when used in warfare, would indeed quite properly be loaded.

Battles and Engagements of British Army on the Western Front

Table 26 shows the names, places and dates of most battles in France and Flanders, 1914–18, involving British soldiers. With the help of guidebooks and good maps the areas can be visited today. What remains to be seen varies from place to place, but an ever-present indicator and reminder of the fighting that occurred are the war cemeteries dotting the landscape in every place. There are literally thousands of those silent cities standing as a stark reminder of the human sacrifice that took place all those years ago.

Further details of the battles, affairs, actions, etc., together with details of the principal units involved, can be found in *A Record of the Battles and Engagements of the British Armies in France & Flanders 1914–1918*.

There were of course other actions that were not named by the Battles Nomenclature Committee in 1921. Some of these were diversionary attacks to draw attention away from large battles elsewhere on the Western Front. To give just one example, on 30 June 1916 three battalions of the Royal Sussex Regiment attacked at Richebourg to draw German attention away from the next day's Battle of the Somme. Despite well over 300 men being killed and a Victoria Cross awarded, the 'battle' was never recognized or even mentioned in the *Official History of the War*. The terms battles, affairs, actions, etc. were those given by the Nomenclature Committee. Some battles at first glance seem to be duplicated but it must be remembered the same ground was often fought over more than once. The remainder of the time when not 'fighting' was officially spent 'holding the line'.

Table 26. Battles and engagements of the British Army on the Western Front

Phase I. The German Invasion 1914

Operations. Retreat from Mons	(23 August–5 September 1914)
Battle of Mons	23–24 August 1914
Action of louges	24 August 1914
Action of Solesmes	25 August 1914
Affair of Landrecies	25 August 1914
Battle of Le Cateau	26 August 1914
Affair of Le Grand Fayt	26 August 1914
Affair of treux	27 August 1914
Affair at Cérizy	27 August 1914
Affair at Néry	1 September 1914
Action of Crépy en Valois	1 September 1914
Action of Villers Cottérêts	1 September 1914
Operations. Advance to the Aisne	(6 September–1 October 1914)
Battle of the Marne 1914	12–15 September 1914
Action on Aisne Heights	20 September 1914
Action of Chivy	26 September 1914
Operations. Defence of Antwerp	(4–10 October 1914)
Operations in Flanders 1914	(10 October–22 November 1917)
Battle of La Bassée	10 October–2 November 1914
Battle of Messines 1914	12 October–2 November 1914
Battle of Armentières 1914	13 October–2 November 1914
The Battles of Ypres 1914 [1st Ypres]	19 October–22 November 1914
Battle of Langemarck 1914	21–24 October 1914
Battle of Gheluvelt	29–31 October 1914
Battle of Nonne Bosschen	11 November 1914

Phase II. Trench Warfare 1914–1916

Winter Operations 1914–15	(November 1914–February 1915)
Defence of Festubert	23–24 November 1914
Attack on Wytschaete	14 December 1914
Defence of Givenchy	25 January 1915
First action of Givenchy	2–21 December 1915
Affairs of Cuinchy	29 January, 1 and 6 February 1915
Summer Operations 1915	
Battle of Neuve Chapelle	10–13 March 1915
Action of St Eloi	14–15 March 1915
Capture of Hill 60	17–22 April 1915

The Battles of Ypres 1915 [2nd Ypres]   22 April–25 May 1915
Battle of Gravenstafel   22–23 April 1915
Battle of St Julien   24 April–4 May 1915
Battle of Frezenberg   8–13 May 1915
Battle of Bellewaarde   24–25 May 1915
Battle of Aubers [Ridge]   9 May 1915
    Attack on Fromelles   9 May 1915
    Attack at Rue du Bois   9 May 1915
Battle of Festubert   15–25 May 1915
    2nd action of Givenchy   15–16 June 1915
    1st attack on Bellewaarde   16 June 1915
Actions at Hooge   19 and 30 July and 9 August 1915
Battle of Loos   25 September–8 October 1915
    Action Piètre   25 September 1915
    Action of Bois Grenier   25 September 1915
    2nd attack on Bellewaarde   25–26 September 1915
    Hohenzollern Redoubt   13–19 October 1915
Local Operations 1916
    Actions of the Bluff   14–15 February and 2 March 1916
    Actions of St Eloi Craters   27 March–16 April 1916
    German attack Vimy Ridge   21 May 1915
Battle of Mount Sorre   2–13 June 1916

Phase III. Allied Offensive 1916
Operations on the Somme   (1 July–18 November 1916)
Battle of the Somme 1916   1 July–18 November 1916
Battle of Albert 1916   1–13 July 1916
    Attack on Gommecourt Salient   1 July 1916
Battle of Bazentin   14–17 July 1916
    Attack at Fromelles   19 July 1916
    Attacks High Wood   20–25 July 1916
Battle of Delville Wood   15 July–3 September 1916
Battle of Pozières   23 July–3 September 1916
Battle of Guillemont   3–6 September 1916
Battle of Ginchy   9 September 1916
Battle of Flers-Courcelette   15–22 September 1916
Battle of Morval   25–28 September 1916
Battle of Thiepval   26–28 September 1916
Battle of Le Transloy   1–18 October
Battle of the Ancre Heights   1 October–11 November 1916
Battle of the Ancre   13–18 November 1916

Phase IV. Advance to the Hindenburg Line 1917
Operations on the Ancre   (11 January–13 March 1917)
   Actions of Miraumont   17–18 February 1917
   Capture of the Thilloys   25 February–2 March 1917
   Capture of Irles   10 March 1917
German Retreat to Hindenburg Line (14 March–5 April 1917)
   Capture of Bapaume   17 March 1917
   Occupation of Péronne   18 March 1917

Phase V. Allied Offensives 1917
Operations. Arras Offensive   (9 April–15 May 1917)
Battles of Arras 1917   9 April–4 May 1917
Battle of Vimy   9–14 April 1917
1st Battle of the Scarpe   9–14 April 1917
2nd Battle of the Scarpe   23–24 April 1917
   Attack on La Coulotte   23 April 1917
Battle of Arleux   28–29 April 1917
3rd Battle of the Scarpe   3–4 May 1917
   Capture of Rœux   13–14 May 1917
   Capture of Oppy Wood   28 June 1917
Flanking Operations. Arras Offensive 11 April–16 June 1917
(a) Round Bullecourt   (11 April–16 June 1917)
   First attack on Bullecourt 11 April 1917
   German attack on Lagnicourt 15 April 1917
Battle of Bullecourt   3–17 May 1917
   Actions on the Hindenburg Line 20 May–16 June 1917
(b) Towards Lens   (3 June–26 August 1917)
   Affairs south of Souchez River 3–25 June 1917
   Capture of Avion   26–29 June 1917
Battle of Hill 70   15–25 August 1917
Operations. The Flanders Offensive (7 June–10 November 1917)
Battle of Messines   7–14 June 1917
   German attack on Nieuport   10–11 July 1917
The Battles of Ypres 1917 [3rd Ypres] 31 July–10 November 1917
Battle of Pilckem   31 July–2 August 1917
   Capture of Westhoek   10 August 1917
Battle of Langemarck 1917   16–18 August 1917
Battle of the Menin Road   20–25 September 1917
Battle of Polygon Wood   26 September–3 October 1917
Battle of Broodseinde   4 October 1917
Battle of Poelcappelle   9 October 1917

First Battle of Passchendaele	12 October 1917
Second Battle of Passchendaele	26 October–10 November 1917
Cambrai Operations:	(20 November–7 December 1917)
Battle of Cambrai	20 November–3 December 1917
Tank attack	20–21 November 1917
Capture of Bourlon Wood	23–28 November 1917
German Counter-Attacks	30 November–3 December 1917
Action at Welch Ridge	30 December 1917

Phase VI. The German Offensives 1918

Operations. Offensive in Picardy	(21 March–5 April 1918)
1st Battles of the Somme 1918	21 March–5 April 1918
Battle of St Quentin	21–23 March 1918
Actions at Somme Crossings	24–25 March 1918
1st Battle of Bapaume 1918	24–25 March 1918
Battle of Rosières	26–27 March 1918
1st Battle of Arras 1918	26 March 1918
Battle of the Avre	4 April 1918
Battle of the Ancre 1918	5 April 1918
Actions at Villers Bretonneux	24–25 April 1918
Capture of Hamel	4 July 1918
Operations. Offensive in Flanders	(9–29 April 1918)
Battles of the Lys	9–29 April 1918
Battle of Estaires	9–11 April 1918
Battle of Messines 1918	19–11 April 1918
Battle of Hazebrouck	12–15 April 1918
Battle of Bailleul	13–15 April 1918
1st Battle of Kemmel	17–19 April 1918
Battle of Béthune	18 April 1918
2nd Battle of Kemmel	25–26 April 1918
Battle of the Scherpenberg	29 April 1918
Action at La Becque	28 June 1918
Capture of Meteren	19 July 1918
Operations. Offensives in Champagne	(27 May–6 June 1918)
Battle of the Aisne 1918	27 May–6 June 1918

Phase VII. Advance to Victory

Operations. Counter-Attack in Champagne	(20 July–2 August 1918)
Battles of the Marne 1918	20 July–2 August 1918

Battles of Soissonais and of the Ourcq	23 July–2 August 1918
Battle of Tardenois	20–31 July 1918
Operations. Advance in Picardy	(8 August–3 September 1918)
Battle of Amiens	8–11 August 1918
Actions around Damery	15–17 August 1918
2nd Battles of the Somme 1918	21 August–3 September 1918
Battle of Albert 1918	21–23 August 1918
2nd Battle of Bapaume 1918	31 August–3 September 1918
Advance in Flanders	(18 August–6 September 1918)
Action of Outtersteene Ridge	18 August 1918
Operations. Breaking the Hindenburg Line	(26 August–12 October 1918)
2nd Battle of Arras 1918	26 August–3 September 1918
Battle of the Scarpe 1918	26–30 August 1918
Battle of Drocourt–Quéant	2–3 September 1918
Battles of the Hindenburg Line	12 September–9 October 1918
Battle of Havrincourt	12 September 1918
Battle of Epéhy	18 September 1918
Battle of the Canal du Nord	27 September–1 October 1918
Battle of St Quentin Canal	29 September–2 October 1918
Battle of Beaurevoir	3–5 October 1918
Battle of Cambrai 1918	8–9 October 1918
Operations: Pursuit to the Selle	(9–12 October 1918)
Operations: Final Advance – Flanders	(28 September–11 November 1918)
Battle of Ypres 1918	28 September–2 October 1918
Battle of Courtrai	14–19 October 1918
Action of Ooteghem	25 October 1918
Action of Tieghem	31 October 1918
Operations. Final Advance – Artois	(2 October–11 November 1918)
Capture of Douai	17 October 1918
Operations. Final Advance – Picardy	(17 October–11 November 1918)
Battle of the Selle	17–25 October 1918
Battle of Valenciennes	1–2 November 1918
Battle of the Sambre	4 November 1918
Passage of Grande Honelle	5–7 November 1918
Capture of Mons	11 November 1918

Chapter 12

RESEARCH SOURCES
AND TIPS

Preamble

The total male British population in July 1914 was estimated at 22,485,501 and by the Armistice well over 7 million had served their country in uniform. But not all served in a theatre of war. And not all were in the Army. The navy and air services too played a vital role. When adding overseas contingents and women that number rose to around 9 million. Statistics, even official ones, can be confusing and seemingly contradictory. Some men served in more than one theatre of war. Some were wounded more than once. A few important statistics are given in Chapter 10, but for enthusiasts, I recommend poring over the plethora of facts and figures crammed into the 880 large pages of the official statistics of the war (see Bibliography).

The introduction offers a few basic tips, amplified a little here. Whenever possible use primary sources of information, which can include family documents and medals. If anything is copied from the original, errors may appear. Sometimes, however, transcripts are all that remain available. Use all sources with caution for everybody makes mistakes.

What can be discovered from various service records? Unfortunately more is often available for those who died than survived. The best you can usually hope for are some basic facts and details of what the man's unit was doing at a particular time. There are of course exceptions to this, such as when an individual soldier is named in a book or official document, whilst playing a part in an action.

There are various excellent specialist books on researching military ancestors and I recommend consulting those shown in the Bibliography. This chapter can only be a summary. I have quoted various establishments, record series, etc. and then attached their popular abbreviated title for future use. As much information is continually being digitalized by official organizations and private companies, it is usually not practical to quote exact references for they often change. Instead, pointers to the type of information and most useful places to consult it are given. Exceptionally I have quoted the main class reference for major document holdings of The National Archives.

With the ever-expanding internet it is highly recommended you search it to see just what has been included. Most major relevant organizations, at home and overseas, have excellent sites that may help. Usually records that can be downloaded, either from commercial organizations or official sites such as The National Archives, have to be paid for. It is necessary to ascertain their current conditions and charges.

What do you Already Have?

The Army had forms for just about everything. Many families have some of these among their heirlooms and they can provide a lot of useful information to expand upon. The more you can initially ascertain, the more can be discovered. First World War medals are engraved with the surname, initials, rank, number and regiment of the recipient. And nearly all those who went to war were issued with them. Where are they now? Many silver war badges (see Chapter 2) were issued. Most can be traced back to the original recipient.

Were any souvenirs brought home and can they be identified? But beware of the badge collector. The badges may not have been officially issued to your relative. Don't jump to conclusions. It is worth questioning relatives and friends of veterans for he may have given them a souvenir, or told anecdotes you were not aware of, that can provide valuable clues to his service. Be sceptical, but nevertheless analyse everything you hear or see.

It was the deliberate policy not to bring home for burial the dead bodies of fallen servicemen. Very few indeed were repatriated. There were nevertheless special church services held in their honour by families and friends. It was common for 'In Memoriam' cards or books to be printed to remember the lost one's life. These cards are frequently found among family documents and can provide quite useful information.

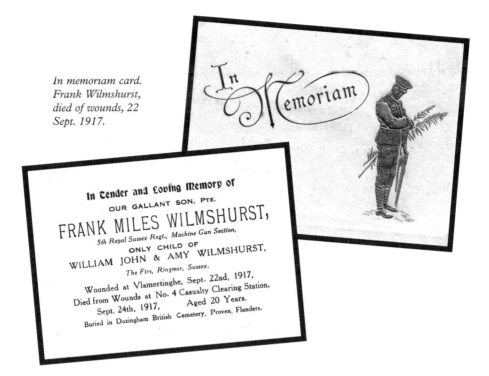

*In memoriam card.
Frank Wilmshurst,
died of wounds, 22
Sept. 1917.*

Well over 32,000 British soldiers died in the British Isles. A few were actually killed here in action fighting German warships bombarding our coastal towns. Many were brought home with a 'Blighty wound'. Some succumbed to their injuries. Other servicemen died as a result of accidents or disease. Bodies were washed ashore from ships and airmen crashed – often with fatal results. These and others were buried in Britain and many, but not all, have a Commonwealth War Graves Commission headstone. It is also not unusual to find an inscription on a family grave commemorating a member of the armed forces who died abroad. The body is not there but the soldier is nevertheless remembered. Sometimes the information, quite literally carved in stone, can be rather illuminating.

Photographs

It was common practice for soldiers to privately have their photograph taken in uniform as gifts to their family and friends. Many were

Many had their photographs taken privately before going to war. Sadly, this man, William Saunders, London Scottish, was killed on 1 July 1916.

photographed just before embarkation and usually indicate the soldier's regiment. Other soldiers had their pictures taken overseas during the war or when home on leave. Often the name and address of the photographer can be found, which may offer a clue to where the man was at the time. These photographs can tell us a lot if examined critically with a good magnifying glass and the insignia correctly identified from reference books. Badges etc. of rank, medals, skills, long service, wounds and regiment may be visible. The diagram shows where each should be located, but there are many anomalies and variations.

Very many photographs were taken during the war but relatively few are of use in researching family history. Most portray battle scenes, but many are in fact set in rear training areas and pretend to show action. To judge whether a photograph is genuine or staged consider the location of the photographer. If he was probably 'in harm's way' the picture was usually staged in some back area. If he was nicely shielded from enemy fire it may represent actual action. The official photographers used unwieldy and slow cameras, generally mounted on large tripods, and would have made a wonderful target. Portraits taken in rear areas can however be quite revealing as insignia on the uniform can tell us much about the soldier. Censorship was strict and in the fighting zones only approved photographers were allowed. However many unofficial snaps were taken on small (but prohibited) pocket cameras.

Colour photographs were very rare in the Great War but some do exist. They were mostly French and used the newly discovered Autochrome process for true colour. When analysing black and white photographs it is worth remembering that red appears darker than blue. To check this look at the roundels used on British and French aircraft. (The British had a red centre spot and blue outer ring – the French had the opposite arrangement.) It is useful to go to a museum and photograph as many exhibits as possible in both colour and black and white and judge for yourself how colours appear in shades of grey. (This is an easy adjustment with most digital cameras.)

Visible Insignia

If cap badges are clearly visible these can be identified to a regiment by reference to one of the many books available on the subject.

Rank

INSIGNIA

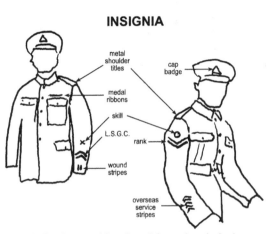

This is evident in the form of chevrons – often called 'stripes': they were worn, point down, on both upper arms. One stripe denoted a lance corporal, two a corporal and three a sergeant. There were naturally other ranks within the non-commissioned officer grouping, such as corporal of horse (equal to a sergeant), to confuse the unwary! Officers officially wore their rank insignia on both cuffs for much of the war before they appeared on the

Sketch showing usual location of the various insignia.

epaulettes. There were however many variations, partly depending upon the seniority and regiment of the officer. Most officers going into action wore standard Tommy's uniforms to disguise their status from enemy snipers.

Regiment

There were brass regimental titles, worn on both shoulder straps of the tunic and greatcoats, unless removed to hide the identity of the unit prior to a battle. Officers in field service dress did not usually wear them. Guards regiments had their regimental insignia embroidered into their uniforms.

Overseas Service Chevrons

These were introduced in January 1918 and a maximum of five were approved. They were worn inverted on the lower right sleeve of the tunic. The one for 1914, if appropriate, was coloured red and sewn nearest the wrist. All other years were represented by blue chevrons and sewn above it.

Long Service and Good Conduct (LSGC)

These inverted cloth chevrons were sewn on the left lower sleeve. One stripe equalling two years, two for six years, three for twelve years and four for eighteen years of, as many old soldiers used to say, 'undetected crime'.

Wound Bars

These were fixed vertically on the left lower arm below any long-service stripes. They were brass and fixed from behind the tunic material. Each wounding qualified for an additional bar and many men had several.

Skill Badges

These can appear on the top right or lower left arm depending upon their significance. Those for an instructor were on the right upper arm whereas skill at arms badges were worn on the lower left arm.

The National Archives (TNA)

Kew, Richmond TW9 4DU (www.nationalarchives.gov.uk/). Formerly called the Public Record Office (PRO), it is the main place to seek information regarding people who served in the Great War. A reader's ticket is required to consult original documents and their website gives full details. It also contains much useful information and I highly recommend that you consult it regularly for updated procedures on accessing records – some of which can be downloaded via the internet.

From time to time The National Archives enters into partnership with outside commercial organizations for the copying and resale of national records. This is an ongoing procedure and changes periodically. Check details of availability with the website.

Catalogue

Discovery, the new catalogue of the collection, can be accessed via the home page. An essential guide to TNA Great War records – what they are and how to use them – is *First World War Army Service Records* by their principal military adviser, William Spencer. There are also 'research guides', both at

The National Archives and available to see online, which give invaluable advice on many aspects of the collection.

Groups of records are commonly called classes. The National Archive classes begin with letters followed by numbers. After that a further number is allocated to each document or file within the collection. The main letter codes concerning us here are:

WO / War Office
ADM / Admiralty: (Royal Navy, Royal Naval Division and Royal Naval Air Service)
AIR / Air Force (Royal Flying Corps and Royal Air Force)
ZJ / 1 *The London Gazette*: Announcements and citations for awards

Searching the 1901 aand 1911 Censuses will often provide useful information on names and family background. Wartime marriage certificates usually give the rank, number and unit of the groom. It is also possible to purchase a death certificate for anyone who died during the war but they rarely show much useful information. Commonly the cause of death is 'killed in action'. Civilian death certificates, issued in respect of men who had already been discharged from the forces, often contain greater information as to the clinical cause of death.

Medal Index Cards (MIC): WO372/

As detailed in Chapter 2, men and women serving in a recognized theatre of war were entitled to campaign medals. The entitlement is summarized on the MIC, which should be available for every qualifying officer and soldier. Each card gives a précis of the unit(s), rank(s), number(s) and regiment(s). On occasion extra notes, perhaps recording the death or entitlement to gallantry medals, were added. The card rarely shows unit details below the regimental or corps name. Sometimes this can be ascertained by examining the full medal rolls. Electronic copies of the MIC can be seen at The National Archives and may be downloaded from their website. Rather better, colour copies, showing both sides of the cards (many have extra information on the back – often showing where the medals were sent) can be downloaded from www.ancestry.co.uk. Usually the full name is given but not infrequently only initials appear. Beware; there may be more than one card for a soldier or officer. If the soldier was sent overseas before 31 December 1915 the card usually shows the first theatre of war he served in and the date he arrived there. Additional information is sometimes given for officers, including, on the rear, the *London Gazette*

Name.	Corps.	Rank.	Regtl. No.
ATKINS. *Tom*	*4/2. Gds.* *C of Wms*	*Pte*	*7094-332* *1/20433*

Medal.	Roll.	Page.	Remarks
VICTORY	*X.CC103 B10*	*635*	
BRITISH	*— do —*	*— do —*	
14 STAR	*C C/4*	*6*	
Clasp + Roses	*IV.2670/C.5 12.21.*	*Clasp. 44003*	
Theatre of War first served in			
Date of entry therein	*1.5. 9. 14*		K 1380.

There really was a Private Tommy Atkins. Typical medal index card.

references for successive promotions. If a soldier (or officer) did not serve in a theatre of war he was not entitled to campaign medals and there will be no MIC for him.

Campaign Medal Rolls: WO329/

The rolls are held by The National Archives and separate series cover the 1914 Star, 1914–15 Star, British War and Victory Medals, Territorial Force War Medal and Silver War Badge. These show the precise entitlement for each soldier and often contain additional information to that shown on the MIC.

Gallantry Medals

There are various lists but the usual place to begin is the *London Gazette* (ZJ/1). Consult the indexes for a reference to the actual gazette where the announcement appears. Detailed citations are given for major awards but it should be noted that there are none for the Military Medal. Sometimes other awards appear by name but no further information is published in the *London Gazette*. The study of medals is a specialist subject and there are many books available to help. Some of these, such as for the Distinguished Conduct Medal, include full citations and/or biographical information.

War Diaries

Each unit of battalion size or greater was obliged to keep a diary of events – from its perspective. Most but not all survive. Higher echelons such as brigades, divisions, corps and armies also kept diaries. Non-infantry units such as artillery brigades (but not usually batteries), engineer and service corps companies, casualty clearing stations etc. also kept diaries. There are literally thousands of them and most are housed at The National Archives under their reference WO95/. It is one of the most important collections concerning the Great War. Other ranks are rarely named in the diaries whereas officers regularly are. The smaller the unit, the more likely it is for a man to be named. Remember that any diary is only as good as the officer who wrote it. On a 'good day' it may be very descriptive. On a 'bad day' it may be very truncated indeed. It will nevertheless often give some idea what your relative etc. probably did on a day-to-day basis. Some diaries are being digitalized and made available through TNA website.

Service Records: Other Ranks

Most First World War army records were destroyed by fire during an air raid on the repository where they were kept in Arnside Street, London, on 8 September 1940. The majority that survived were damaged. They are in class WO/363 and referred to as 'burnt records'. It was vital that certain records, mainly for pensioners, were reconstructed from other government files. These are kept separately in class WO/364 'Unburnt records'. Both sets of records can be viewed on microfilm at The National Archives or via www.ancestry.co.uk. The information they show varies considerably but often includes attestation papers, conduct, military history and medical history sheets. The attestation documents usually contain much personal information, including a physical description of the soldier. An especially useful form is Army Form B103 (Casualty Form – Active Service). It summarizes basic details and records transfers, promotions, embarkations, leaves and injuries. The papers in 'unburnt records' often contain details of the injuries etc. resulting in the grant of a pension. Whilst the odds are not good, it is always worth searching the service records in the hope the ones you seek may have survived the fire.

Officers' Records

These were in three parts and typically only the correspondence section survives. Usually this consists of arguments over monies due the officer (or War Office). The records of service and confidential reports are mostly lost.

They are still interesting however and there are exceptions; so it is worth checking the files under classes WO/338 (index to WO/339) for Regular Commissions and WO/374 for Territorial Army officers. There are other classes covering small groups of officers. Consult The National Archives for details.

Other Records in The National Archives

It is also possible to obtain records of service of Royal Flying Corps, Royal Naval Air Service, Royal Air Force and Royal Navy personnel. Some of these can be downloaded from TNA website which give also full details of the various classes where the records are stored.

There are other records, too many and varied to cover in detail here, but unfortunately usually only samples remain; for example, pension records and medical records, the bulk having been destroyed over the years. Consult The National Archives for more information.

Soldiers with various visible insignia such as cap badge, medal ribbons, rank, unit, long-service and wound. The photographer's details are also visible.

Imperial War Museum

Lambeth Road, London SE1 6HZ (www.iwm.org.uk). There are other branches, including the former RAF airfield at Duxford where many aircraft and larger exhibits are housed. The website gives full details of branches and access to collections. This museum accommodates not only a vast amount of wartime artefacts but also a library of military books, maps, photographs, sound archives, films and other records, mainly concerning the two world wars. Their collections of documents, diaries and personal reminiscences, many deposited by or on behalf of veterans, are priceless.

Regimental Museums

These usually have extensive collections of medals and artefacts and tell the traditions of the regiment. Additionally they often have libraries which include copies of relevant war diaries, documents and correspondence with officers and men over the centuries. The files are rarely adequately indexed and it is worth contributing to regimental funds and befriending the curator – usually a fount of knowledge – to see just what can be found. The location of these museums can generally be found on the internet.

Army Lists

There are monthly and quarterly lists. The most useful are the monthly lists, which are indexed. It is possible to progress through them and follow an officer's career from commissioning, to any subsequent promotions, and also to see in which unit he served. It will not usually show temporary detachments to another unit. Copies are available in The National Archives, Imperial War Museum and National Army Museum.

Postmarks

The many postcards sent home during the war went through the British Army Postal Service. The postmarks are coded but can be translated to show from where the card was sent. See Bibliography for details.

Red Cross Lists of Missing

Each month the British Red Cross and Order of St John published an ongoing 'Enquiry List of [Officers and Soldiers Reported] Missing'. Those subsequently found or presumed dead were omitted from the next month's list but more were added as time went on. It is valuable, for unlike other sources, it usually shows not just the name, rank, number and battalion but also the man's company and platoon, together with the date he was posted missing. No complete run of these volumes exists but the Imperial War Museum probably houses the best surviving collection.

Voluntary Aid Detachments

VAD nurses came under the British Red Cross. Record cards of service during the Great War exist with the British Red Cross. Write to: Museum and Archives Department, British Red Cross, 44 Moorfields, London. EC2Y 9AL. Because of the time a search takes, please be prepared to donate at least £10.00 to the Red Cross.

County Record Offices

These sometimes house the records of the local regiment and also copies of the relevant war diaries. Using the constantly updated website 'Access to Archives' (A2A) hosted by The National Archives, it is possible to see what each record office holds.

Other useful documents include local newspapers, which are worth scouring for mention of actions involving your family, etc. Although there was strict censorship, that did not seem to prevent publication of often lurid accounts involving the deaths of the chums of the contributor. Families with several members serving commonly appear together with their stories and photographs. Also seen are lists of men enlisting from various schools and other establishments.

Trade and other directories may be helpful.

Voters' lists for 1918 are very useful. They will list as absent voters, servicemen aged 21 or more, still serving in the armed forces. If it survives, the Absent Voters List itself will show the unit and regimental number of the man.

It is always worth checking local lists and card indexes to see if your man appears. Not everything will be catalogued on A2A.

Prisoners of War

A list is available (see Bibliography) of British officers taken prisoner which shows their name, unit, date missing, date repatriated and sometimes other information, such as where held or details of death. There is no complete list of other ranks captured and the records at The National Archives (WO/161) are incomplete, as are those few lists published over the years. It does seem however that over 195,000 British and Commonwealth officers and men were taken prisoner of war. A large proportion of these were captured during the March/April German Offensives of 1918. Although not so well publicized as for the Second World War, some prisoners nevertheless did escape and get home. The Red Cross in Geneva does have more information about prisoners of war. All applications must be in writing and include the full name, nationality and unit of the prisoner, plus any other details held. Because of other commitments, a long delay is to be expected and usually a substantial donation is expected. Write to: Archives Division and Research Service, International Committee of the Red Cross, 19 Avenue de la Paix, Geneva, CH-1202, Switzerland.

Soldiers (and Officers) Died in the Great War

This is the official casualty list for the British Army. It was originally published in 1921 in eighty-one volumes but has now been digitalized and can be examined in detail on CD-ROM. It is also available on the internet but can only be searched there by surname whereas the CD-ROM can be searched by any of its thirteen fields. These include, where the information is available, besides the name, regiment and battalion etc., the date of death, the places of birth, enlistment and residence, the rank and regimental number and often the man's previous service details. Using it one can extract precise details of who and how many were killed, when and in which theatre of war. The causes of death differentiate between killed in action, died of wounds and died. A few are more elaborate. The numbers and names of men from any particular town who died can easily be ascertained and there are many more features. It has huge potential for statistical research. The CD-ROM, *Soldiers Died in the Great War*, can be consulted at major reference libraries throughout the country or purchased from Naval & Military Press Ltd. It can also be viewed on their website www.military-genealogy.com or at www.findmypast.com.

Royal Naval Division

Extensive details relating to over 10,000 fatal casualties may be viewed online on at least two main family history websites. Use your search engine to obtain the current details.

Commonwealth War Graves Commission (CWGC)

2 Marlow Road, Maidenhead SL6 7DX (www.cwgc.org/). This most excellent organization is responsible for British and Commonwealth war graves and memorials of the two world wars and some other conflicts. They keep them to an extremely high standard. The most important purpose of their records is to provide information so that the next of kin may know the resting place or place of commemoration of their relatives. The CWGC records are therefore designed to identify the casualty and trace the cemetery or memorial. They give the location of the grave or memorial to aid a visit and thus provide a most valuable service.

The basic CWGC data consist of surname, initials, number, unit, date of death and burial or commemoration details. In 60 per cent of cases the next of kin supplied additional information, which can be most useful. The records can be consulted most easily on that organization's website. They also publish an excellent map showing the *Cemeteries and Memorials in Belgium and Northern France.*

Neither *Soldiers Died in the Great War* nor the records of the Commonwealth War Graves Commission stand alone. They complement each other with similar, but generally different, information other than the basic military identification details.

Published Sources

Both during and soon after the war many memorial books were published. Some contain thousands of entries. Initially some authors and organizations attempted to detail all the dead but soon gave up, as the task was just too big. In more recent times many books have been written, some containing extensive biographies and photographs, dedicated to 'local' men and women who made the ultimate sacrifice. Almost all are the result of extensive research and are truly labours of love. As some were published privately there is no comprehensive catalogue for them but generally enquiries, perhaps to the local Royal British Legion, should reveal where to find a copy.

Regimental histories and histories of various units of the army, navy and air services are another source of information and literally hundreds have been published. Many are long out of print but others are constantly being reprinted. Check your search engine to see just what is available.

War Memorials

These come in two main variations. Those on or near battlefields throughout the world commemorate the men who have no known grave. Memorials on shore to those lost at sea fill a similar role. Traditional war memorials at home (wherever that may be) honour local people who died in the war whether or not they have an identified grave.

Arras memorial for flying services.

Memorials on the battlefields to the missing are arranged in regimental order of preference, then by rank and then in alphabetical order. Local town or village memorials most often are in alphabetical order but other arrangements, such as date of death or rank order are not uncommon. Often there will be a companion memorial in a nearby church, village hall or library and it is worth checking for uniformity or extra information. Don't forget stained-glass windows and separate plaques or memorials in or near churches. Cricket or football clubs, workplaces, etc., frequently contain more personal details and can be most informative.

The main naval memorials to their missing are at Chatham, Portsmouth and Plymouth. They are organized first in ship order, followed by rank then names. There are many other smaller memorials. The Merchant Navy is primarily honoured at Tower Hill, London – but again there are other memorials such as Hollybrook, Southampton. Missing airmen from the Great War are commemorated on the Flying Services Memorial at Arras, France.

The Commonwealth War Graves Commission can advise where any casualty is buried or commemorated on one of its memorials.

Records for who was included or excluded on local war memorials are uncommon as there was no national policy on this aspect of commemoration. It was left to local people to make these decisions, along with how to fund the memorial. Sometimes relatives of those who died did not want their fallen to be on the memorial and that wish was usually respected. Some men were not commemorated because their families had moved away. Surviving records of those named on the memorial can occasionally be located in the relevant county record office or local library but most seem to be missing. I suspect any still in existence are in the personal archives of the descendants of the then chairman of the war memorial committee. What are worth checking however are newspaper accounts of the unveiling of the local war memorial.

East Hoathly, Sussex. Typical of thousands of village war memorials.

At the ceremony it was the custom to place wreaths, along with a dedication card, to the family's fallen. After the ceremony the local newspaper reporter frequently copied down the details from those cards for publication in the next week's paper. Names in print sell newspapers! Find out when 'your' war memorial was unveiled and check the local papers.

There is a United Kingdom National Inventory of War Memorials being compiled under the umbrella of the Imperial War Museum. It is an ongoing project and more information, both on the memorials and those named on them, is constantly being added. The current web address is: http://www.ukniwm.org.uk/

One should not forget school, college, railway, post office, company or town hall records or memorials either. In short anywhere men were educated, worked, lived, worshipped or played may be a source of additional data.

Internet Family History Sites

It is well worth regularly checking exactly what the major family history sites have available. Three large ones, containing information especially useful to researching Great War dead are: www.ancestry.co.uk www.findmypast.co.uk and www.military-genealogy.com Their collections increase all the time. Occasionally their name or web address may change, for the internet is a very fluid medium. It is however most unlikely that they will cease to trade. Any good search engine will find the latest location. From there see what is on offer and decide the type of subscription you wish to enter into. The major sites have sophisticated search facilities whereby you can enter brief identifying criteria and be taken to various sources of information within the entire collection.

Many local villages and parishes throughout the land have excellent websites covering local people, places and events. It is always worth trying to see what is currently available. I suggest initially entering on a search engine the parish where he or she was born, lived or died together with the name of the person you are researching.

Whatever digital sources you search I suggest there is one golden rule to adopt: 'less gives more'. I am also a great believer in the maxim of using a 'mark one eyeball and a modicum of commonsense'. If you search *Soldiers Died in the Great War*, for example, for my cousin 'Harold Bridger', who was killed in action on 18 November 1914, you will not find him. He served under the name of 'Harry Bridger'. If you had entered just his initial the record would have been displayed. Should your first search produce too many hits you can gradually eliminate those not required. If however the list does not include your relation then perhaps the assumption will be drawn that he is not there. That may not be true. It is worth using a little lateral thinking. For example at the time of the Great War the name 'Bert' was very popular. However, who was 'Bert'? He could have been Albert, Bertie, Bertram, Gilbert, Herbert, Hubert, Robert, Wilbert or even just Bert. There were over 65,000 men who perished during the War whose first names included 'Bert' in one shape or other. And was your William perhaps a Willie or a Bill? Much better to just enter a single initial to start with – assuming you are not looking for J Smith that is! Be careful with hyphenated names and also those containing an apostrophe. Mac can be awkward. It could be Mac or Mc and then there are variations on the capitalization of the next part of the name. Try each in turn for greater chances of getting a hit.

What's Left?

There are so many other minor sources of information that it is impossible to list them all here. Many archives in museums and universities hold material relating to the Great War. The books by Simon Fowler and Norman Holding referred to in the Bibliography detail many of them. Track down private collectors and enthusiasts near you with specialist knowledge. So many people are interested in the Great War that collectively, their knowledge base is truly awesome. There are also several forums, some hosted by the Western Front Association, that you could join and ask your question.

Postscript

Don't reinvent the wheel but remember there is no such thing as perfect research and the ultimate answer. More records become available as time goes on, although some are occasionally still being destroyed. There is usually more to be discovered – keep researching and good luck.

BIBLIOGRAPHY

General Books on the Great War

Abbott, P E and Tamplin, J M A. *British Gallantry Awards* (London: Nimrod, Dix & Co., 1981).

Banks, Arthur. *Military Atlas of the First World War* (London: Heinemann Educational Books Ltd, 1975).

Baynes, John. *Morale: A Story of Men and Courage* (London: Cassell & Co. Ltd, 1967).

Bridger, Geoff. *The Battle of Neuve Chapelle* (Barnsley: Leo Cooper, Barnsley, 2000).

Bull, G V and Murphy, C H. *The Paris Guns and Project Harp* (Herford and Bonn: Verlag E S Mittler & Sohn, 1988).

Chasseaud, Peter. *Artillery's Astrologer: A History of British Survey and Mapping on the Western Front 1914–1918* (Lewes: Mapbooks, 1999).

Fraser, Edward and Gibbons, John. *Soldiers and Sailors Words and Phrases* (London, 1925).

Hogg, Ian and Thurston, L F. *British Artillery Weapons and Ammunition 1914–1918* (London: Ian Allen, 1972).

Jäger, Herbert. *German Artillery of World War One* (Marlborough: Crowood Press, 2001).

James, Edward A. *A Record of the Battles and Engagements of the British Armies in France and Flanders 1914–1918* (Aldershot, 1924); *British Regiments 1914–1918* (London: Samson Books Ltd, 1978; combined edition).

Lewis, Captain Cecil. *Sagittarius Rising* (London: Peter Davies Ltd, 1936).

Oram, Gerald. *Death Sentences Passed by Military Courts of the British Army 1914–1918* (London: Boutle Publishers, 1998).

Petre, F, Ewart, W and Lowther, C. *The Scots Guards in the Great War 1914–1918* (London: John Murray, 1925).

Proud, E B. *History of British Army Postal Service*, vol 2. *1903–1927* (Dereham: Proud-Bailey Co. Ltd, 1983).

Rawling, Bill. *Surviving Trench Warfare* (Toronto: University of Toronto Press, 1992).

Simpkins, Peter. *Kitchener's Army* (Manchester: Manchester University Press, 1988).

Strachan, Hew. *The First World War* (London: Simon & Schuster, 2003)

Williamson, Howard. *Collector and Researchers Guide to the Great War*: pt 1. *Medals*; pt 2. *Small Arms, Munitions, and Militaria* (Harwich: Anne Williamson, 2003).

Young, Michael. *Army Service Corps* (Barnsley: Pen & Sword, 2000).

Books Useful for Researching Military Genealogy

Fowler, Simon. *Tracing your Army Ancestors* (Barnsley: Pen & Sword, 2006).

Fowler, Simon. *Tracing your First World War Ancestors* (Newbury: Countryside Books, 2003).

Hobson, Chris. *Airmen Died in the Great War 1914–1918* (Suffolk: J B Hayward & Son, 1995).

Holding, Norman. *World War 1 Army Ancestry* (Bury: Federation of Family History Societies, 2003).

Holding, Norman. *Location of British Army Records 1914–1918* (Bury: Federation of Family History Societies, 1999).

Holding, Norman. *More Sources of World War 1 Army Ancestry* (Bury: Federation of Family
   History Societies, 1998).
*List of British Officers taken prisoner in the various Theatres of War between August, 1914 and
   November 1918* (London: Cox & Co., 1919).
Spencer, William. *First World War Army Service Records* (London: The National Archives, 2008).

Official Publications
Field Artillery Training 1914 (London: War Office, 1914).
Field Service Pocket Book 1914 (London: War Office, 1914).
Infantry Training 1914 (London: War Office, 1914).
King's Regulations and Orders for the Army 1912 (London: HMSO, 1912 and amendments).
Location of Hospitals and Casualty Clearing Stations, British Expeditionary Force 1914–1919
   (London: Ministry of Pensions, c.1923).
Manual of Military Law (London: War Office, 1914).
Official History of the War: Military Operations: France and Belgium (14 vols plus appendices and
   map vols; London: various authors on behalf of Committee of Imperial Defence, various
   dates). (Similar Official Histories exist for other theatres of war and other arms of service.)
Order of Battle of Divisions, compiled by Major A F Becke (5 vols; London: HMSO, 1935–45).
Order of Battle of Divisions [Dominions, etc.], compiled by F Perry (2 vols; Malpas, Gwent: Ray
   Westlake – Military Books, 1992).
Order of Battle of the British Armies in France [at] November 11th 1918 (London: GHQ, 1918).
Statistics of the Military Effort of the British Empire during the Great War 1914–1920 (London: War
   Office, 1922).
Textbook of Small Arms 1929 (London: HMSO, 1929).
The Army List (London: War Office, monthly throughout the war).
The London Gazette (also *Edinburgh* and *Belfast Gazettes*) (London: HM Government, regularly
   throughout the war).
Vocabulary of German Military Terms and Abbreviations (London: War Office, 1918).

Organizations
Web addresses current at date of publication:
   Western Front Association: *http: //www.westernfrontassociation.com/*
   Gallipoli Association: *http://www.gallipoli-association.org/*
   Orders and Medals Research Society: *http://www.omrs.org.uk/*
   Cross and Cockade International: *http://www.crossandcockade.com/*

Digital Sources
British Trench Map Atlas (Uckfield: Naval & Military Press, 2008).
LinesMan [Trench maps] (Orpington: Great War Digital Ltd (Memory Map), 2007).
Soldiers Died in the Great War (Uckfield: Naval & Military Press, 1998).

Websites
Because of the ever-changing nature of the internet I am reluctant to recommend many
unofficial websites. Some are excellent and improve over the years. Others fade away. Others
change their name and consequently amend their web address. In addition organizations often
amend their mailing address when secretaries etc. change. The better sites remaining current
will usually appear on the first few pages of a good search engine and common sense should
tell you the quality of the site you are viewing. Generally the more bibliographical references
and fewest advertisements for unrelated material the better the site will be.

INDEX

Bold type is used for the main discussion of a topic and *italic* for illustrations.

The Poems of Gerard Manley Hopkins: A Sourcebook edited by Alice Jenkins
Charles Dickens's David Copperfield: A Sourcebook edited by Richard J. Dunn
Charles Dickens's Bleak House: A Sourcebook edited by Janice M. Allan
Charles Dickens's Oliver Twist: A Sourcebook edited by Juliet John
Charles Dickens's A Tale of Two Cities: A Sourcebook edited by Ruth Glancy
Herman Melville's Moby-Dick: A Sourcebook edited by Michael J. Davey
Harriet Beecher Stowe's Uncle Tom's Cabin: A Sourcebook edited by Debra J. Rosenthal
Walt Whitman's Song of Myself: A Sourcebook and Critical Edition edited by Ezra Greenspan
Robert Browning by Stefan Hawlin
Henrik Ibsen's Hedda Gabler: A Sourcebook edited by Christopher Innes
George Eliot by Jan Jedrzejewski
Thomas Hardy by Geoffrey Harvey
Thomas Hardy's Tess of the d'Urbervilles edited by Scott McEathron
Charlotte Perkins Gilman's The Yellow Wallpaper: A Sourcebook and Critical Edition edited by Catherine J. Golden
Kate Chopin's The Awakening: A Sourcebook edited by Janet Beer and Elizabeth Nolan
Edith Wharton's The House of Mirth by Janet Beer, Pamela Knights and Elizabeth Nolan
Joseph Conrad by Tim Middleton
The Poems of W. B. Yeats: A Sourcebook edited by Michael O'Neill
E. M. Forster's A Passage to India: A Sourcebook edited by Peter Childs
D. H. Lawrence by Fiona Becket
Samuel Beckett by David Pattie
W. H. Auden by Tony Sharpe
Richard Wright's Native Son by Andrew Warnes
J. D. Salinger's The Catcher in the Rye by Sarah Graham
Ian McEwan's Enduring Love by Peter Childs
Arundhati Roy's The God of Small Things by Alex Tickell
Angela Carter's Nights at the Circus by Helen Stoddart
Joseph Conrad's Heart of Darkness by D. C. R. A. Goonetilleke
Martin Amis by Brian Finney
Ted Hughes by Terry Gifford

Kazuo Ishiguro

Wai-chew Sim

Routledge
Taylor & Francis Group

LONDON AND NEW YORK

First published 2010
by Routledge
2 Park Square, Milton Park, Abingdon, Oxon OX14 4RN

Simultaneously published in the USA and Canada
by Routledge
270 Madison Ave, New York, NY 10016

Routledge is an imprint of the Taylor & Francis Group, an informa business

Typeset in Series Design Selected by
Taylor & Francis Books
Printed and bound in Great Britain by
TJ International Ltd, Padstow, Cornwall

British Library Cataloguing in Publication Data
A catalogue record for this book is available from the British Library.

Library of Congress Cataloging in Publication Data
Sim, Wai-chew.
Kazuo Ishiguro / Wai-chew Sim. – 1st ed.
    p. cm. – (Routledge guides to literature)
Includes bibliographical references and index.
1. Ishiguro, Kazuo, 1954—Criticism and interpretation. 2. Ishiguro, Kazuo,
1954—Handbooks, manuals, etc. I. Title.
    PR6059.S5Z895 2009
    823'.914–dc22
                        2009011539

ISBN10: 0-415-41535-7 (hbk)
ISBN10: 0-415-41536-5 (pbk)
ISBN10: 0-203-86999-0 (ebk)

ISBN13: 978-0-415-41535-4 (hbk)
ISBN13: 978-0-415-41536-1 (pbk)
ISBN13: 978-0-203-86999-4 (ebk)

For J., S. L., and J. L.

Contents

4: Chronology   **165**

Acknowledgements

Chia Ying Mei and Rashmi Lad helped me to get important documents at key moments in my research and writing. I owe them a debt of gratitude. Special thanks go to Benita Parry for her continued guidance and for helping to launch this project. I would like to thank Liz Thompson, Polly Dodson and Emma Nugent at Routledge for their encouragement and support. Thanks are also due to a great bunch of colleagues at NTU's English division – somehow they make the work less onerous and more worthwhile.

Abbreviations and referencing

PVH	*A Pale View of Hills*
AFW	*An Artist of the Floating World*
ROD	*The Remains of the Day*
UC	*The Unconsoled*
WWO	*When We Were Orphans*
NLMG	*Never Let Me Go*

All references are to the Faber & Faber editions of Ishiguro's novels.

Introduction

This book examines the literary career of Kazuo Ishiguro, who is generally considered to be one of the finest writers working today. Part 1 provides a survey of the pertinent familial, historical and social context. It links these details to a general account of the trajectory of Ishiguro's work and authorial reception. Part 2 provides convenient synopses of the novels as well as detailed, closely referenced accounts of their salient features and concerns. A review of Ishiguro's short story and screenplay work is given in the final sub-section, 'Other creative works'. Part 3 offers an account of the main trends in the critical reception of Ishiguro's writing. It identifies a number of clearly defined areas: Ishiguro's style and narrative theory; Ishiguro, multicultural Britain and postcolonial studies; Ishiguro and psychoanalytic criticism; Ishiguro as an international writer, and other readings. The major readings in each area are reviewed with the aim of providing a state-of-the-field survey of the major directions in Ishiguro criticism. A final sub-section, 'Film adaptation', provides in addition a review of the reception given to the 1993 film adaptation of *The Remains of the Day*. This sub-section complements Part 2, 'Other creative works' by venturing beyond the usual novel-centred discussion of Ishiguro's work. Throughout the volume, cross-reference is made between different sections and sub-sections so that readers can get a sense of the multiple links between texts, contexts and analysis. This *Routledge Guide to Literature* volume thus provides a synopsis of Ishiguro's life and contexts, an authoritative introduction to his *oeuvre*, and a comprehensive account of the principal directions in Ishiguro criticism and commentary. Read through, it is a detailed introduction to Ishiguro's work and its recurrent thematic and stylistic concerns; alternatively, cross-references between the sections make it possible to pursue a particular line of enquiry within the book, supported by an extensive bibliography.

1

Life and contexts

Kazuo Ishiguro is fast emerging as an important cultural figure of our times. He has produced six varied and interesting novels, all of which possess great emotional impact and intellectual verve. His work has been translated into over thirty languages. The existential issues addressed in his writing clearly strike a deep chord with readers. As the growing body of criticism on Ishiguro's writing attests, he is seen as representing certain large sociocultural trends and developments. Among them, his reception dovetails with the increased visibility of Anglophone writing from non-traditional sites. When Ishiguro first emerged on the literary scene over twenty-five years ago, his bicultural status was presented as an epitome of British multiculturalism. His reception was hailed as a sign of a more confident and inclusive society less riven by the conservative identity politics [52, 158] of the preceding era. Since then he has carved out a distinct position within British literature as well as a host of academic sub-fields that claim him as their own. These include Asian diasporic writing, minority writing, cosmopolitan literature, postcolonial writing, world literature and comparative literature. And furthermore it could be said that this development is not surprising, because among other things Ishiguro strives to breach geographical and cultural boundaries that many take for granted and are having to question in an era of increased globalization and cross-cultural exchange.

To help readers achieve a nuanced understanding of the recurrent and developing concerns in Ishiguro's fiction, this section runs through some of the family and social background details pertinent to his choice of vocation and early development. A brief survey of Ishiguro's *oeuvre* will be followed by an explanation of the trajectory of his writing, relating in the process his acknowledged creative and formative influences. This review of authorial development puts the emphasis on Ishiguro's movement towards and occupation of a unique cosmopolitan terrain manifested among other ways in his self-ascription as an international writer. The narrative concerns underwriting Ishiguro's early work are also recounted.

Life and works

Born in 1954 in Nagasaki, Ishiguro came to England in 1960 when his father, an oceanographer, joined a British government research project on the North Sea. His family settled in the town of Guildford, southern England, where he grew up attending British schools but speaking Japanese at home with his parents. Ishiguro states in several interviews that the expatriation was originally intended to be short-term. Well into his adolescence, his family expected that they would one day return to Japan. With the passage of time, however, the sojourn became permanent.

After leaving school in 1973, Ishiguro took up a variety of sundry jobs including working for a brief period as a grouse-beater for the Queen Mother at Balmoral Castle, Scotland. In April 1974, he travelled to the US and hitchhiked around the west coast for several months. As Ishiguro recounts it, this was a time of carefree, youthful idealism. In a recent interview, he states that in his encounters with fellow travellers, 'the third question, after "What bands are you into?" and "Where are you from?" was "What do you think is the meaning of life?"' (Hunnewell 2008: 37). Later that year Ishiguro took up a course of study at the University of Kent in Canterbury. After a year he decided to take another year out and spent six months working as a volunteer community worker on a housing estate in Renfrew, Scotland. This was a time of declining manufacturing and widespread structural unemployment and Ishiguro recounts that the experience had a sobering effect on him: he 'grew up a lot' because he had been brought up in 'a very middle-class environment in southern England' (Hunnewell 2008: 37). At the University of Kent, he attended classes in English and Philosophy, and after earning a Bachelor of Arts degree in 1978, Ishiguro went back to social work. For a while he was based in London and worked for the Cyrenians, an organization that seeks to meet the needs of the homeless [100]. His initial dreams about becoming a songwriter having come to naught, he enrolled in 1979 in a famous creative writing course run by Malcolm Bradbury at the University of East Anglia [87] in Norwich, where the writer Angela Carter was also another teacher and mentor. Ishiguro graduated from the course in 1980 having obtained an advance from Faber and Faber for a novel in progress.

That novel, A Pale View of Hills, was published in 1982. A precocious first book, it tells the story of a middle-aged Japanese woman who has settled in England and whose grown-up daughter from her first marriage has committed suicide. Her manner of coming to terms with the tragedy is to recount the story of a friend she had back in Nagasaki just after the war. The friend wants to leave Japan and move to the United States; she also has a young troubled daughter whose behaviour echoes the protagonist's own experiences with her daughter. This narrative arrangement gives the novel an uncanny doppelganger dimension and helped Ishiguro win the prestigious Winifred Holtby Prize awarded by the Royal Society of Literature. The impact of the first novel can also be gleaned from Ishiguro's inclusion in 1983 in *Granta* magazine's list of the twenty best young British novelists [99] as names to watch out for in the future, although the accolade was slightly premature. Ishiguro only took up citizenship later that year, something that had been on the cards because, as he puts it, he 'felt British' and thought that his 'future was in Britain' (Wroe 2005).

A subplot in *A Pale View of Hills* features a retired teacher who has to rethink his values in the aftermath of the war. This scenario was transformed and expanded in Ishiguro's second novel, *An Artist of the Floating World*, which appeared in 1986. Set entirely in post-war Japan, the book recounts the experiences of a painter who had supported militarism in the 1930s with propaganda artwork. In a radically altered post-war environment, he is forced to question the certainties of the antebellum period. Among other things, the novel deals with the themes of collaboration, self-deception and self-betrayal. Its garrulous, back-and-forth narration marks an ambitious attempt to capture the texture of memory. The novel was shortlisted for the Booker Prize and won the Whitbread Book of the Year award. It subsequently appeared on bestseller lists around the world.

Ishiguro earned an international reputation in 1989 when his third novel, *The Remains of the Day*, won the prestigious Booker Prize. The book recounts the experiences of an emotionally stilted butler who discovers late in life the costs of his misplaced adherence to hierarchical notions of duty, service and vocational excellence. The novel is Ishiguro's best-known work and has arguably become a classic of the contemporary literature canon. Explaining the award, the chair of the selection panel, David Lodge [106], called it 'a cunningly structured and beautifully paced performance', one that 'renders with humour and pathos a memorable character and explores the large, vexed themes of class, tradition and duty' (Lewis 2000: 137). In a review of the book, Salman Rushdie praised it for daring to pose 'Big Questions' like what is 'greatness', what is 'dignity', and what is 'Englishness' – all of it done with 'a delicacy and humour that do not obscure the tough-mindedness beneath'. For Rushdie, the twist that it gives to the country-house novel genre [54, 79, 117, 126] makes it 'a brilliant subversion of the fictional modes from which it at first seems to descend' (Rushdie 1991: 244–5). The novel was subsequently made into a movie by the famous Merchant Ivory production team. Released in 1993, it starred Anthony Hopkins and Emma Thompson; it garnered eight Academy Award nominations and won three awards.

Ishiguro's most openly experimental novel, *The Unconsoled*, was published in 1995 to decidedly mixed reviews. Its lengthy dream-like sequences and opaque construction left many critics nonplussed. At the same time, it also drew the support of some prominent commentators [113]. Lengthwise, the novel is almost as extensive as Ishiguro's three previous novels combined. It allowed him to push into a new post-realist phase and also to surprise readers with his reach and coverage. In the same year, Ishiguro received an OBE for his services to literature. He was also named Chevalier de l'Ordre des Arts et des Lettres by the French government in 1998.

Ishiguro's fifth novel, *When We Were Orphans*, was published in 2000. While not a conventional realist text, the novel makes a sizeable retreat from the out-and-out fabulism that characterizes the previous work. Set in London and Shanghai, it relates the experiences of a detective who tries to unravel the mystery of his parents' disappearance in the early years of the previous century. On one level a rewrite of Dickens's *Great Expectations*, it directs attention on the protagonist's psychological manoeuvres rather than on the spadework that one might expect from a conventional detection novel. In this sense it also gives a twist to the crime fiction genre.

Ishiguro's most recent novel, *Never Let Me Go*, captured the runner-up spot in the 2005 Booker Prize awards and raises the topical issue of cloning and bioethics. It tells the story of a trio of clones who in some speculative society are bred to furnish body parts for 'original' humans. The title of the novel is also the title of the chief protagonist's favourite song, which she interprets as a mother's love song to her infant. In formal terms, it braids together science fiction and dystopian fiction [118, 156]. Critics and reviewers have commented on its striking ability to stoke existential angst and deliberation [118]. Already the novel is starting to attract innovative readings addressing a number of pressing issues and challenges. Among other things, it taps into and explores deeply held yearnings for radical change in society. With the passage of time, it could conceivably become Ishiguro's most culturally and intellectually important book.

Compared to the novels, Ishiguro's other creative works have not received much critical attention. He has published a number of short stories, some of which acted as trial runs for the books. An early batch of three appeared in 1981 in *Introduction 7: Stories by New Writers*. The most recent story, 'A village after dark', appeared in 2001 in the *New Yorker* magazine. Ishiguro also wrote two original screenplays for Britain's Channel 4 television: *A Profile of Arthur J. Mason* (broadcast in 1984) and *The Gourmet* (broadcast in 1986). Both plays were directed by Michael Whyte. Told in a semi-documentary style, the former relates the experiences of a butler who late in life suddenly becomes famous when a book he wrote decades ago is rediscovered and published to great acclaim. The latter is a black comedy about a sophisticated, wealthy gourmand who travels the world searching for 'extreme' culinary experiences and who faces a crisis when he runs out of things to satisfy his bored palate. Part of the play recounts his travails in a church that provides shelter for the homeless. This portion of the play appears to draw on the social work that Ishiguro did before he became a full-time writer.

In addition, Ishiguro also wrote a screenplay that was substantially reworked for a movie directed by the avant-garde film-maker Guy Maddin, as well as the screenplay for another movie directed by James Ivory. Maddin's film, *The Saddest Music in the World*, was released in 2003 and revolves around an international music competition held in Depression-era Winnipeg, Canada. Its objective is to determine which folk music tradition has the most tragic melody. Ivory's film is titled *The White Countess*, and was released in 2005. It tells the story of a group of White émigrés who, displaced by the Russian civil war, fetch up in Shanghai in the mid-1930s. One of them – the female lead played by Natasha Richardson – falls in love with a blind former diplomat played by Ralph Fiennes, who sets up a nightclub for her.

After his first three novels, Ishiguro was branded a supplier of Japanese and English authenticity [60] despite his efforts to probe cultural claims and assumptions made about these nations. In some circles, he was read in a manner diametrically opposed to the universalist and cross-cultural thrust of his fiction. Since then he has sought to write in a mix of realist and non-realist styles so that his works would be read as 'parables' and he wouldn't be saddled with literalist readings that tied them severely to a national, cultural or historical setting. Ishiguro explains in a 1990 interview that, 'if there is something I really struggle with as a writer ... it is this whole question about how to make a particular setting actually take off into the realm of metaphor [60] so that people don't think it is just about Japan or Britain' (Vorda and Herzinger 1993: 16).

Three books later, in a recent extended interview in the *Paris Review*, Ishiguro gives some tantalizing glimpses into his forthcoming novel. His remarks show him still apprehensive about this driving issue, still trying to come up with innovative solutions so that his settings can take off into a figurative realm. He states that he considered France after World War Two and post-invasion Britain (*c.* 450 AD) as potential settings for his new novel. The latter covers the period after 'the Romans left and the Anglo-Saxons took over, which led to the annihilation of the Celts'. He figured that 'the further you go back in time, the more likely the story would be read metaphorically ... as a modern parable' (Hunnewell 2008: 43) [109].

Elsewhere in the *Paris Review* interview, Ishiguro talks about how *The Remains of the Day* got its name [135]. He states that a piece of juvenilia he wouldn't mind publishing relates the experiences of two young people working in a fish-and-chip restaurant who fall in love. In response to the interviewer's comments that in his writing he doesn't do 'what is so common now', namely to fictionalize his life, to write about how it was like 'growing up in a Japanese home in England', Ishiguro replies that he *did* do it, but only 'half-hearted[ly]', because at that point in his life his main priority was writing songs that 'went over the same territory' (Hunnewell 2008: 38) [19, 74]. Ishiguro currently lives in London's Golders Green district with Lorna Anne MacDougal, his partner of over twenty years, and his teenage daughter, Naomi.

Early development and influences

As a number of commentators have noted, the experience of displacement and dislocation has a great impact on Ishiguro's fiction. His first two novels, set wholly or partially in Japan, can be read as works that enact an imaginative or 'fictional' return to a birthplace (Boehmer 1995: 199). They explain the exilic tone that often accompanies his writing. In his interviews on this subject, Ishiguro reveals that migration and exile had prompted his decision to take up writing as a career:

> Actually, until I was about twenty, I did a lot of reading about Japan and whenever there was a Japanese movie, I would go see it. Looking back now, it had a lot to do with my wanting to write at all. Japan was a very strong place for me because I always believed I would eventually return there, but as it turned out, I never went back. This very important place called Japan which was a mixture of memory, speculation, and imagination was fading with every year that went by. I think there was a very urgent need for me to get it down on paper before it disappeared altogether.
>
> (Krider 1998: 150)

Elsewhere, he explains that weakened family connections and a keen sense of loss underpin his understanding of what creative work entails, and hence his belief that art is basically a form of consolation for writers. These ideas are important because they provide insight into Ishiguro's artistic goals and objectives; they also come to the fore in his tellingly titled fourth book, *The Unconsoled*:

> For me, the creative process has never been about anger or violence, as it is with some people; it's more to with regret or melancholy ... [I]t's to do with the strong emotional relationships I had in Japan that were suddenly severed at a formative emotional age, particularly with my grandfather. I lived with my grandparents for the first five years of my life; it was a three-generational family, and my father was away for three of my first five years. So my grandfather was the head of the household, the person I looked up to. It's only in the past few years that I've begun to appreciate the importance of what happened then. I've always been aware that there was this other life I might have had ... [H]ere was a very important bond. It didn't get severed, because I always thought I was going back, but it faded away. Then he died when I was still in England.
>
> (Shaffer and Wong 2008: 116)

I think most writers do write out of some part of themselves – that is, I wouldn't say 'unbalanced', but where there is a kind of lack of equilibrium ... Writing is kind of a consolation [64] or a therapy. Quite often, bad writing comes out of this kind of therapy. The best writing comes out of a situation where I think the artist or writer has to some extent come to terms with the fact that it is too late. The wound has come, and it hasn't healed, but it's not going to get any worse; yet, the wound is there. It's a kind of consolation that the world isn't quite the way you wanted it but you can somehow reorder it or try and come to terms with it by actually creating your own world and own version of it ... I think serious writers have to try, in some way or the other, to keep moving in a direction that moves them toward this area of irresolution.

(Vorda and Herzinger 1993: 30–1)

Taken as a whole, these remarks allow us to discern shifts and changes in Ishiguro's work, and also its overarching concerns and direction. Ishiguro has stated that he writes in the 'Western tradition' (Mason 1989b: 336) and was influenced by in particular the 'full-blooded nineteenth century fiction' that he first started to read in university (Hunnewell 2008: 53). He cites as his favourites: Chekhov, Dostoevsky, Charlotte Brontë and Dickens, with the first two often named as formative influences (Hunnewell 2008: 53; Shaffer and Wong 2008: 4, 50, 82, 173). As well, Ishiguro tends to reject any comparison of his work with Japanese writers, although he reads its literature in translation [144] and appears to have substantial knowledge of certain works and styles (Shaffer and Wong 2008: 47, 81–2; Sinclair 1987: 37) [147].

There is, however, one area of Japanese culture that he readily admits to being influenced by, namely the *shomin-geki* [93] or domestic-drama films made by Yasujiro Ozu (1903–63), and Mikio Naruse (1905–69). Part of the reason for their appeal appears to be that they help meet a certain exilic or nostalgic longing. Ishiguro states that: 'The visual images of Japan have a great poignancy for me, particularly in domestic films like those of Ozu and Naruse, set in the postwar era, the Japan I actually remember' (Mason 1989b: 336). More importantly, he states that he learned from 'seeing movies by film makers like Ozu' and from 'watching the plays of Chekhov' (and reading his stories):

the courage and conviction to have a very slow pace and not worry if there isn't a strong plot ... It is almost assumed that plot has to be the central spine around which the story is fleshed, and that is almost the definition these days [of fiction]. When you actually think about Chekhov, it is really hard to actually see his pieces as plots with flesh on it.

(Vorda and Herzinger 1993: 25–6)

In an interview conducted shortly after the publication of *An Artist of the Floating World*, Ishiguro was asked what he takes from the 'Japanese' tradition. His remarks are notable for their adamant rejection of melodrama – a hallmark of the film-makers identified above – as well as for the effort to assert everyday unremarkable humanity. Ishiguro states:

> [I]f I borrow anything from any tradition, it's probably from that tradition that tries to avoid anything that is overtly melodramatic or plotty, that tries basically to remain within the realms of everyday experience.
>
> I'm very keen that whenever I portray books that are set in Japan, even if it's not very accurately Japan, that people are seen to be just people. I ask myself the same questions about my Japanese characters that I would about English characters, when I'm asking the big questions, what's really important to them. My experience of Japanese people in this realm is that they're like everybody else. They're like me, my parents. I don't see them as people who go around slashing their stomachs.
>
> (Mason 1989b: 343)

The influence of Chekhov hasn't been followed up yet in the criticism on Ishiguro. However, the Yasujiro–Ozu link has attracted some attention and is worth recounting. In an article assessing this issue, Gregory Mason argues that Ishiguro's first two books:

> deal with the classic *shomin-geki* domestic configuration of conflict between parents and children in an extended family setting with certain comic overtones. His boisterous, sometimes disrespectful children, like Mariko in *A Pale View of Hills* and Ichiro in *An Artist of the Floating World*, find clear precedents in *shomin-geki* classics like Ozu's *Good Morning* (1959). The affectionate relationship between the father, Ogata, and his daughter-in-law, Etsuko, in *A Pale View of Hills* directly parallels the situation in Ozu's *Tokyo Story*.
>
> (Mason 1989a: 45–6)

Mason's observations have been backed up by other commentators (Petry 1999: 42; Lewis 2000: 69–70; Zinck 2004: 146–7). Given the connection, Ishiguro's television and movie screenplay work may well draw on his familiarity with *shomin-geki* conventions, although more research would be needed to establish the correlation.

Initial literary reception

There are several things happening here and it is worth taking the trouble to tease them out, taking into account the references above about how Ishiguro joined the writing profession and about his assorted creative influences. Ishiguro has stated that he speaks a kind of 'five year old's Japanese' with his parents (Sexton 1987: 16; Mason 1989b: 336). On another occasion, he states that having been brought up by Japanese parents, he 'understood very deeply how a Japanese family works and about parent/child relationships, marriages, and so on', but was in no position to comment on 'the economic situation in Japan or [on] what Japanese people did or didn't do in the '80s' (Krider 1998: 149).

When Ishiguro first emerged on the literary scene, a large portion of the reading public and media appeared to see him as a spokesman for Japanese culture, a native informant who could not only offer expert opinion on Japanese society and more, but also explain its assumed eccentricities and mysteries. This led Ishiguro to complain about one egregious situation where he was asked to appear on television to discuss rumours about an impending trade war between the US and Japan, to present 'things from the Japanese side' (Bryson 1990: 44). As Clive Sinclair points out, Ishiguro was considered to be 'the premier explicator of post-war Japan' (Sinclair 1987: 36).

Commenting on *An Artist of the Floating World*, one reviewer in the *New York Times* claimed that Ishiguro could even provide auto-translations that would help smooth over difficult issues of cross-cultural communication and exchange:

> Often with Japanese novels the Western reader may suspect he is missing the point and feel that important references may be getting by him. That is not a problem here. Mr Ishiguro, though born in 1954 in Nagasaki, has lived in England since 1960. He writes in English and does not require that the reader know the Orient to understand his book ... True to a traditional Oriental delicacy and circumspection, the characters are forever emitting small laughs, saying, 'indeed', while essentially disagreeing. As the author never fails to reveal their true intentions, they seem no more 'inscrutable' than any of us. The tensions stay tight. And this is what makes Mr. Ishiguro not only a good writer but also a wonderful novelist.
>
> (Morton 1986: 19)

As Ishiguro's comments suggest, however, something more complex is happening in his early work. There is the assertion of a dual cultural heritage through the naming of Chekhov and Ozu as co-equal influences. The rejection of anything 'melodramatic or plotty' stems from both West and non-West, and this might be said to question in itself the Manichean assumptions underlying the *New York Times* reviewer's conviction that East and West are irrevocably separate entities. The preference that Ishiguro expresses for Ozu and Naruse suggests that their works allowed him to engage in a filmic retrieval of his birth culture [99]. These directors are famous for their visual work: visual imagery from the place from which one has been displaced is poignant because it answers a need for roots revivalism. Such effort can be accounted an aspect of immigrant self-fashioning, of the process of coming to terms with one's dual heritage which can mean in a sense coming to terms with loss and deracination. There is a need to get down on paper certain experiences before they disappear. And this is then channelled or redirected into beautifully paced writing awash with nostalgia and affect, writing that Ishiguro calls a mixture of 'memory, speculation and imagination'. This work is miles away from Hollywood eye-candy like *Memoirs of a Geisha* or the top-knotted, bullet-dodging Tom Cruise of *The Last Samurai*. But it is also removed from readers' hopes that cultural non-familiarity will be removed in a flash of blinding insight. It betokens perhaps a homage and a leave-taking. It sets the scene for Ishiguro to move on to other kinds of writing, a process that other immigrant or second-generation immigrant writers also go through (e.g. Hanif Kureishi, Salman Rushdie). In light of Ishiguro's comment that writing is a kind of consolation for some wound or lack of equilibrium and that creativity is tied to regret and melancholia, the prospect is raised that the complex mournfulness of much of his writing stems from the experience of displacement and dislocation. The exilic undertones of Ishiguro's remarks about the appeal of the writing life suggest that the creation of self-sufficient fictional worlds is in some respects a compensation for the loss of formative emotional ties, for the loss of language, of self, of 'this other life' that one might have had, for becoming marginal. As stated earlier, the word 'consolation' appears in negative form in the title of Ishiguro's fourth book, and this has also led one critic – linking it with his comments about why writers write – to wonder if 'traumatic rupture' or some kind of 'poetics of the wound' might be used to explain what happens in that novel (Reitano 2007: 362).

In the area of Japanese studies, Ross Mouer and Yoshio Sugimoto argue that one thing that impedes communication between Japan and the West is the romantic notions that some individuals hold about the former. Mouer and Sugimoto argue that this contributes to an Orientalist mindset. They suggest that the issue arises because individuals hold 'narrow ethnocentric visions of Western industrial society' and 'romantic notions [115] of what has been lost to materialism' as a result of industrialization. These two aspects 'interact to create in our minds images of something traditional that we *want* Japanese society to have been in the past or to be now and in the future' (Mouer and Sugimoto 1990: 185, emphasis added).

One feature of the early reception of Ishiguro's work was a critical *idée fixe* on tracing the *Japaneseness* of his novels [113]. It is arguable that the romanticism identified by Mouer and Sugimoto plays a part in the formation of these views. Reviewers and commentators focused on finding Oriental style in a way that displaced everything else, including the possibility that this 'style' – how it arises as an indicator of cultural uniqueness or eccentricity – might be the focus of authorial inquiry. If it is the case that romanticism stems from the envy that Japan somehow balanced a tradition and modernity lost to the West, as Mouer and Sugimoto imply, there was little cognizance that, stemming from the wholesale overhaul of its society during the Meiji restoration (1868–1912), Japan also became expansionist – it too wanted to play the Great Game and to build an empire.

Questioning stock assumptions

In a 1989 interview conducted in Canada, Ishiguro was asked how his novels were being received in different parts of the world. After the success of *The Remains of the Day*, a lot of his time was spent on taxing promotional tours, with little time to write. He replied that in Germany, *An Artist of the Floating World* seemed to be read as non-fiction, as 'a further contribution to some debate'. The questions he got during his tour stops were 'over-whelmingly about fascism'. In England, the situation was 'almost the antithesis':

> People have not paid much attention to the ideas and just treated it as an exotic kind of little thing, and drawn comparisons to Japanese painting and brushwork, carp splashing about in still ponds. I've had every kind of Japanese cliché phrase – even Sumo wrestling.
>
> (Kelman 1991: 76)

At one point in his career, the artist protagonist of this novel works at a commercial outfit selling kitsch. Commissions received at this outfit typically call for 'geishas, cherry trees, swimming carps, [and] temples'. The 'essential point' about these commissions is that 'they look "Japanese" to the for-eigners to whom they [are] shipped out' (*AFW* 69). The novel makes clear that this sojourn for the protagonist is unpleasurable. Ishiguro arguably tries to signpost here the need for readers to be more self-reflexive about his work. He questions rigid or Manichean cultural assumptions premised in part on romanticism and sentimentality. In this regard, Ishiguro's early fiction can be read as an attempt to clear space for meaningful cultural interchange, a process that should ideally involve close scrutiny (and therefore heightened understanding) of one's assumption about oneself and others. Ishiguro's books are in a different semantic zone from Japanese writing and need to be understood in this regard. However, his lament about being sidelined by cliché phrases calls to mind the concerns of the critic Masao Miyoshi, who argues that the terms which pepper many First World responses to Japanese fiction – 'delicate', 'lyrical', 'suggestive', etc. – are actually 'pseudo-comments' that 'conceal the absence of [a cultural] encounter by cluttering up the field of reading and distracting the reader from the text'. Miyoshi states uncompromisingly that these reading practices are actually techniques of neutralization. For readers who indulge in them, 'One opens a book in order to close it, as it were' (Miyoshi 1991: 10). There is no need to pay attention to its ideas.

Arguably, however, some of these romanticizing responses to Ishiguro's early work were aimed with a sideways disapproving glance at the more vulgar commonplaces about Japanese persona and society circulating during the 1980s, when Ishiguro's books first appeared, and with detectable effects on his fiction. The reason for Ishiguro's stylistic aversion to melodrama was intimated in a 1989 panel exchange between him and Japanese Nobel laureate Kenzaburo Oe. The occasion for these remarks was Ishiguro's visit to Japan as a guest of a cultural exchange foundation. This was the first time in almost thirty years that he had visited his birthplace. At one point during the conversation, Ishiguro asks Oe what he thinks about the Japanese writer Yukio Mishima (1925–70). Ishiguro states that: '[M]y suspicion is that the image of Mishima in the West confirms certain stereotypical images ... He fits certain characteristics ... [I]n the West he is being used to confirm some rather negative stereotypes.' Mishima had killed himself in 1970 after a failed attempt to initiate a coup at a Tokyo military base. He took over the commandant's office of the base with a group of followers and tried to rally the troops to his side. When this didn't work he committed *seppuku*, and since then he has achieved a dubious, cult-like status among some of his readers. In his reply to Ishiguro, Oe, one of the most revered figures in world literature, quotes Edward Said's term 'orientalism' to describe Mishima's mindset:

> He [Mishima] said that your image of the Japanese is me. I think he wanted to show something by living and dying in exact accordance with the image. That was the kind of man he was and why he gained literary glory in Europe and the world.
>
> (Ishiguro and Oe 1991: 113–14, emphasis original)

It helps to understand why these concerns are highlighted if the larger historical background is quickly sketched in. To make this point is also to suggest that these ideas have receded from mainstream culture and might not be readily appreciated. Japan's mercantilist economic policies were tolerated for most of the post-war period because it was the big anti-communist partner of the US in East Asia. Its economy benefited tremendously from the Korean and Vietnam wars. By the 1980s, however, these policies were being read as straightforward revanchism, as attempts to regain lost territory or standing. Japan's growing economic prowess was considered an existential threat; its very name operated as a figure of danger in the popular cultural and political imaginary. It wasn't uncommon to find media reports saying that the economic foundations of the West were being undermined by samurai warriors dressed in business suits. Michael Crichton's 1992 novel *Rising Sun* basically deploys this idea. This idea is also reiterated in a 1989 reprint of a famous book on Japan by the American ethnographer Ruth Benedict. Titled *The Chrysanthemum and the Sword*, the book was a bestseller when it first appeared in 1946. As the double metaphor in its title suggests, Benedict offers hyper-aestheticism and militarism as timeless (and therefore 'returnable') attributes of a posited Japanese ethno-national character. She also offers a notorious distinction between the 'guilt culture' said to designate the US, where behaviour is regulated by 'absolute standards of morality', and the 'shame' culture of Japan, where behaviour is regulated by 'external sanctions', by fears about being punished or about looking bad in the front of the group (Benedict 1989: 222–3). In a foreword to this reprint, the American scholar Ezra Vogel [93] sings its praises and suggests that 'understanding the Japanese is perhaps just as critical now, when Japanese progress is made by troops of suited businessmen, as it was when troops of khaki-clad soldiers were advancing'. Benedict's book is vitally important because she reveals, 'The mysteries of [the] Japanese character ... for those who wish to know' (Vogel 1989: xii).

An illuminating insight into how cultural otherness is reproduced even when individuals seek change is given by Tessa Mayes and Megan Rowling. In an essay examining press attitudes, Mayes and Rowling interviewed fifteen Japan-based correspondents working for a range of British newspapers [29, 117]. One of them recounted the pressures faced by a colleague who covered the 1995 sarin gas attacks on the Tokyo subway. Among the instructions given, he was told to write about what aspects of 'the Japanese character' these attacks revealed. The reporter produced the required 1,100 words and filed his piece. But here his editor apparently called him back saying:

> 'This is fine but it's 1,100 words long and you haven't mentioned kamikaze and our readers expect – you know it's Japan – they expect kamikaze [92] to be in there somewhere!' So, he said 'Do it yourself', and they did.
>
> (Mayes and Rowling 1997: 129)

The upshot, according to David Pollack, is that our customary picture of Japan is often made up of a panoply of images with little reference to reality. Its components include 'exotic dramas, bloody revenges, delicate emotions, [and] inscrutable suicides'. All in all, it is a 'pastiche' with little logical coherence unless caught against the backdrop provided by *Madame Butterfly* or *The Mikado* (Pollack 1992: 1).

If we return to Ishiguro's remarks about the influence of *shomin-geki* films made by Ozu and Naruse, it becomes clearer why he chose these directors. As the *kanji* name of this genre indicates [148], its chief focus is on the lives of common ordinary working people, on the multitudes. It is neo-realist in orientation and its artistic precepts reject melodrama, including the samurai and ousted *ronin* figures that are common motifs in other areas of Japanese film-arts (Zinck 2004: 146). This genre discards 'the big passions of wrath, valor and rapture to focus on small joys and a passive endurance of the world' (Mason 1989a: 45). If it is the case that Ishiguro's work is influenced by these domestic dramas, he also appears to replicate those features of Japanese culture that he knows at a personal level. But as well there is an element of protest and affiliation. Even if his books are 'not very accurately Japan', as stated above, his concern is 'that people are seen to be just people'. His effort to assert unremarkable domesticity implicitly questions the othering and stereotyping propensities generated by inter-capitalist competition.

These historical and contextual details are useful because they explain the climax of Ishiguro's much-anthologized short story 'A family supper' [91], which first appeared in the discontinued journal *Quarto* in 1980. This story is arguably inflected with elements of the *shomin-geki* form and prefigures the narrative sensibility underpinning Ishiguro's first two books. Ishiguro's first novel, *A Pale View of Hills*, questions in particular the conventions of exotic fiction and echoes among other things Puccini's *Madame Butterfly* [33, 117, 125]. *An Artist of the Floating World* queries a tendency to portray Japan's Second World War aggrandizement in *sui generis* or isolationist terms. The anti-exoticist and proto-universalist thrust of these works allow us to understand why *An Artist of the Floating World* bears many similarities with *The Remains of the Day*, meaning that the continuation of theme [49] between Ishiguro's first three books is also not an innocent detail. In the passage from the second to the third book, Ishiguro repeats theme and story idea while changing the field of vision from East to West: both books portray a man rethinking his values in the aftermath of war. In this regard, Ishiguro tackles the notion, common around the time, that Japanese culture is inveterately odd or expansionist. By transferring over at the same time the understandably elegiac tones of the first two novels, however, Ishiguro arguably miscalculated its impact on certain readers. Something that arises from displacement and immigrant self-fashioning became overlaid with something that arises from ersatz nostalgia, from the proto-elitist veneration of class and caste. For some readers, the stately home world depicted in *The Remains of the Day* represents national heritage par excellence. British historian David Cannadine asserts however that such a stance is paradoxical or incongruous. He is surprised that:

> the stately-home world that most of us never knew has become the world we ourselves have lost, and thus the world we desperately want to find once more: the only paradise we seek to regain is the one which was never ours to lose in the first place.
>
> (Cannadine 1997: 100)

As a result of that transfer of elegiac feeling, *The Remains of the Day* was mis-categorized in some quarters as a tribute piece, a paean to the social order that it depicts. And this also explains the change of direction instantiated by *The Unconsoled*. The non-realist elements of this book help launch a new phase in Ishiguro's career [60]. It acknowledges at some level that the first three books have cumulatively reached a kind of impasse. With *The Remains of the Day*, a key feature of Ishiguro's writing also comes into its own, namely a propensity to refine [49] the substance of earlier works, to take their popular and critical reception as the occasion for a reworking and reiteration of the material in a sequel work. If *An Artist of the Floating World* was considered an exotic kind of little thing, Ishiguro confronts readers with a similar story in the sequel work. He invites a reassessment of the earlier stance. Ishiguro explains in a 1995 interview with the *Boston Globe* that this is a kind of 'rephrasing' [144]. The interview was conducted after the release of *The Unconsoled* attracted some negative reviews. Ishiguro states that he is prepared to go through the same material in a different way. His relationship with readers is a kind of 'conversation', he said. If they don't understand him, he has to find 'a different way' of saying it (Kenney 1995: 47). This is also to say that single-novel readings of Ishiguro's work might overlook the links between one book and the next. Part of the conversation mentioned above might be missed. More perhaps than for other writers, this attribute is a potential interpretive concern in Ishiguro's fiction.

Reaching an international audience

In light of the above, it is easier to understand why Ishiguro after his first three books elects to stake out a place as a cosmopolitan writer, a citizen of the world as it were. The background to this development can be traced to Ishiguro's 1989 panel conversation with Oe, where he states tellingly that his bicultural status [9, 74] also makes him 'a kind of homeless writer'. He had 'no obvious social role' because he wasn't a 'very English Englishman' and he 'wasn't a very Japanese Japanese either'. As a result, Ishiguro states, 'I had no clear role, no society or country to speak for or write about. Nobody's history seemed to be my history. And I think this did push me necessarily into trying to write in an international way' (Ishiguro and Oe 1991: 115). Ishiguro's desire to take off into the realm of metaphor thus stems from this situation where he is located within and between two different social formations. Its artistic ramifications can be gleaned from a British Council pamphlet published around 1988 in which Ishiguro states that he hopes to be accounted an author who writes 'international novels' [155]. He gives in that pamphlet an elaboration of what that term means to him. For our purposes, this document is useful because it is virtually an artistic manifesto. After producing three books, Ishiguro appears to have settled on his writing goals.

The statement is worth quoting in full because its core ideas have been repeated in numerous interviews since its publication:

> I am a writer who wishes to write international novels. What is an 'international' novel? I believe it to be one, quite simply, that contains a vision of life that is of importance to people of varied backgrounds around the world. It *may* concern characters who jet across continents, but may just as easily be set firmly in one small locality.
>
> There are numerous implications for a novelist wishing to write 'internationally'. One must not make foolish assumptions concerning the reader's knowledge; one does not, for instance, attempt to describe characters by listing the brand names of clothes they wear or commodities they utilise – a ploy not only meaningless to all but a narrow group of readers, but also one quite redundant for future generations. Nor does one depend on clever linguistic devices – especially puns – that cannot hope to survive translation. (In my opinion, any writer who assumes his or her language to be the only one in the world fully deserves a limited readership!) Most crucial of all, one must be able to distinguish those themes that are of genuine international concern.
>
> It is a truism that the world is becoming ever more internationalised. We have already long passed the stage when any discussion of politics, commerce, patterns of social change or the arts can be conducted intelligently without reference to the international context. If the novel survives as an important form into the next century, it will be because writers have succeeded in creating a body of literature that is convincingly international. It is my ambition to contribute to it.
>
> (Brandmark n.d., emphasis original)

Part of the consequences of this artistic programme as implied above is that Ishiguro avoids making vernacular references. In an interview at the Sorbonne in 1999, Ishiguro gives further insight into the publicity side of the writing life, into what the fiction publishing industry demands of its charges. He offers as an example a sojourn in Norway (although he will cite other places in other interviews), where on a typical stopover he would spend two to three days giving lots of interviews in hotels, part of which entails having to explain his book to 'literary journalists'. He fleshes out the stricture above about avoiding linguistic devices such as puns because, back home, he sometimes recalls these visits. In the middle of writing something he might realize that a particular audience 'wouldn't understand' what he wants to achieve (Shaffer and Wong 2008: 145). Ishiguro states elsewhere that, in toto, these encounters create for him an imagined reader who is a 'conglomerate' of various visits and interviews. He suggests that 'the wider one is made to travel, the more one is made to answer to people from different cultures with different priorities'. In the process, this imagined reader who guides his writing gets increasingly 'confused and complicated', and sometimes this can be 'inhibiting and paralyzing' (Shaffer and Wong 2008: 180–1). Nevertheless, Ishiguro seems committed to this rather ambitious goal. His remark about writing being a communicative event that requires reiteration or 'rephrasing' was cited earlier. Promotional work to satisfy this extended readership apparently takes up about a third of Ishiguro's working time (Hunnewell 2008: 47), but it also allows him to gauge and weigh a 'communicative process' that he appears to take seriously:

> All this kind of public does have an effect, because I do think of writing these days as a kind of communication process. Partly because of this business of having to go on the road and meeting readers … It's not just that I happen to produce this thing and that accidentally, other people have come across it. I am actually trying to gauge how people receive certain things I do, what they understand, and what they don't understand, what they find too much, what they find funny or don't find funny.
>
> I think these things are important, because in a way, this is how I learn about other people and how similar or not they are to me in my response.
>
> (Wong 2001: 317)

At the same time, this attempt to reach an international audience – to write novels that survive translation – is already prefigured in Ishiguro's early work. Commenting on the Japanese chief protagonist of *An Artist of the Floating World*, Ishiguro states in an early interview that he speaks in a language that is 'almost like a pseudotranslation'. He can't be too fluent or use too many 'Western' colloquialisms. His manner of speaking has to be 'almost like subtitles' so that it can suggest a foreign tongue operating 'behind' the English language. Ishiguro calls this a kind of 'translationese' and states that he paid great attention to maintaining the effect as he wrote the novel (Mason 1989b: 345). Furthermore, this point is reiterated in an article that Ishiguro wrote after the death of his mentor, Malcolm Bradbury, in late 2000. In an article commemorating Bradbury's contributions in the *Guardian* newspaper, Ishiguro states that one of the most important things he learned from him was, 'Never assume that English is the only language' (Ishiguro 2000b: 5). In addition, the cosmopolitan dimension of Ishiguro's work is closely related to the conditions of his initial literary reception. Ishiguro asserts that one of the reasons he made his career rapidly in Britain in the 1980s was because of the specific needs of that era. There was then 'a great hunger' for anything that could be labelled a 'new internationalism'. As he sees it, publishers and critics were on the lookout for cosmopolitan artists who could signal a move away from an 'inward-looking, postcolonial post-Empire phase' (Richards 2000).

Whether pressed into nomadism by unhomely conditions, post-imperial malaise, publishing industry demands, or by the internal thrust of his writing (or by a combination of all these factors), this aspect of Ishiguro's work chimes with large socio-cultural trends and developments. It explains the settings that he uses after *The Remains of the Day*. *The Unconsoled* is set in Kafka country somewhere in middle Europe. One critic claims that it can be read as a 'European Union' novel (Stanton 2006: 20) [61, 120]. *When We Were Orphans* is partly set in an evocatively named 'International Settlement', an enclave that was part of the political set-up of Shanghai during the inter-war years. As a cloning story set in a speculative universe, *Never Let Me Go* is even more unlocatable. The account of *The Unconsoled* given in this volume suggests that among other things it can be read as a pastiche of the international book promotion tour. It is arguable that this novel registers the confusion and disorientation Ishiguro initially faced with the extended readership created by its Booker Prize-winning predecessor, even as he tries to direct the chaos to serve his own narrative purposes. With his works from *The Unconsoled* onwards, the idea that this situation entails responsibility as well the possibility of artistic and ethical renewal appears to have taken hold. In his first three novels, Ishiguro explores human limitation or finitude as an attendant factor in the development of reactionary political stances: the three books feature protagonists whose illiberal attitudes are challenged by widespread social change. But since then human finitude is posed in more varied and resonant terms: as a means to assert artistic autonomy (for the historical author), as a way to raise the issue of idealism or radical change, and as a means to promote existential deliberation and autonomy. The short story cited earlier, 'A village after dark', can also be read as a sign of this change or modulation in artistic programme. This story is discussed in detail in Part 2.

In crafting his works through some dialogic or polyphonic interchange with an imagined conglomerate reader, Ishiguro underscores the importance of genuine cross-cultural communication and exchange. In the terms suggested by Christopher Prendergast, this would be 'a complex human encounter, a meeting of categories in which there will of course be many cognitive mishits and conflicts of value but where an exchange nevertheless takes place' (Prendergast 2000: 88). In his encounters with different audiences when he travels, Ishiguro would then know from the questions posed whether he succeeded in achieving his goals, or whether his ideas were getting through. Given the fractious nature of contemporary politics Ishiguro's interest in this subject is ambitious and far-sighted. It deserves our unstinted support.

Further reading

Shaffer and Wong (2008) bring together many important interviews and profiles in their collection, which also features the above-cited panel exchange between Ishiguro and Japanese Nobel laureate Kenzaburo Oe. The collection has a comprehensive index. Wilkinson (1991), Littlewood (1996) and Hammond (1997) examine popular myths and assumptions about Japan and explain how cultural otherness is reproduced as received wisdom.

2

Works

This section provides a general introduction to Ishiguro's writing. The sub-sections that follow provide convenient synopses of the novels as well as their main or salient features and concerns. In some cases historical contextualization is provided to flesh out the issues addressed by the text. Where relevant, reference is made to Part 1 where the personal and social background to composition and publication is reviewed, and to Part 3 which covers the critical debates inspired by the works as well as the 1993 film adaptation of *The Remains of the Day*. Where authorial comments are introduced the intention is not to set up the historical author as the final arbiter of meaning, but to provide one of a range of voices that can be taken into account where appropriate. Authorial commentary can be considered a cultural sampler which itself requires examination and analysis, hence allowing a more nuanced or sensitive understanding of the texts. Ishiguro's short story and screenplay work is addressed in the final sub-section.

A Pale View of Hills

A Pale View of Hills is a beguiling and precocious first novel whose cumulative impact bespeaks a mastery of craft and technique. Much of its novelistic effects are achieved by innuendo and indirection. Ishiguro shows great skill in the by turns poignant and perplexing twist that he puts into the ending. The novel engenders empathy and a desire for verisimilitude which it frustrates in its resolution. It is in addition a compelling double story, with a secret-sharer relationship between two of its main protagonists. It also has strong intertextual connections with Puccini's *Madame Butterfly*. In the discussion below, these claims will be elaborated and explained. Emphasis is placed on the cultural recuperative dimensions of the book and on the related use of doppelganger figuration.

The novel tells the story of Etsuko, a widow living in the English countryside, who receives a visit from her second daughter, Niki. Niki's visit acts as a frame story for the multiple, discontinuous flashbacks that constitute the bulk of the narrative, as Etsuko mulls over her life in Nagasaki in the early 1950s when she was pregnant with her first daughter, Keiko. The occasion for these reflections is the recent death by suicide of Keiko, who, estranged from her family, had left home and gone to live in Manchester. Niki's visit lasts five days, during which time Etsuko reflects on her life with her first husband, Jiro, and her father-in-law, Ogata-San. She also recounts her mysterious friendship with a woman named Sachiko, who has a troubled daughter named Mariko.

Oblique glimpses of Etsuko's personal history are provided during these flashbacks. We learn that she lost her paramour, Nakamura, during the war. It appears that she lost her family as a result of the nuclear bomb dropped on Nagasaki, that Ogata-San took her in and became her benefactor, and that presumably that was how she met Jiro. Etsuko's return to a period when she was still mourning the death of her loved ones forms part of her efforts to cope with present tragedy, with Keiko's death. From the sections recounting Niki's visit in the frame story we also learn about Niki's father, Sheringham, a journalist who had reported on Japan. Sheringham has a theory that Keiko and Niki are completely different creatures with opposed personalities. Etsuko believes that he is wrong. At a key moment in the novel she addresses this issue. In one of the few times that she allows herself to comment directly on Keiko's death, she says that Niki's 'aggressive regard for privacy':

> [R]eminds me very much of her sister. For in truth, my two daughters had much in common, much more than my husband would ever admit ... In fact, although he never claimed it outright, he would imply that Keiko had inherited her personality from her father. I did little to contradict this, for it was the easy explanation, that Jiro was to blame, not us. Of course, my husband never knew Keiko in her early years; if he had, he may well have recognized how similar the two girls were during their respective early stages ... And yet, one has become a happy, confident young woman − I have every hope for Niki's future − while the other, after becoming increasingly miserable, took her own life. I do not find it as easy as my husband did to put the blame on Nature, or else on Jiro. However, such things are in the past now, and there is little to be gained in going over them here.
>
> (PVH 94)

A little before this, Etsuko states that, 'in truth, despite all the impressive articles he wrote about Japan, my husband never understood the ways of our culture' (90). What underpins this disparity is suggested in the opening of the novel when Etsuko reflects on how Niki got her name [115]. Sheringham chose Niki because he believes that it has 'some vague echo of the East about it'. For Etsuko, however, the name is a 'compromise' reached with Sheringham because she didn't want a name that might remind her about the past (9). She adds a bit later that:

> Keiko, unlike Niki, was pure Japanese, and more than one newspaper was quick to pick up on this fact. The English are fond of their idea that our race has an instinct for suicide, as if further explanations are unnecessary; for that was all they reported, that she was Japanese and that she had hung herself in her room.
>
> (PVH 10)

One of the novel's thematic concerns is thus the set views that we might have about other cultures, about the semantic category 'East' or 'Japan'. Niki and Keiko are given figurative emphasis as metonyms for respectively the 'West' and 'Japan'. Etsuko's disagreement with Sheringham's view that Niki's name has some echo of the East about it parallels her disagreement with his opinion that Keiko was a difficult person by nature. It also mirrors her rejection of the idea that Keiko's death could be attributed to her being 'pure [ly]' Japanese with some dyed-in-the-wool propensity to kill herself (10).

More importantly, the novel repudiates these strictures by staging a posthumous reconciliation between Niki and Keiko. Keiko, we are told, went through a troubled adolescence. She remained in her room for days on end, refused to eat with her family, and took her meals alone. She was also estranged from Niki. After Sheringham died, Keiko did not attend his funeral and, in retaliation, Niki did not attend Keiko's wake. In one of the novel's more affecting moments, however, Niki decides at one point to 'read through all her father's newspaper articles' about Japan and rifles through the drawers and bookshelves of the house in order to unearth them (91) [17, 117]. What she learns as a result of that reassessment is suggested later when she tells Etsuko that, 'I suppose Dad should have looked after [Keiko] a bit more, shouldn't he? He ignored her most of the time. It wasn't fair really' (175). This insight is given figurative emphasis when Niki goes into the garden of Etsuko's cottage to feed some goldfish in a pond, and also to straighten some young tomato plants that have languished as a result of neglect. These deeds are Niki's most interventionary acts in the novel and suggest that her change of mind contains a wider didactic thrust. The associative logic of the text repudiates absolutist notions of cultural distance, with Sheringham and Niki set up as, respectively, negative and positive examples.

Apart from the relationship between the sisters, another key feature of the text is its expert use of doppelganger figuration. Very quickly into the novel, we realize that Sachiko is Etsuko's alter ego. When Etsuko recounts Sachiko's experiences as those of a friend she happens to remember, there is a hint that she is using Sachiko to talk about herself. She seems to exemplify our propensity to act in these ways, to see the self in the other. The novel confronts us with various parallels between their life trajectories: Etsuko ends up living in England whereas Sachiko wants to go to the United States. Sachiko is a focus of gossip and, like her, Etsuko keeps herself aloof from her neighbours. The parallels between the troubled Mariko and Keiko also encourage us to see Etsuko and Sachiko as secret-sharers. Etsuko appears to stage through the Sachiko–Mariko relationship her own misgivings over Keiko. It also transpires that the novel is filled with several doppelganger-like characters. Mariko is haunted by a woman who lives in the densely forested part of the riverbank across from her cottage. This woman may or may not be imaginary, for Mariko had witnessed a young, apparently crazed mother committing infanticide in the war ruins of Tokyo before coming to Nagasaki. Etsuko describes herself at one point as a 'mad girl' (58). This was just after the war when she went to stay with Ogata-San. There is, in addition, a serial killer stalking the neighbourhood, one who targets children. Another woman also stares disconcertingly at Mariko on the bus back from a day-trip that they took to Inasa, the hill-park overlooking Nagasaki Bay.

Such a treatment of character means that an element of the uncanny is injected into the novel. An eerie atmosphere is also imparted by a large stretch of waste ground that lies between Etsuko's high-rise residence and Sachiko's riverside cottage. This psychically suggestive setting contributes to a sense of foreboding that increases as the narrative progresses, all of which heightens the frisson of the uncanny that accompanies the twist in the resolution, when Keiko suddenly emerges in place of Mariko. By this time, Sachiko and Etsuko have become firm friends. Etsuko is often entrusted with Mariko's care when Sachiko goes out to town. Mariko has a habit of running off into the undergrowth and forested area near her cottage when she fights with her mother or when she gets bored. In an episode pregnant with mystery and figurative implications, Sachiko, in a fit of anger, drowns some of Mariko's pet kittens when she misbehaves. In response, Mariko runs off into the undergrowth and Etsuko goes to look for her. Eventually, Etsuko finds her and tries to persuade her to come back. Without anything in the way of obvious signposting, she suddenly shifts into her own reveries. She tells Mariko – who appears to have been transformed into Keiko – that '[i]f you don't like it over there [overseas], we'll come straight back. But we have to try it and see if we like it there. I'm sure we will' (173). Etsuko holds a piece of rope in her hands as she says this. She tells Mariko that she picked it up after it got caught around her foot. However, this situation mirrors an earlier scene when Etsuko had also found Mariko after she ran off into the bushes, and Mariko had questioned her about a piece of rope in her hands (83–4). The unexplained repetition adds an element of the macabre to the proceedings even as it heightens the frisson of the uncanny.

In the same puzzling or inexplicable manner, this mis-remembering or slippage of memory also continues into the frame story. Speaking to Niki just before she goes back to London, Etsuko mentions that Keiko had once gone on a trip to Inasa and that she had been 'happy' there (182). Yet the only day-trip recounted in the novel is undertaken by Sachiko, Mariko and Etsuko. This surfacing of Keiko in place of Mariko comes as a great shock because the text doesn't prepare us for it. But in retrospect, we realize, Etsuko's narrative has all along been about her. It is organized in a bid to achieve the figurative rebirth of Keiko in the person of Mariko [96, 110]. An indirect manner of approach allows Etsuko to confess her misgivings over the issue. It allows her to bear the pain of recounting to herself her misgivings over her unmet or unmade promise to bring Keiko back if she didn't like England. What lends the novel its compelling poignancy is the shock of recognition achieved through such an ending, one that plausibly combines pain, guilt, regret, self-flagellation and perhaps a touch of self-exculpation. In this regard, A Pale View of Hills works against an established migrant–narrative paradigm, one that tracks the protagonist's heroic migration to the West.

One effect of this complex mode of characterization and organization is that it raises questions about the ontological status of Sachiko. We wonder whether she is a figment of Etsuko's imagination, whether beliefs and experiences ascribed to Sachiko are actually things that happened to Etsuko. However, the novel's carefully wrought circularity – and this is surely one of its strengths – precludes a definitive answer. A Pale View of Hills is written as a first-person narrative, so everything we know about Sachiko stems from Etsuko's recognizably unreliable testimony. The presence of huge gaps in Etsuko's narrative means readers will tend to look to Sachiko to fill these gaps. We don't know exactly why Etsuko left Jiro, how she met Sheringham, and why and how she left Japan. Etsuko appears to sees herself writ large in Sachiko. Not surprisingly we do the same, and this is also to say that the novel exploits our desire for circumstantial detail to link the two together like Siamese twins.

Thus while Sachiko's ontological status is raised as a puzzle, it is difficult to figure out to what extent she arises from or is a figment of Etsuko's overwrought imagination. One way to gain purchase on this issue is to note how Etsuko's narrative privileges the word 'premonition' [95] when she spots a car moving across the above-mentioned waste ground towards Sachiko's cottage. She says first that memory is an 'unreliable thing'. Then she says that she obtained a premonition of how Keiko would turn out when she saw the car (156). In a sense, her entire narrative has been working towards this moment. In The Remains of the Day, the narrative also follows a similar pattern, with the chief protagonist working in a roundabout manner towards an account of his meeting with an important character named Harry Smith [48]. The arrival of the car marks the abandonment of Sachiko's plans to leave her boyfriend, an American named Frank, and go to live with her uncle. Frank had cheated on her but the arrival of the car shows that she had patched up with him. It is supposed to take her and Mariko to Kobe and from there the three of them are supposed to make their way to the US. Sachiko shows how determined she is to pursue her new plans when she drowns Mariko's pet kittens in the river. She does this because in their new home in Kobe they won't have enough space for the cats. The word 'premonition' is important because it suggests a principle of selection driving Etsuko's narrative. Like all of Ishiguro's novels, A Pale View of Hills is relatively plotless. However, Etsuko's narrative seems to be driven by a desire to pull together a series of events detailing violence done to children or done by children, and colouring them as so many premonitory incidents, so many warnings and shots across the bow that she could have noticed and in fact should have noticed, all of which heightens the impact of her story because it tells us how emotionally charged her recollections are. Sachiko's ontological unreliability is linked to this wider use of unreliable narration. It is part of the supporting structure of the novel.

The above provides one reading of the double story inscribed in A Pale View of Hills. On this reading, the novel provides insight into affective and psychological processes pursuant to a situation where memory tries to cope with tragedy. Etsuko's projection of herself into Sachiko is an extreme instance of a more general emotional and psychological propensity. It shows us how memory uses the past in order to address present needs and concerns.

At the same time, it is also worth considering Sau-ling Cynthia Wong's argument that doubles when used in Asian diasporic writing should not be construed in a wholly universalist fashion with de rigueur references to Robert Louis Stevenson's Dr Jekyll and Mr Hyde (1866), and a concentration on 'how a common set of psychological mechanisms operate in us all' (Wong 1993: 115). For Wong, the problem is that, under the current dispensation, double stories tend to be read as 'case studies in the intricacies of human psychology' (114). Socio-historical particulars are downgraded in favour of a focus on human nature in the abstract, and this tends to 'flatten the materially shaped contours of a double story to quasi-mythic patterns' (85). Wong allows that 'at a very high level of abstraction, the defense mechanisms of repression and projection may safely be considered universal'. The terms that saturate doppelganger studies – 'personality', 'the civilized self', 'antisocial tendencies' – have however never been 'neutral or unmarked' for minority or immigrant writers (78, 85). Historically, they tend to trail social denigration and exclusion pressures that result in subjects projecting their 'undesirable "Asianness" outward onto a double', on what she calls a 'racial shadow' (78). Alter-ego scenarios encountered in fiction will thus tend to reflect the tensions and negotiatory acts of individuals who hold bicultural affiliations and affinities.

Wong's paradigmatic example is drawn from Maxine Hong Kingston's semi-autobiographical novel *The Woman Warrior* (1975), in particular the last chapter where the namesake character Maxine tortures a quiet Chinese girl in the school toilet. Wong points out that the Chinese girl and Maxine are actually very similar. Maxine's treatment of the girl represents 'a crisis in self-acceptance and self-knowledge'. She disowns her putative *Asian* attributes by projecting them outwards onto an antithetical double or second self. The quiet girl represents that 'residue of racial difference' whose 'irreducibility' impedes her assimilationist stance and makes her mad (82, 89). Confrontation with the quiet girl is important because it sets the scene for Maxine's painful re-examination of her behavioural code and her realization that she needs to formulate an identity encompassing both aspects of her bicultural heritage. Analysis which seeks to explain double stories as 'parables of human nature in the abstract' will tend to overlook the features described here (114).

If we move on to ask how this racial shadow topoi might apply to *A Pale View of Hills*, it is interesting that the huge gaps in Etsuko's narrative, the parts that Sachiko presumably 'fills in', are also those parts that echo Puccini's 1904 opera, *Madame Butterfly* [18, 117, 125]. Etsuko is haunted by various doppelganger figures in the novel and Sachiko, it could be said, is haunted by Puccini's protagonist. The genealogy of the opera has been traced to Pierre Loti's 1887 novel, *Madame Chrysanthème*, which according to Jean-Pierre Lehmann initiated a craze for a genre known as the 'novel of desertion' (Lehmann 1978: 92). The genre calls for 'naval officers' to visit Japan, acquire partners, and later leave them (Miner 1958: 48). This template appears to fits Sachiko's paramour, Frank, whose name recalls the middle name of Puccini's protagonist: Benjamin Franklin Pinkerton. After the arrival of the American car that sparks Etsuko's 'premonition', Sachiko tells Etsuko that Frank has been offered a job aboard a cargo ship, thus reiterating the genre's marine associations. The plan is that he will return to the States first and come back later to fetch Sachiko and Mariko, and this also echoes the promise made by Pinkerton to Cho Cho San (Butterfly). Another parallel is that, like *A Pale View of Hills*, the opera is set in Nagasaki. Furthermore, the day-trip that Etsuko, Sachiko and Mariko take to Inasa is noteworthy. Puccini apparently modelled his fictional Pinkerton on a nineteenth-century British merchant. The mansion in which he stayed lies in the vicinity of Inasa ('Nagasaki').

So argued, the scene where Mariko's drawing of a 'butterfly' elicits the response 'delicious' from an American woman named Suzie-San may be read as a metonym for cultural encroachment and misrepresentation (114). The incident occurs during the Inasa trip: Mariko has been drawing in her sketchbook and Suzie-San, another visitor to the park, happens to be passing by. Suzie-San has an imperfect command of Japanese and presumably uses 'delicious' because she doesn't know the term for pretty or lifelike, but given the echoes of *Madame Butterfly* described above, the scene arguably portrays the hijacking of a native, indigenous act of self-representation [146]. Mariko's drawing is annexed, changed from a visual register to a gustatory one.

In response to that annexation, Ishiguro arguably rewrites the opera emphasizing not so much the male–female relationship but the one between parent and child. In the opera, Cho Cho San kills herself because Pinkerton returns not as promised to bring her over but to claim their child for himself and his new American bride. For *A Pale View of Hills*, in contrast, the focus is on the child, on Keiko, and on Etsuko's attempt to come to terms with her death years after achieving the dream of a move overseas. Whatever *A Pale View of Hills* 'tells' us about post-war Japan is on this reading overlaid with its *simultaneous* configuration as a story of immigrant self-fashioning, meaning that Ishiguro disowns a prominent 'racial shadow' by rewriting it. This manner of proceeding is in a sense the opposite of the narrative movement described by Wong above. It is the stock, exoticist account that is 'disowned' rather than the birth culture. Ishiguro in effect appropriates the *Madame Butterfly* story. He takes it on board and gives it a twist. He changes the conventions of exotic fiction [79, 116] to suit his own narrative goals.

The above suggests that *A Pale View of Hills* shares on one level the concerns of Asian-American playwright David Henry Hwang [124, 145]. It repeats what Hwang does in his 1988 Broadway hit, *M. Butterfly*. Hwang's play inverts Puccini's opera by making the male protagonist, Gallimard, the unwitting dupe of a Chinese spy named Song Liling, who is actually a man masquerading as a woman. As a result, China is able to influence Western policy in Vietnam through Gallimard, a French diplomat, part of the reason being that Song plays up to cultural and gender stereotypes. On this account, *A Pale View of Hills* is one of those works where a Euro-American canonic text (*The Tempest*, *Jane Eyre*, *Robinson Crusoe*) is rewritten from a cultural recuperative perspective. Hwang's rewriting of Puccini's opera is the better-known version; but Ishiguro's rewriting is interesting in its own right and arguably deserves greater critical attention.

In addition, this desire to open up a space for self-representation is arguably highlighted through Niki, who near the end of the novel makes an interesting request of her mother. Niki, we may recall, is the focus of narrative wisdom because she is willing to reassess Sheringham's adamantine views about Keiko and, by extension, Japan. She later tries to reassure her mother that she was right to leave home and settle in England. She says that a 'friend' of hers wants to write a poem about Etsuko. For about the only time in a novel suffused with melancholia, Etsuko shows a flash of anger. She says that it is 'presumptious' (*sic*) of Niki to feel that she 'would need reassuring on such matters' (89–90) [95]. Later on, however, she relents. In response to Niki's request for a keepsake to help her friend write a laudatory poem, Etsuko provides a calendar-photo of Inasa [86]. The calendar is one of those that in the original offers 'a photograph for each month' (179). It is this photo that prompts Etsuko to say right at the end of the novel that it gives a view of Nagasaki harbour from the Inasa hill-park. More importantly, she tells Niki that it reminds her of the time when Keiko went on a day-trip there, that she was 'happy that day' (182). According to Roland Barthes, the photograph unlike other art forms has a necessary relationship to reality. The 'photographic referent' is 'not the *optionally* real thing to which an image or a sign refers but the *necessarily* real thing which has been placed before the lens, without which there would be no photograph' (Barthes 1998: 76, emphasis original). By insisting on the autonomous reality of the object photographed and by making it a gift, Ishiguro offers a different dynamic from the one that sees Mariko's sketch of a butterfly being appropriated by Suzie-San.

Finally, the subplot involving Ogata-San [42] also deserves a quick mention. Ogata-San's retrograde stance towards the Second World War is suggested by the language he uses when he plays chess with Jiro. He tells Jiro that rather than show 'defeatism' when he loses, he should plan his defence so that he can 'survive and fight ... again' (129). Ogata-San later has a falling out with Jiro, who is not interested in chess and, by implication, in his father's views about the conflict. Most importantly, Ogata-San is upbraided by a former pupil for his role in the imprisonment of five anti-war dissidents (148). His implicit acknowledgement of the younger generation's greater probity on this issue is suggested when he tries to mend fences with Jiro. He tells Jiro that it is time he ended his summer visit with him and Etsuko: it isn't right for him to sit in their apartment all day 'thinking about chess' (155) [94].

FURTHER READING

For readers interested in the subject, Miner (1958) provides a survey of the use of Japanese motifs and themes in British and American literature. Forsythe (2005) discusses the mother–daughter relationship in the novel. Lewis (2000) argues that the novel is structured around what it does not or cannot say or broach directly, namely the nuclear holocaust visited upon Japan. Lyne (2002) tracks the century-old development of exoticized ethnicity, covering, in the process, *Madame Chrysanthème*, *Madame Butterfly* and the 'China doll' figure. The gestation of several ideas in the novel can be seen in a story that Ishiguro published in 1981 titled 'A strange and sometimes sadness', including the use of doppelganger figuration. Ishiguro also published an article in the *Guardian* newspaper in 1983 where he commented on the reception of the novel. Both texts are discussed in Part 2, 'Other creative works' [90–102].

An Artist of the Floating World

An Artist of the Floating World is a compelling work of art with an unsettling ending, one in which Ishiguro introduces an element of radical indeterminacy. Partly as a result, it raises normative issues and the question of the link between public and private history. Japan's Second World War aggrandizement is sometimes presented in *sui generis* terms in metropolitan culture, and among other things this novel gives a historical context to that episode without suggesting that it endorses an expansionist ethos. To the extent that it succeeds in highlighting such concerns the novel raises the question whether we ourselves comprehend the large socio-historical forces that no doubt affect our actions. The chief protagonist's appreciation of blameworthiness with regard to his wartime role is the focus of much of the discussion below. In the final part of the sub-section, two suggestions will be provided as to how we might read or approach the ambiguous conclusion to the novel.

The novel opens around three years after the end of hostilities and is couched as a first-person narrative. It relates the experiences of a retired painter, Masuji Ono, who had supported Japan's war efforts with propaganda art pieces, and who in the aftermath of the war is led to re-examine his militarist views. In the narrative present, Ono spends his time engrossed in genial pursuits: he tends to his garden; he receives a visit from his eldest daughter, Setsuko; he brings his grandson to watch monster movies; he visits old friends, and he goes drinking with Shintaro, an ex-pupil. He also tries to arrange a suitable match for his younger daughter, Noriko. Afraid that the disclosure of his status as a prominent war supporter will derail the delicate nuptial negotiations, Ono confesses his misdeeds before the family of the prospective groom (123–4). However, his confession appears insincere and even hypocritical. It appears to be prompted by the revelation that the younger brother of the prospective groom is a student at the college where a former student of Ono teaches art (121). Ono appears to fear that the brother has learned about his treatment of this ex-student, Kuroda, and might expose him. Towards the end of his time with Ono, Kuroda started to develop anti-fascist sympathies and deviated from some of his teachings. Hoping that they would give him a warning, a 'talking-to for his own good', Ono reported him to state security agencies run by the 'Interior Department' (182–3). As a result, Kuroda was imprisoned and spent the war in prison. He was also subjected to repeated 'beating[s]' (113).

Related to this issue are two instances where Ono claims to have supported artistic independence and autonomy. He speaks at one point about how he rushed to defend an ex-colleague named 'the Tortoise' (67). The commercial art establishment that they worked for stressed quantity rather than quality, and fellow colleagues had rounded on him for not painting fast enough. In his recall of this episode, Ono states that he scolded them for failing to appreciate the 'artistic integrity' shown by the Tortoise, by his refusal to 'sacrifice quality for the sake of speed' (68). A while later, Ono claims that as an established artist he told a group of his pupils that 'while it was right to look up to teachers, it was always important to question their authority'. This was the important lesson that he learned from his sojourn with the commercial art establishment. In essence, it taught him 'never to follow the crowd blindly' (73). However, these two claims appear far-fetched and unreliable. Ono's recollection of events seems forced and selective. It appears to be driven by self-interest, by current needs and concerns rather than by a genuine desire to attain self-understanding.

Nevertheless, Ono's narrative also contains stretches where a more considered examination of that sordid history takes place, one that he approaches through a series of flashbacks and indirect recitation. This reassessment is partly caused by the scale of post-war change in Japan, although Ono has only a limited appreciation of its significance. He concedes that 'something has changed in the character of the younger generation in a way I do not fully understand, and certain aspects of this change are undeniably disturbing' (59). His grandson is enthralled by American cultural icons such as the 'Lone Ranger', a development that bewilders him (30). Ono's wife died in an Allied bomb raid and his son, Kenji, died fighting in the war in Manchuria. But it is only in an exchange with former combatants such as Setsuko's husband, Suichi, that he comes face to face with anti-war sentiments. Suichi expresses bitterness about the wasted lives of the '[b]rave young men' who died fighting for 'stupid causes' (58). Other related developments such as the ideological desertion of Shintaro also cause Ono to revisit the past, to ask questions that he had never thought to consider.

From the self-scrutiny thus engendered, Ono appears to realize that in his treatment of Kuroda he had repeated the pattern of his own repressive treatment at the hands of a former teacher, as well as of his father. His father, a businessman, forbade him from becoming an artist and humiliated him when he learned about his ambitions (44–8). Ono's imperfect understanding that he was privy to a transfer of violence is linked with the rhetoric used by Chishu Matsuda, the person who converted him to the militarist cause. In the sections recounting Matsuda's influence, some of the language used by him plays on Ono's vulnerabilities, including his insecurities and blind spots towards his father. Ono's self-understanding is also given a historical gloss when Matsuda argues that Japan can only solve its internal problems through overseas expansion. In some of the key lines of the novel, Matsuda echoes the social Darwinist rhetoric used to justify European expansionism [97]:

'Listen, Ono, Japan is no longer a backward country ... In the Asian hemisphere, Japan stands like a giant amidst cripples and dwarfs. And yet we allow our people to grow more and more desperate, our little children to die of malnutrition ... Can you imagine any of the Western powers allowing such a situation? They would surely have taken action long ago.'

'Action? What sort of action do you refer to, Matsuda?'

'It's time for us to forge an empire as powerful and wealthy as those of the British and the French. We must use our strength to expand abroad.'

(AFW 173–4)

These remarks come just before the highpoint of Ono's meandering narrative, the incident that he has been circling around, moving away from and then doubling back to, namely Kuroda's capture and imprisonment. True to the hierarchical protocols that govern apprentice relations in Japan, Ono acknowledges that teachers who invested time and resources in their students might be disappointed when they take deviationist paths. Some of them might even destroy the works of their pupils, as his own teacher once did. But in an apparent moment of genuine contrition and insight, Ono admits that 'such arrogance and possessiveness on the part of a teacher – however renowned he may be – is to be regretted' (181). With the recognition plot seemingly secured, the novel ends on a note of resignation as Ono gazes at the pleasure district he knew as a youth, now razed to the ground and converted into a business quarter. He sits on a bench looking at the scene and admits a nostalgic longing for those 'brightly lit bars' where he spent his youth. Nevertheless the sight of the rebuilt city fills him with 'genuine gladness'; he extends good wishes to the young people around him and hopes that they will avoid the errors that he made (206).

In this way the novel develops a recurrent theme in Ishiguro's fiction: the concern that individuals may find themselves adhering to a set of beliefs that appear self-evidently correct, but that with the passage of time are shown to be problematic or even repugnant. On this matter, *An Artist of the Floating World* maintains a close overlap between private memory and public history. Through its depiction of a social landscape crammed with apprentice relations, the novel floats the idea that Japanese expansionism had followed a similar master–apprentice pattern. In consonance with this theme, Ono has a dim recognition that he was both imitative *and* culpable in his treatment of Kuroda. The key to this reading lies in a ten-page span where Ono relates, one after the other: his final parting with his former teacher, Seiji Moriyama; his assessment of the 'vindictive' treatment Moriyama meted out to him (180), and his own treatment of Kuroda culminating in him being hauled to prison. When Ono deviated from his teachings, Moriyama or Mori-san seized some of his most cherished paintings and insulted him, suggesting that if Ono left his patronage he would have to find work 'illustrating magazines and comic books' (180). The earlier-quoted remarks about 'arrogance and possessiveness' on the part of the teacher being something to be 'regretted' form part of Ono's response to Moriyama. By the logic of association, this pejorative assessment is allowed to colour Ono's own account of his efforts to cashier Kuroda. The extent of the hurt caused by a former teacher presumably validates the acknowledgement of blameworthiness in the case of the student. Ono ponders whether the words 'exploring curious avenues' were those that Mori-san used to reprimand him, or those that he used to reprimand Kuroda (177). He concedes that 'this is probably another example of my inheriting a characteristic from my former teacher', thus suggesting that he has attained important if belated reflexivity on his actions (177–8). The Oedipal undertones of this chain of events are also underlined when state security officials ransack Kuroda's home and burn his paintings (183). The violence mirrors an earlier scene where Ono's father burns his paintings when he discovers his artistic ambitions (47–8).

In addition, the master-apprentice metaphor is reinforced through the language used to describe Ono's artistic development. Ono's career goes through three phases. In the first phase, he works at the commercial outfit mentioned earlier. Commissions received at this outfit typically call for 'geishas, cherry trees, swimming carps, [and] temples'. The 'essential point' about these commissions is that 'they look "Japanese" to the foreigners to whom they [are] shipped out' (69) [117]. In the second phase, Ono works at the artists' colony run by Mori-san. The significant thing about this colony is their collective efforts – following Mori-san's lead – to update the legacy of the Tokugawa painter and printmaker Kitagawa Utamaro (1753–1806). The title of the novel refers to a characteristic Utamaro motif, the demi-monde denizens of the Japanese pleasure quarter known as the 'floating world'. It is only in the third phase under Matsuda's tutelage that Ono starts to produce propaganda artwork for the ultra-nationalist Okada-Shingen society. This organization later becomes one of many 'victims' of the anti-fascist purges organized by the occupying forces (88).

In some readings of *An Artist of the Floating World*, there is a tendency to focus on Ono's middle period and read it as an Eden-like or rustic idyll [114]. However, close reading establishes that even this middle period is not untainted by the outside world. It already contains in embryonic form what Ono tries to do later. In the first stage of his career, Ono arguably provides kitsch for foreign buyers. In the third stage, he supplies propaganda, but even in the second stage the influence of Western art is paramount and is presented as an antecedent to the third stage. Mori-san is called by others 'the modern Utamaro' because he is trying to 'modernize' or update Utamaro's legacy (140). Ono states tellingly that:

> Mori-san made extensive use of the traditional device of expressing emotion through the textiles ... But at the same time, his work

was full of European influences, which the more staunch admirers
of Utamaro would have regarded as iconoclastic; he had, for
instance, long abandoned the use of the traditional dark outline to
define his shapes, preferring instead the Western use of blocks of
colour, with light and shade to create a three-dimensional appearance. And no doubt, he had taken his cue from the Europeans in
what was his most central concern: the use of subdued colours.

(AFW 141)

When Ono starts producing propaganda its key feature is his retention *and*
intensification of just this European- or Western-initiated use of 'blocks of
colour', which although stemming from abroad becomes with adaptation
even more of a 'central' concern. At one point in the narrative present, Ono
talks about a painting for which he harbours an obvious affection. The
painting is titled *Eyes to the Horizon* and bears the slogan 'No time for
cowardly talking. Japan must go forward' (169). Ono, addressing the reader,
states that anyone new to the city might not know the work. But those who
lived there during the war would have been 'familiar' with it because it
received widespread praise for its 'vigorous brush technique and, particularly, *its powerful use of colour*' (169, emphasis added)

This shift from the use of 'traditional dark outline' to define shapes to
the use of 'subdued colours' at the Mori-san outfit and finally 'powerful'
ones for propaganda work means that the *internal* grammar of Ono's
artistic development contains in a nutshell the thesis of Japanese modernization and aggrandizement achieved on the Western model. Ishiguro takes
pains to overlap private and public, to tie Ono's career to the historical
frame provided in the conversation with Matsuda, namely Japan's attempt
to match the European empires through the seizure of colonies in Korea
and China. In its direct address of the implied reader and in its overwrought use of 'but' and 'of course' (169), Ono's language draws illuminating attention to itself. His pride in this painting is also suggested a bit
earlier when he says that as a print in the 1930s it had 'achieved a certain
fame and influence' throughout the city (168).

Given that the *internal* grammar of Ono's artistic career carries a figurative association with imperialist competition, one of the objectives of the
novel might be to influence our customary ways of reading and understanding 'Japanese' culture, to locate it not in some timeless, ahistorical
essence called 'art' but in the messy and complicated accommodations of
history. What appears quintessentially 'Japanese' (69) is already 'full of
European influences' (141). One text relevant to the argument here is a
story that Ishiguro wrote, titled 'The summer after the war' [96], which
acted as a kind of trial run for the novel.

Nevertheless, this aspect of the novel does not appear to endorse an
exculpatory stance towards Japan's Second World War aggrandizement,

merely to place it in a wider historical context. Couching it in a more prolix manner, we might say that *An Artist of the Floating World* offers a shock of recognition aimed at those like Sheringham, a character in *A Pale View of Hills*, who believes that 'Japan' and the 'West' are complete opposites. The fuller dimensions of this artistic goal can be gleaned perhaps from a preface that Fredric Jameson wrote to a book by the Japanese critic Kojin Karatani. The book is titled *Origins of Modern Japanese Literature*, and Jameson recommends it because:

> it is not even an 'alternate history' which is offered us by this ... analysis of the institutions of the modern self, writing, literature and scientific objectivity that were constructed and imposed by the Meiji Revolution. Rather, it is as though that great laboratory experiment which was the modernization of Japan allows us to see the features of our own development in slow motion.
>
> (Jameson 1993: ix)

One reason for this desire to highlight history rather than timelessness might be adduced from the period in which Ishiguro's early fiction appeared, and which was spelt out in Part 1. By locating the referent 'Japan' in historical time rather than in some timeless cultural or artistic essence, Ishiguro arguably engages in immigrant self-fashioning, which is also addressed in the section.

Apart from the above, the radically indeterminate or ambiguous features of *An Artist of the Floating World* also need to be addressed. So far in our discussion the novel seems relatively straightforward. Ono gains a limited but appreciable insight into the contours of his life. The past cannot be re-made. The realization that one has wasted large portions of one's life can nevertheless be borne with dignity. Put in a different way, the novel appears to endorse a version of psychological realism, albeit an attenuated one. Taking up an established model of narration, it seems to chart the growing self-understanding of Ono. Yet it is also at this moment that Ishiguro throws a spanner into the works by introducing an element of radical indeterminacy. As a result everything established up until this point is put in doubt. A reading that ignores this sharp reversal runs the risk of being incomplete.

This change in the narrative occurs after the section where Ono relates the ransacking of Kuroda's home by state security officials. The twenty-odd pages between this incident and the closure stand out structurally from the rest of the novel. The mystery relates to the question whether Ono was involved in the first place in militarist work of any substantial import or consequence. Earlier in the novel, Setsuko had counselled Ono to take 'precautionary steps' so that Noriko's nuptial arrangements could be completed without hindrance (49). Ono takes this to mean that she is alluding to his pre-war activities and goes to see Matsuda for help. One customary practice stemming from these negotiations is the use of detectives to check up on the family background of the prospective partners. Ono asks Matsuda to dissimulate on his behalf if thus approached for information: in effect, to play down his pre-war activities. Matsuda promises that he will have 'only the best of things' to report about that era (96). However, in a subsequent conversation, Setsuko tells Ono that everyone was astonished at his confession during dinner a year earlier with Noriko's eventual partner and in-laws. Ono had said then that much of his wartime activities were 'ultimately harmful' to Japan (123). Setsuko states that Noriko wrote to her after the dinner 'expressing surprise' at Ono's conduct; she also denies telling Ono to take 'precautionary steps' over the marriage negotiations (191). Since our only access to events is through Ono's recollections, his narrative appears to be compromised by self-contradiction.

The reversal introduces a number of interpretive questions. There are multiple implications. One is that Ono has all along overstated his pre-war eminence: his story is a kind of folie de grandeur. Or else he is so guilt-ridden his mind plays tricks on him with regards to what was said during various conversations. What is definite is that Ono is markedly different from Ogata-San in *A Pale View of Hills*. *An Artist of the Floating World* expands the Ogata-San subplot into a full-fledged recognition plot. However, the rebuttal of Ogata-San's stance in the earlier novel is handled in a relatively straightforward manner [35]. His acceptance of the younger generation's views about the war is intimated at one point in the novel when he tells his son and daughter-in-law that it is time he ended his summer visit with them: it is time for him to return home.

One way to respond to the interpretive challenge posed by *An Artist of the Floating World* is to re-assimilate it to a realist frame. The interchange where Setsuko denies urging Ono to take 'precautionary' steps happens just before they discuss the recent suicide of a well-known writer of patriotic songs named Naguchi. Naguchi killed himself in apparent atonement for his work, and Setsuko observes that his songs had an 'enormous prevalence at every level of the war effort'. In comparison, Ono is 'wrong to even begin thinking in such terms about himself', since he was 'after all, a painter'. Predictably, perhaps, Ono reiterates his standpoint. He states that 'I am not too proud to see that I too was a man of some influence, who used that influence towards a disastrous end' (192). On this reading, it could be said, Setsuko and Noriko downplay Ono's role in the war because they want to shield him from self-harm. They fear that he will kill himself, like Naguchi. Hence they deny his pre-war status, which then gives the impression that Ono's narrative is contradictory and inconsistent.

Another realist-oriented reading, but this time social rather than psychological, is suggested by the exigencies of cold war *realpolitik*. This account puts the emphasis on the founding of the People's Republic of

China in 1949, which meant that in foreign policy terms the United States lost the opportunity to secure China as its big anti-communist ally in Asia. As Bruce Cumings explains, this development bolstered the conviction that there was a need to strengthen occupied Japan to take up that role. As a result, a change of direction was initiated there in accordance with the 'global policy' objectives of the Truman presidency (Cumings 1993: 37). A strategic decision was made to rehabilitate many of the Japanese war leaders who had earlier been targeted by anti-fascist purges. At the same time, a 'Red purge' was conducted against socialists and communists who had earlier been freed from prison. Emancipatory energies released in the immediate post-war period by US occupation forces were thus crushed by those same forces, by what historians call the 'reverse course' in occupational history (Dower 1999: 272–3). Conservative elements returned to power as a result and Japan was to remain an essentially single-party polity well into the 1990s.

These historical details explain the complaint made by Miyake, one of Noriko's prospective grooms, about the 'plenty of men already back in positions they held during the war', some of whom are 'no better than war criminals'. Immediately after sharing these recollections, Ono wonders if these words might have come from someone else. He wonders if he might have 'confused' them with 'the sort of thing Suichi will come out and say' (56). This lack of clarity [136] about who said what as well as Ono's manner of being simultaneously blameworthy (but less so) might be said to reference these about-faces and disavowals.

On this reading, Ono's narrative tracks the gaps and fissures in the dominant historical representation of the period. Rather than being an instigator of a beneficent and thoroughgoing democratic political revolution [114], his splintered narrative captures the sense in which US occupation authorities made positive changes but also supervised the rehabilitation of former fascists and criminalization of progressive elements. His see-sawing narrative is the novel's manner of capturing that fateful switch in occupational history, one whose make-up and impact is still hotly contested among scholars and historians. These contextual details make it difficult to close the novel in a determinate fashion. In both artistic and historical terms an indeterminate ending is a more satisfying choice.

FURTHER READING

Dower (1999) gives an excellent account of the historical period referenced by the novel. Scanlan (1993) and Sarvan (1997) discuss Ono's split or fractured subjectivity. Zinck (2004) traces the influence of Japanese literature and art on the novel and on its precursor, A Pale View of Hills. Gluck (1997) addresses what is left out when the Second World War is grasped through the lens of a 'neat moral calculus' where the attack on Pearl Harbor is balanced against the atomic bombings of Hiroshima and Nagasaki, namely the Asian continental aspects of the conflict. In the line of development from *An Artist of the Floating World* to *When We Were Orphans*, Ishiguro arguably unsettles such a neat calculus.

The Remains of the Day

The Remains of the Day won the Booker Prize in 1989 and is Ishiguro's most well-known and best-loved work. It has attracted more criticism than any of his other novels. Its technical and artistic virtuosity can be appreciated from the fact it has been taken up in a slew of fields and sub-fields. After reading the novel while it was still in galleys, Harold Pinter optioned the film rights for it, something that he confessed he had 'never done' before (Jones 1993: 3). It was subsequently made into a movie by the Merchant Ivory team starring Anthony Hopkins and Emma Thompson, with the film winning three Oscars after being nominated for eight. It features on many school and university syllabi and it is not an exaggeration to say that it has become something of a contemporary classic.

In the discussion below, a synopsis of the novel will be followed by a review of its recognition plot. The question of how it achieves its appeal will be addressed. Three additional features will also be reviewed, namely the nature of the relationship between the novel and Ishiguro's previous works, the way in which it brings together public history and private recollection, and, related to that, the sense in which it operates as a condition-of-England novel. Emphasis will be placed on the last because it dovetails with a gathering critical consensus on the novel [126, 155].

Written in the form of a *journal de voyage*, the novel relates six days in the life of an English butler, Stevens, who works for a Mr John Farraday, an American businessman and owner of the stately home where Stevens plies his trade. Set in the 1950s, it is a first-person account by Stevens but harks back constantly to the 1920s and 1930s when the home was the seat of his previous employer, Lord Darlington. For a time during this period Stevens was close to the housekeeper, Miss Kenton. The novel suggests that they had deep feelings for each other although their relationship never progressed beyond convivial 'cocoa' evenings when they met in Miss Kenton's parlour to discuss the smooth running of the estate (147). When the novel opens, Stevens is on his way to meet Miss Kenton (now Mrs Benn) in Cornwall, some twenty years after she left Darlington's service. He travels to see her ostensibly to relieve a staff shortage, to ask if she will come out of retirement and work for Farraday. As he travels, various chance encounters prompt him to revisit the important events of his life. He questions, perhaps for the first time, his lifelong adherence to a singular conception of duty, dignity and vocational propriety. All along he had believed that 'A "great" butler can only be ... one who can point to his years of service and say that he has applied his talents to serving a great gentleman – and through the latter, to serving humanity' (117). In the name of duty, he had eavesdropped on guests so that he could pass items of information on to Darlington, an advocate of appeasement and an admirer of Hitler's regime. On instructions from Darlington he had sacked two Jewish maids [132]. He failed to realize his relationship with Miss Kenton, and he also failed to attend to his father as he lay dying in an upstairs bedroom during a diplomatic conference held at the hall in 1923.

When Stevens finally meets Miss Kenton and learns that her marriage has been unhappy and that she too wishes they had made their feelings known to each other, the costs of his misguided investment in an ethos of self-abrogation are brought painfully home to him, even as the realization comes too late for him to profit from it. The novel ends with him seated on a bench on a seaside pier in Weymouth, southwest England, holding sadly to the shreds of his dignity. Finally giving in to tears, he speaks to a stranger and laments that whereas Darlington in the course of his life 'made his own mistakes', he couldn't even say that about himself. He notes that 'All those years I served him, I trusted I was doing something worthwhile. [But] I can't even say I made my own mistakes. Really – one has to ask oneself – what dignity is there in that?' (243) [102, 154].

The Remains of the Day has a strong empathetic impact on readers, and it is helpful to consider for a moment where its appeal lies. Part of it would seem to derive from its clever use of unreliable narration [105], its successful treatment of character and adroit use of language. With great economy, Ishiguro delineates a character who was in many respects a bystander and who wasted large portions of his life. Through large parts of the narrative, Stevens's formal diction keeps us at a distance. At crucial moments, however, the narrative provides slight departures from formality that hint at the emotional turmoil taking place beneath a seemingly placid exterior. One good example would be when Stevens comments on various incidents that later became the great 'turning points' of his life: he allows that they seemed 'crucial' in retrospect but insists that they didn't give that impression then; there was 'nothing to indicate' that those small incidents would 'render whole dreams forever irredeemable' (179).

Ishiguro shows great craft in delineating this self-understanding that emerges tacitly and against the grain of a first-person account. These interspersed and oftentimes equivocal moments are to some extent the high points of the novel's recognition plot, the moments that readers respond to. One of novel's striking features is the way it solicits the reader's inquiry into how much self-understanding or insight Stevens possesses. The fact that it takes the form of a confession enhances our connection with the text. Despite the rhetorical and emotional defences that he throws around himself, the impression is given that Stevens realizes the scale of his errors.

It appears that at some level he appreciates the great mistake he made when he internalized a rationalization of his role in an exploitative class system. Another reason for its appeal might be its promise of a 'below-the-stairs' peek into the lives of the great and the good. Stately homes like Darlington Hall were the centre of the world when the world was run by a confraternity of diplomatic and governing classes drawn from the old European aristocracy. The novel underlines this feature through the unofficial gatherings organized by Darlington during the inter-war years to discuss the situation in Europe, and also through the powerful or influential 'real-life' figures who feature on his guest lists. These include Maynard Keynes, Oswald Mosley, George Bernard Shaw, Joachim Ribbentrop, Lord Halifax [111], Stanley Baldwin, H. G. Wells and Anthony Eden. This world of tea on lawns, unhurried elegance and polite, self-effacing butlers – in short, an entire culture linked with the stately home world – plays a prominent role in the imagination of many individuals, driven perhaps by middle-class fantasies of inclusion or of escape. As the historian David Cannadine points out, 'No artifact in modern England has been the object of such fanciful, romanticized and well-articulated veneration as the country house' (Cannadine 1997: 99). To some it is synonymous with English national culture and heritage.

Paradoxically, perhaps, the novel also combines the appeal of imaginary access to a luxurious life with a confirmation of the idea that modern-day Britain is less riven by class and social stratification. The novel affirms the more progressive features of contemporary society by putting readers into a situation where they track from a more advanced socio-historical vantage point Stevens's gradual divestment of his hierarchical mindset. These insights are intermeshed with the flashbacks that he makes as he journeys through southern England to meet Miss Kenton. As he motors around the country, Stevens uses a guidebook written by a certain Jane Symons, titled *The Wonder of England* (11). Symons was a frequent visitor to Darlington Hall, and like Darlington was a full-fledged member of the aristocratic order that in Stevens's opinion occupies 'the hub of this world's wheel' (126) [143]. That privileged position meant that Darlington was tasked with world-historical responsibilities – the inter-war crisis in Europe, for instance – which he tries to resolve by organizing two informal diplomatic conferences, the one mentioned above and another one in 1936. It was at these conferences that Stevens made the fateful decisions of his life, first when he failed to tend to his dying father, and, subsequently, when he failed to express his feelings for Miss Kenton after her future husband proposed to her. His regard for that gentlemanly order made him choose his career over his private life. Stevens's use of the guidebook is thus figuratively an effort to justify the way of life that it represents, to say that the values which had sustained a narrow sliver of culture – hierarchy, old school ties, noblesse oblige notions of service – were as valid in the post-war years as in the inter-war period. Despite the enormous changes the country underwent as it created the welfare state and began the retreat from Empire, the guidebook frames his journey under the spiritual patronage of the old landed-gentry order. It insists that Darlington Hall and those of its ilk are still the irreplaceable hubs or centres of the world.

The motif of travel usually generates narratives that are concerned with self-realization in geographical space, with getting the 'truth' about oneself confirmed, as it were, by encounters with landscape, buildings and diverse individuals. Symons's guide is presumably entrusted with generating encounters that endorse the lordly order supported by Stevens. However, it fails to deliver on that score. Of note are two incidents that together sound the death-knell of Stevens's reverence for the stately home world. The first occurs just after he enters Dorset when his car breaks down. The second occurs after he runs out of petrol near a secluded farming village. These misadventures in turn lead to other encounters where Stevens is prompted to confront his errors. The associative logic of the novel suggests that the principles figured by the guide have got him lost in the past and are doing so again.

In the first incident, Stevens's radiator boils over and he goes to seek help at a country estate. The person helping him, a chauffeur, starts to pry into his service history when he learns that he works at Darlington Hall. To get himself out of a tricky situation, Stevens says that he didn't serve Darlington, who after the war was vilified for his pro-appeasement stance. This encounter in turn prompts a recollection of an incident a few months earlier when Stevens similarly denied serving Darlington when pressed by an American couple – the Wakefields – who were then visiting Farraday. The Wakefields had questioned the pedigree of the estate, insisting that a lot of its features were 'mock period piece[s]' (123). Stevens recalls that when the news of his denial filtered back to Farraday, he had asked him:

> I mean to say, Stevens, this *is* a genuine grand old English house, isn't it? That's what I paid for. And you're a genuine old-fashioned English butler, not just some waiter pretending to be one [153]. You're the real thing, aren't you?
>
> (124, emphasis original)

The changed social environment means that Stevens's esteem for Darlington is now politically anachronistic. The incipient commodification of the stately home world by American new money hints at this wider development. Farraday's innocent query over whether he bought the 'real thing' heightens the impression of social obsolescence. In the irony attached to his questioning of Stevens's professional status, Farraday gently registers the direction of Stevens's own queries and observations.

It is with the second incident, however, that what might be called the conceptual climax of the novel occurs. After running out of gas Stevens has to abandon his car on a lonely hill road and get help. He winds up at a small village called Moscombe where he meets the Taylors, a couple who offer him hospitality. Stevens's arrival attracts the attention of various villagers, who congregate at the Taylor residence and engage him in conversation. The irony and humour raised by the earlier questioning of Stevens's status are continued here: Stevens's refined deportment and speech (a condition of his vocation) cause the villagers to mistake him for a gentleman and to question him about foreign affairs matters as well as his knowledge of certain prominent politicians. Stevens's difficulty in extracting himself from a false situation generates humour. But there is a serious side to the use of the mistaken identity motif, for Stevens also meets a villager named Harry Smith [31], who, as his name implies, is a kind of everyman or John Bull figure. Smith inadvertently aims a broadside at Stevens's cherished beliefs when he proclaims that dignity is not a preserve of the upper class. It is something 'every man and woman in this country can strive for and get' (186). In his opinion:

> That's what we fought Hitler for, after all. If Hitler had ... [won the] whole world would be a few masters and millions upon millions of slaves. ... [I]t's one of the privileges of being born English that no matter who you are ... you can express your opinion freely, and vote in your member of parliament or vote him out. That's what dignity's really about.
>
> (ROD 186)

This is a key moment because Smith presents a different understanding of 'dignity' from its association in Stevens's mind with service and deference. Smith's version is more in tune with post-war egalitarian ideals. It is in mulling over this encounter, the novel suggests, that Stevens finally recognizes his status as a mere auxiliary figure in the antebellum social order. Only then is he able to countenance Darlington's betrayal in the past when he allowed other guests to bully him despite his adherence to hierarchical codes of service. Stevens tries to defend Darlington as he recounts this episode. However, his attempt comes across as a last-ditch effort to hold back a breaking dam. Together with the pain generated by his meeting with Miss Kenton, these two incidents underline certain home truths for Stevens. They show how far he has travelled since the start of his journey. They set the scene for the epiphanic moment that closes the novel, when Stevens acknowledges that in relinquishing autonomy he had also surrendered his dignity.

Apart from the events and motifs outlined above, three other things about *The Remains of the Day* are important and worthy of attention.

These are: the nature of its relationship with Ishiguro's earlier works sense it which it operates as a condition-of-England novel, and the wa which it brings together public and private history.

With regard to the first feature, it is useful to consider the sense in which *The Remains of the Day* is in some respects an arch performance by Ishiguro, one meant to be weighed in tandem with his previous novels. Together, that cumulative reading experience was apparently meant to open up new avenues for authorial development. Up to this point in his career, Ishiguro had been labelled a supplier of Oriental style and manners. In *The Remains of the Day*, he resists this label with the counter-example presented by a chief protagonist who exudes Victorian qualities. Accustomed to Manichean notions of cultural distance and dissimilarity, readers are invited to consider the continuation of theme [18] between Ishiguro's first three books, including the similarities between Stevens, Masuji Ono of *An Artist of the Floating World* and Ogata-San of *A Pale View of Hills*.

Given these commonalities, its change of setting while replicating theme would seem to be an integral part of the meaning of *The Remains of the Day*. The propensity to relinquish autonomy is presented as a philosophical or existential dilemma and not necessarily a culturally specific one. By having Stevens share these features, Ishiguro in effect 'rewrites' or refines [19] his earlier works. The idea that they are necessarily particularist (they are only about Japan) is contested. This is also to say that *The Remains of the Day* gains an additional layer of meaning when grasped within an enlarged interpretive horizon that incorporates these other texts.

In an interview conducted in 1990 in the US, Ishiguro was asked what he thought about the relationship between *The Remains of the Day* and the work of 'traditional' (interviewer's term) writers such as Somerset Maugham, Evelyn Waugh, E. M. Forster and Joyce Cary. He replied tellingly in the following manner:

> Sometimes it looks like or has the tone of a very English book, but actually I'm using that as a kind of shock tactic: this relatively young person with a Japanese name and a Japanese face who produces this extra-English novel or, perhaps I should say, a super-English novel. *It's more English than English.* Yet I think there's a big difference from the tones of the world in *The Remains of the Day* and the worlds created by those writers you mentioned because in my case there is an ironic distance.
>
> (Vorda and Herzinger 1993: 13–14, emphasis original)

Extrapolating from these remarks, it can be argued that *The Remains of the Day* is on one level a response to authorial typecasting. The super-English configuration of Stevens is a 'shock tactic' meant to initiate a kind of critical double-take in readers so that they will question – and hopefully alter – the expectations they bring to Ishiguro's works. If granted, this sense in which the novel is concerned with clearing a path for artistic development is arguably troped in a humorous episode where Stevens and Miss Kenton squabble over the significance of a misplaced porcelain item. Miss Kenton tells Stevens that for some time now certain 'Chinaman' figures have not been cleaned properly and, worse, that they have started to appear in 'incorrect positions' (59). She means to say that Stevens's father, who also works at Darlington Hall, has been entrusted with too many responsibilities: he is responsible for these mistakes and needs a rest. Stevens has idealized notions about his father and refuses to contemplate that prospect. But given Ishiguro's remarks above, it would seem that the episode has metafictional import: it can be read as an authorial in-joke [60] anticipating puzzlement or critical astonishment over his shift of vision from Japan to Britain.

In addition, *The Remains of the Day* can also be read profitably as a state-of-the-nation or condition-of-England novel [128] with intimate links to the decade in which it appeared. This aspect of the novel has been lucidly stated by Ishiguro, who said that one of his objectives with the book was to 'rewrite P. G. Wodehouse with a serious political dimension' (Kelman 1991: 74). In the 1990 interview cited earlier, Ishiguro adds that he hopes to unsettle a certain dominant mythology:

> *The Remains of the Day* is not an England that I believe ever existed ... What I'm trying to do there, and I think this is perhaps much easier for British people to understand than perhaps people abroad, is to actually rework a particular myth about a certain kind of England [consisting of] ... sleepy, beautiful villages with very polite people and butlers and people taking tea on the lawn ... [A]t the moment, particularly in Britain, there is an enormous nostalgia industry [60] going on with coffee table books, television programs, and even some tour agencies who are trying to recapture this kind of old England. The mythical landscape of this sort of England, to a large degree, is harmless nostalgia for a time that didn't exist. The other side of this, however, is that it is used as a political tool ... a way of bashing anybody who tries to spoil this Garden of Eden [128]. This can be brought out by the left or right, but usually it is the political right who say England was this beautiful place before the trade unions tried to make it more egalitarian or before the immigrants started to come or before the promiscuous age of the '60s came and ruined everything.
>
> (Vorda and Herzinger 1993: 14–15)

These remarks explain the semantic loading of the term 'great' [125] in two key passages near the start of Stevens's journey when the anti-pastoral thrust of Ishiguro's project is intimated. On the evening of Stevens's first day of travel, he mulls over a view of the 'rolling English countryside' that he had enjoyed earlier that day from the top of a hill (28):

> For it is true, when I stood on that high ledge this morning ... I distinctly felt that rare, yet unmistakable feeling – the feeling that one is in the presence of greatness. We call this land of ours *Great* Britain, and there may be those who believe this a somewhat immodest practice. Yet I would venture that the landscape of our country alone would justify the use of this lofty adjective.
>
> (*ROD* 28, emphasis original)

A while later Stevens tellingly links this 'whole question' of what makes Britain 'great' to his manifestly painful deliberations over the direction of his life. National greatness, he says, is 'akin to the question that has caused much debate in our profession over the years', namely the question of what makes a butler 'great' (29). He elaborates subsequently what that professional tag entails:

> It is sometimes said that butlers only truly exist in England. Other countries, whatever title is actually used, have only manservants. I tend to believe this is true ... Continentals – and by and large the Celts, as you will no doubt agree – are as a rule unable to control themselves in moments of strong emotion, and are thus unable to maintain a professional demeanour other than in the least challenging of situations ... In a word, 'dignity' is beyond such persons.
>
> (*ROD* 43)

What is at stake in the two indented passages above is thus arguably the performance-cum-examination of a discourse of English pastoralism – a 'Garden of Eden' in Ishiguro's words – in which elements of the countryside and the stately home milieu are reconfigured as floating metaphors for a certain kind of fundamental Englishness, one that excludes other denizens who have somehow made their way to its shores. During his hill-top deliberations, Stevens explicitly contrasts the restrained English landscape with that of 'America' and 'Africa' (29), and it is possible to argue that these terms signify in an exclusionary fashion the Afro-Caribbean immigrants who came to work in the London transport sector and to help set up the National Health Service. Dominic Head points out that their arrival in the late 1940s is usually taken to denote the beginning of 'multicultural' or multiracial Britain (Head 2002: 164) [124]. Stevens's use of the Symons guide is arguably an attempt to yoke together the countryside and stately home as a final bastion threatened by foreign incursion. Intrinsic to this discourse is a certain level of anxiety even as spaces marked 'foreign' are screened out, as can be seen in

Stevens's address of the implied reader ('as you will no doubt agree'). As Rob Nixon suggests, it basically denies the experience of history:

> As an imaginative tradition, English pastoral has long been both nationally definitive and fraught with anxiety. At the heart of English pastoral lies the idea of the nation as garden idyll into which neither labor nor violence intrudes. To stand as a self-contained national heritage landscape, English pastoral has depended on the screening out of colonial spaces and histories, much as the American wilderness ideal has entailed an amnesiac relationship towards the Amerindian wars of dispossession.
>
> (Nixon 2005: 239)

For the purposes of this sub-section, the Black British writer Mike Phillips provides a useful personal gloss to Nixon's more abstract exposition:

> I remember going as a boy to the National Maritime Museum in Greenwich, and finding all these monumental sculptures and paintings very oppressive. You go to a stately home, then, and you're either looking at the insolent display of a nabob who's whipped the ass off all his slaves, or an innocent display of domestic magnificence which by its nature excludes your history ... this heritage is for us not the same innocent heritage it is for an English person. As history it is deeply compromised.
>
> (Coster 1991: 6)

As explained by Paul Gilroy, the conservative identity politics [5, 158] of the 1970s and 1980s used a rhetoric of law and order to rewrite Britain's imagined community along exclusive lines. This was done so that 'modern conservatism could voice populist protest against Britain's post-imperial plight and marshal its historic [voting] bloc' (Gilroy 1987: 48). Part of this move involved an extensive deployment of the analogy of war, which was used to characterize 'black immigration and settlement' as an 'encroachment of aliens'. It pulled together 'the politics of crime and domestic political dissent', as a result of which '[i]ndustrial militants and black settlers' both came to share the designation, 'The Enemy Within' (Gilroy 1990: 266). In Gilroy's opinion, a consideration of the 1987 British general elections allows these themes to be seen with 'a special clarity':

> The theme of patriotism was well to the fore and a tussle over the national flag was a major feature of the campaign. The Labour party pleaded for Britain to heal its deep internal divisions and become 'one nation again', whereas the Conservatives underlined their success in 'putting the Great back into Britain' by urging the

electorate not to let the Socialists take this crucial adjective out
again. Significantly, this language made no overt reference to race,
but it acquired racial referents. Everyone knows what is at stake
when patriotism and deference to the law are being spoken about.

(Gilroy 1990: 268–9)

In light of these points, The Remains of the Day can be read as a plea for a
more fully inclusive or pluralist society [125, 145]. It questions through its
recognition plot the prelapsarian mindset that says, in Ishiguro's words,
England was this 'beautiful place' before organized labour sought a more
egalitarian society, before the immigrants arrived, and before the 1960s
social revolutions took place. The entire movement of the novel asserts that
formality and repression have truncated Stevens's life. To the extent that
such a super-Victorian deportment undermines the clarion calls made
throughout the 1980s for Britons to emulate 'Victorian values' (Marsden
1990: 2), it therefore mounts a trenchant critique of the dominant discourse
of that period.

   This reading – its questioning of Thatcherite authoritarian populism
[127] – potentially explains why the colonial stories [160] shared in the novel
contain an undertow of self-critique. As explained by Gordon Marsden, one
of the political purposes underlying the propagation of Victorian values in
the 1980s was its attempt to exploit a residual nostalgia for Empire [61]. The
notion that Empire represented a 'golden age' of power and influence was
essential to the Conservative Party's promise to bring it back in some attenuated form. Given that 'self-help, self-reliance, entrepreneurship, individual
charity (rather than a state dole), law and order, family discipline and a
stricter sexual morality' were the principles underlying the imperial achievements of the Victorian era – so the argument goes – then they also endorsed
a 'similar philosophy' pursued by Margaret Thatcher in the 1980s and 1990s
(Marsden 1990: 2).

   In this context, Stevens's father has a favourite story about how a butler
in India killed a tiger without fuss so that it wouldn't disturb the equipoise
of a colonial tea-party (36). However, the novel also hints that he dies from
overwork. On his deathbed, his dedication to duty is arguably parodied by
his son's failure to attend to him – a stance that draws strength from precisely the same colonial anecdote. In addition, the novel reveals early on
that Stevens's elder brother, a soldier, was killed during the Boer War. He
'died quite needlessly' during 'a most un-British attack on civilian Boer
settlements' (40). Subsequently, Stevens's father had to serve the general
responsible for this carnage when he visited his employer, Mr Silvers.
Through these negative portrayals of Empire, The Remains of the Day
endorses a different, more participatory society outlined above.

   Connected to that social ethos, it is also noteworthy that the novel is set
in the same month and year – July 1956 – as the Suez crisis. As a result it

links together public and private history in a manner suggestive of *An Artist of the Floating World* [36–44]. The Suez crisis refers to the diplomatic standoff that led to a joint operation by Britain and France to seize control of the Suez Canal after it was nationalized by Egypt. Partly because of logistic problems and partly because of the lack of US support, the mission was eventually aborted. Now accounted a failed bid to roll back the retreat from Empire (and hence marking its death-knell), it subsequently dogged the reputation of the then prime minister Anthony Eden (1897–1977).

Anna Marie Smith has asserted that the symbolic meaning of the Suez crisis for Britain 'can be compared to that of "Vietnam" for the Americans' (Smith 1994: 11) and, taken from that perspective, the crisis is hinted at in the novel but relatively underplayed. At one point during the conversation at the Taylor residence, the villagers prise from Stevens the fact that he 'knows' Mr Eden, meaning that he had served him as a guest of Darlington Hall (*ROD* 191). This item of information attracts the attention of a Dr Carlisle, who to the apparent dismay of Harry Smith supports the dissolution of Empire – of the notion of 'all kinds of little countries going independent' (192). In this regard, *The Remains of the Day* takes appreciable efforts to undermine Smith's status as one of the sources of narrative wisdom on the question of egalitarianism, a status conferred earlier by his homily about why Britain fought Hitler. This about-turn is one of the interpretive conundrums of the novel, an area of incongruence that solicits the reader's attention. One way to handle this incongruence is to consider Carlisle's function in the novel. Carlisle is the one who rescues Stevens from the embarrassment of being accounted a high-born gentleman. He asks Stevens the day after his confrontation with Harry Smith whether he is a 'manservant' of some kind, and Stevens is happy to acknowledge his perspicacity (207). 'Manservant' is the word Stevens used earlier when he said that certain breeds incapable of 'emotional restraint' could only aspire to that category as opposed to the butler vocation (43). The novel indicates that Carlisle went to Moscombe in 1949 to help set up the National Health Service (210). His sense of mission and fellow-feeling is thus linked to the post-imperial ethos described earlier, to the novel's use of colonial stories to challenge contemporaneous efforts to romanticize Empire and the Victorian age.

Finally, it helps to consider how Ishiguro tends in a self-reflexive manner to questions of genre and literary heritage. As stated above, he claims that *The Remains of the Day* sets 'an ironic distance' between itself and other works written by so-called 'traditional' writers. Raymond Williams has argued that 'the true fate of the country-house novel [7, 79, 117, 126] was its evolution into the middle-class detective story' (Williams 1973: 249) [77, 117]. In making this claim, Williams indicts stately home culture for offering a false notion of community divorced from any nourishing or recuperative tributaries.

Ishiguro appears to track this line of development in his fifth book, *When We Were Orphans*.

FURTHER READING

Arguably the two most important readings of *The Remains of the Day* are the ones by Robbins (2001a) and Phelan and Martin (1999). The latter is useful for pedagogical purposes because of its precision of analysis and because its authors discuss their own disagreements about the text. The former has been influential in moving Ishiguro criticism towards a consideration of the cosmopolitan themes that underpin his writing. Williams (1973) gives one of the best analyses of the English pastoral tradition. Lowenthal (1991) explains succinctly the link between British national identity and the English landscape. Gilroy (1987) and A. M. Smith (1994) give penetrating accounts of the conservative discourse referenced above. Strongman (2002) addresses the novel in the context of a wider argument tracking the legacy of Empire and its impact on the Booker Prize. Raphael (2001) gives an important feminist reading of the novel. McCombe (2002) situates the novel against its mid-twentieth-century historical setting. Hewison (1987), P. Wright (1985) and Lowenthal (1998) provide telling insights into the heritage or 'nostalgia' industry referenced by the author.

The Unconsoled

The Unconsoled marks a surprising departure for Ishiguro. After three novels that in the main upheld conventional notions of novelistic verisimilitude, this sprawling, disorienting and oddly surrealist work quickly drew the ire of reviewers [112]. In its use of teutonic character names, its lack of geographical references and its recurrent depiction of unconsummated action and curtailed agency, *The Unconsoled* echoes the disturbing allegorical worlds of Kafka's *Trial* and *The Castle*. At one point in the novel, the chief protagonist, Ryder, is accosted in the centre of town by a journalist who wants to interview him. Ryder deposits his son, Boris, in a coffee shop and tells him to order a snack (164–5). He wanders off with the journalist and they journey further and further away from town. Eventually, Ryder fetches up at a roadside truck-stop, 'the sort of place one might imagine lorry drivers stopping for a sandwich' (192). Yet in the very next moment he walks through a door at the back of the truck-stop and is back again with Boris (203–4). Near the beginning of the novel, Ryder drives out to a mansion in the countryside, wanders around in it, and is suddenly back in the hotel left behind in town. In this way, the novel displays the elastic temporal and spatial features that also characterize Kafka's works. And, incidentally, similar odd slippages also occur in Ishiguro's subsequent novel, *When We Were Orphans*.

At the same time, *The Unconsoled* is more than an artistic or stylistic homage to European high modernism [79]. Its peculiar mix of straight realism and out-and-out fabulism is intriguing and provocative. It can be read as an allegory of the commodifying propensities of the book trade, of the way in which authors are packaged as ersatz gurus who can solve all manner of existential concerns. It bears some relation to Ishiguro's personal experience as a writer, and can be read as an attempt to escape artistic sequestration. It is on one level a pastiche of *The Remains of the Day*. It proffers an alternative way of writing a memoir or a biography, and in this respect can be said to have expanded the frontiers of the novel [113]. This is also to say that it offers a different way of 'doing' characterization and plot. These features will be reviewed in the discussion below.

At over five hundred pages long – almost as large as the combined length of Ishiguro's three previously published novels – *The Unconsoled* is not an easy book to summarize. Set in an unnamed central or eastern European city, it relates the experiences of Ryder, a famous classical pianist who comes to give a concert. The inhabitants of the city have oddly exalted notions of what he can achieve during his visit. They see him as a Herculean figure who will transform the city's cultural life and restore its former civic glory. They expect him to give existential ballast to their lives, to succeed where someone named Christoff had failed (99). The language is rife with semi-parodic comments about how '[t]hings were good here in the good old days' (103). Some sort of '*crisis*' or deep cultural malaise is constantly being intimated (271, emphasis original). The town dwellers say that they hope to 'reverse the spiral of misery gaining ever greater momentum at the heart of our community' (112). Yet the reason for that pessimism and dejection is never reliably established. Like an agony-aunt figure, the town's denizens expect Ryder to mend their many broken relationships. But everything Ryder does is a false start, everything an exercise in futility, with the novel wringing a dry, mordant humour from its relentless enactment of curtailed agency and inconsequence, as Ryder lurches from one outlandish errand to another.

Over the course of three days, Ryder judges musical recitals, tries to reconcile estranged families and attends a movie screening where the audience doesn't pay attention to the film. He attends dinners where he pleads the cause of a disgraced, bibulous ex-conductor named Brodsky. When he stands up to deliver a speech his gown gapes open to reveal his naked body (143). He meets old university and childhood friends who have a tendency to pop up in his vicinity (302). He meanders across town and comes across streets whose 'entire breadth' is blocked by brick walls (387). He causes public disquiet when he accidentally intervenes in local politics, in some farrago over a man named Max Sattler (369–75). He asks a stranger for instructions to an art gallery and is told to tail after a red car driven by a man who lives close to it (244). He tails the car through miles of open fields. After several diversions he eventually reaches the gallery, and it just happens that in a field next to it are the remains of his 'old family car', one that his father had 'driven for many years' (261). Ryder also meets Brodsky's former partner, a Miss Collins, and tries without success to get her to resume her relationship with Brodsky (276). At times he can relate in a telepathic manner what happens with other characters, an example being the episode where he reports on a conversation between Miss Collins and a young pianist named Stephan Hoffman (56–61). The novel also allows a kind of dual characterization. Its ontological coordinates are elastic and insecure: Sophie and Boris, whom Ryder meets in the town, are actually his wife and son. As the novel progresses, we get the impression that Stephan echoes aspects of Ryder's own life experiences, especially in the lack of parental support for his artistic endeavours. Brodsky also 'echoes' his experiences, or at least his fears about how he may end up as an artist.

Through it all, Ryder is unable to refuse the interminable requests thrown at him. Eventually he loses his temper and shouts at his interlocutors to 'stop asking favours of me' (330). In Chapter 25, he finally gets to practise for his concert. For some unaccountable reason, however, his piano is located in a little wooden shed at the top of a hill (356). It transpires that he is actually participating in a burial ceremony for Brodsky's recently deceased pet dog, Bruno, for which his 'piano accompaniment' is meant to be 'the sole embellishment' (358). Predictably as well, Ryder doesn't get to give his grand performance, although the novel does end with a concert. Ensconced in a 'small black cupboard' (476) that gives him a surrealistic bird's-eye view of an auditorium, Ryder sees Stephan give a rendition of a piece called 'Glass Passions' (481). He sees Brodsky conduct an orchestra, providing an interpretation of another piece called 'Verticality' (491). He listens to the town librarian give a poetry recital with many of the poems recounting in mock-heroic manner episodes from Brodsky's life. After the concert, the audience quickly disappears and is next glimpsed in a large sunlit conservatory having breakfast (523). Nobody comes to ask Ryder why he didn't perform, why he missed the concert. His attempts to get attention are studiously ignored (502). As the novel closes, Ryder is on his way to Helsinki, apparently to continue his tour. His estranged relationship with his family has not been mended. He also fails to mend the many broken relationships among the town dwellers, or to noticeably impact upon their lives.

The above synopsis gives an idea of the novel's comic range, absurdist features and surrealist tenor. It hints at the way it tests our novelistic suspension of disbelief as well as its wider allegorical and figurative dimensions. However, it should be noted that the novel's formal, cognitive and intertextual depths have yet to be fully explored or enumerated. Its depiction-cum-exploration of various psycho-social processes is also fascinating and deserves further commentary. Ishiguro has suggested, apparently in jest, that *The Unconsoled* 'could be seen to be about the third week of an American [book promotion] tour' (Tonkin 2000: 9). He has stated that promotional work to satisfy his extended readership takes up about a third of his working time (Hunnewell 2008: 47). After the success of *The Remains of the Day*, he had to spend a lot of time on the road. In a 1990 interview with the *Washington Post*, he bemoaned the fact that he had been 'doing very little except publicity' and had not written anything since 1988 (Streitfeld 1990: E1). Interestingly, the profile piece is headlined: 'The author's life as a salesman; Ishiguro, on tour with no time to write'. Ishiguro adds in a separate interview that *The Unconsoled* gestures at the 'complexity of the issues which confront the world'. This is portrayed in an 'abstract' manner through the notion of 'a community in decline because it had been worshiping the wrong musical values. So when this pianist stumbles into town, they look to him to lead them to correct musical values.' As such the book is 'a metaphor for how communities look to experts to solve their problems because the issues facing them seem so complex and the cost of democratic participation is so great' (Kenney 1995: 47).

Given the above, *The Unconsoled* might be said to spoof on one level contemporary celebrity culture as well as the commodifying propensities of the culture or book-publishing industry. It allows Ishiguro to depict in a cloaked manner his concerns about artistic compromise and betrayal, to register his awareness of being put in a false position because of the need to 'do' publicity. Such a construal of the novel fits the town dwellers' exaggeration of Ryder's role and function. It explains the interminable requests made of him, the repeated contention that he offers key existential insights and solutions. It fits the name given to Ryder's predecessor, Christoff, suggesting that artists are being imbued with proto-spiritual qualities. It gestures at the media circus that cheapens contemporary cultural life, including the way in which writers are pulled into disparate controversies through the line of questioning pursued in interviews. This state of affairs appears to be referenced at one point when Ryder unsuspectingly gets his name and picture into the front page of a local newspaper, in an article headlined, 'RYDER'S RALLYING CALL'. No mention is made of what he actually said or endorsed, and we are told that there is apparently 'no other text at all on the front page' (267, emphasis original).

Two incidents may be read as apogees or high points of this burlesque of expert–celebrity culture. A hullabaloo develops at one point over what would be a fitting way to honour the memory of Bruno. The discussion takes place between participants at a formal dinner party. An unnamed, distinguished-looking man addresses Brodsky in over-inflated, hilarious language. He says that:

> Your Bruno, sir, was not only much loved by those of us who saw
> him going about his business around our town. He came to

achieve a status rare among human beings, let alone among our quadrupeds. That is to say, ... he came to exemplify for us certain key virtues.

(*UC* 139)

After this comically overblown tribute, a heated discussion ensues over whether a bronze statue should be erected in Bruno's memory or whether a street should be named after him, for Bruno had been 'the greatest dog of his generation' (142). This discussion indicts in a humorous fashion the hagiography fostered by modern celebrity culture.

The second incident would be when Stephan's father, Hoffman, gives exaggeratedly detailed instructions to Ryder for a public conference that he hopes to organize. The manager of the hotel where Ryder stays, Hoffman comes across as a publicist from hell:

And now we come to the moment, sir ... of your appearance ... I have borrowed from our sports centre ... the electronic scoreboard that usually hangs over the indoor arena ... [A] single spot will come on, revealing you standing at the centre of the stage ... [A] voice will boom out across the auditorium, pronouncing the first question. The voice will be that of Horst Jannings ... [H]e will read out each question slowly. And as he does so ... the words will be spelt out simultaneously on the electronic scoreboard fixed directly above your head.

(*UC* 381)

Hoffman's speech goes on in an interminable fashion for almost four pages. Nothing is mentioned of what Ryder might want to say in response to the posed questions. Hoffman claims that everything he says depends on Ryder's approval, but Ryder can't get a word in edgeways. With great comic brio his status as cultural luminary is reduced to that of making signals and gestures. Hoffman wants him to make 'some sort of inconspicuous signal' as he approaches the end of each question, a 'modest shrug of the shoulder', perhaps, so that the question-and-answer session can proceed smoothly – and eventually Ryder capitulates to the verbal onslaught. He states that 'a curious, dreamy sense of unreality came over me as I realised just how unprepared I was'. He tells Hoffman that everything 'sounds splendid' and that he has 'thought the whole thing out very well' (382–3). Hoffman's suggestion that Ryder use an electronic scoreboard appears to uncover the awkward truth that art has become a business much like sport. It gestures at a situation where razzmatazz outweighs substance, or where form prevails over content.

Since *The Unconsoled* is one long delineation of an artist failing in what he sets out to do, it can also be read as a wry self-burlesque, a parody of

Ishiguro's own experiences of artistic emasculation. Ishiguro explains in the following manner his expressed desire to make his settings 'take off into the realm of metaphor' [9]:

> [I]f you make [a particular setting] too concrete and too tied down to something that might exist in reality, that fictional work doesn't take off at that metaphorical level and people start saying, 'Oh, that's what it was like in Japan at a certain time', or, 'He's saying something about Britain in the 1930s'. So, for me, it is something that I feel I haven't quite come to terms with yet, but I'm trying to find some territory, somewhere between straight realism and that kind of out-and-out fabulism, where I can create a world that isn't going to alienate or baffle readers in a way that a completely fantastic world would – but a world which, at the same time, can actually prompt readers to say that this isn't documentary or this isn't history or this isn't journalism. I'm asking you to look at this world that I've created as a reflection of a world that all kinds of people live in.
>
> (Vorda and Herzinger 1993: 16–17)

In another interview with the writer Bill Bryson, Ishiguro states tellingly that 'I sometimes feel that if I had written a book like Kafka's *Trial*, people would say to me, "What a strange judicial system the Japanese have"' (Bryson 1990: 44). The drift and tenor of these comments allow us to understand that one of the aims of *The Unconsoled* is again to clear new ground for aesthetic development. Ishiguro courts incomprehensibility in a bid to achieve this goal. He rejects the supplier-of-authenticity tag [9] by pushing into a European or incipiently internationalist milieu represented by Kafkaesque expressionism. As part of that undertaking, he combines realism and fabulism in order to challenge the literalist interpretations [112] that have historically shadowed his fiction. He confounds those reading practices by making Ryder say at one point to Sophie, 'I still have more trouble with French than I do with Japanese. Really. I get by in Tokyo better than in Paris' (249). Appearing only once in a novel over five hundred pages long, this detail can be read as a kind of autobiographical red herring or authorial in-joke [50]. In its use of non-realist techniques, *The Unconsoled* rehearses some of the stylistic attributes that have come into greater prominence in Ishiguro's recent work. It arguably demarcates a new, more mature phase in his writing.

At the same time, it might be said, Ishiguro also responds to the problematic reception accorded *The Remains of the Day* by repeating what he said in a different key. If the precursor novel's critique of the heritage or nostalgia industry [50] was read in a diametrically opposed fashion as an attempt to unearth a lost essential Englishness [116], Ishiguro repeats himself by lampooning declinist attitudes in *The Unconsoled*. The text is filled with individuals obsessing over some mysterious ailment or 'crisis' (289), who keep expressing the hope that they have reached some 'turning point' (107, 232, 482) where decline will be reversed so that they can push on to 'a new mood [and] a new era' (112). Through the town dwellers' exaggerated lament and consequent turn to purported cultural saviours, Ishiguro pokes fun at the attitudes that fuel heritage consumerism and ersatz nostalgia. No weighty reason is ever given for their overstated mourning although its real-life context – post-imperial cultural adjustment – is suggested by the town dwellers' fears about being unable to measure up to the likes of 'Stuttgart' (128) and 'Antwerp' (374).

Ishiguro provides a *reductio ad absurdum* of the declinist stance through, for instance, Hoffman, who is oppressed by the idea that he is not the social and artistic equal of his wife, and who insists that his situation is 'desperate' (353). Hoffman is one of many in the novel oppressed by a deep-set and yet unwarranted malaise. The entire town's population exemplifies this problem. Their pervasive pessimism and mourning are shown to be unjustified, and in this way Ishiguro suggests a need to move beyond declinist attitudes. The continental European setting of *The Unconsoled* is perhaps not insignificant here, for a push towards a truly post-imperial arrangement would require an appreciation and expansion of regional ties for Britain [22, 120].

This allusion to Britain's post-imperial travails comes across keenly at one point when Ryder peruses a list of 'Lost Property' items [86] on a wall chart in a room. Initially the entries are for the usual lost pens and wallets. Halfway down the list, however, they become increasingly facetious, and Ryder spots an entry for 'Genghis Khan', who had apparently lost the 'Asian Continent' (471). In this way, Ishiguro undercuts a residual nostalgia for Empire [53] by pointing out its incongruous and contradictory elements.

Not insignificantly, then, *The Unconsoled* also appears to parody *The Remains of the Day* through a porter named Gustav. Gustav is one of the first people who Ryder meets when he arrives in the city. He is also Ryder's father-in-law. As stated earlier, the novel allows this kind of arresting double characterization. One of our immediate impressions of Gustav is that he echoes Stevens of *The Remains of the Day* as well as his father, Stevens senior. On first encounter, he launches into an interminable description of his luggage-handling policy, much as Stevens talks incessantly about butlering. Gustav complains that the town dwellers do not respect his profession, that they think anyone can do his job because at some point in their lives they had the experience of 'carrying luggage from place to place' (6). He invites Ryder to call on the hotel porters' association that meets every Sunday afternoon in the Old Town (7), and this association appears to be a send-up of the 'Hayes Society' of butlers eulogized in *The Remains of the Day* (*ROD* 31).

In an extraordinary set-piece scene that is one of the comic highlights of *The Unconsoled*, Gustav and his fellow porters stage a dance-cum-weight-lifting display called a 'Porters' Dance' when Ryder finally meets up with them (396). The dance involves Gustav hoisting increasingly heavier suitcases and bags as he shuffles atop a café table (399–407). When we encounter Gustav earlier in the novel he is always overladen with luggage (280, 294). The dance exhausts him and he eventually dies from the gargantuan effort put into its enactment, just as Stevens's father appears to die from overwork in *The Remains of the Day*. In response to the accusation that he is delinquent for not appearing at Gustav's deathbed, Ryder replies that he is due on stage 'very shortly'. Moreover, he has to answer 'complex questions about the future of this community' (473). His actions echo Stevens's failure to attend to his father as he lies dying in a bedroom at Darlington Hall. He parodies Stevens's exaggeration of his role and impact, the way he sacrifices his emotional life for ostensibly communal purpose.

The satire of the precursor work also appears to colour the depiction of Gustav's relationship with his daughter, Sophie. At one point, he recounts the accidental death of Sophie's pet hamster when she was a child, and of how he dallied outside her bedroom wondering whether he should go in to express solicitude (83–5). His hyperbolic deliberations echo and exaggerate Stevens's emotional ineptitude following the death of the aunt of his colleague, Miss Kenton, when he had also dallied in the corridor outside her room, afraid that if he went in to offer his condolences he would 'intrude upon her private grief' (*ROD* 176). Gustav says that he has some '*understanding*' with his daughter that explains their alienation. Furthermore she knows this 'arrangement' and respects it (*UC* 82, 85, emphasis original) [164]. Taken as a whole, the episode might be considered an absurdist presentation of some of the emotionally handicapped or even masochistic aspects of Stevens's personality.

In addition, this pastiche of *The Remains of the Day* is arguably extended to cover Brodsky, who is in some respects an alter ego of Ryder, a projection of his fears about artistic failure and betrayal of principles. Brodsky's suitability for the retrograde role given to him by the town dwellers is underscored through description: he has a habit of perusing 'turgid-looking volumes of history' in the town library; he also seems to be afflicted with melancholia for the 'old country' (110). Ishiguro extends the pastiche through a town official named Pedersen who shares with Ryder a recollection of Brodsky sitting in the library one day staring into space with 'a droplet [dangling] on the end of his nose' (111). In *The Remains of the Day*, the same sardonic or de-valorizing language is used by Miss Kenton when she argues that less work should be assigned to Stevens's father. She says that she has spotted him going about his duties with 'a large drop on the end of his nose dangling over the soup bowls' (*ROD* 60).

This unflattering depiction and also Ryder's attempt to resuscitate Brodsky's career raises our curiosity about him. Brodsky's unsuccessful relationship with Miss Collins mirrors aspects of the relationship between Stevens and Miss Kenton; and Miss Collins gives insight into the main issue at stake when she laments that years after reaching adulthood, Brodsky is still plagued by a wound sustained in a childhood accident (464). With the passage of time his wound has healed but he is still obsessed about it. In some of the key lines of the novel, Miss Collins reproaches Brodsky in the following manner:

'Your wound,' Miss Collins said quietly. 'Always your wound.' Then her face contorted into ugliness. 'Oh, how I hate you! How I hate you for wasting my life! ... Your wound, your silly little wound! That's your real love, Leo, that wound, the one true love of your life! ... Me, the music, we're neither of us anything more to you than mistresses you seek consolation from. You'll always go back to your one real love. To that wound!'

(UC 498)

If it is the case that *The Unconsoled* spoofs the ersatz nostalgia that fuels heritage consumerism, that in some ways it urges readers to reassess essentialist views about Ishiguro's precursor work, one of its high points would be the scene where Brodsky addresses a group of mourners at a funeral and tells them to 'caress' their 'wound' while it is still 'raw and bleeding'. In effect, he is telling them to stoke their grief in order to prolong it (372). Furthermore, Miss Collins's rebuke in the indented passage above allows us to understand the psychological process that underpins the prolongation of grief. Like many of the town dwellers, Brodsky is plagued by some phantom wound. At the concert which takes place just before Miss Collins's denunciation, Brodsky goes on stage not just to conduct an orchestra, but actually to hobble around on one leg using an ironing board as a crutch (488–9). His performance is a kind of 'sordid ... exhibitionism' (492). His value to the audience arises from this display of a phantom wound given, as it were, a literal rendition. Brodsky needs a crutch because he wears a prosthesis on one leg, a result of the childhood accident mentioned above. He apparently lost his prosthesis in a recent car accident, but the novel withholds this item of information in order to create ghoulish tension during its recounting of the episode. What is actually a long-past event – losing a limb – is presented as a current event, for it appears that Ryder in this scene absentmindedly gives permission to a doctor to amputate without anaesthetic one of Brodsky's limbs (439–43).

Having Brodsky hobble around on stage displaying an old injury implies that he is unhealthily obsessed with it, and Miss Collins suggests as much when she says that it is his one true love. Furthermore, his situation can be understood in terms of the distinction that Sigmund Freud makes between mourning and melancholia. In his classic essay on this subject, Freud argues that healthy mourning entails a kind of reality testing where the mourner progressively reduces libidinal attachment to the lost object of love. The lost object may be a loved person or 'some abstraction which has taken the place of one, such as one's country, liberty, an ideal, and so on' (Freud 1957: 243). In Tammy Clewell's useful elaboration, the mourner engages in a kind of 'hyperremembering, a process of obsessive recollection during which the survivor resuscitates the existence of the lost other in the space of the psyche, replacing an actual absence with an imaginary presence':

> This magical restoration of the lost object enables the mourner to assess the value of the relationship and comprehend what he or she has lost in losing the other ... [B]y comparing the memories of the other with actual reality, [the mourner] comes to an objective determination that the lost object no longer exists. With a very specific task to perform, the Freudian grief work seeks, then, to convert loving remembrances into a futureless memory. Mourning comes to a decisive and 'spontaneous end', according to Freud, when the survivor has detached his or her emotional tie to the lost object and reattached the free libido to a new object, thus accepting consolation in the form of a substitute for what has been lost.
>
> (Clewell 2004: 44)

Brodsky's manifest inability to accept true consolation in the form of his substitutes (what Miss Collins calls his 'mistresses') suggests that his mourning has become melancholic, meaning that it is pathological and injurious. His disposition mirrors that of the other characters in the novel, and, as suggested by its title, that disposition is one of its primary focus of interest.

In light of Ishiguro's revelation that he turned his hand to fiction writing because it offered a kind of 'consolation [11] or a therapy' (Vorda and Herzinger 1993: 30), the daisy chain of compromised or sequestered artist-characters in *The Unconsoled* can perhaps be read in a metafictional or self-reflexive manner. They allow Ishiguro to explore his *own* entanglement in the cultural nostalgic mode that he had sought to criticize in his precursor novel, one where expatriate or diasporic/minority writers tackling the exigencies of migrant self-fashioning are ensnared by the heritage industry and by its need to assuage phantasmal wounds. With *The Unconsoled*, therefore, Ishiguro distances himself from a certain retrograde reading of *The Remains of the Day*.

It might seem odd that a writer wishes to put some space between himself and his most successful book, and it may be helpful here to note that the 1993 release of the Merchant Ivory adaptation of *The Remains of the*

Day puts Ishiguro in an odd, conflictual position. The novel and its filmic avatar [157] arguably clash with one another. Ironically, what the former warns us against is served up on a platter in the latter. Through a pastiche of the precursor work, therefore, Ishiguro invites its rereading and re-contextualization.

This distancing and re-contextualization effort is perhaps glossed through the use of intertextual reference, for Ryder is also the name of the chief protagonist of Evelyn Waugh's 1945 novel, *Brideshead Revisited*. Waugh's book was made into a hit television series in the 1970s, one that was arguably the forerunner of the cultural nostalgic mode associated with the Merchant Ivory label. By giving us another version of the character Ryder in his novel, Ishiguro undermines the earlier, more problematic or retrograde associations of that name.

Our elucidation so far has concentrated on the critical and reiterative features of *The Unconsoled*. At the same time, and perhaps most importantly, there is a sense in which the novel also allows Ishiguro to pursue recurrent concerns from a different direction. As the remarks below suggest, the novel allows him to experiment with a different way of writing a memoir or a life story. For the purposes of this sub-section, it is helpful to cite from a number of different sources:

It's a biography of a person, but instead of using memory and flashback, he bumps into other versions of himself – projections of how he fears he might end up.

(Jaggi 1995: 28)

This way of telling a story was something I've been wanting to do for some time ... I wanted to have someone just turn up in some landscape where he would meet people who are not literally parts of himself but are echoes of his past, harbingers of his future and projections of his fears about what he might become.

(Steinberg 1995: 105)

This character appropriates people, the people he runs into stand for various parts of his life. They exist in their own right but they are also being used to tell the narrator's story ... It's just a different way of telling someone's life and if people don't grasp it the book will seem to be directionless or disparate.

(J. Smith 1995: 17)

A character wanders into a situation where the people he meets in some way illustrate him and his relationships in the past, or in the possible future. They aren't literally him as a child or whatever, but he appropriates them. This has always appealed to me, partly because it's an exaggeration of the way people relate anyway. We use others to orchestrate the things we're talking to ourselves about.

(Walton 1995: AB4)

We can appreciate the scope of the novel's ambition in tandem with Ishiguro's attempt to fashion an alternative, non-realist way of writing 'biography'. This 'appropriat[ion]' method has according to Ishiguro a psycho-social provenance – it's an exaggeration of how we relate to each other. Furthermore, in terms of craft, the method is provocative and unusual. By peppering his novel with doppelgangers (echoes, harbingers and projections of Ryder), Ishiguro in effect obviates the need for flashbacks. A flashback detracts from the forward momentum of narrative. Its placement and arrangement is a major challenge for writers. By obviating the need for flashbacks, Ishiguro offers a radically new stylistic innovation. The past is intermeshed with the present, and this also shows the importance of memory in Ishiguro's work. Memory comes alive and is layered together with the narrative present. Conventional signposts between the two are eliminated so that we get purely imagistic transitions between them. As a result, a vertiginous quality is introduced into the narrative. Ryder can peer into a home in an estate that he visits with Boris and suddenly he will realize that he is looking at something that 'resembled exactly' the parlour of a house that he lived in long ago in Manchester (214).

This alternative method of 'doing' characterization means that plot in the novel also follows a non-realist logic. Put in a different way, it could be said that Ishiguro discovers in *The Unconsoled* a new or different emplotment technique. The novel follows the logic of dreams, as some commentators have suggested [134]. But it can also be read as a rendition of how classical music operates. In classical music, a piece develops from a motif or theme that is played. From this brief melodic or rhythmic formula – a melodic line – longer passages are developed. Passages of tonal music are basically heard as elaborations or more complicated versions of simpler passages. Plot in *The Unconsoled* appears to follow this organizational logic. The idea of a wound is elaborated in various ways in the novel and affects an entire town. Another favourite motif is the notion of inconsequence or ineffectiveness. When he tries to give a speech on Brodsky's behalf, Ryder's gown, as stated earlier, gapes open to reveal his naked body (143). Later on, when he visits a childhood friend, he is unable to intercede on her behalf. He is there in an official capacity, but when he tries to speak he loses his voice and catches sight of himself in a mirror, his face 'bright red and squashed into pig-like features' (240). At the end of the novel, Ryder doesn't get to give his concert or even to rehearse properly for it. In this way, the logic of association gains precedence over the traditional plot arc with its formulaic placement of climax, inciting incidents, and rising and falling action. Without exaggeration it should be said that all this is really quite remarkable. Ishiguro's sustained, bravura performance is arguably one of the more powerful efforts to cross-pollinate one art form with the organizational logic of another. There are depths to *The Unconsoled* that criticism has yet to uncover. Ishiguro gives us a novel that repays close attention and analysis.

FURTHER READING

Accessible readings of the novel are available in Adelman (2001), Childs (2005) and Lewis (2000). More challenging accounts include those by Reitano (2007), François (2004) and Pégon (2004). Rorty (1995) and M. Wood (1995) give useful reviews of the novel.

When We Were Orphans

When We Were Orphans is an intriguing hodgepodge of a novel that shows Ishiguro pushing the envelop in terms of craft and thematic focus. Like *The Unconsoled*, it is one of the more ambitious works of recent times. It explores and articulates what transcultural or transnational fellow feeling might entail. This gives it a utopian dimension and makes it a provocative commentary on our times. Stylewise, Ishiguro pulls back from the out-and-out fabulist construction of *The Unconsoled* but doesn't return to the broadly psychological realist framework that characterizes his first three novels. The result is a combination of the solipsistic and the real that can be considered a fresh phase in Ishiguro's development as a writer. The key features of the novel are: its rewriting of Dickens, its troping of Great Power collaboration, its use of the childhood topos [90] and the twist that it gives to the detective narrative form; its publishing history is also interesting and will be elaborated together with these features after a fairly lengthy synopsis of the novel.

On first encounter, *When We Were Orphans* gives the impression of being a conventional detective thriller. Christopher Banks is a celebrated detective much in demand for his expertise as well as in London high society. He solves a number of cases that have the police shaking their heads. References are made to the 'Mannering case', 'the Roger Parker murder', 'the Studley Grange business' and 'the mystery of Charles Emery's death' (19, 30–1, 36). Ahead of Banks, however, lies his biggest challenge, namely the mystery surrounding his parents' disappearance in old Shanghai when he was around ten. Banks's father, an opium trader, and his mother – ironically an anti-opium campaigner – had disappeared within the space of a few weeks from their palatial home in the city's International Settlement. Their apparent kidnapping and murder destroyed what was in many respects a halcyon childhood for Banks, much of it spent devising ornate games with his friend and neighbour, a Japanese boy named Akira. After his parents disappear, Banks is sent 'home' to an England he has never seen, to his aunt in Shropshire (28). He goes to boarding school and attends university. The early chapters of the novel describe him setting up practice in London, meeting old school friends, and quickly achieving professional success. A tentative liaison is formed with a woman named Sarah Hemmings, an orphan like himself. However, some strange, elemental force seems to be directing him to return to Shanghai. On a case out in Somerset, a police inspector suggests that Banks should go there to do his duty, thus continuing a pattern in *The Unconsoled* where veritable strangers voice at times the secret preoccupations of protagonists. After attending a lecture on whether 'Nazism pose[s] a threat to Christianity', a cleric waylays Banks and suggests that he can help avert some civilizational 'crisis' whose 'real heart' lies not in Europe but in Shanghai (136–7). Banks himself appears to see his early career as a preparation for him to pick up the trail of his parents' disappearance. So in 1937 he sets off for the city. In the interim Sarah has married a diplomat and fetches up there as well. Banks's decision to go to Shanghai appears to be connected with a desire to see her again.

From here the novel takes an unusual turn. What was merely off-kilter up to this point becomes increasingly surrealistic and implausible as the novel begins to violate the realist protocols it has so far appeared to endorse. By now the Sino-Japanese war has reached Shanghai and the city is in chaos. However, the well-heeled denizens of the International Settlement seem oddly unconcerned. They hold a party in the penthouse ballroom of a hotel overlooking an area being shelled by the Japanese. The party features showgirls and a jazz orchestra. As he watches this, Banks is repulsed by the indifference of the party-goers, by their 'pathetic conspiracy of denial' and their refusal to acknowledge 'culpability' and 'responsibility' for the 'maelstrom threatening to suck in the whole of the civilised world' (162). He meets a city official who asks him how he wants to conduct a 'welcoming ceremony' for his parents after they're found (158). He visits his old house in the settlement, now converted into a Chinese home, and finds himself 'oddly comfort[ed]' by the smell of 'incense mingled with that of excrement' in the air (185). He talks to the owner, a Mr Lin, who says that it is 'quite natural' that Banks wishes to 'restore' the house to 'just the way it was' when he was a boy (193). He also tracks a mysterious informant named 'Yellow Snake' (157).

Eventually Banks undertakes an extended trek through the slum warrens of the old city where he gets caught up in the confused fighting between the Chinese communists, Chiang Kai-Shek's army and the invading Japanese. With the fighting echoing around him, he wanders in and out of ruins and through zones controlled by different forces. He finds Akira, now a soldier in the Japanese army, injured and alone, and saves him from a mob.

Against all rational precepts, he believes that his parents are still held captive in an abandoned house in the warren. Together with Akira he finds the house and enters it, but the place is empty save for a young girl whose family lies dead around her, killed by the shell fire. She asks them to save her injured dog and when he hears this Banks breaks down sobbing. It appears that in order to cope with traumatic loss he had built up the childhood games devised with Akira into a kind of alternative, palliative universe. At last he is made to confront what appears to have been a decades-long denial of loss. He acknowledges as much when he says that childhood is 'hardly a foreign land to me. In many ways, it's where I've continued to live all my life. It's only now I've started to make my journey from it' (277). In this way, Ishiguro pursues his favourite topic – self-deception and the attainment of insight. Rather than the political bad faith and emotional sterility arraigned in *The Remains of the Day* [44–55], however, he deploys a recognition plot in *When We Were Orphans* to explore what might be called a 'mummification' of childhood. This term was used by the psychiatrist John Bowlby to describe individuals who respond to bereavement by, for instance, refusing to allow the deceased's room to be redecorated or changed in any way (Bowlby 1991: 150–1). Banks appears to have mummified his childhood in just such a fashion.

In a penultimate chapter equivalent to the disclosure scene of a detective novel, Banks finally meets Yellow Snake, the man he has been stalking. As expected, he turns out to be 'Uncle Philip', a former friend of the family. From Philip he learns that his father had not been kidnapped, that he didn't convert to the anti-opium cause and pay the price of betrayal. Instead he had run away with his mistress. Two years after his supposed disappearance he had contracted typhoid fever in Malaya and died. His mother kept those details from him in order to spare him hurt. More shockingly, Banks learns that during her anti-opium campaign his mother had crossed a Chinese warlord named Wang Ku, who then kidnapped her with the help of Philip. Philip did this because she spurned his advances. Banks learns as well that his mother submitted to humiliation, concubinage and 'compliance' as part of a 'financial arrangement' reached with Wang Ku (292). All along Banks believed that the money which paid for his education and leg up in life came from his aunt. Finally he learns the identity of his 'real benefactor' from Philip, who tells him that: 'Your schooling. Your place in London society. The fact that you made of yourself what you have. You owe it to Wang Ku. Or rather, to your mother's sacrifice' (293).

The final chapter acts as a coda and is set in Hong Kong in the 1950s. The narrative suggests that Banks experiences a breakdown of sorts after his discovery about his parents. He is nursed back to health by Jennifer, an orphan he has adopted. We learn that Banks's mother somehow survived turmoil and revolution and was shipped to Hong Kong when China closed its doors. Banks goes to Hong Kong and meets up with her at Rosedale

Manor, a hilltop sanatorium. However, she has lost her wits and seems to be trapped in a mental fog. She fails to recognize him. It is only when he cites his childhood nickname, Puffin, that he manages to provoke a response from her. He asks her whether she can forgive Puffin and she replies: 'Whatever for? ... That boy. They say he's doing well. But you can never be sure with that one. Oh, he's such a worry to me. You've no idea' (305). Banks decides to leave his mother in Hong Kong rather than to bring her back because she has 'lived all her life in the East' and seems contented there (306). He settles for the consolatory thought, as he tells Jennifer, that his mother 'never ceased to love [him], not through any of it' (305). At one point during his sojourn in Shanghai, Banks makes plans to elope with Sarah, whose diplomat husband ill-treats her. However, nothing comes of it. Sarah in her subsequent letters suggests that she has found happiness with someone else, although Banks doesn't appear to appreciate or to countenance that possibility. On the last page of the novel, he says, referring to Sarah and himself, that they were fated to

> face the world as orphans, chasing through long years the shadows of vanished parents. There is nothing for it but to try and see through our missions to the end, as best we can, for until we do so, we will be permitted no calm.
>
> (313)

The fact that *When We Were Orphans* is a rewriting of Dickens's *Great Expectations* (1861) [118] is easy to miss in a quick perusal of the novel. Nevertheless, it is signposted in Banks's encounter with a Japanese colonel during his trek through the slum warrens, who tells him that he is 'especially fond of your Dickens' (276). The clincher is the revelation in the closure that the source of Banks's wealth is the warlord Wang Ku and not his aunt, as he had all along believed. In this way, *When We Were Orphans* mirrors *Great Expectations* whose hero, Pip, is rocked by the discovery that the person responsible for his ascension to gentility is not the elderly gentlewoman, Miss Havisham, but the ex-convict, Magwitch. Philip asks Banks to consider what 'made possible' his 'comfortable life in England' (294), and thus the reader is encouraged to pursue a question that Dickens had also raised.

Ishiguro, it might be said, extends Dickens to fit a contemporary globalizing world environment. Dickens indicts Victorian class society when he reveals that Pip's vaunted 'expectations' are underpinned by tainted colonial spoils, by a less than genteel logic where transportation (of offenders overseas) and the debtors' prison await large numbers of the struggling masses. Ishiguro similarly presents for consideration a slice of the economic logic connecting different parts of the world. He figures the relationship between the global South and the North, suggesting that the lopsided dimensions of that relationship need to be addressed.

This account is supported by the effort that the novel takes to set up an expropriation motif and to link it decades later to the climax when Banks enters the abandoned house in the Shanghai slum warren. The theft occurs one day while Banks and Akira are playing in Akira's house. In their overwrought childish imagination, they believe that Akira's Chinese manservant, Ling Tien, is not who he seems to be. He is actually a fearsome warlock who concocts spells and mutilates human beings. They believe that a bottle of medicine in his room is actually a magic potion and decide to steal it. However, they are afraid to enter Ling Tien's room and need to stoke up their courage by linking their arms together. Staging the scene this way means that it acquires larger symbolic or figurative overtones. Earlier on we are told that Akira likes to boast about Japanese economic and military achievements. He likes to proclaim that it has become a 'great, great country just like England'. On these occasions Akira would 'try to start arguments about who cried the easiest, the Japanese or the English'. When Banks stood up for the latter, Akira would insist that they 'put things to the test' by putting him in one of his 'dreadful arm-locks'; and he wouldn't stop until Banks 'capitulated or gave in to tears' (78). These contest-of-strength games appear to trope Great Power rivalry operating in the international arena. They figure the geopolitical jostling for power and influence in the period leading up to the Second World War. But this means that the reverse also holds true, meaning that when the two boys 'linked arms' to steal a bottle from Ling Tien's room, Great Power collaboration is underscored. In his recall of the episode, Banks states that he and Akira might have run away from fear but for Akira saying at the crucial moment: 'Come on, old chap! We go together!' (95). It was such Great Power collaboration that led to the partitioning of China into various European and Japanese spheres of interests in a development known as the 'scramble for concessions'. The historical precedent for this event was the late nineteenth-century 'scramble for Africa' when the continent was partitioned between various European powers. The expatriate enclave that Banks and Akira stay in − the International Settlement − stems from that process of imperial encroachment.

It is interesting as such that Banks's search for his parents is figured as a bid to return the bottle. The important point here is that the boys become contrite shortly after stealing it. Despite their fear of Ling Tien's sorcery, they resolve to 'join arms again' to return it. In Banks's retrospect, tinged with the pathos of subsequent events, they had believed that 'nothing bad' would happen to them if they did it 'together like that' (100). However, they never get a chance to return the bottle because on the day that they are supposed to do so, Banks's father disappears (102–3). As the language of his subsequent recollection suggests − '[t]hat was when Akira and I committed our little theft − an impulsive act whose wider repercussions, in our excitement, we failed entirely to anticipate' (93) − Banks associates the loss of his parents with this failure to return the bottle. The incident is framed as a childhood fantasy involving warlocks and sorcery but has a deeper psychological resonance. At the climax when he finds the abandoned house, Banks tellingly alludes to the manner in which he and Akira stole the bottle. Before entering the house, Banks tells Akira that he wants them to 'do it together, arm in arm. Just like that other time, going into Ling Tien's room' (267). As they cross the threshold Banks 'reache[s] a hand down to [his] friend' and says, 'Akira, this is it ... Let's go in now together' (269).

At the libidinal level, Banks's imaginary enactment of what they never got a chance to accomplish as children operates as a kind of symbolic restitution. The bottle has great psychological resonance for him. He believes that if he 'returns' it his parents will somehow be restored to him. The pathos elicited by this manifestly childlike view of the world is heightened for us because Banks *does* return to a kind of normalcy after he enters the house. After he symbolically returns the bottle, he is able finally to confront his losses. He has a breakdown, just like Pip in *Great Expectations*, but later recovers from it. At long last he can move beyond his 'mummification' of childhood.

In figurative terms, the return of the bottle can be read as the conceptual equivalent of a move beyond current exploitative and expropriative conditions. The associative logic of the novel pulls together the rewriting of Dickens signalling the transfer of wealth, the childhood prank-theft and desire for symbolic restitution, and links it with Banks's recovery and attainment of self-knowledge. In so doing, Ishiguro provides a cosmopolitan or transnational vector to British cultural identity by following a logic *already* embedded in Dickens's novel. He tracks these links by framing his concerns under the heading 'connectedness' (WWO 6) [139], which means that he also takes a big risk because one easy response would be to say that he is naïve or jejune. Right from the beginning of *When We Were Orphans*, nevertheless, this word is offered as the organizing rubric of the book. Banks as a child used to badger 'mercilessly' a schoolmate named Osbourne about the meaning of the phrase 'well connected'. Banks presumably does this because, as an orphan, he is naturally curious about social networks, and because in Osbourne's words, he's a bit of 'an odd bird' (5). When they meet up in the narrative present, Osbourne invites Banks to a ball organized by his uncle for a tycoon friend, the one where Banks meets Sarah for the first time. Osbourne hopes to show him what well-connected *really* means, what one of the guests later describes as a chance to get 'a leg up in life' (15). For Osbourne, it is an unremarkable matter. It involves the usual class privileges and the benefits of the old boy network. However, the novel uses this oddly jejune question – what is connectedness? – to offer an alternative social network, to prefigure its ending and to challenge the idea that our sympathies and sense of fellow feeling must be tied to fixed geographical boundaries [102]. It calls on us to imagine in a different way our customary attachments and affiliations.

Banks's return to Shanghai is, for instance, prompted by the previously mentioned encounter with the police inspector in Somerset, who tells him that he needs to go back there to fight the *real* source of crime. Banks has been called in to investigate an incident. He calls it 'one of the most dispiriting crimes' that he has ever encountered, although its nature is kept helpfully vague in order to encourage a figurative reading (134). In an example of the novel's use of a melodramatic yet beguiling register, the inspector says that this crime has also '[t]ruly sickened' him (134). He compares it to a great 'serpent' or hydra, a 'beast with many heads'; each time a head is lobbed off another three grow 'in its place' (135). Hence it was better that Banks address the problem at source. He himself will do his best to fight it in England. Rather than waste time 'wrestling with its many heads', however, Banks should go after 'the heart of the serpent' and 'slay the thing once and for all' (136).

This connectedness concept is repeated in the serpent–hydra imagery because the associated term – chasing the dragon – is a Chinese trope for opium consumption. What Banks unveils when he chases after the heart of the serpent is literally 'the Great Opium Dragon of China' (60), namely the transfer of funds from Wang Ku to Banks. The novel asks us to consider the economic logic connecting different parts of the world. But perhaps most strikingly it says that Banks and Akira are outsiders in their respective cultures and nationalities. In another instance of the novel's deployment of an idealistic, child's-eye view on the world, Akira believes that his parents do not get along because he is 'not enough Japanese' (73, *sic*). He influences Banks, who before long also starts to think that the relationship problems between *his* parents stem from him 'not behaving sufficiently like an Englishman' (73). Akira when he goes home to Japan for a visit is bullied in school for having picked up foreign ways. When Banks brings up this issue with Philip, the latter's comments are illuminating and indicate the thematic affinity of the novel. The setting of the novel, the International Settlement in Shanghai, contributes to this motif. Philip asks Banks whether he thinks he really ought to be more English and Banks replies, 'I can't tell really, sir' (76). Philip's response is arguably the key passage of the novel:

> No, I suppose you can't. Well, it's true, out here, you're growing up with a lot of different sorts around you. Chinese, French, Germans, Americans, what have you. It'd be no wonder if you grew up a bit of a mongrel ... You know what I think, Puffin? I think it would be no bad thing if boys like you *all* grew up with a bit of everything. We might all treat each other a good deal better then. Be less of these wars for one thing.
>
> (*WWO* 76, emphasis original)

Responding to Philip's words of encouragement, Banks points to the window blinds in his office and says confusingly that 'if the twine broke.

Everything might scatter' (76). He again shows the influence of Akira and a boy's view of the world, for Akira had told him earlier when they were discussing their parents' troubles something that a Japanese monk had told him and which explain their exaggerated sense of responsibility for the tribulations at home, namely that:

> We children ... were like the twine that kept the slats [of a window blind] held together. A Japanese monk had once told him this. We often failed to realise it, but it was we children who bound not only a family, but the whole world together. If we did not do our part, the slats would fall and scatter over the floor.
>
> (WWO 73)

In response to Banks's non sequitur about blinds and twine, Philip qualifies his earlier stance. He tells Banks that:

> You might be right. I suppose it's something we can't easily get away from. People need to feel they belong. To a nation, to a race. Otherwise, who knows what might happen? This civilisation of ours, perhaps it'll just collapse. And everything scatter, as you put it.
>
> (WWO 76–7)

Banks and Philip are talking at cross-purposes here, and this might be the sense in which Ishiguro registers his understanding of the scale of the task set by the novel. Nevertheless, in this intermeshing of British and Japanese cultural elements, *When We Were Orphans* puts across some large cross-cultural themes and issues.

Through these variations on the theme of connectedness – serpentine imagery, climactic allusion to Dickens, twine imagery, the 'International Settlement' as a proto-utopian space [89] – Ishiguro suggests a different way of understanding terms such as 'allegiance', 'ethics' and 'action'. Philip's remarks about Banks being a bit of a mongrel echo Akira's counsel about the responsibility of children because they both contain the idea that childhood is different from the status quo. The cliché that children don't harbour the prejudices shared by adults is relevant here, as shown by the friendship between Banks and Akira. In framing Akira's counsel as something that stems from a Japanese monk, Ishiguro arguably gives equal weight to both sides of his bicultural heritage [9, 19]. He takes pains to suggest that both East and West possess cultural resources that can help address current ethico-political challenges, many of which require multi-national cooperation and collaboration.

As Ishiguro explains in an interview, the meaning of 'orphans' in the title of the novel is tied to the issue of radical change. He wants to explore how much remains of our childhood after we leave it behind. For the purposes

of this sub-section, a lengthy citation is helpful because it gives cogency to
the ideas presented earlier:

> What I was interested in exploring here was the journey that we
> all must have made out of a protective childhood bubble where we
> didn't know about the harsher world ... Christopher Banks, the
> main character, lives in this relatively sheltered cocoon or child-
> hood, and he has a child's view of the world ... Suddenly, he is
> plunged into the big world. It's that question: when we go out into
> the harsher world do we perhaps carry with us some sense of
> nostalgia, some sense of memory of that time when we believed
> the world to be a nicer place? Perhaps we were misled by adults;
> perhaps quite rightly, we were sheltered from these things.
>   When we go out into the larger world to find that there are
> nasty things, difficult things. Sometimes perhaps, we still carry
> some memory of that more innocent view that we had as a child,
> and we have an urge to reshape the world, heal the world, to make
> it the way we once thought it was as children.
>   So, this latest book is very much about someone who loses that
> childhood garden of paradise very suddenly ... [H]is big aim in life
> is to fix that thing that went wrong then, so that he can pick up
> where he left off.
>   When I say 'orphan', it's in that very broader sense of having
> left the protective world of childhood that I am referring to.
>
> (Wong 2001: 319–20)

Ishiguro elaborates in another interview that he means by nostalgia something different from its typically negative portrayal as something that 'skirts
around the darker side of Empire', something that highlights its 'glories and
comforts' without taking into account its 'true costs'. Instead, he means it as
'a positive thing in that it's a kind of emotional equivalent to idealism'
(Shaffer 2001: 7). At one point after they enter the Shanghai slum warren,
Akira says that: 'When we nostalgic, we remember. A world better than this
world we discover when we grow. We remember and wish good world come
back again' (*WWO* 263, *sic*). Elsewhere as well, Ishiguro's attempt to give a
new take on nostalgia can be seen in the encounter with the Japanese
colonel – the one responsible for signposting the Dickens allusion – who,
commenting on the generally underappreciated importance of childhood,
quotes a Japanese court lady to the effect that 'our childhood becomes like a
foreign land once we have grown [up]' (277). Ishiguro overlays Japanese and
British culture here because the quote echoes the famous first line of L. P.
Hartley's novel, *The Go-Between*, 'The past is a foreign country: they do
things differently there' (Hartley 2002: 17). It is as the emotional equivalent
of idealism that such nostalgic references work to foreground the issue of

radical change. And this would also explain those moments in *When We Were Orphans* when Banks displays an oddly monumentalized desire to save the world, when he expresses a desire to fight 'encroaching wickedness' (30) and to combat 'evil of the insidious, furtive kind' (21).

For a novelist writing in an age of restricted horizons, Ishiguro appears to have given himself some outsized objectives. As Bill Martin explains, the dominant mindset of our times is cynicism [89, 98, 109] because 'people are not *citizens*, in any significant sense, but instead primarily consumers, customers, and spectators' (Martin 1998: 132, emphasis original). He calls this the common sense of contemporary society:

> [S]peak in any way about fundamental problems with existing social structures, the sort of problems that cannot be addressed with mere reforms and band-aids, and you will immediately be told that 'you can't change the world', you are 'unrealistic', 'utopian', etc.
>
> (Martin 1998: 133)

The scale of Ishiguro's ambition means that he faces the risk of being dismissed in the way spelt out by Martin. Whether or not Ishiguro succeeds in crafting a novel that achieves in artistic terms the vision that he articulates is also a moot point. In turning to the topos of childhood, however, Ishiguro is basically on the right path. He investigates an idea raised by the American critic Fredric Jameson, namely that the origin of radical or 'revolutionary' action lies in the plenitude of psychic gratification – in happiness – experienced early in life. Furthermore, it is intimately linked with memory, a key motif for Ishiguro:

> Now the origin of Utopian thinking becomes clear, for it is memory which serves as a fundamental mediator between the inside and the outside, between the psychological and the political … It is because we have known, at the beginning of life, a plenitude of psychic gratification … that memory … can fulfill its profound therapeutic, epistemological, and even political role … The primary energy of revolutionary activity derives from this memory of a prehistoric happiness which the individual can regain only through its externalization, through its reestablishment for society as a whole.
>
> (Jameson 1971: 113)

It is worth noting that Ishiguro returns to this idea in his subsequent novel, *Never Let Me Go*. This work takes up again the topos of childhood and depicts the growing-up experiences of a trio of clones with an extraordinary ability to cling on to hope despite the mandatory early death dictated by their society, since they are slated to become spare parts for 'original' humans. Their idealism comes close to the jejune or even gullible qualities displayed by Banks in *When We Were Orphans*. It provokes a feeling that something is deeply wrong with *our* world. In this respect, Ishiguro pursues from a different direction what he tries to convey through utopia-inflected metaphors such as the 'International Settlement' [99, 139] in *When We Were Orphans*. Like Banks, Jennifer and Sarah, these clones are another set of orphans looking for direction and meaning in life.

Returning to *When We Were Orphans*, there are two additional features that need to be addressed, starting with the novel's creative use of the detective narrative form [54, 117]. One of our first impressions of *When We Were Orphans* – and one that sticks with us – is that it violates genre conventions. Detective writing can be grouped into two broad categories. The first, epitomized by Arthur Conan Doyle's Sherlock Holmes, highlights the use of inductive reasoning. Wonderfully ingenious links are established between seemingly disparate items of information. The second, epitomized by Raymond Chandler's Philip Marlowe, calls for a detective who chases multiple leads and at times uses violence and intimidation to get his way. Despite the mention of some big name cases that are said to improve his reputation, however, we never get to see Banks exhibiting ratiocinative brilliance or engaging in intricate spadework. Both facets of the genre are missing in what is ostensibly a detective novel. The account given so far implicitly assumes that this twist to the detective narrative form – the way it fails to meet our expectations – helps to advance its consciousness-raising goals. Unlike conventional 'detective' works, *When We Were Orphans* refuses to restore order and sanity in its closure. This feature underscores its wider thematic concerns.

In this regard, the proposed reading follows the critic Franco Moretti, who argues that 'the dominant cultural oppositions of detective fiction are between the individual (in the guise of the criminal) and the social organism (in the guise of the detective)'. Moretti contends that detective fiction 'exists expressly to dispel the doubt that guilt might be impersonal, and therefore collective and social' (Moretti 1988: 134–5). It helps to reinforce status quo conservatism by imposing on individuals a set of mental or ideological blinkers. Responsibility, exculpation, redemption, forgiveness and hope cannot be posed as public interest issues because detective fiction redirects our attention somewhere else. Through its experiments with form, however, *When We Were Orphans* challenges these perhaps deeply held assumptions and premises. It questions the cynicism referenced by Martin above. It is necessary to add, however, that the literary sociology [117] of detective fiction can be understood differently, meaning that different interpretations are possible. An alternative to Moretti's stance is the idea that artistic experimentation is important in its own right, and Ishiguro's book certainly fulfils this condition. On this account, *When We Were Orphans* solicits our attention because it helps to extend the boundaries of the novel.

Finally, the controversy over Ishiguro's use of a company name should also be recounted. When the novel first appeared the name of the firm that employs Banks's father was given as 'Butterfield and Swire'. This title is actually the name of the former Shanghai subsidiary of the London-based trading group, John Swire and Co., which took umbrage at the suggestion that it had participated in the opium trade. It took legal action against Ishiguro and his publisher, Faber and Faber, but eventually an 'amicable settlement' was reached between the parties concerned and the matter was dropped. The settlement carried the stipulation that future editions of *When We Were Orphans* would drop the name 'Butterfield and Swire' and use an entirely made-up one: 'Morganbrook and Byatt' (Milmo 2000). Aside from the mistake made with the Swire group, another extant company is cited in the first and subsequent editions of the novel as a participant in the trade, but that detail has not been contested. The critic Roland Barthes has suggested that the Western cultural imaginary indelibly associates Chineseness or 'Sininess' with opium consumption (Barthes 1973: 84). If so, *When We Were Orphans* gives a context to that association. The account given here suggests that this act of historical retrieval is part of a larger and more ambitious undertaking.

FURTHER READING

Trocki (1999) gives a penetrating account of the opium trade in Asia. Veyret (2005), Vinet (2005) and Zinck (2005) explore how memory operates in the novel. Bickers (1999) and F. Wood (1998) provide illuminating insights into the experiences of the British expatriate community in China. Thompson (1993) explores the development of the crime fiction genre and explains how it links up with the growth and expansion of Empire.

Never Let Me Go

Never Let Me Go won the runner-up spot in the 2005 Booker Prize awards and has a number of striking and thought-provoking attributes. It is a science fiction or dystopian novel which departs strikingly from its ostensible forebears. It has strong existential motifs that bring to a head the previous treatment of this issue in Ishiguro's work. It has, less obviously, a strong ecological dimension and mounts among other things a trenchant critique of modern conspicuous consumption and the throwaway culture that it inculcates [100]. In an age of lowered political horizons, it also provides a space to ponder and imagine the radical transformation of society. Before moving on to these features it is helpful to consider for a moment the parallels between the novel and a Hollywood movie, *The Island*, which appeared in the year in which it was published. Making this comparison allows us to appreciate the nature of the stylistic innovations introduced by Ishiguro, and also the way he uses them to highlight certain key thematic concerns.

Directed by Michael Bay, *The Island* relates the story of a couple who go on the run after they discover that they are actually clones bred in a facility secluded from the world. This scenario occurs in the near future when wealthy individuals can pay to be cloned so that they can harvest their body parts in the event of disease or accident. After escaping to the real world and finding out the truth about their origins, however, one of the clones manages to kill his 'original'. Together with his partner, whose 'original' has been mangled in an accident, he fights and eludes his pursuers. Despite the hi-tech arsenal deployed against them, they manage to come out on top; eventually they escape to safety in South America.

Like *The Island*, it could be said, *Never Let Me Go* appears well poised to milk for dramatic effect a similar moment of recognition or *anagnorisis* where its protagonists find out that they are actually clones. The novel tells the story of a trio of clones – Kathy, Ruth and Tommy – who are brought up in a facility called Hailsham. They are bred to furnish humans with body parts. Like the movie, the book exploits a topical story-idea. It explores a hotly contested and controversial issue, namely the ethical implications of the ongoing advances in biomedicine and genetic technology. In a typical Ishiguro contrarian move, however, the novel fails to meet the conventions of the incipient sub-genre. The previous sub-sections have discussed the 'twist' that Ishiguro gives to exotic fiction [34, 116], to the country house novel [7, 54, 117, 126], to the high-modernist European novel [56] and to detective fiction [77]. Instead of following the paths sets by established genres, he likes to alter their configuration to suit his own narrative purposes. With *Never Let Me Go*, as stated above, we might expect a showdown scene where the clones discover their true identity. However, Ishiguro refuses to meet such expectations. The shock of recognition that one is a copy or simulacra does not occur. Kathy, Ruth and Tommy do not go on the run, although Kathy and Tommy do try to ask for a 'deferral' (140). Long before the halfway point of the novel, the contours of their world have already emerged both directly and in the interstices of Kathy's first-person narration; and the most shocking thing about it is that the protagonists accept so matter of factly the horrific fate ordained for them. They know that they are 'copied at some point from a normal person' (127). They know that they are there to act as 'donors'; they understand what the euphemism means (3). After graduating from Hailsham, which operates as a kind of boarding school, they go to another facility called 'the Cottages' where they are expected to live independently (109). The sojourn at the cottages lasts about two years, and some time after that they expect to be notified about their first donation. The number isn't stated explicitly but it appears that they will make around four donations each to a variety of recipients. Some will die after three or even two donations from complications arising on the operating table. After undergoing their full slate of donations, they die, or rather they will 'complete' (255).

Another astonishing feature of this world is that some of the clones are chosen for special training as 'carers'. These are taken out of the roster of operations and are tasked to provide palliative care for fellow clones, to nurse them through the trauma that ensues after each donation so that they can shorten their 'recovery times' and be prepared to undertake another donation (3). Kathy is a carer who is coming to the end of her tenure. The novel opens with her introducing herself; and her words are remarkable because they exemplify how it consistently tones down, dampens or makes banal its potentially lurid material:

> My name is Kathy H. I'm thirty-one years old, and I've been a carer now for over eleven years ... Now I know my being a carer so long isn't necessarily because they think I'm fantastic ... There are some really good carers who've been told to stop after just two or three years ... But then I do know for a fact they've been pleased with my work, and by and large, I have too.
>
> (NLMG 3)

One of the most intriguing features of *Never Let Me Go* is that this composed placid tone hardly ever varies. Kathy never gets overwrought or distraught. The clones never complain in a direct way about their plight. At the end of the novel after narrating Ruth's and Tommy's completion as well as what passes for a plot – the failed efforts of herself and Tommy to get a deferral – Kathy indulges in a little escape from routine. However, this purported moment of immoderation shows through its diffident character the limited range and closed horizons of the clones. As a carer, Kathy gets to live in a flat in town, to own a car and to drive to various facilities around the country where her charges are housed. One day about two weeks after she hears that Tommy has completed, she drives miles out of her scheduled route to a secluded spot in Norfolk, a place that has a special meaning for them. Here, in the novel's final paragraph, she allows herself a little 'fantasy', a little dream that she might get to see Tommy again. She alights at a deserted spot where she can see 'acres of ploughed earth' stretching before her. The only things 'breaking the wind for miles' are a fence and a cluster of trees. Caught on the barbed wire of the fence are all kinds of 'rubbish' akin to the debris that we might find on a seashore. '[T]orn plastic sheeting and bits of old carrier bags' are also caught on the limbs of the trees (263). As she takes in this 'strange rubbish', Kathy ends her narrative in the following manner:

> I was thinking about the rubbish ... [and I imagined that] if I waited long enough, a tiny figure would appear on the horizon ...

and gradually get larger until I'd see it was Tommy, and he'd wave, maybe even call. The fantasy never got beyond that ... and though the tears rolled down my face, I wasn't sobbing or out of control. I just waited a bit, then turned back to the car, to drive off to wherever it was I was supposed to be.

(*NLMG* 263)

This consistently battened-down tone is key to the powerful emotional impact of *Never Let Me Go*. The novel does raise existential questions, as in *The Island*, but not so much from the discovery that one's assumption of uniqueness and individuality is vitiated by the fact of being a copy. Instead it raises them by, as it were, the obverse, by the fact that even the most rambunctious among the clones accept so placidly the fate arranged for them by society. This fatalism captures our attention and stokes our curiosity: the fact that they never question their allotted purpose in life and at the most only ask for a deferral. The clones unsettle and disconcert us because they lack volition and agency and because they completely accept the social order they find themselves in. In some ways perhaps they remind us of ourselves, of the pressures that modern society puts on us.

Because there is no questioning of social arrangements and no possibility of the clones having a separate agency or alternative fate, there is no need to separate them from the 'outside' world. In *The Island*, an elaborate charade is concocted to keep the clones in the dark about their fates. The film's title refers to a holiday destination that is the ostensible winning prize in a lottery in which all the clones participate. The lottery is rigged and winning is presented as a kind of escape to a tropical paradise in order to disguise the fact that the supposed winners are being carted off for harvesting. But with *Never Let Me Go* there is no need for such subterfuge. As they grow up at Hailsham, they are supervised by teachers who are called 'guardians' (5). They take classes in a variety of subjects including geography, from which it appears they become habituated to their dreadful fate. At the cottages they live entirely without supervision. There doesn't appear to be any censorship about their societal function. While living in the cottages they decide one day to go into town. They mingle with the denizens without eliciting surprise or hostility. They go into high street shops to buy things and interact with the proprietors. They look exactly like the 'normal person[s]' from whom they are copied (127). They are even prepared to persist with the artifice encouraged by the guardians, namely that they are students and that they should so describe themselves if questioned by the town dwellers.

The clones have, it would appear, a large amount of negative freedom, which can be defined as the lack of coercive force that might prevent them from doing what they want. Once they leave Hailsham, they are relatively free from interference, whether by other people or by some constituted authority. The chains that hold them in place are primarily ideological or mental. The novel doesn't say what might happen if one of them does decide to go on the run, and this becomes one of those questions that dogs us powerfully as we read. But the point is that this scenario would never occur to any of them. Even the wishes that they express while in town observing its denizens are workaday and pedestrian. Ruth says that her 'dream future' is to work in an 'open-plan' office (131). Some of the others say they wish they could work as a postman or on a farm. Or else they dream about becoming 'drivers of one sort or other' (130). The innocuous nature of these declarations increases sympathy for the clones. We feel for their truncated lives, for the spectacle of the young dying before their time. But they also encourage through understatement our own self-scrutiny, our own assessment whether in our dreams and plans we are pursuing what really matters or what is important.

In his introduction to a collection of early short stories, the American writer Thomas Pynchon observed that '[w]hen we speak of "seriousness" in fiction ultimately we are talking about an attitude toward death – how characters may act in its presence, for example, or how they handle it when it isn't so immediate' (Pynchon 2000: 5) [138]. In this regard, it might be said, *Never Let Me Go* captures our attention because it places the fact of mortality squarely in our faces. It breaks down our myriad ways of denying, repressing or ignoring this eventuality. The inexorable, unalterable fate which awaits the clones as well as their lack of volition and agency works powerfully to foreground this issue. In the terms suggested by the philosopher Heidegger, it stresses that death is '*that possibility which is one's ownmost, which is non-relational, and which is not to be outstripped*' (Heidegger 1962: 294, emphasis original). The cumulative impact of such an arrangement is that the novel raises in a powerful way a number of pressing existential and normative issues. It conveys in its cognitive and formal design what another philosopher calls the '[t]error before the abyss of the self' (Adorno 2000: 65).

It is worth considering for a moment how *Never Let Me Go* achieves such an impact. One of the reasons it is able to do so is because it immerses us in the commonplace. The opening chapters exemplify this feature of the novel. They are dotted with descriptions of the physical environs around Hailsham. Kathy reminisces about what was, paradoxically, a halcyon childhood. She talks about growing up in Hailsham, about school routine, about how and when she first met Tommy and Ruth, and about how Tommy has a temper and is sometimes bullied. We learn that the students have 'some form of medical almost every week' (12) and that the school puts great emphasis on arts and crafts. Kathy describes the 'Exchanges' held by the students so that they can sell their artwork and poetry to one another. She contrasts these with the 'Sales', where mass-produced items from outside Hailsham can be purchased, but which are often 'a big disappointment' despite the 'excitement' they generate (38). She talks about the privileges they enjoy when they move from junior to senior year, of how they get to sleep six to a dorm instead of fifteen, and of how they get to hold the 'most intimate conversations' as they lie in their beds at night (14).

For what is ostensibly science fiction or speculative fiction, what strikes us is the sheer workaday or quotidian nature of the events portrayed in the book, with Ishiguro courting triteness in order to make this point. If it is the case that science fiction has a built-in penchant for escapism, *Never Let Me Go* counteracts this tendency through immersion in the commonplace. By the overturning of genre expectations, we are forced back to reading it as a story about present times, about *our* era. Kathy's narrative is prefaced by a laconic phrase telling us that it is set in 'England, late 1990s'. Obviously the book doesn't portray an extant society where cloning has achieved widespread currency. In this way, it rejects the convention that 'science fiction' must strive to portray a near future or imaginary future society. *Never Let Me Go* gets to balance intriguingly between what is real and what is imaginary. And this also means that it is easier for Ishiguro to achieve his stated goal of getting readers to 'take off' into the realm of metaphor. The book invites us to question contemporary society by relocating it to the present but non-place of science fiction. Such a setting allows it to acquire wider, allegorical dimensions, to avoid the literalist interpretations that have shadowed Ishiguro's fiction. The novel becomes a story about us, about what we wish or need to do before we die.

A comparison with Aldous Huxley's classic science fiction novel, *Brave New World*, is also instructive. The opening pages of Huxley's book describe the use of embryo stores, conveyor belts, incubators and fertilizing rooms. It gives us enough evocative details so that a facility called the 'Central London Hatchery and Conditioning Centre' can be an everyday item of furniture (Huxley 1977: 1). In contrast, however, cloning technology is kept off-stage in Ishiguro's novel. Apart from the euphemisms mentioned earlier, the novel does attempt for plausibility's sake to elaborate some features of a world where the harvesting of body parts is a regular occurrence. At one point, one of the older students at Hailsham teases Tommy about a section on their elbows where the skin can be 'unzip[ped] like a bag opening up'. Tommy has just received an injury on his elbow and is worried about becoming 'skeletally exposed' (77–8). He becomes the butt of students' jokes over the next few days. At another point one of the teachers makes oblique remarks about the 'terrible accidents' that occur on the operating table during donations; she suggests that students should be informed about these eventualities sooner rather than later (71). Nevertheless, moments such as these are rare. In the course of the novel even oblique remarks like this are conspicuous by their absence. Science is arguably pushed to the background in this novel [118] so that it can explore what human-ness means [156].

Apart from failing to meet genre expectations, the novel also supports its themes by handling time and plot in a special way. The most interventionist act in the novel occurs when Kathy and Tommy decide to go and ask for a deferral for Tommy. As mentioned earlier, this quest is the closest equivalent in the novel to a plot. However, their actions are conspicuously ineffectual. Plot in some respects becomes anti-plot. There is effectively no forward narrative movement because we sense that failure will be the only outcome. As a result, the novel hinders and obstructs any sublimation or refocusing of psychic energy towards the future and away from its thematic concerns, from the question of one's life purpose. There is no future, no possibility of things getting better. There is only an ever-present, radically truncated now that encourages tough-minded soul-searching and values clarification.

According to a lore that had developed among the clones, couples who are 'really, properly in love' and who can 'show' it should be able to obtain a three- or four-year deferral from their slate of donations. This is apparently a privilege given to Hailsham clones (140). This self-styled 'rumour' has an independent life of its own and 'couples' from other establishments will appear sometimes on the doorsteps of Hailsham asking whether the privilege can be extended to them (235). Within the thematic design of the novel, Hailsham functions as a symbol of hope, of the human need for sustaining stories and dreams. Despite great effort by the guardians to stamp it out, the rumour always manages to crop up again. However, the interesting thing in *Never Let Me Go* is that hope is in some respects channelled towards the past rather than the future.

As Kathy and Tommy discuss the rumour at the cottages they convince themselves that it is true. They conclude that to get a deferment they will have to find a mysterious woman known only as Madame. This lady turns up periodically at Hailsham to examine the students' artwork, essays and poems. She selects outstanding works from a selection of the best 'four or five items from each Junior and Senior year' (30). These items go into something known as the 'Gallery', although the precise details are never made known to the students (28). Kathy and Tommy speculate that the gallery is linked to an actual deferral policy. Since there is no way to ascertain whether a couple are 'really telling the truth' about being in love, the guardians *need something to go on* when deciding whether to grant deferrals. They need to peer into the 'souls' of the clones by scrutinizing 'the art they've done over years and years'. In this way – Kathy and Tommy believe – they would be able to tell whether a particular relationship is 'a good match' or 'just a stupid crush' (161, emphasis original).

When Kathy and Tommy finally meet up with Madame or 'Marie-Claude', their hopes are predictably dashed (234). Whatever the suspension of disbelief summoned by readers, a small, insistent voice has been saying that all this deferment talk is a chimera. In the resolution of the novel,

Tommy and Kathy learn that the gallery was meant for something else. It had nothing to do with any deferral policy but it did have a humane purpose. Their former principal, Miss Emily, lives with Marie-Claude; and she tells them that their artwork, poetry and essays were put into an exhibition that toured the country. They were part of a campaign aimed at overhauling the system of upbringing for clones, to highlight the need to treat them in a tolerably benevolent manner. Hailsham apparently spearheaded a reform movement that wished to demonstrate the practical benefits of providing the clones with an education, with access to culture, with some structure to their lives, and with what was recognizably a childhood. It was miles ahead of other institutions where clones were kept in terrible conditions. Unaware of the contradictory nature of her words – since she doesn't envisage stopping the donations – Miss Emily explains that for those who doubted the need for reform, the gallery helped to 'reveal what [the clones] were like ... inside'. It helped '*prove*' that they had '*souls*' (238, emphasis original). It showed that 'if students were reared in humane, cultivated environments, it was possible for them to grow to be as sensitive and intelligent as any ordinary human being'. It allowed her to say to doubters that the children were also 'fully human' (239).

Eventually, however, their campaign failed because of two things. Experiments conducted in a 'remote part of Scotland' by a certain James Morningdale stoked eugenicist fears among the general public. By raising the prospect of designer babies with '[s]uperior intelligence [and] superior athleticism', Morningdale went 'far beyond legal boundaries' (241). He is the narrative counterpart of Mary Shelley's Frankenstein, who also arrogated the same god-like powers to himself in a laboratory located in the Orkneys, in northern Scotland. Through him, the novel registers the idea that genetic engineering might conceivably inaugurate a post-human scenario [138, 156], meaning that it also underscores its humanist concerns. At the same time, the reform movement failed because they couldn't return the genie to the bottle once they got it out. In Miss Emily's forceful words the 'overwhelming concern' of most individuals was that their loved ones did not die from terminal disease, and thus they 'did their best' not to think about the clones (240).

The social theorist Sven Lütticken has argued that there are two kinds of perspectives on the current social order: a radically democratic one and a liberal one that despite its many important insights helps to maintain the status quo, to keep things as they are. The second perspective – the dominant one – sees lines of development leading to biological and ecological disaster but cannot imagine changing substantially the economic system, the reason for that crisis. That system has become 'second nature' for us, so deeply ingrained and taken for granted that the idea of changing it causes great anxiety; paradoxically, it creates more anxiety than the idea that first nature – the living world around us – might collapse altogether. The economic system 'appears as a second nature whose collapse would be more dramatic than that of the physical environment'. This means that disaster or dystopian narratives, no matter how painstakingly detailed, capture only part of the picture. Unless we get at this mental block, we cannot address the *real* issues. The situation becomes as it were a runaway train, and, for Lütticken, most writers are 'unable to think beyond this limit' (Lütticken 2007: 117).

The innovative thing about *Never Let Me Go* might be that Ishiguro *does* try to think beyond this limit. He plays around with genre and form so that he can get at this mental block. In its final arresting image of old carrier bags and debris caught along lines of barbed wire, the novel arguably relates the fate of the clones to an entire socio-economic order and to a throwaway culture encouraged by that order. What makes this novel different from other cloning stories is that bioethics is not raised in a stand-alone manner. By telling a cloning story, it taps into our moral disquietude over prodigious advances in the biomedical sciences. Various government panels have been set up around the world to address this issue and to regulate the sector. But the point is that *Never Let Me Go* doesn't just broach the bioethics issue. Or rather, it links it to the wider social environment. It confronts the fundamental impasse described by Lütticken and tries to go beyond it.

With her term as a carer coming to an end, Kathy gets ready to face death herself by returning to Norfolk one last time to dream. Her dream is that she will see Tommy, who has recently died. She believes that Norfolk is the 'lost corner of England' (155) analogous to a lost-and-found cupboard. Tommy is merely misplaced and will eventually turn up there. This analogy stems from an in-joke among the clones, from Miss Emily who taught them geography using pictures taken from calendars [35]. Miss Emily had a large collection of these calendars but for some reason 'none of them had a single picture of Norfolk' (59). The county became in their imagination the lost corner of England and was linked, by extension, with the other banal 'lost corner' cupboard [61] they had in school (60). At one of the few points where *Never Let Me Go* talks about the 'science' behind cloning, it states that Tommy's elbow can be 'unzip[ped] *like a bag* opening up' (77, emphasis added). As expendable or disposable human beings the sympathies of the clones are extended first to themselves. But the novel also registers their affinity with other disposable things, with the assorted rubbish, carrier bags and torn plastic sheeting that turn up in the last scene of the novel like debris caught on a seashore. After losing the cassette that contains the song she loves, the one that gives the novel its name, Kathy finds it significantly in a 'second-hand' store in a 'seaside town' located in Norfolk (157, 136). In Kathy's imagination, Norfolk is a giant space where all kinds of refuse finds, so to speak, a second life. The clones and the other 'strange rubbish' (263) of this society may be considered expendable, but like things that go into a lost corner cupboard they are precious to the original owners. Norfolk was where Ishiguro learned his trade, at the University of East Anglia [6] located in its capital, Norwich. Ishiguro took a postgraduate creative writing course there in the late 1970s, so perhaps the locale has an added significance.

But the important point is that in painting a dystopian scenario to encourage reflection, Ishiguro also addresses how modern society *causes* this problem. He relates the commodification of human beings to a culture where the demands of corporate profit-making penetrate all aspects of social life and trump all considerations. He links the novel's bioethical concerns to, less obviously, an ecological theme. Human beings are part of nature, after all, and are only threatened when the latter becomes entrenched in its cultural insignificance, when it is merely a 'resource' used with no thought to whether the earth can sustain such a rate of use. Only in such a society can a vast network of causes and forces culminate in human organs being put on a shelf like canned goods in a store. Pharmaceutical companies nowadays offshore clinical trials for drugs to the Third World [102], and the serious point that Ishiguro is making is that humanity is *already* segregated into a two-tier system. Great damage is already being done in *our* name. For *Never Let Me Go*, it might be said, the end point is portrayed in order to draw attention to the interim damage.

To understand why this might be a preferred reading, we need some knowledge about previous works written by Ishiguro. And the ones pertinent to *Never Let Me Go* are: *When We Were Orphans* [67], its immediate precursor; *The Gourmet* [99], a television play that Ishiguro wrote in the 1980s; and *The Saddest Music in the World* [101], a screenplay that Ishiguro started also in the 1980s. Knowledge of these texts engenders an appreciation of the emphasis that Ishiguro puts on social equality in both national and international terms. *The Gourmet* in particular describes a tramp killed by an unnamed party in 1904 because it needed 'human organs' for 'research purposes' (Ishiguro 1993a: 120) [101], so there is conceptually a straight line leading from it to *Never Let Me Go*.

If we return to *Never Let Me Go* and join the dots ourselves, the urgency of its critique of consumerism and throwaway society becomes clear. The mindset described by Lütticken may be so ingrained in us that changing 'our' economic system is mentally out of bounds. Thinking about it creates great anxiety for us. But Kathy, we may recall, explicitly contrasts the Hailsham art-exchange with its sales. Sales are events where they can buy mass-produced items – a jacket, say, or a watch. They are oftentimes a 'big disappointment' despite the excitement they generate (38). Speculating about the purpose of the gallery, Kathy wonders at one point, referring to Madame, if '[m]aybe she sells them. Outside, out there, they sell everything' (28). Through this contrast, we understand why Hailsham is made a symbol of hope, because it offers the dream of an alternative social logic, one where corporate profit-making doesn't trump all considerations. Every three months, a large exhibition-cum-sale of all the items made by students during that period is held at Hailsham. Students exchange paintings, drawings, pottery and sculptures that they have made themselves during these events. For each item they put into the pool, they are paid in 'Exchange Tokens', with the guardians deciding how much a particular piece merits. Then on the given day they use the tokens to buy what they like (14).

These exchanged items possess great significance for the clones. They use them to decorate the walls around their beds and to place on their desks as they move around from room to room in school (15). They have a practice of keeping them under their beds in little wooden chests tellingly engraved with their names. They take 'enormous care' over these 'collections' and agonize over whether particular items should be taken out for display. Whenever old Hailsham students gather they 'sooner or later' become 'nostalgic' about them (35). And, furthermore, these practices are an endless source of fascination for non-Hailsham students, for whom they have a near-spiritual connotation [156]. Early in her career, Kathy meets a clone who wants 'not just to hear about Hailsham, but to *remember* Hailsham, just like it had been his own childhood' (5, emphasis original).

The art-items are obviously important because they allow the clones to assert their individuality. They use them to personalize their environment, and this is also the means by which they challenge subconsciously their assigned status as expendable things. If outside Hailsham 'they sell everything', Hailsham preserves a space for something else. We use the phrase 'sentimental value' to describe things that cannot be priced. This phrase captures something of what the Hailsham exchanges mean to the clones. This important theme is raised retrospectively as Kathy mulls over the fact that, apart from artwork, they could also hand in original poems for the exchanges. In the narrative present, Kathy is intrigued that they accorded great importance to juvenilia, to 'nine-year-old stuff, funny little lines, all misspelt, in exercise books' (15). If they liked someone's poetry, they could have borrowed their books and copied the poems. Yet when an exchange came along they were as likely as not to stand there 'torn between Susie K.'s poems and those giraffes Jackie used to make' (16). With the prospect of the human body entering the circuit of exchange (what the 'sales' imply), the question of what *really* typifies humanity becomes critical. Kathy's curiosity over their willingness to grant poetry a *sui generis* status highlights the issue. They could have copied the poems but it was important to them to keep afloat the idea of uniqueness. These ideas supply the backdrop to the following remarks made by Kathy, in what are also arguably the most important lines of the novel:

> Looking back now, I can see why the Exchanges became so important to us ... I can see now, too, how the Exchanges had a

more subtle effect on us all. If you think about it, being dependent on each other to produce the stuff that might become your private treasures [i.e. 'collections'] – that's bound to do things to your relationships.

(*NLMG* 15)

In her meditation on the meaning of Hailsham, Kathy also quotes Ruth saying that the 'Exchanges' were 'all part of what made Hailsham so special … [t]he way we were encouraged to value each other's work' (15). It doesn't surprise us that Ishiguro posits the ability to create and appreciate art as the heart of what defines human-ness. What is more penetrating is that human-ness – the quality represented by the poetry and other 'stuff' that might become one's 'private treasure' – is cast as a function of a larger social arrangement that allows intimacy and closeness to develop. It requires a society calibrated on a human scale, one where economic activity caters to the demands of locality and precinct rather than to the needs of corporate gigantism. The 'subtle effects' mentioned by Kathy are a reference to the intimacy and regard that develops between the clones. Despite moments of awkwardness and difficulty, Ruth's final act in the novel is self-sacrificing. At this point in its presentation of ideas, *Never Let Me Go* is less about inexorable death than about the larger meaning of Kathy's vocation as a 'carer'. Despite the humanity denied them, it is ironically Hailsham that offers a different logic, suggesting the need for a radical overhaul of society. Only in such a society can the needs of individual development be met, the implicit contrast being our way of life, the way it fosters competition and the battle of all against all. In assigning a proto-utopian [74] weight to Hailsham, Ishiguro criticizes modern pessimism and cynicism [76, 98, 109].

The argument was made earlier that *Never Let Me Go* resists the typical forward movement of plots and that this design blocks psychic energy from being channelled to an undefined palliative 'future' where things are supposed to get better. Such a design increases our level of anxiety as we read. We keep wondering why the clones don't just run away. The reason for such a design can now be better appreciated, for this refusal of directionality is how the novel moves beyond current mental and ideological limits. Lütticken suggests that the dominant narratives in our society champion the following scenario: if ecological collapse is a 'by-product' of the 'incredible inventiveness' set free by the economic system, the economic system will also 'create the means' to fight this crisis: 'There are opportunities for growth even in the green sector' (2007: 116).

In refusing a forward-moving plot, *Never Let Me Go* in effect refuses to accept these narratives. It refuses to allow ecological and biological disaster to be reintegrated into the story of shopping and growth for growth's sake. It assigns prominence to art-exchanges where a different kind of society is envisaged. This isn't to say that barter is offered as an alternative, only that, if it exists, the solution will be something radically different from the current status quo. This is perhaps why the novel generates great existential distress in readers [118], because it refuses to accept the ideological fiction of progressivism buried deep in our collective psyche. It taps into our own conflicted understanding that something is deeply wrong (deeply inhuman) with this picture of growth that never stops, the dreams we sometimes have about turning our backs on society, joining an artisan community, making things with our hands, finding time for conversation again. And this is also another reason why Ishiguro returns to the childhood topos [67] in this novel after exploring it in *When We Were Orphans*. Having a plot that doesn't move forward says in a sense that abstract things like 'technology', 'progress' and 'modernity' will *not* provide a cure. The economic regime that caused the problem will *not* solve it. In a situation where corporate gigantism dominates, small *is* beautiful. More than the collapse of the physical environment, this refusal of progressivism is the true scandalous proposition of Ishiguro's novel. In a world where consumerism is tragically the only thing left to 'buy into', refusal to consume becomes subversive in its own right. The American critic Fredric Jameson has argued that in an age of lowered political horizons and piecemeal reformism, science fiction plays a key role in sustaining important visionary and emancipatory perspectives. It offers 'a kind of mental space in which the whole system can be imagined as radically different' (2005: 16). *Never Let Me Go* in certain respects fulfils this function.

FURTHER READING

Kass (2002) gives an important standpoint on the bioethics controversy. Squier (2004) explores tellingly the cultural impact of the medical transformation of human life.

Other creative works

One salient feature of Ishiguro criticism is the paucity of attention on his work outside the novel genre-form. In addition to the six novels discussed earlier, Ishiguro has written a number of short stories, two television plays and two movie screenplays. While the focus on the novels is understandable because of the novel's key role in contemporary intellectual and cultural life, to neglect these other works overlooks the possibility at the least that they might help improve our understanding of the longer works. They can help us achieve a nuanced understanding of Ishiguro's artistic programme, to appreciate whether the change of direction instantiated by *The Unconsoled* is as unprecedented as it is generally taken to be, for instance, or give us pointers about general philosophical and aesthetic development. In the case of the short stories, it is pertinent to say that the modern form requires great metonymic focus: an item described early in the text is not likely to be there just to add scenic content or verisimilitude. Ideally, the various literary elements – characterization, plot, tone and so on – should contribute to a climax or epiphany packed into the closure or ending. As such, Ishiguro's shorter works may contain, in more recognizable form, motifs, themes and ideas that in the longer works are more diffused and oblique. They may prefigure a change or modulation in the wider authorial project.

Setting aside the journeyman texts, the important stories will be reviewed first in the discussion below, followed by the television and movie screenplay work. For the stories, 'A family supper' is elucidated as a text that anticipates some of the key concerns of Ishiguro's first two novels. 'A strange and sometimes sadness' and 'The summer after the war' operate as dry runs for, respectively, *A Pale View of Hills* and *An Artist of the Floating World*. 'A village after dark' provides illuminating insights into the direction of Ishiguro's recent work. These stories are surveyed in the order presented here.

Apart from these works, Ishiguro also published as a story in 1985 an extract from the novel then in progress, *An Artist of the Floating World*. The story is titled 'October, 1948', which is also the title of the first diary entry of the chief protagonist of the novel. It appeared in an issue of *Granta* magazine dealing with the topic of war and is extracted from pages 19 to 28 of the Faber and Faber edition of the novel, starting on page 19 with the words, 'I have never at any point', and ending on page 28 at the section break.

SHORT STORIES – 'A FAMILY SUPPER'

'A family supper' first appeared in a discontinued journal, *Quarto*, in 1980, and opens with an account of the narrator's mother dying a painful death after eating fugu fish at the home of an old school friend. The dish is famous because it requires expert preparation to deactivate the poison inside. For a while after the war it was extremely popular. Before 'stricter regulations' were imposed it was 'all the rage to perform the hazardous gutting operation' at home and then to 'invite neighbours and friends round for the feast' (Ishiguro 1983a: 123). The narrator has been living in California estranged from his parents because he will not work in the family firm. He only learns these gruesome details surrounding his mother's death when he returns to Tokyo two years after she died, his father supplying the information as they drive in from the airport. The narrator's sister, who is away at university, is also coming home for dinner.

The eponymous meal appears to be an occasion for father and son to mend ties. However, the conversation between them is forced and awkward. The father's 'general presence' does not encourage 'relaxed conversation', we are told, and neither are 'things helped much by his odd way of stating each remark as if it were the concluding one'. Sitting opposite his father, the narrator recalls a boyhood memory of his father hitting him several times around the head for chattering like an old woman. At a pause in the conversation, the narrator says that he is sorry to hear about the collapse of the family business. The father replies that, in fact, 'the story didn't end there', for after its collapse, his partner of seventeen years, Watanabe, killed himself because he 'didn't wish to live with the disgrace'. Watanabe was a 'man of principle and honour' whom he 'respected ... very much'. The son asks whether he will go into business again and he says, no: it is too 'different' nowadays and would mean having to deal with 'foreigners' and '[d]oing things their way' (124). At this point, the narrator's sister arrives and the father goes off to prepare dinner.

As brother and sister take a turn in the garden, they discuss a well located there that is apparently haunted by a female ghost. The sister contemplates travelling to the US with her boyfriend but is not sure whether she wants to spend a great deal of time with him. A ghoulish parallel is drawn between their deceased mother and the female ghost (126–8). More importantly, the sister volunteers the information that Watanabe killed his wife and two young daughters before killing himself: 'He turned on the gas while they were all asleep. Then he cut his stomach with a meat knife.' The sister is disgusted when the brother reveals that their father describes Watanabe as 'a man of principle' (127). With the dinner preparations almost finished, the father takes the son on a tour around the house, leaving the sister in the garden. The father declares mysteriously that his wife's death was 'no accident' (128). They see a plastic model of a battleship on a low table in a corner of a room and he explains that since the firm folded he has more time on his hands for such hobbies. During the war, in fact, he spent time on ships like this although his ambition, he says, was 'always the air force'. He explains that: 'I figured it like this. If your ship was struck by the enemy, all you could do was struggle in the water hoping for a lifeline. But in an aeroplane – well – there was always the final weapon' (129) [17]. By the time they sit down to dinner, the impression is firmly established that the father blames the son for failing to help with the family business and for causing the mother's death. With tension at a heightened pitch, we learn that the main dish is fish that the father has prepared himself. A strong presentiment of approaching disaster ensues. The father seems to want to emulate Watanabe and the supper they have partaken might well be their last. At the dinner's end, the reader is left wondering how long fugu fish poison takes to work through the system; and the point is that such a macabre notion is allowed to be pleasurable. Yet against the run of expectation, we get the following snatch of dialogue (131):

'Father,' I said, finally.
'Yes?'

'Kikuko tells me Watanabe-San took his whole family with him.'

My father lowered his eyes and nodded. For some moments he seemed deep in thought. 'Watanabe was very devoted to his work,' he said at last. 'The collapse of the firm was a great blow to him. I fear it must have weakened his judgement.'

'You think what he did – it was a mistake?'

'Why, of course. Do you see it otherwise?'

'No, no. Of course not.'

'There are other things besides work.'

'Yes.'

A few paragraphs later, the father expresses the hope that his daughter will come to stay with him after finishing her studies and the story ends. In bare outline like this, the above account doesn't capture the story's pacing and adept choice of detail, how it builds up tension and suspense. Nevertheless, it should be clear that it aims at an anti-climax that deflates the desire for melodrama. In this context, the story can be read as, so to speak, a variant on the *shomin-geki* form [11]. On this view, it is a story about an old man who fears loneliness. The father's wish that his daughter will come and stay with him – the story makes it clear that the chances are low – resonates with something he said earlier when the narrator saw the plastic battleship and found the idea 'odd', since his father had always been such a busy man. 'Too busy perhaps,' the father says. 'Perhaps I should have been a more attentive father' (128).

As Ishiguro explains in an interview, this story is 'basically just a big trick' [124]:

> It's never stated, but Western readers are supposed to think that these people are going to commit mass suicide, and of course they do nothing of the sort … The Japanese are in love with these melodramatic stories … but people in Japan don't go around killing themselves as easily as people in the West assume.
>
> (Mason 1989b: 343)

By deflating the expectation that some kind of mass suicide will occur, Ishiguro encourages readers to question assumptions they bring to the text. Through the father's proclamation that there are 'other things besides work', he confutes the warning raised by Ezra Vogel [17], namely that the West is threatened by a society of self-denying economic animals. The father's blasé censure of his business partner shows up the sweeping or essentializing nature of those proclamations. In this regard, 'A family supper' hints at the narrative sensibility underpinning the first two novels set wholly or partially in Japan.

Taken as a 'return from exile' story, however, the interesting point is that the narrative presents its *own* authority as fallible. The Japan-born narrator (who has spent time abroad) did not expect his father to endorse his opinions [125] about Watanabe. The story suggests through metafictional reference to Ishiguro's own authorial position the need for a nuanced reading of his texts. It problematizes its *own* point of view and also the responsibility foisted on Ishiguro to explain the assumed complexities and mysteries of Japanese culture and society.

SHORT STORIES – 'A STRANGE AND SOMETIMES SADNESS'

'A strange and sometimes sadness', as stated earlier, prefigures *A Pale View of Hills*. It is in a sense the absent centre of the novel, something that Ishiguro took out or rejected as an option for development in the longer work. It raises the issue of ventriloquism, which is also raised in the novel. It is pertinent to an article that Ishiguro published in the *Guardian* newspaper in 1983 where he complains about how *A Pale View of Hills* was being received. It also prefigures the use of doppelganger figuration in Ishiguro's fiction, both in *A Pale View of Hills* and in subsequent works. Ishiguro states in an interview that this story is written from the 'point of view' of a woman who is 'rather like' Etsuko, the chief protagonist of *PVH* (Shaffer and Wong 2008: 22). The Etsuko role is undertaken by a middle-aged Japanese woman named Michiko, now living in England, who recalls a three-day visit by her Britain-born daughter, Yasuko, at the start of the summer just past. Yasuko's visit awakens in Michiko memories of a childhood friend, also named Yasuko, who had grown up together with her in the Nakagawa district of Nagasaki. Michiko had a troubled pregnancy with Yasuko and had named her after her friend, hoping that she would be 'as gentle and [as] kind' as her (Ishiguro 1981a: 14). In the flashback portions of the story, Michiko narrates, among other things: Yasuko's worries about her fiancé, Nakamura, who is away at war; her easy friendship with Yasuko's father, Kinoshita, who is a prototype of Ogata-San [35] in *A Pale View of Hills*; their life as factory girls, which Yasuko finds difficult to settle into; their regular evening walks and the things they talk about; their fears about Kinoshita, who having lost his wife and son now only has his daughter; their dreams about the end of war, and Yasuko's dreams about starting a family but also her wavering about marriage because of her allegiance to Michiko, who had been close to Nakamura. The hint that they are willing to sacrifice for each other over this matter shows the depth of their friendship and amity. They also discuss a stray American plane that dropped a single bomb somewhere east of the city.

One evening while talking on a garden bench, Michiko has a fright when she sees 'Yasuko staring towards [her] with an expression so ghastly it completely distorted her face. The eyes were staring so frantically they trembled with tension. Her jaw was quivering, her teeth starting to bare'

(23–4). Alarmed, Michiko asks her what has happened but her friend's face suddenly resumes its normal visage. The following day, Yasuko, her father, and many thousands of others are killed by the atom bomb dropped on the city. Yasuko appears to have had a forewarning or premonition [31] of some kind. Michiko herself is spared. Her children – Yasuko and an older daughter – are born healthy; they are unaffected by radiation poisoning. Until her daughter's visit at the start of summer, Michiko had not thought about her friend, 'the first Yasuko', for many years. But since then she crosses her mind often. Michiko says that, 'My memory of her is not clouded with nostalgia, nor does it bring me pain. Rather, it brings me an oddly disturbing kind of sorrow, a strange and sometimes sadness I find hard to place.' She contemplates returning to Japan and maybe teaching English there, but recognizes that she has settled down well in England. 'And besides, my daughters are here,' she says (26). She also thinks about taking up painting again.

At one point before this elegiac ending, Michiko narrates a key incident that took place about a year before the narrative present, when Yasuko visited her seeking her signature for a petition against nuclear weapons. Although Yasuko 'mentioned various facts and figures', Michiko says that she 'never mentioned Nagasaki', as if she had 'forgotten' her mother's presence in the city during the conflagration (25). This incident mirrors an episode in *A Pale View of Hills* where Niki comes to see Etsuko and tries to reassure her that she was right to leave Japan. She says that a 'friend' of hers wants to write a poem about her, to commemorate her courage because she 'appreciates what it must have been like, how it wasn't quite as easy as it sounds'. For the only time in the novel, Etsuko shows a flash of anger, saying that it was 'presumptuous' (*sic*) of Niki to feel that she needs reassurance on this matter (*PVH* 89–90) [34]. In this way, Ishiguro registers his concern about ventriloquism and misrepresentation.

Ishiguro reiterated these concerns in non-fictional terms in the above-mentioned news article, which was headlined 'Bomb culture'. He states that while the lure of preserving childhood memories made him set *A Pale View of Hills* in Nagasaki, it was being cast unaccountably as a book 'about the bomb'. He speaks about learning 'cynical professional lessons' from the publicity generated by such a label – which happened because the threat of 'nuclear annihilation' had 're-emerged as an issue on a scale unseen since the Sixties' (Ishiguro refers here to the Euro-missile crisis triggered by the stationing of American Cruise and Pershing missiles in response to the deployment of SS20 missiles by the former Soviet Union). This gave his book 'an easy kind of global significance', one that happened to coincide with changes in literary taste. He notes that 'the British literary world', having grown tired of the 'Hampstead novel' [109] (usually concerning 'failed relationships among members of the London media'), was now turning to books with 'the large global theme'. As a result, however, a fad for nuclear-themed works might emerge. If that happens, it would basically be a new form of 'escapist entertainment'; over the long run it could conceivably desensitize readers to the horrors of nuclear warfare (Ishiguro 1983b: 9).

In showing the road not taken in *A Pale View of Hills*, 'A strange and sometimes sadness' allows a better appreciation of the episode where Niki's 'friend' offers to write a poem about Etsuko – to, in effect, represent her experiences *on her behalf*. As the use of language suggests – the friend 'appreciates' its nature and understands that it 'wasn't quite as easy as it sounds' – the potential is already there for it to be trivialized, cheapened or misrepresented. Ishiguro's move to fend off the threat of ventriloquism is also an effort to preserve the decency of witness. He speaks elsewhere about the experiences of family members affected by the holocaust (Sexton 1987: 17). In this regard, the story is an important step in the development of greater maturity shown in the novel. The fact that Yasuko had somehow 'forgotten' her mother's presence in the city registers his concern – belatedly understood – that the experiences of an older generation might be (mis) appropriated by their progeny. The news article shows a related fear that in the cross-cultural re-articulation of this issue to address current concerns something is potentially lost, perhaps the pacifism that is a genuine feature of post-war Japanese society. It also suggests a level of anxiety about Ishiguro's own use of a freighted word and locale, as well as a desire to keep the past free from contamination by the present. In addition, the figurative rebirth of Yasuko in the person of another Yasuko (Michiko's daughter) mirrors the figurative rebirth of Keiko in the person of Mariko in *A Pale View of Hills* [31, 110].

SHORT STORIES – 'THE SUMMER AFTER THE WAR'

Published in 1983, 'The summer after the war' prefigures certain ideas in *An Artist of the Floating World* [36] and allows us to appreciate the expanded historical perspective sought by the novel. Told from the point of view of a young precocious child, it relates a summer holiday spent by the protagonist with his grandfather. The boy likes to ask about things that the adults of the household prefer to leave well alone. 'I thought Oji was a famous painter ... Where are his paintings?' he asks at one point (Ishiguro 1983c: 123). One day the grandfather receives a visit from one of his most brilliant protégées. In the same way in which Shintaro comes to ask Ono for a character reference in *An Artist of the Floating World*, the visitor asks the grandfather to vouch for his political credibility. With regard to Japan's 'China campaign', he prompts his former teacher, 'Don't you remember, Sensei? I said that it was no business of ours to employ our talents like that' (128). However, the sensei refuses to help. Having benefited from his name when it was 'revered', his ex-pupil should 'face up' to the music now that the world has a 'different opinion' of him, he says (129). The protagonist has been playing in a 'Western-style room' at the top of the house – the only one decorated in a non-Japanese manner – when their heated exchange draws him out to the balcony and he overhears the conversation (128). He keeps pestering a young servant girl to explain 'the China campaign' after the visitor leaves. The girl admits that war is 'not a good thing, everyone [knows] that now' (131). A while later the two discover one of the grandfather's propaganda artworks in the previously mentioned 'Western' room. The painting sports the same message as the one for which Ono harbours a strong recidivist affection in *An Artist of the Floating World*. It too bears the slogan, 'No time for cowardly talking. Japan must go forward' (Ishiguro 1983c: 133; *AFW* 169). The grandfather thereafter suffers a stroke and is bedridden for several months. When he finally starts to recover, the boy gives him a sketch of a maple tree. The grandfather says that it will help him get better and the story ends.

The significance of this story in the genesis of *An Artist of the Floating World* lies in the metaphor of a 'Western-style room' (128) or 'Western room' (133) located *within* a Japanese house. The metaphor stages in spatial terms what Chishu Matsuda proffers in the novel when he echoes the social Darwinist attitudes used to justify European expansionism [37]. His use of language suggests that an expansionist ethos has been adopted and indigenized for local consumption. It operates in the same manner as the architectural metaphor. The motif of a Western-style room located in a Japanese house also appears in *When We Were Orphans*.

SHORT STORIES – 'A VILLAGE AFTER DARK'

'A village after dark' was published in 2001 and is potentially of great interest because it hints at the direction in which Ishiguro's writing is headed. Set in an unnamed English village but with overtones of the geographical non-place of all his novels since *The Remains of the Day*, it relates the experiences of a gifted man named Fletcher. At one point in his life, Fletcher wielded great influence over the inhabitants of the village as well as a great number of individuals living in other places. He tried to achieve certain large objectives but he ultimately failed. Since then he has lived a nomadic life and become a bit of a tramp, moving from place to place trying to undo some of the damage that he has caused. The action of the story begins when he enters the unnamed village. It takes him a while to recognize that he actually spent a few years there. Quickly the inhabitants recognize him and start to take sides concerning his legacy and whether any good will come from his return. The older inhabitants believe he is a spent force but also a potentially negative influence on the younger, more impressionistic inhabitants. The younger ones seem to find him fascinating and worth listening to, at least. He acknowledges that he has changed his mind about many things and made large errors. Nevertheless, the striking quality about Fletcher is an irrepressible belief in the need to press on, which he conveys to his doubters in the following manner:

> [Y]ou'll be interested to know I'm going to do the very thing you feared. I'm going this moment to the young people's cottage. I'm going to tell them what to do with all their energy, all their dreams, their urge to achieve something of lasting good in this world. Look at you, what a pathetic bunch. Crouching in your cottage, afraid to do anything, afraid of me ... Afraid to do anything in the world out there, just because once we made a few mistakes. Well, those young people haven't yet sunk so low, despite all the lethargy you've been preaching at them down the years. I'll talk to them. I'll undo in half an hour all your sorry efforts.
>
> (Ishiguro 2001: 88)

The interesting thing here is the lack of dramatic irony. There is no intimation that the text harbours a different attitude towards Fletcher's sense of mission. As he makes his way to the above-mentioned 'young people's cottage' he meets an ex-schoolmate, Roger Button, whom he knows from a two-year sojourn spent in Canada before his family moved back to England. They were in their early teens then and Fletcher had been wont to bully Roger, who idolized him. Roger says, however, that he has moved on. He doesn't bear any grudges and perhaps even benefited from that treatment. He tells Fletcher that the young people's cottage is located some way out of the village and that he needs to take a bus to get there. As they walk to the bus stop, Fletcher shares his fear that the young people might not bother to wait. Roger tells him not to worry. They will, because 'They've so little else to believe in these days, you see'. He assures Fletcher that while he may get lonely waiting for the bus, the experience once he gets on it will be wonderful. It will be 'brightly lit', full of 'cheerful people, laughing and joking' and pointing to things outside the window. 'Once you board it, you'll feel warm and comfortable, and the other passengers will chat with you, perhaps offer you things to eat or drink.' After Roger goes off, Fletcher is there alone in the night with no indication of any approaching vehicle. The story ends with Fletcher telling himself that even so, 'I had been cheered by Roger Button's description of the bus. Moreover, I thought of the reception awaiting me at my journey's end – of the adoring faces of the young people – and felt the stirrings of optimism somewhere deep within me' (91).

As mentioned, this story signals certain ideas explored in Ishiguro's recent works. It suggests a change or modulation in his artistic programme. He appears more concerned with probing contemporary cynicism and the sharply lowered horizons of the times [76, 89, 109]. The title of the story, 'A village after dark', puts forward the idea that having progressed through a period of widespread cultural pessimism or darkness, it is time for us to seek the higher planes. The story also resonates when compared with *When We Were Orphans*. At one point in the novel, the chief protagonist, in conversation with his childhood friend, says that he considers the Shanghai International Settlement [77, 139] to be his 'home village' (*WWO* 256). Both texts give a utopian slant to this idea. The village in the story is equivalent to the global village concept bandied about in the media. Ishiguro suggests that to be a meaningful entity it has to reach out to those located 'outside' its borders; it shouldn't be a privileged enclave. If it is to be more than just a marketing slogan, it needs, like Fletcher, to take a bus and reach out to the rest of the world.

TELEVISION AND MOVIE SCREENPLAYS

The influence of the movie makers Yasujiro Ozu and Mikio Naruse on Ishiguro was discussed in Part 1. Their films arguably allowed him to undertake a retrieval and recovery of his birth culture [13]. Commenting critically on *A Pale View of Hills*, Ishiguro notes that 'dialogue interspersed with stage directions' could be considered the 'base unit' or structuring principle of this novel, and this suggests that in his early fiction he was still trying to get out from under their sway (Shaffer and Wong 2008: 24–5). Of the two television plays that Ishiguro wrote, the script for one of them, *The Gourmet*, is publicly available. It was screened in 1986 on Britain's Channel 4 television and published in 1993 in another issue of *Granta* magazine commemorating the twenty best young British writers – Ishiguro was still young enough to make the grade after achieving the accolade a decade earlier [7].

The Gourmet

Readers and critics interested in incorporation imagery should have a field day with *The Gourmet*. The play is a black comedy about a sophisticated, wealthy epicure, Manley Kingston, who travels the world searching for 'extreme' culinary experiences. He moves in a social set made up of similarly obsessed individuals – all men – who hold him in awe. They understand that compared to him their achievements are trivial and insignificant. He has eaten everything, including, it is rumoured, human flesh. Just when it seems that Manley might have to face the crisis of dealing with a bored palate, he meets a mysterious old man, Rossi, who has followed his career with interest. Rossi declares that Manley is his 'true son' and that he is his 'true father'. Rossi has tasted everything and more, the last referring to something 'not of this earth' (Ishiguro 1993a: 106). It turns out that he once tasted the flesh of a ghost. The great game is thus on again as Manley seeks to catch and eat one too. Nine years later, he comes within sight of his quarry. He joins a queue of homeless people outside a church offering food and shelter. After they settle down for the night, he enlists one of the vagrants in his task. Later that night they catch and butcher a ghost that appears regularly in the vestry. It is apparently the ghost of a tramp killed in 1904 by an unnamed party that needed 'human organs' for 'research purposes' (120). As Manley cooks his catch in a wok he stares greedily at it. His face is '[i]mpatient and lecherous' and he 'smiles in anticipation' (123).

We see Manley again early next morning in a back alley near Charing Cross, violently ill, clutching his stomach and vomiting into a bin. He reaches an underpass where some homeless people live, their 'places' marked by a jumble of 'cardboard boxes' (124). A homeless man thinks that he has had too much to drink and expresses his solicitude. Manley responds, according to the stage directions, 'with dignity'. He tells the man that 'I was hungry. I ate. Now I am sick.' The homeless man again offers his sympathies; he thinks that Manley has been eating rubbish-bin leftovers. 'Right, right. See what you mean,' he says, and adds a while later, 'Well. We all get hungry, don't we?' Manley replies disdainfully: 'You have no idea what *real* hunger is' (125, emphasis original). His driver then picks him up in a Rolls-Royce and he zooms away. In the car, he tells his driver that the experience wasn't as 'extraordinary' as he hoped it would be. It was a 'disappointment all in all' and he might have to 'take a trip up to Iceland again' to assuage his need for stimulus and variety. His last words to the driver are: 'So dreary, Carson. [*Pause*] Life gets so dreary once you've tasted its more obvious offerings' (126).

The last scene returns to the church vestry, to the tramp who helped Manley catch the ghost. He picks up a piece of ghost meat lying in Manley's wok, brings it to his face, and, revolted by the smell, flings it away. He catches sight of something in the back room where they caught the ghost. What he saw was himself, his image reflected in a full-length mirror left 'abandoned' against a wall: 'He looks at his appearance with an empty expression. Then he sighs, shrugs and turns away, once again rubbing the back of his neck.' The last shot is of a Rolls-Royce moving through the streets of early-morning central London (127).

Several things are immediately striking about this play. It has a manifestly strong vein of social criticism. Manley is in his fifties, has a 'large, formidable British upper-class presence [and] … wears a habitual expression of disdain and boredom' (93). His obtuseness and the mirror shot at the end underscore the issue of social inequality and the hypocrisies that surround this topic. Manley's ennui and the quality-of-life gulf in the play arguably indict modern conspicuous consumption and its attendant throw-away culture [78]. It also appears to draw on Ishiguro's experience doing social work in Renfrew, Scotland, and in London [6]. The homeless in the play are so to speak the real 'ghosts', their plight unnoticed and invisible. This critique of social neglect acts as a backdrop to the examination of the stately home order in *The Remains of the Day* and the rewriting of *Great Expectations* in *When We Were Orphans*. [70, 118]. The argument that *The Remains of the Day* is a homage to a class-directed social order is difficult to sustain if we know this play [115–16, 157].

Another prominent feature of the play is its absurdist and fabulist elements. The black humour, the conceit about catching a ghost and the related 'extreme' gourmet social set suggest that the non-realist features of *The Unconsoled* are not as atypical as they are often taken to be. The play solicits a moderation of the radical switch argument and suggests that stylistic change in the novel was undertaken to track certain cognitive or thematic objectives. In addition, *The Gourmet* also prefigures *Never Let Me Go*. The tramp-ghost caught by Manley was killed to provide organs for research purposes [87], and this echoes the plight of the chief protagonists in the novel. Given that the tramp motif reappears in the central character of 'A village after dark', there is a suggestion that Ishiguro connects social marginality to the development of a social inclusivist or cosmopolitan ethos. In addition, the driver in the play, Carson, anticipates the use of various servant figures in *The Remains of the Day*. The use of a ghost motif also echoes 'A family supper', which has a similarly deflationary ending. The characters in 'A family supper' face the prospect of being turned into 'ghosts' through mass poisoning. However, nothing comes of it. Manley eats the flesh of a ghost in *The Gourmet* but fails to obtain the gustatory epiphany that he seeks.

Other screenplay work

Commenting on Guy Maddin's movie, *The Saddest Music in the World*, one reviewer suggests that, 'Whatever Ishiguro's original scenario was like, Maddin and George Toles have presumably rewritten it beyond recognition, transplanting the story to Depression-era Winnipeg, "the world capital of sorrow"' (Romney 2004: par. 3). The movie was released in 2003 and was based on a screenplay that Ishiguro started in 1987 and completed around 1991 (Shaffer and Wong 2008: 43, 212). Ishiguro states that it was originally intended to be the third part of a three-play series for Britain's Channel 4 television, to complement the two that he wrote. However, it became 'too big' for television and had 'drifted around for a long time' before Maddin took it up. He adds that it is 'very much Guy's film' – his role 'became that of a script editor' (Shaffer and Wong 2008: 212–13). Maddin has made some telling remarks about his treatment of the script and the sizeable changes that he made to it. His comments are useful because they allow us to appreciate the thematic focus and ethos of the original:

> My latest film is a giant orgy of self-pity, where every nation of the
> world sends delegations of musicians to vie for the title of the

'saddest music in the world'. In Kazuo Ishiguro's script, it's a political allegory [158]. Like panhandlers who do some sort of limbo of pathos, the countries see who has the saddest song to sing and is therefore the neediest and most worthy of international charity. It's a story about how Third World countries can survive only by losing all their dignity [45, 154], or keep their dignity by panhandling in a very clever way. I didn't want to make this a political satire, so we inserted a family melodrama in the foreground, in which various family members – all musicians – are also manipulating each other through self-pity, fake pathos.

(Quandt 2003: 161)

As a script meant to complement *The Gourmet*, it could be said that *The Saddest Music in the World* extends the proto-cosmopolitan social vision of the former. Following the logic inscribed therein, the commentary on Third World conditions [87] in the First World (the plight of the homeless in London) is extended to encompass the global South, to take in the 'panhandlers' of humanity and their search for 'dignity', a major motif in Ishiguro's fiction. In tandem with 'A village after dark', this development arguably provides certain pointers about the direction of Ishiguro's work. This line of argument underpins the claim made in Part 2, '*When We Were Orphans*', namely that *When We Were Orphans* draws attention to the international transfer of wealth and resources [142] because it seeks to enlarge our sense of sympathy and fellow feeling [72].

The White Countess was released in 2005 and tells the story of a group of White émigrés who are displaced by the Russian civil war and fetch up in Shanghai in the mid-1930s. One of them falls in love with a blind former diplomat played by Ralph Fiennes, who sets up a nightclub named *The White Countess* for her. Ishiguro states in an interview that the script draws on 'a whole lot of research' that he did not get to use in *When We Were Orphans* (Shaffer and Wong 2008: 212). It features together for the first time in a film the famous actress-sisters Vanessa and Lynn Redgrave.

FURTHER READING

Some of Ishiguro's short stories are discussed in Lewis (2000), Walkowitz (2001) and Cheng (2005a).

3

Criticism

This section provides an account of the major trends and directions in Ishiguro criticism. It identifies a number of clearly defined areas: Ishiguro's style and narrative theory; Ishiguro, multicultural Britain, and postcolonial studies; Ishiguro and psychoanalytic criticism; Ishiguro as an international writer; and other readings. Closely referenced accounts of the major readings in each area are provided so that readers can appreciate the scholarship, issues and debates raised in the different fields. For readers who want a further synoptic take on Ishiguro's fiction, the dedicated books addressing his writing include: Shaffer (1998), Lewis (2000), C. Wong (2000) and Sim (2006). In addition, an issue of the journal *Études britanniques contemporaines* was devoted to a discussion of Ishiguro's writing (December 2004, issue 27). The nine essays in this volume offer many keen and varied insights and are notable for their attention to works other than *The Remains of the Day*. The issue includes an authorial interview conducted at the Sorbonne in 2003.

Ishiguro's style and narrative theory

This sub-section provides a survey of the criticism on Ishiguro's style – his prose style, his use of memory, history, genre and unreliable narration – and also of the way in which his work is addressed in the field of narrative theory. It relates in the process some of the responses to Ishiguro's early fiction and to the radical departure undertaken in *The Unconsoled*. We will begin with a review of the pertinent commentary on Ishiguro's prose style and then move on to the rest of the listed topics.

All of Ishiguro's novels use first-person narration. His ability to create complex, believable characters is one of the reasons why he attracts a considerable readership. The prose style of these works is tied to the narrating consciousness that the text seeks to render and would presumably vary from book to book. Nevertheless, they are underpinned by a distinctive authorial voice which has been variously described as: elegant, spare, tight, elliptical, clipped and restrained. Referring to Ishiguro's first three books, one critic asserts that they are 'distinguished by an exquisite precision'. Ishiguro is a writer who 'works scrupulously within self-imposed limits, achieving his effects by understatement and the adroit deployment of his material' (Massie 1990: 64). This prose style obviously enhances the verisimilar impact of Ishiguro's most famous creation, Stevens, of *The Remains of the Day*. It underpins his 'butlerspeak', as the writer David Lodge correctly points out (Lodge 1992: 155) [7]. It also draws differing comments from critics. Lodge suggests that '[v]iewed objectively', its 'fussily precise [and] stiffly formal' contours have 'no literary merit whatsoever'. It lacks 'wit, sensuousness and originality'. Its 'effectiveness as a medium for [the] novel resides precisely in our growing perception of its inadequacy for what it describes' (1992: 155). Dominic Head contends that Stevens's 'reticence' and 'taciturnity' show how much he buys into the 'ideology' of the stately home order (Head 2002: 158). Nevertheless, these are also the features that make readers empathize with him. For Head:

> It is in this sense that the novel's own undemonstrative style (presented as Stevens's narrative) can be defended. Within this subtly ambivalent style there is a utopian impulse, stemming from such features as Stevens's involvement of the reader in his situation of disempowerment ... (which inspires dissent), and from Ishiguro's overlaying of different cultural codes of 'politeness' ... He is hinting at a post-imperial, post-industrial world in which the individual must manoeuvre with ingenuity to retain ownership of those cultural codes that are subject to 'incorporation' in the world of multinational enterprise.
>
> (Head 2002: 158)

For Kana Oyabu, this taciturn mode is intimately tied to the fact that Ishiguro in his early books wrote 'cross-cultural' fiction that partakes in part in Eastern metaphysics (Oyabu 1995: 261) [147]. Eastern metaphysics offers a different understanding of speech, writing and silence from that which predominates in the West. It solicits, according to Oyabu, an 'attitude of anti-expression' that seeks 'the empowering of silence over expression' (59, 259). Despite the presence of 'stereotypical Japanese images' in Ishiguro's early works, Oyabu contends that their use of a spare language privileging gaps and silences helps to 'convey a culture and society' and to dissolve 'essentialism in cultural representation' (205). In contrast, Michael Wood examines the larger idea that 'silence is what literature longs for but can't reach, not only because its very condition is language but because a complicated fidelity to silence is one of literature's most attractive attainments'

(M. Wood 1998: 1). In his opinion, 'the sheer bareness' of Etsuko's language in *A Pale View of Hills* is in itself 'a kind of richness' (177). Ben Howard asserts in turn that the 'balanced syntax and precise diction' of Ishiguro's elegant style embodies in 'civil' speech and voice a 'continuity of values' both moral and aesthetic (Howard 2001: 400). Ishiguro offers in the civil voices of his narrators 'emblems of stability, balance, and restraint' (417). As a result, he shores up 'the forces of civilized order and cultural tradition' (400).

Ishiguro has also commented on his prose style and on its difference from the more exuberant syntax and diction found in, for instance, the works of Salman Rushdie and Timothy Mo. He notes in an interview that Rushdie and Mo tend to have 'quirks' in their writing where 'it explodes in all kinds of directions' (Vorda and Herzinger 1993: 9). Singling out Rushdie for elaboration, Ishiguro asserts that his writing reaches out to 'express meaning that can't usually be expressed through normal language'. Rushdie's language 'just grow[s] in every direction at once, and he doesn't particularly care if the branches lead nowhere' (9–10). Ishiguro adds that:

> I respect Rushdie's writing enormously, but as a writer I think I'm almost the antithesis. The language I use tends to be the sort that actually suppresses meaning and tries to hide away meaning rather than chase after something just beyond the reach of words. I'm interested in the way words hide meaning. I suppose I like to have a spare, tight structure because I don't like to have this improvised feeling remain in my work.
>
> (Vorda and Herzinger 1993: 10)

This manner of approach – language hiding meaning for certain ends – entails a kind of character evasiveness (and growth) that Ishiguro has made very much his own. Several of his books employ forceful recognition plots where the narrator moves in a series of stops and starts towards some roughly glimpsed idea that has been troubling him or her. Genuine insight is difficult for the narrator because it involves a radical readjustment of his or her world view. We see before us a crisis of some kind whose implications and significance are still being worked out. What Mark Wormald says about *A Pale View of Hills* is in this context applicable to several of Ishiguro's compellingly unreliable narrators:

> The text draws attention to the temporal as well as physical distance between its own multiple but discontinuous acts of retrospection and the somewhat hazy memories these acts of retrospection seemed designed to contain. To contain here means to hold in check as well as to clarify. The impulses to reveal and to suppress compete for dominance in a disturbing dynamic, a calm eye for some long remembered detail and a calmer turn of phrase

often standing in for some crucial but suppressed circumstance in the story's present. A compulsion to confess competes, in tone, with a casual but devastating tendency to disguise.

(Wormald 2003: 228)

Stanley Cavell has suggested in an oft-quoted comment that 'a first-person account is, after all, a confession; and the one who has something to confess has something to conceal. And the one who has the word "I" at his or her disposal has the quickest device for concealing himself' (Newton 1995: 243). Ishiguro's familiarity and skill with the genre means that he has a powerful and effective tool, one that can be used to raise issues of bad faith, responsibility and ethics.

Nevertheless, this situation doesn't necessarily increase the distance between reader and text. Rebecca Suter suggests that there are several instances in *The Remains of the Day* where the reader and the narrator (Stevens) switch places, as it were. Stevens is *himself* put into a reading or interpretive situation, and this increases our ability to understand his plight. These role-reversal swaps include Stevens's attempts to read further into the letter [159] that Miss Kenton sends to him from Cornwall, and in which he detects what he believes to be nostalgia for Darlington Hall, and presumably fondness for himself. When their relationship deteriorates during the 1923 conference at the hall, they send notes to each other. Stevens also mulls over various homilies where his father, also a butler, sought to transmit to him the true essence of the butler tradition. Suter adds that Stevens isn't an effective reader. He often projects onto the text that he is reading 'his own wishes' (Suter 1999: 245). Even so, this role reversal means that the reader often finds him or herself 'in the same condition as the narrator, struggling to find a "truth" behind the filter of his hazy memory'. There is great empathy for Stevens because as readers we are basically put in the same situation (246).

Apart from these renditions of acts of reading, Andrew Teverson (1999) extends the list to include the travel guide that Stevens consults as he travels through southern England, the romances that he likes to read surreptitiously in his spare time, and also the encyclopedia volumes that Darlington pretends to peruse when he has something sensitive or embarrassing to tell Stevens. If we accept Suter's argument, therefore, these would all be situations where the role reversal between audience and narrator heightens the empathetic impact of the novel.

At certain key moments in *The Remains of the Day*, Adam Newton argues in addition that Stevens's voice 'conspicuously changes registers'. His language contains the 'poignancy of incipient realization' and is also 'without irony's safety-net' (Newton 1995: 273). A good example would be the semi-epiphanic moment when Stevens laments on Weymouth pier his failure to exercise autonomy. We might add that these responses show how difficult it is to ascertain how much self-knowledge Ishiguro's narrators possess. Even as readers feel compelled to pursue this question it is difficult to separate the concealing self from the narrating self. It is important to stress, however, that since *The Remains of the Day* the impression of duplicity has altered or has receded. In the novels since *The Remains of the Day*, unreliability stems more from a lack of local or social knowledge. It appears to be shaped by a larger textual desire to broach the issue of social change and to offer alternatives to contemporary cynicism and pessimism [76, 89, 98].

A confessional style that uses a balanced syntax to hide meaning and explore remorse would be striking if Ishiguro writes what on one occasion he calls 'Hampstead' novels, or books dealing with relationships between members of the London media social set (Ishiguro 1983b: 9) [95]. Right from the beginning, however, he has crafted works where abundant flashbacks and retrospection take place in locales undergoing large-scale social change, with the Second World War acting as a backdrop in many of them. Tying together private recollection and public historical narratives gives additional layers of meaning to Ishiguro's work. Furthermore, it appears to be a favoured modus operandi. Ishiguro states that in his early work his usual approach was to scour history books for potential settings in the way that a film director might search for suitable locations for a script. He explains that:

> I would look for moments in history that would best serve my purposes, or what I wanted to write about. I was conscious that I wasn't so interested in the history per se, that I was using British history or Japanese history to illustrate something that was preoccupying me.
>
> (Ishiguro and Oe 1991: 115)

In a recent interview, Ishiguro adds that he considered post-war France and post-invasion Britain (*c.* 450 AD) as potential sites for his forthcoming novel (Hunnewell 2008: 42–3) [9]. He appears to have continued thus with this approach, which insists on one level that the locales of his stories are essentially interchangeable or fungible.

For Christoph Henke, the manifest importance of memory in Ishiguro's work is a key feature of contemporary British fiction and is intimately tied to the question of identity. Henke argues that the two are co-implicated or co-extensive with each other. Quoting earlier work in this area, he states tellingly that, 'The core meaning of any individual or group identity, namely, a sense of sameness over time and space, is sustained by remembering; and what is remembered is defined by the assumed identity' (Henke 2003: 79). According to Henke, the fields of autobiographical memory, constructivist philosophy and cognitive psychology teach us that 'remembering is a complex cognitive process which bears no direct relation to events experienced in the past'. The individual's 'inner story' is structured in response to present needs and 'undergoes continual rewriting and editing'. It entails 'a continual "self-creation" of the ego' (80). In addition, literary texts don't just exploit stories circulating in the national realm. They may also 'have such an influence on them that [they become themselves] a medium of cultural memory, contributing to the formation as well as the perpetuation of cultural identity' (82). In this context, Henke argues, the goal of *The Remains of the Day* is the activation of a series of remembrances that chart a 'profound identity crisis'. As a result, 'a whole set of long-standing stereotypes of aristocratic Englishness comes under scrutiny as well' (85). Aside from Henke, other critics also bear out the importance of memory in Ishiguro's fiction. The argument that it operates in a half-submerged or palimpsest-like manner has been made by Guth (1999), Jirgens (1999), Évain (2004), Zinck (2005) and Veyret (2005).

For Cynthia Wong, in addition, memory as a retelling of an inner story doesn't just generate self-creation or 'self-mastery' (Wong 1995: 128). It is also for her a kind of estrangement. Drawing on the work of the French theorist Maurice Blanchot, Wong argues that the narrators of Ishiguro's first three books share a similar interest in 'self-dispossession'. They all undertake a 'turning away' or 'inverting' of the past so that they can 'unburden themselves' of it (128, 131, 144). They all face a pressure to obsessively remember, to 'reconfigure' past events 'owing to a subsequent emotion which the reader will identify as their shame about the past' (131). They 'remember in order to forget; they reconstruct the past in an effort to obliterate it' (128).

In the case of Etsuko in *A Pale View of Hills*, Wong writes insightfully that her narrative is organized in a bid to achieve the 'figurative rebirth' (135) [31, 96] of Keiko in the person of Mariko. That rebirth allows Etsuko to 'forget the premonition of death [that] she connects with that period'. In '[r]emembering the pain of the past, she is able to forget, momentarily, the horror of her daughter's demise' (129). Wong adds that Etsuko's version of events is unreliable because of her own 'awareness' of being mad in the period immediately following the bombing. Yet it is also 'filled with lucid observation of the way historical circumstances produced one's sense of self in those times'. It is this anachronistic or paradoxical feature of her narrative that 'extends the personal story': faced with that anachronism, readers are encouraged to explore 'the sociohistorical aspects which inform it' (132–3).

The striking connection between private and public that is a feature of Ishiguro's fiction is also usefully elucidated by James Lang. Lang concurs with Wong that 'self-interest' plays a large role when Ishiguro's narrators 'reconstruct, through private memories, a public historical context which they have experienced' (Lang 2000: 144). They do this in order to explain away or to excuse their past behaviour and actions. Nevertheless, referring to Ishiguro's first four novels, Lang states that each novel 'seems to assert the important role that private memories can play in helping us recapture and relive the openness and contingency of historical moments in the face of the deterministic tendencies of the national collective memory' (143).

Lang's particular concern is with how *The Remains of the Day* tracks recent changes in historical practice and writing. The novel moves away from so to speak the big man version of history and opts to pay attention to those 'living on the social margins' (147). Just as importantly, it moves away from an obsession with clarifying what amounts to be a fixed timeline, with the idea that things 'must have occurred as they did'. For Lang, the novel resists 'the creation of the retrospective illusion of fatality with its insistent critique of the discourse of, in the novel's phrase, "turning points"'. In the process, it gives us a 'richer sense of history', one that places the contingency of things at the centre of its account of events. It signals that things 'could have been different' and that 'the future admits of various paths' (154). Despite his faults, therefore, Stevens allows us to express 'a guarded faith in the ability of private memory to help recapture history', meaning that it challenges official narratives that encourage status quo conservatism (163).

As for the historical research that might have gone into *The Remains of the Day*, both Ekelund (2005) and Veyret (2005) note the parallel between its title and the title of the late Earl of Halifax's memoirs. One of the 'real-life' historical personages who features on the guest list of Darlington Hall, Halifax's autobiography, *Fulness of Days*, appeared in 1957 [46, 135, 137]. In the novel, he plays a key role in Stevens's attempt to shore up a crumbling self-image. Stevens remembers that Halifax praised the quality of the cutlery or silver on display during one of the 'unofficial' meetings arranged by Darlington between himself and the German foreign minister Ribbentrop – it had helped to lift his sombre 'mood' just before entering the meeting (*ROD* 135). For Stevens, the incident represents one of those situations where effort put into something as trivial as silver-polishing might have played a 'small' yet significant part in the making of history (*ROD* 138). Other critics – Bhabha (1995: 14) and Walkowitz (2007: 218) – have also commented on this silver-polishing episode. Veyret asserts that, despite their title, Halifax's memoirs contain nothing more than 'disconnected shallow remarks' and 'empty talk'. In this regard,

> *The Remains of the Day*, although embodied by a fictional character provides a more political statement than *Fulness of Days*: it is the voice of the margin speaking about the centre of events, addressing ethical questions about the nature of one's political responsibility in the face of chaos.

(Veyret 2005: 168–9)

The influence of the Second World War on Ishiguro's fiction is also addressed by Cheng (2006b), who discusses its use as a backdrop to *A Pale View of Hills*, *An Artist of the Floating World*, *The Remains of the Day* and *When We Were Orphans*.

Returning to the use of unreliable narration in *The Remains of the Day*, its depiction of what might be described as a split or fractured subjectivity [130] has, not surprisingly perhaps, been linked to developments in continental philosophy. Margaret Scanlan relates the indeterminate stories of Ono and Stevens to the work of Foucault and Derrida (Scanlan 1993: 139–40, 147). She concludes that Ishiguro offers a 'posthumanist' notion of the subject in the novel (139). Derrida's notion of 'différance' is also used by Jean-Pierre Naugrette to investigate *When We Were Orphans* (Naugrette 2004: 79). Kathleen Wall provides on her part a narratological reading of *The Remains of the Day* but also appends an idea that echoes Scanlan's conclusion, namely that older definitions of unreliable narration 'reflect a liberal humanist view of literature' (Wall 1994: 20) [156]. In crafting a novel that is in certain respects 'thoroughly indeterminate', Wall contends that Ishiguro challenges these older definitions even as he 'foregrounds the problem of "truth", perhaps challenging us never to figure out "what really happened"'. The upshot is that we might have to settle for an 'ironic pleasure in reaching what few conclusions come our way' (30). Charles Sarvan (1997) and Molly Westerman (2004) also register the tie between unreliable narration and the fractured subjectivity of, respectively, Ono and Stevens. They reference the work of the French psychoanalyst Jacques Lacan and are reviewed in greater detail in Part 3, 'Ishiguro and psychoanalytic criticism'. Daniela Carpi also discusses *The Remains of the Day* in relation to the broader cultural uncertainty about subjectivity. She explores what she calls the crisis of the 'social subject' as manifested in contemporary British literature (Carpi 1997: 168). Her analysis compares *The Remains of the Day* with two other novels that feature butlers: Muriel Spark's *Not to Disturb* (1971), and Rose Tremain's *Sadler's Birthday* (1976).

LITERALIST INTERPRETATIONS AND EXPECTATIONS

After Ishiguro's first three books, much controversy was generated when *The Unconsoled* failed to meet the expectations of reviewers. James Wood in the *Guardian* said that it 'has the virtue of being unlike anything else; it invents its own category of badness' (Wood 1995: 5). Amit Chaudhuri in *The London Review of Books* said that the novel is marred by its 'refusal' to engage with the 'social shape of our age' (Chaudhuri 1995: 31). James Walton declared in the *Daily Telegraph* that '[f]or months now, there have been rumours that [Ishiguro] has followed up *The Remains of the Day* – 1989 Booker Prize-winner, international bestseller, major motion picture – with "a stinker"' (Walton 1995: AB4). Commenting on the book's use of

motifs and vocabulary drawn from classical music, the American composer
Ned Rorem said that he found them 'aimless'. Its 'oversimplified' deployment of those terms meant that they amounted to 'high-sounding gob-
bledygook'. As for the chief protagonist's dream-like account of his
experiences, Rorem states, 'Let his nightmare be *his* problem. For nothing is
more boring than another person's dream. When that person is himself a
bore, the result is fatal' (Rorem 1996: 158–9, emphasis original).

Interestingly, the novel also found some prominent defenders [7]. The
philosopher Richard Rorty raised the possibility that Ishiguro might have
'found his voice and expanded the frontiers of the novel' [56], although he
found the work itself obscure, given its odd representation of time and
space. He concluded that '[s]ometimes all a reviewer can do is express
appreciative puzzlement' (Rorty 1995: 13). Anita Brookner called it a
'superb achievement' and said that '[t]he logic of [its] procedure is never in
doubt' (Brookner 1995: 40). Michael Wood adds that the novel 'takes the
opportunity that fiction so often resists, and pursues the darker logic of a
world governed by our needs and worries [134] rather than the laws of
physics' (M. Wood 1995: 18). John Carey argues that 'the book may cause
puzzlement at first', but 'once you have got used to its ruptures of reality it
becomes tense and absorbing' (Carey 2000b: 165). In a poll conducted in
2006, the *Observer* newspaper gave it joint third place in a survey of 'the
best British, Irish or Commonwealth novel from 1980 to 2005'. Around a
hundred and twenty individuals representing an impressive cross-section of
British cultural life apparently took part in the poll (McCrum 2006). *The
Unconsoled* won third spot, together with four other novels including
Anthony Burgess's *Earthy Powers* (1980) and Salman Rushdie's *Midnight
Children* (1981). First place went to J. M. Coetzee's *Disgrace* (1999) and the
runner-up was Martin Amis's *Money* (1984), so, surprisingly perhaps, Ishiguro's novel found itself in quite illustrious company. At least among wri-
ters, it appears to have garnered a heavyweight reputation of some kind.

As for the critical reception of Ishiguro's early works, one of its salient
features is its zeal for tracking the *Japaneseness* of his writing [14]. One
reviewer said that *A Pale View of Hills* is 'typically Japanese in its compression,
its reticence and in its exclusion of all details not absolutely essential to its
theme' (F. King 1982: 25). Another commentator argues that Ishiguro's
'gradual revelation' of the main protagonist's personality in *An Artist of the
Floating World* is influenced by 'the gentle restraint of Japanese culture and
is an integral feature of his art' (Mallett 1996: 19). In some cases, this concern was carried over to *The Remains of the Day*. In a review published in
1989, Gabriele Annan argues that Ishiguro's first three books are 'explanations,
[and] even indictments, of Japanese-ness'. The people that Stevens meets on
the road – Smith, Dr Carlisle – are 'specimens of ordinary, warm-hearted,
decent humanity'; they act as a foil to Stevens's stilted mannerisms and
implicitly indict Japanese persona and psyche. The former encapsulate 'an

argument for spontaneity, openness, and democracy, and against Japaneseness'. Thus the 'message' of the novel – which Annan faults for its parochial focus on Ishiguro's birth culture – is an injunction to be 'less Japanese, less bent on dignity, less false to yourself and others, less restrained and controlled' (Annan 1989: 3–4). Another reviewer suggests that Ishiguro carries over into *The Remains of the Day* the 'Japanese' tonal qualities of the first two books. These are listed as: 'taciturnity', the use of 'subtle brush strokes', and 'the aim to evoke form rather than create it' (Kauffmann 1995: 43).

In addition, Rocio Davis claims that in *The Remains of the Day*, Ishiguro 'revisions Japan in a novel that is not even set in Japan but has as its theme six unexceptional days in the life of that most English of characters, a butler'. Davis is impressed with Ishiguro's use of 'Japanese subtlety' (Davis 1994: 144). Pico Iyer asserts on his part that *The Remains of the Day* has the distinction of being 'the most revealing' among the genre of books 'purporting to explain Japan to the West' (Iyer 1991: 585). The novel achieves this distinction because its portrayal of an obedient, self-effacing English butler 'lights up the Japanese mind from within' (587). For David Gurewich, Stevens is notable for his love of 'ritual', his 'stoicism in performing his duties', and his 'loyalty to his master that conflicts with his humanity'. These qualities stand out in the novel's portrayal and are indeed 'prominent aspects of the Japanese collective psyche' (Gurewich 1989: 80). Claude Habib argues as well that in *The Remains of the Day*, 'Ishiguro has managed to translate into purely British terms the crucial problem of Japanese identity: what happens to the values of perfectionism when confronted with the values of democracy? (Connor 1996: 107) [43].

Related to this critical proclivity, some readings of *An Artist of the Floating World* tended to focus on the middle period of the artist-protagonist, Ono. His sojourn at an artists' colony is read as a lament for a lost paradise, a tribute to a bucolic, prelapsarian Eden [39]. Wendy Brandmark argues that the 'central irony' of the novel is Ono's rejection of 'the art of the floating world' (a reference to his sojourn at the colony) for being 'too ephemeral'. He discovers after the war that the political goals through which he sought transcendence 'were indeed transitory' (Brandmark n.d.). Ono's middle period is also described by Brian Shaffer as a 'stereotypically bohemian world ... cut off from an inhospitable, materialistic, aesthetically shallow, mainstream society'. When Ono breaks up with his mentor, Mori-san, it is 'precisely the "real world" in general, and Japanese economic and military aspirations in particular, that Ono hopes to shape and reflect' (Shaffer 1998: 52–3). In a review of the novel, Anne Chisholm states as well that:

> One would like to think ... that it is always the Floating World, the world of love, beauty and art, that endures, and that the 'real' world of action, of politics and war, turns out to be treacherous and temporary. But the Floating World, in Japan as elsewhere, is

always under threat; the old man's longings for his past become a
universal lament for lost worlds.

(Chisholm 1986: 162)

For Hermione Lee, however, any concern with finding and fixing Oriental
style in Ishiguro's work is already disputed in the *first* paragraph of his *first*
book [28]. In her review of *A Pale View of Hills*, Lee quotes its first paragraph, which is given below:

> Niki, the name we finally gave my younger daughter, is not an
> abbreviation; it was a compromise I reached with her father. For
> paradoxically it was he who wanted to give her a Japanese name,
> and I – perhaps out of some selfish desire not to be reminded of
> the past – insisted on an English one. He finally agreed to Niki,
> thinking it had some vague echo of the East about it.
>
> (PVH 9)

She argues that it contains a cautionary reading conundrum integral to its
promise of cultural knowledge:

> Part of Ishiguro's appeal is the novelty he seems to provide of a
> 'translation', a little bridge, between Japanese culture and English
> writing. But the abbreviation at the start of the first novel sets up
> the paradoxes here. The Japanese-looking name is actually a
> mixed-product of the narrator's desire to get away from Japan to
> England, and of her husband's romantic attraction (like the
> attraction some of Ishiguro's Western readers feel?) [143] to 'an
> echo of the East'. What looks to a Western reader like a Japanese
> text may have a Western content for an Oriental reader.
>
> (Lee 1990: 37)

Ishiguro's stance on this matter is suggested in an interview with the writer
Bill Bryson:

> I found it disturbing that many of the reviews of my first two
> books were saying things like, 'Read this book if you want to
> understand how Japanese people think'. That was worrying to me
> because I didn't have that kind of authority ... Before I knew
> anything about the [third] book, I knew that it wasn't going to
> have anything to do with Japan or Japanese people.
>
> (Bryson 1990: 44)

In the case of *The Remains of the Day*, some readers felt additionally that
it was animated by a spirit of fealty and imitative cultural reverence.

Exemplifying that outlook, a letter to *The Times* questioned its historical and descriptive veracity, averring that 'port would never be handed round by a butler after dinner, but would be circulated clockwise by the dining gentlemen' (Lewis 2000: 77). One reviewer also urged readers to show a bit of patience and tolerance: 'It is a difficult undertaking for someone born in Nagasaki in 1960 to attempt to impersonate an English butler in 1956', he said. As such there would be times when, 'inevitably and excusably, Ishiguro gets things wrong' (F. King 1989: 31). Addressing such attitudes, Steven Connor argues that one commonplace view of the book was that 'the alien eye of the Japanese immigrant writer' had revealed 'a once-present but now lost essential Englishness' (Connor 1996: 111) [60]. Their impact was to deny Ishiguro the opportunity to comment on the country he grew up in, something that Connor identifies as 'a form of cultural repatriation' (107).

Confronted with that repatriation, *The Unconsoled* breaks new ground and moves beyond a realist framework. Among its experimental features, its chief protagonist, Ryder, has the ability to access the thoughts of certain characters. Claire Pégon points out that this attribute is scandalous when viewed in narratological terms. It means that Ryder 'usurp[s] the powers of an omniscient narrator and provide[s] logically inaccessible background material to embellish his narrative' (Pégon 2004: 182). Mark Wormald asserts as well that:

> Gustav, the extraordinarily hyper-dignified hotel porter in [*The Unconsoled*], rehearses and pushes to a tragi-comic conclusion that commitment to his profession that Stevens had communicated merely through his wooden prose in *The Remains of the Day*. At one point he turns in a brilliant performance of dancing on a table top while laden down with implausibly heavy bags.
>
> (Wormald 2003: 235) [62]

Ishiguro does a lot of promotion work for his books and grants a lot of interviews. He has stated tellingly that, 'Publicity for me has to a large extent been fighting the urge to be stereotyped by people' (Chira 1989: 13).

USE OF GENRE

At the same time, it should be noted, the experimental aspects of Ishiguro's fiction are not solely confined to one book. Arguably a key feature of his writing from the beginning is the way he takes readers' expectations about form, topos and motif and reworks them or gives them a twist. In the process, he performs a subversive rewriting of entrenched genres. With his first two books, it could be said, Ishiguro appropriates the conventions of exotic fiction [34, 79] for his own narrative purposes. Thus, in the review cited earlier, Hermione Lee observes that 'Sachiko is a version of Madame

Butterfly' (Lee 1990: 38) [18, 33, 125]. Barry Lewis argues that, 'One means by which the novel obstructs realist readings is by persistently echoing Giacomo Puccini's *Madam Butterfly*' (Lewis 2000: 22). Lewis's wariness about this issue is shared by Megumi Arai, who finds telling Etsuko's comment that Sheringham, her husband, 'never understood' the ways of her culture despite the impressive news articles [17, 29] that he wrote about Japan (*PVH* 90). The novel presents in this regard, 'the classical coupling of the mysterious and elusive oriental and the well-meaning but non comprehending Westerner, [thus making it] another variation on the Madam Butterfly–Pinkerton theme' (Arai 1990: 29–30). Chu-chueh Cheng contends on her part that Ono in *An Artist of the Floating World* caricatures the penchant for *Japonaiserie*. At one point in his career he spends time painting geishas, cherry trees, temples, swimming carp and the like. These paintings are commissioned by foreign buyers because they look 'Japanese' to them (*AFW* 69) [39]. For Cheng, this episode is a 'metafictional moment' that explicitly targets 'the eagerness of foreign consumers who prize contrived exoticness' (Cheng 2005b: 164).

This use of genre for authorial purposes is also carried over to *The Remains of the Day*, which can be considered among other things an appropriation of the country house novel form [7, 54, 79, 126]. Its wider connection with issues of multiculturalism and with postcolonial studies is addressed in Part 3, 'Ishiguro, multicultural Britain and postcolonial studies'. Following *The Unconsoled*, Ishiguro continued to experiment with form and genre. Christopher Banks in *When We Were Orphans* is a detective who violates the conventions of the detective narrative form [54, 77]. One reviewer says in this context that the novel highlights the escapist proclivities of the genre: 'The hand-me-down conventions of detective fiction are shown to be too neat: brilliant feats of detection don't work in a wider, messier world' (Francken 2000: 37). For Timothy Weiss, the novel can be read as 'an attempted innovative extension of the [detective] genre' (Weiss 2004: 140). Brian Finney suggests that Ishiguro performs a 'burlesque [of] different genres' in his recent work (Finney 2002: par. 1). Hélène Machinal adds that *When We Were Orphans* presents two different versions of the sociology of detective fiction [77]. On the one hand, the detective is 'a reassuring agent of social cohesion' because he knows the layout of the city, including its 'darkest recesses'. He provides an antidote to the fragmentation introduced by industrialization and modernization. On the other hand, the novel also criminalizes all kinds of behaviour deemed 'deviant and transgressive' by presenting 'a manichean representation of society' (Machinal 2004: 62–3).

Building on earlier work by Raymond Williams, Caroline Patey has suggested that the 1923 conference held at Darlington Hall in *The Remains of the Day* tracks an internal development in the country house novel genre. It shows how it 'reluctantly and imperceptibly' acquires 'some features of the detective novel and ... the espionage story'. According to Patey, this 'gradual sliding into the *roman policier*' can be seen in the way that Stevens eavesdrops on the conversations of guests for Darlington, the presence of bodyguards around the mansion, and the overall secrecy and heightened tension (Patey 1991: 143, emphasis original). In this regard, Patey raises presciently an intellectual link that Ishiguro explores in *When We Were Orphans*.

In addition to the above, Henry Cuningham argues that Sarah Hemmings in *When We Were Orphans* is like Estella in Dickens's 1861 novel *Great Expectations* [70]. Sarah, like Estella, is 'a cold, elusive beauty who is worshipped from afar' and who hankers after a position in 'high society'. Cuningham adds that throughout *Great Expectations* Joe Gargery, a friend of the hero, Pip, calls him 'old chap', and this is paralleled as well by Akira, who calls Banks by that name, although he initially mispronounces it as 'old chip' (Cuningham 2004: 4–5). Also sharing this emphasis, Frederick Holmes observes that 'like Pip in Dickens' *Great Expectations* ... [Banks] learns that the inheritance which enabled him to be educated as a gentleman had its source in crime'. Banks is 'inextricably enmeshed in the very evil that he is impotent to defeat' (Holmes 2005: 19).

It is with *Never Let Me Go*, however, that this key attribute of Ishiguro's style comes most strikingly to the fore. This novel braids together the science fiction form and the dystopian tale [8, 156]. Again, Ishiguro unsettles formal expectations by pushing 'science' to the background in a work about cloning [83]. Bruce Robbins asserts in this context that *Never Let Me Go* is 'an inspired piece of genre modification'. Ishiguro according to him takes the:

> bland, squeaky-clean idiom of the middle-class boarding school novel, with its beguiling motivational assumption that the world is just and that effort will eventually be rewarded, and infuses it with a dark, late-twentieth century punk or slacker vision of 'no future'.
>
> (Robbins 2007: 201)

In the process, Ishiguro establishes through what is ostensibly a cloning novel the centrality of class [141] in any understanding of society and of the dynamics of social change.

Like other commentators, Robbins is also struck by the novel's ability to provoke existential anxiety and deliberation [90]. We might add that *Never Let Me Go* showcases why Ishiguro takes entrenched genres and gives them a twist – because it allows him to address recurrent concerns. Robbins puts his observations in first-person terms. He states that 'I depend for my daily dose of contentment on a blinkering of awareness that I myself in my better moments would find outrageous and shameful'. It is plausible as such that one of the aims of the novel is to push us to contemplate 'the Big Picture' (Robbins 2007: 201).

This feature has also been noted by the writer M. John Harrison, who asserts that the book is about 'why we don't explode' (Harrison 2005: 26). His comments are worth quoting in full because they capture its nebulous, yet powerfully visceral impact:

> By [the end of this novel] readers may find themselves full of an energy they don't understand and aren't quite sure how to deploy. *Never Let Me Go* makes you want to have sex, take drugs, run a marathon, dance – anything to convince yourself that you're more alive, more determined, more conscious, more dangerous than any of these characters ... [It is about] why we don't just wake up one day and go sobbing and crying down the street, kicking everything to pieces out of the raw, infuriating, completely personal sense of our lives never having been what they could have been.
>
> (Harrison 2005: 26)

In a related vein, Sarah Kerr argues that while the novel doesn't move us to 'outright heartbreak', it 'delivers images of odd beauty and a mounting existential distress that hangs around long after we read it' (Kerr 2005: 16). Lev Grossman adds that in its essence *Never Let Me Go* is an 'existential fable about people trying to wring some happiness out of life before the lights goes out' (Grossman 2005: 62). Over the course of his career, it could be said then that Ishiguro unsettles the conventions of: exotic fiction (*A Pale View of Hills* and *An Artist of the Floating World*); the country house novel (*The Remains of the Day*); the high-modernist European novel (*The Unconsoled*); crime fiction (*When We Were Orphans*); and science fiction (*Never Let Me Go*). It should be interesting to see if this penchant for generic modification is continued in his subsequent works.

It needs to be said, however, that critics have proposed alternative explanations for the genre variation undertaken in *Never Let Me Go*. Toker and Chertoff suggest that while in many dystopian tales, 'love is a subversive force that threatens the stability of the system', this topos is reworked 'almost beyond recognition' in *Never Let Me Go*. The upshot is that the novel raises consciousness about bioethical issues (Toker and Chertoff 2008: 173). Deborah Britzman asserts in contrast that *Never Let Me Go* escapes many of the categories or sub-categories that we might use to describe it. Among other things it can be read as an allegory for 'interiority', as a parable about child-rearing, or as a comedy about 'parental wishes' (Britzman 2006: 312). Perhaps most memorably, Keith McDonald asserts that the novel is a 'speculative memoir': it questions our customary assumptions about how autobiography operates (McDonald 2007: 74). These comments hint at the depth and fecundity of *Never Let Me Go* and suggest that it will have a sustained cultural and intellectual impact.

On the topic of experimentation, finally, Ishiguro states that he finds 'tedious ... the kind of book whose *raison d'être* is to say something about literary form'. He states that his interest in literary experiment extends only insofar as it allows him to explore 'certain themes with an emotional dimension' (Mason 1989b: 346).

He adds that while 'the nature of fiction or fictionality' is something that writers might need to know in order to write properly, it isn't something that he 'turn[s] to novels and art to find out about' (Vorda and Herzinger 1993: 22–3). Without privileging a decisionist or voluntarist stance on the relationship between writers and their works, it might be helpful to consider Ishiguro's latest works as a search for what Raymond Williams calls 'emergent' forms of culture that can challenge dominant social structures and practices. For Williams, an emergent culture is 'never only a matter of immediate practice'; its development 'depends crucially on finding new forms or adaptations of forms'. Such innovation 'is in effect a *pre-emergence*, active and pressing but not yet fully articulated' (Williams 1977: 126, emphasis original). Williams's take appears to underpin Katherine Stanton's claim that *The Unconsoled* is a 'European Union' novel and as such belongs to an important 'emergent genre' (Stanton 2006: 20) [22, 61]. In this sense, it could be said, Ishiguro's recent works embody a moment of anticipatory social reconfiguration.

NARRATIVE THEORY

Apart from the topics addressed above, *The Remains of the Day* has also attracted substantial attention from the field of narrative theory. David Lodge (1992) used the novel to illustrate 'the unreliable narrator' in a series of newspaper articles that he wrote in the early 1990s highlighting various literary devices pertinent to the art of fiction. Since then this feature has been studied in a more systematic manner in narrative theory, in what is also a testimony to the novel's exemplary craft and technique. Narratology seeks among other things to make general statements about how narratives operate. The key readings in this area are the ones offered by Doyle (1993), Wall (1994), Phelan and Martin (1999), Newton (1995) and Marcus (2006). In the rest of the sub-section, these readings will be reviewed in the order presented.

For Waddick Doyle, a sense of alterity or otherness arises in the novel because of Stevens's use of defamiliarizing vantage points or viewpoints. Doyle is interested in their thematic implications. Near the start of his journey, Stevens muses over the view of the English countryside glimpsed from the top of a hill. At this point in the narrative, according to Doyle, his remarks about national and professional 'greatness' are straightforwardly secure – 'butlerhood operates as a type of synecdoche for Englishness' (Doyle 1993: 71–2). As the journey progresses, however, the novel complicates this claim using, among other things, multiply embedded stories – where

Stevens is both protagonist and narrator – so that like an 'infinite regression of observation' these devices increasingly subvert his assertions (72). Ultimately, they allow him to be 'an other' to himself, to gain an external perspective on his views and to question their initial clarity (70). In addition, Doyle asserts that:

> Each of the following five chapters [following the one titled 'Salisbury'] is named after points of narration, and at each his vision becomes more and more obscured by climatic elements. At Mortimer's Pond in Dorset, his vision is hindered by branches and shadows. In Taunton, Somerset, he is unable to discern figures because of excessive sunlight. In Moscombe, Devon, it is twilight and fog that makes his way unclear. By the time he reaches Little Compton where he will meet Miss Kenton, visibility disappears altogether due to heavy rain. As he moves further from Darlington Hall the formerly all-seeing, self-effacing butler, becomes less and less able to observe and more and more observed (by villagers, passers-by, people he meets on his way). From the high position from whence he started his journey with the best view in the whole of England he has descended into the fog-bound valley of Moscombe.
>
> (Doyle 1993: 74)

Near the start of the novel, Doyle adds that the reader 'determines that the narrator is inauthentic' or unreliable. Much of the subsequent tension arises from the question whether the narrator will 'come to agree' with the reader (74). This question is answered in the final point of view of the narration which occurs in Weymouth. Located 'on a pier projected off the mainland in the very south of England', Doyle argues that Stevens is so to speak 'no longer quite in England'. As a result, he can finally 'see himself as [an entity] distinct from it' (75).

Kathleen Wall's article was cited earlier in the discussion about split or fractured subjectivity. The bulk of her essay on *The Remains of the Day* challenges the traditional understanding of unreliable narration. Wall contends that:

> [T]he novel challenges our usual definition of an unreliable narrator as one whose 'norms and values' differ from those of the implied author, and questions the concept of an ironic distance between the mistaken, benighted, biased, or dishonest narrator and the implied author, who, in most models, is seen to communicate with the reader entirely behind the narrator's back.
>
> (Wall 1994: 18)

As opposed to older theories that emphasize distance between implied author and narrator, Wall asks what happens when narrators 'admit their unreliability'. Furthermore, she asks, 'What bearing does it have upon our perception of unreliability if the narrator provides the means for correcting his or her unreliability – consciously or unconsciously?' (21). These questions are taken up in an illuminating discussion of Stevens, who according to Wall is unreliable in the following ways. He uses certain verbal markers – in particular the appellation 'you' – when he makes problematic judgements (24). His description of events clashes with the interpretation that he gives to them (24–8). The order in which events are narrated in the novel provides clues about things that he finds difficult to deal with, and hence might misrepresent or gloss over (30–4). These instances yield the general headings: 'Discourse' (23), 'Scene and Commentary' (24), and 'Order and Duration' (30), to which Wall adds a fourth, 'Naturalization', to refer to the reader's use of general and historical knowledge to sort out discrepancies (28). She offers these four categories as a new and better way to ascertain and explore unreliable narration in texts, as opposed to older theories which she effectively dismantles and undermines.

In an influential article on *The Remains of the Day*, Phelan and Martin also take up the question of unreliable narration which they link with the closing sequences of the novel. Using the text as a case study, the authors suggest that traditional notions about unreliable narration need to be supplemented by other considerations. Apart from focusing on whether 'the kind of unreliability' is about 'facts, values, or both', they suggest that narrators can also be wrong about matters involving 'knowledge and perception' (Phelan and Martin 1999: 91–2). Along these three distinct axes of communication, narrators can be unreliable in two different ways. They either fall short or they distort. Consequently, Phelan and Martin distinguish six different kinds of unreliability: misreporting, misreading, misregarding, underreporting, underreading and underregarding (95). They add that this taxonomy is meant to be a 'heuristic' tool rather than a fixed template (96). Just as importantly, they propose that narrative theory should move beyond strictly formal concerns to adopt a rhetorically conscious stance, one that focuses on 'the ethics of reading' (100). They distinguish themselves from Wall on this basis.

This proposed approach is illustrated through an in-depth discussion of Ishiguro's novel. At certain key moments in the text, Phelan and Martin argue that the responsibility for disambiguating unreliable text is transferred 'from Ishiguro and the signals in the narrative to the flesh-and-blood reader' (102). They discuss in this context their own conflicting interpretations about the text. They propose that the 'deciding factor' in how readers disambiguate is '*individual ethical beliefs as they interact with* [one's] *understanding of Stevens as a particular character in a particular situation*' (103, emphasis original). In this regard, the novel activates the reader's 'desire' for a storybook ending; it also hints that it 'cannot be fulfilled' (105).

The link between narrative and ethics is also pursued by Adam Newton, who was cited earlier about the use of first-person narration. Newton's larger concern is with the ethical consequences of reading. Taking his intellectual bearing from Levinas, Bakhtin and Stanley Cavell, he argues that, independent of any paraphrasable content that one may draw from stories, the very act of reading entails ethical response and engagement – '[t]he story is its own lesson' (Newton 1995: 17). Newton sets out to explore 'narrative *as* ethics', by which he means 'the ethical consequences of narrating story and fictionalizing person, and the reciprocal claims binding teller, listener, witness, and reader in that process' (11, emphasis original). He suggests that there are three types of ethical structure prevalent in narrative: the narrational, the representational and the hermeneutic. Narrational ethics refers to 'the exigent conditions and consequences of the narrative act itself'. Representational ethics refers to 'the costs incurred in fictionalizing oneself or others by exchanging "person" for "character"'. Hermeneutic ethics refers to 'the ethico-critical accountability which acts of reading hold their readers to' (17–18). *The Remains of the Day* fits this schema in a section of Newton's book where he explores 'the tie between narrational and hermeneutic ethics' (246). He argues that as a 'fictive' autobiography that examines the nature of autobiography (what happens when people share stories about themselves, taking others into their confidence), Ishiguro's novel helps to 'train readers in an ethics of secrecy' as 'vigorously moral' as any of the texts produced by Victorian society (275). The novel solicits from readers an 'ethical surplus'. It 'presumes on our sympathy [and] our tact'. Ultimately it shows that 'reading sometimes demands the contrary sign of looking away, of stopping short, of realizing that texts, like persons, cannot be entirely known' (284–5).

Finally, the use of unreliable narration in *The Remains of the Day* is also addressed by Amit Marcus. Marcus brings together narrative theory and the investigation of self-deception undertaken in analytical philosophy. In contrast to the commentators above, he points out that Stevens oscillates between 'reliability and unreliability' in the text. 'As a result, the reader oscillates between clues that reinforce Stevens's version [of events] by making it cogent and reasonable, and clues that undermine it' (Marcus 2006: 134). In this regard, Stevens also complicates the analytical understanding of self-deception. Two different explanations of self-deception are given in this area of study, both of which assume that 'the beliefs of the subject are *relatively stable*'. For Marcus, Stevens's oscillating narrative suggests that there is a need to revisit those assumptions (145, emphasis original).

FURTHER READING

Phelan (2005) provides a user-friendly introduction to narrative theory. His book contains an edited version of the Phelan and Martin (1999) essay outlined above. Nunning (2005) gives a good overview of some recent developments in the study of unreliable narration.

Ishiguro, multicultural Britain and postcolonial studies

In the early 1980s, Ishiguro was often grouped with Timothy Mo and Salman Rushdie and the three collectively labelled as writers to watch because they added new contours to the British literary landscape. The critic Bruce King commended them for bringing a 'new internationalism' to the general cultural milieu (B. King 1991: 192). No doubt they attracted attention because they brought new, non-Anglo voices to the mainstream literary discussion. However, their prose styles [105] and thematic concerns are markedly different, and the alacrity with which they were lumped together suggests that literary commentators were themselves responding to social inclusion concerns generated by an increasingly multicultural populace. Arising from the influx of immigrants from the Commonwealth that started around 1948, Britain faced a slew of socio-cultural challenges, a need to redefine its whole sense of self. This debate over 'multicultural' Britain [51] acquired great urgency because conservative politicians in the 1970s and 1980s tended to scapegoat minorities for the distempers of the time. According to one commentator, the language of imperial nostalgia that they deployed carried at times a 'subliminal racism': the term 'greatness' played a significant role in this discourse and in certain respects operated as 'a tacit but widely recognized code for white England' (Su 2002: 563). We don't get with Ishiguro works that articulate a collective immigrant narrative. The term 'Anglo-Japanese' lacks the semantic density of its 'across-the-pond' equivalent Japanese-American or Asian-American [34, 145]. There is little of that reading experience that a non-Anglo name on the book cover sometimes signals, as writers explore the dramatic possibilities offered by protagonists wrestling with the Scylla and Charybdis of enclavism on the one hand and absorptionism on the other. Nevertheless, bicultural affiliation and migrant self-fashioning issues have a substantial place in Ishiguro's work. In the discussion below, these concerns and the pertinent readings will be reviewed, followed by an elaboration of how Ishiguro's work is addressed in the field of postcolonial studies.

Like the fiction of some migrant or minority writers located in the West, some of Ishiguro's early fiction seeks to create conditions that allow genuine cross-cultural dialogue and interchange. The short story 'A family supper' addresses this issue using what Ishiguro calls a 'big trick' (Mason 1989b: 343) [93]. Furthermore, Rebecca Walkowitz points out that it is not just readers who are set up for a deflationary ending. The Japanese narrator, who has spent time overseas, is himself surprised at his father's condemnation of his work-obsessed business partner. He has 'assumed' that he knows 'what his father's values are' – they are diametrically opposed to his – and is surprised to find his father endorsing his opinion (Walkowitz 2001: 1060) [94]. Walkowitz writes insightfully that, 'By addressing Japanese stereotypes within his work, Ishiguro prefigures and theorizes the interpretations that have come to pursue him' (1053). Chu-chueh Cheng (2005b) concurs as well that the repudiation of stock or simplistic motifs is an important feature of Ishiguro's work. The way in which *A Pale View of Hills* rewrites a canonic work – Puccini's *Madame Butterfly* [18, 33, 117] – in order to counter exoticist discourse echoes as well some of the writing strategies used in diasporic and postcolonial writing.

Ishiguro's position on this matter is registered in an open letter that he wrote to Rushdie in 1993. The letter was one of over twenty solicited from various artists and published on the third anniversary of the *fatwa* proclaimed against Rushdie. It formed part of a collective gesture of support. Ishiguro states in his letter that he bought Rushdie's controversial 1988 novel, *The Satanic Verses*, and read it on a recent train journey. When he got home he 'continued to read it right through to the end'. He said that he found 'marvellously expressed' in it themes such as the 'longing for love, the warring forces within one who both embraces and rejects his origins, [and] the search for moral parameters in a world of chaos and flux'. He adds that 'Having myself settled in a country other than the one of my birth, I could identify with many of your characters' feelings'. In an age marked by 'migration' and 'multi-culturalism' he was convinced that 'countless others' around the world would discover in Rushdie's novel 'a valuable exploration of their hopes and sadnesses' (Ishiguro 1993b: 79–80).

It is with *The Remains of the Day*, however, that Ishiguro offers his most powerful appeal for social inclusion [53, 145]. The writer Caryl Phillips recognized as much when he selected a nine-page section from the novel for an anthology that he edited, titled *Extravagant Strangers: A Literature of Belonging*. Published in 1997, the collection showcases the work of thirty-nine British writers born outside Britain. The earliest extract is taken from a work published in the eighteenth century. Phillips explains in a preface that 'For many British people, to accept the idea that their country has a long and complex history of immigration would be to undermine their basic understanding of what it means to be British'. One of his objectives for the collection was that 'readers will come to accept that as soon as one defines oneself as "British" one is participating in a centuries-old tradition of cultural exchange' (Phillips 1997: xv–xvi). The extract from *The Remains of the Day* spans pages 23 to 31 of the Faber and Faber edition of the novel and tellingly includes the section where Stevens shares his hilltop deliberations about national 'greatness' (*ROD* 28) [50]. Phillips explains further that while Ishiguro's life appears 'unencumbered by the trappings of empire', his work exhibits 'an often microscopic concern with the nature of Britishness' (xv).

In its broad outlines, the above appears to form part of a gathering critical consensus [44, 155] on *The Remains of the Day*. Rushdie's oft-quoted comment that the novel subverts 'the fictional modes from which it at first seems to descend' was taken up by critics (Rushdie 1991: 244), and the twist that Ishiguro gives to the country house novel form [7, 54, 79, 117] is now an acknowledged feature of the book. For Barry Lewis, 'One of Ishiguro's main motivations for writing *The Remains of the Day* was to produce a book which was not only about Englishness, but also engaged with recognisable English literary traditions' (Lewis 2000: 11). Luke Strongman adds that through its 'satire of [the] British gentlemanly tradition', the novel 'carries the implicit suggestion of a need for a more culturally encompassing British national identity'. As Stevens 'awakens to empire's twilight', he also casts a 'metonymic silhouette on a multicultural British nation' (Strongman 2002: 174). John Su argues that because of the way it undercuts Stevens's allegiance to the elitist order represented by Darlington Hall, the novel 'demand[s] a notion of Englishness that accommodates a wider class spectrum'. Su adds that, despite his limitations, Harry Smith's 'demand for a more inclusive *ethos* envisions a future that would have a place for difference and marginality in ways excluded by earlier estate novels like [Evelyn Waugh's] *Brideshead Revisited*' (Su 2002: 570, emphasis original). For Sarah Gibson, *The Remains of the Day* 'employs the trope of the English journey in order to deconstruct the dominant heritage myth of Englishness in the Thatcherite 1980s' (Gibson 2004: 44). Steven Connor asserts in addition that:

> The purpose of the performance of national identity that is *The Remains of the Day* is ... to let in what such a restricted imagining of identity relies on keeping out. It aims to enlarge the possibilities for narrating identity across and between cultures and their alleged essential characteristics and conditions by performing the impossibility of a more constrained, coherent imagination of Englishness.
>
> (Connor 1996: 112)

For Brian Shaffer, the novel doesn't just present Stevens's repressive and 'deceptive self-conception', it also targets 'an entire nation's mythical self-identity' (Shaffer 2006: 174). Dominic Head contends that the novel is 'a devastating portrait of repressed Englishness and an exploration of those national characteristics that must be expunged before an authentic post-nationalism can emerge' (Head 2002: 156). Head uses his discussion of the novel to preface a chapter on 'Multicultural personae' in a book discussing contemporary British fiction. Similar ideas are expressed by Bruce King (1991) and Laura Hall (1995). And moreover these readings fit Homi Bhabha's observation that *The Remains of the Day* is a 'temporal montage' made up of a 'three-leveled palimpsest'. According to him, it layers together: 'the authoritarian populism [53] of the Thatcherite late 1980s (its moment of enunciation)', the 'Suez-centered mid 1950s with its post-imperial "confusions" (the historical "present" of the narrative)', and 'the countryhouse, patrician fascism of the fellow-travelers of late '20s and '30s' (Bhabha 1995: 13–14).

Apart from its deliberation under the rubric multicultural Britain, Ishiguro's fiction has attracted a fair amount of attention from the related (and overlapping) area of postcolonial studies. The fit is an inexact one in one respect and needs to be clarified. As a shorthand for writers linked by birth or affiliation to the formerly colonized parts of the world, it is inapplicable to Ishiguro. Japan itself offers an unusual example of secondary imperialism, when in response to ominous incursions by the West it modernized itself in one generation, defeated the Russian navy in 1905 and embarked on its own programme of expansion. At one stage it even had its own equivalent to the United States's Monroe Doctrine, declaring through the Amau Doctrine that China was vital to its economic and political interests, and signalling a desire to assert hegemony there, just as the Monroe Doctrine warned the European empires to keep their hands off South America (Dower 1999: 471).

As a big-tent, internally divergent term for migrant literature and for what a post-imperial world and attendant culture(s) might entail, however, the term 'postcolonial writing' carries weight when assigned to Ishiguro and is worth consideration. His fiction has perhaps a double belonging when put under this heading. It belongs to British literature and it also participates in the more recent growth and promotion of Anglophone writing from non-traditional sites. Ishiguro calls himself an 'international writer' [20] and there is a sense in which the postcolonial label dovetails with that designation. Some of the readings referenced earlier already intersect this field of inquiry. Other important readings include those offered by George (1996), Tamaya (1992), Griffiths (1993), Cheng (2006a), O'Brien (1996) and Ekelund (2005). In the rest of this sub-section, these accounts of *The Remains of the Day* will be reviewed. Postcolonial accounts of *The Unconsoled* and *When We Were Orphans* will then be referenced, after which larger disciplinary considerations will be addressed.

For Rosemary George, *The Remains of the Day* belongs to an alternative canon or counter-canon that she calls 'global English' (George 1996: 1). Focusing on the parallels between Ishiguro's novel and Joseph Conrad's *Heart of Darkness*, George argues that the latter provides a 'strategic fault line' or 'fictional originary for a whole genre of *international* twentieth-century writing in the English language' (90, emphasis original). George takes the phrase 'strategic fault line' from Fredric Jameson. She argues that the specifics of Conrad's 'personal location' and 'the terrain covered by his fiction' mean that his writing can be usefully conceived as a 'generative' site for global English. For her, 'Conrad best serves the genre of fiction in English ... as a site for global writers and readers to enter, experience and exit the western world. The terms of this travel are constantly being transformed and contested in the writing' (89, 98). *The Remains of the Day* according to George fits this category.

In contrast, Meera Tamaya is more concerned with the empathetic impact of *The Remains of the Day*. She argues that Ishiguro is 'unique among post-colonial writers' because he uses 'that consummately economical and British literary form – the novel of manners – to deconstruct British society and its imperial history' (Tamaya 1992: 45). In addition, she asserts that:

> The brilliance of Ishiguro's narrative strategy is such that, just as Lord Darlington has convinced Stevens of the importance and nobility of his diplomatic maneuvering, the intimate tone of the narrative beguiles the reader into a curious complicity with Stevens' point of view; this enables one to empathize with Stevens even as the butler is completely taken in by Lord Darlington. Thus Ishiguro makes it possible for the reader to *experience* every nuance of the cruelly comic hoax which lies at the core of the master/servant, colonizer/colonized relationship.
>
> (50–1, emphasis original)

Like George above, Melanie Griffiths also undertakes a comparative reading of *The Remains of the Day*. She pits it against V. S. Naipaul's 1987 novel, *The Enigma of Arrival*, and notes that both works devote considerable space to an examination of stately home culture. These homes provide 'a powerful social myth of harmony and order in the "Edenic" garden of the English countryside' [50]. They have an 'iconic' function. They are 'ground[s]' over which different constructs of "English values" ... [are] contested', and thus both novels may be said to address the 'postcolonial condition of England' [50] question (Griffiths 1993: 489, 502). For Griffiths, however, *The Enigma of Arrival* is damaged by its patrician affectations. Naipaul's semi-autobiographic narrator makes 'implicit judgements on the social order' represented by the stately home milieu, but he also identifies excessively with the 'malaise it symbolizes'. He fails to 'separate himself from a fascination with the power it once represented'. In contrast, Stevens in *The Remains of the Day* 'takes us directly into a particular social order and system of values, exposing their contradictions despite his limited consciousness' (502). Griffiths adds that there are limitations to Ishiguro's approach. 'His choice of narrator precludes his direct engagement in the heat and passion of the questions raised' (493). For example, the novel broaches without examination the question posed by Harry Smith, namely that of self-determination for the colonies. According to Griffiths, these lacunas arise because of Ishiguro's method of approach. His ploy is to 'suggest important issues and the debate around them' rather than to address them directly. Nevertheless, she is struck by the incisiveness of the novel's examination of the 'restricted' notion of 'Englishness' championed by Darlington Hall (493). This incisiveness makes *The Remains of the Day* 'a muted example of the kind of tactics needed to allow the maneuvering subversive right into the house of fiction' (502).

Like Griffiths, Cheng also brings together *The Remains of the Day* and *The Enigma of Arrival*. She reads them as postcolonial texts that contain unexpected links with late Victorian literature. For Cheng, these two novels present views that were expressed during the colonial era, but that socially and ideologically could not be heard. 'Contemporary Britons' are, for Cheng, 'delayed readers who at last have the ears to listen to what earlier colonial discourse condemned as cacophony' (Cheng 2006a: 5–6). In literary-historical terms, therefore, Cheng suggests that Ishiguro should be 'dually canonized' as both a 'late Victorian' and a 'postcolonial' writer (12).

Opposed to the readings surveyed so far, Susie O'Brien (1996) and Bo Ekelund (2005) argue that *The Remains of the Day* is ultimately complicit with the social order that it portrays. Their accounts stand out from the generally positive reception given to the novel. In an important article, O'Brien asserts that Ishiguro's book is compromised by an over-simplified distinction between Stevens's 'Victorian' deportment and commonplace notions about 'America' – 'freedom, nature, and individualism' – as exemplified by Farraday's more informal demeanour, and especially by his love of bantering (O'Brien 1996: 788). O'Brien argues that this thematic opposition contributes to readings which nonchalantly marshal Ishiguro under a seemingly progressive rubric – e.g. 'polycultural[ity]' – but which in effect fuel a '"world" fiction industry' that works to neutralize and domesticate difference (788). These readings invoke 'a monolithic colonial Britain against which visions of a "noisy and polyglot and many-hued" global village have powerful graphic and ... political appeal' (800). Conveniently 'ignored' in this celebration is the fact that 'the ambivalently constituted force of capitalism' nowadays has the ability to operate in just such a protean and multi-pronged fashion (802). For O'Brien, therefore, an over-amplified distinction between Stevens and Farraday supports the further penetration of the world by transnational capital with all the attendant problems that it causes.

Ekelund concurs with O'Brien on this issue and claims in addition that the novel layers together five different genres: the travelogue, the political memoir, the country house romance, farce and the essay on values (Ekelund 2005: 73). Ishiguro performs a 'labor of transformation' of these genres to suit his own narrative purposes, but ultimately, according to Ekelund, he fails to question contemporary realities (88). 'By deciding to start from the bad old repressed days of Lord Darlington, Ishiguro certainly seems to imply that we are now living in the good new liberated ones with Mr Farraday' (87–8). For Ekelund, the genres cited above bring with them 'a complicitous history'. Ishiguro makes a 'profound investment in the formal maneuvers of evasion, distortion, and self-justification' when he incorporates them into his novel (79). In the end, this means that his novel is ironic but 'not ironic enough'. It excuses itself from 'its own inquiring' or its own field of vision; it fails to recognize the formal limitations that undermine its critical and social insights (90).

Like the other approaches surveyed in this section, *The Remains of the Day* has attracted the bulk of the attention from the postcolonial interpretive field. However, Ishiguro's other works have also attracted some attention from this area. In the case of *The Unconsoled*, Barry Lewis argues that it is strongly postmodernist in its configuration. He asserts that '[p]ostmodernist fiction is defined by its temporal disorder, its disregard of linear narrative, its mingling of fictional forms, and its experiments with language – all of which are to be found abundantly in Ishiguro's novel' (Lewis 2000: 125). Building on Lewis's formulation but also taking issue with it, Pierre François contends that these purportedly postmodernist features are undercut by what he calls a 'spectral return of depths' (François 2004: 77). It hints from a postcolonial ethical and aesthetic vantage point that a strong version of the postmodernist rejection of subjectivity [112] is ultimately untenable. In this regard, François argues, the novel 'draws upon modernist [representational] strategies to indict the postmodernist rejection of depths (on the psychic plane) and community (on the social plane)' (77). Ryder in his estimation 'has never learnt to look inwards for a better comprehension of inner self and outer world'. In consequence, he 'projects his own splintered psyche on his fellows'. Because '[o]nly exponentially expanding chaos can ... result from the projection of chaos', this means that *The Unconsoled* expresses a certain 'pathos of the human condition' rooted in Ishiguro's nostalgia for a time when '"the complexities of a still unified self" were being explored in fiction, and "the convention of psychological depth" had not [yet] been jettisoned' (89). Comparing *The Unconsoled* with the work of the Guyanese writer Wilson Harris, François adds that chaos can be understood differently. For Harris, the 'artistic experience of fragmentation is a creative process involving an opening of the channels of primordial memory', and this then endorses a rekindling of 'the flame of community'. This process gives the lie to the idea that man can be a 'self-sufficient social animal' (90) [147]. Through the 'chinks' in *The Unconsoled*'s 'schizoid narrative', therefore, 'a post-colonial alternative (ethical and aesthetic) can be discerned for postmodernity's alleged spiritual predicament' (77).

As for *When We Were Orphans*, the account given in Part 2 asserts that it rewrites a canonic text in order to highlight the colonial spoils underpinning the social mobility enjoyed by the chief protagonist. By implication, it also stresses the neocolonial arrangement of the current world system. To the extent that it successfully conveys these ideas, the novel engages with some of the key concerns of postcolonial studies. For Brian Finney, the novel is also notable for its insights into colonialist discourse and behaviour. In the course of the novel, Finney argues,

> Ishiguro forces the reader to recognize that the representatives of colonialism, [Banks and others], while attempting to foist onto the colonized the stigma of eternal childishness, are in fact themselves childlike, having evaded maturation by projecting the unacceptable within themselves onto the subjects of their colonial discourse.
>
> (Finney 2002: par. 2)

On her part, the writer Joyce Carol Oates observes in a review that Banks has a habit of forgetting things. She suggests that 'Banks's growing amnesia ... is symptomatic of a generalized cultural amnesia regarding British and European exploitation of China' (Oates 2000: 21).

Apart from individual text-centred readings, the wider theoretical implications of Ishiguro's fiction have been addressed by Nico Israel (2006), Homi Bhabha (1995) and Neil Lazarus (2005). Israel contends that Ishiguro represents a kind of boundary or limit case for postcolonial studies [145]. His fiction raises, according to Israel, 'thorny questions concerning identity and representation that have gnawed at the foundations of postcolonial theory since its inception'. In particular, it raises the question whether the label 'postcolonial literature' hinges on the 'ethnic' identification of the author, 'thereby extending segregated categories produced ... [by] colonialism itself', or whether it applies to any writer who depicts 'colonial or postcolonial experience' (Israel 2006: 95).

Bhabha's observation on *The Remains of the Day* being a three-levelled palimpsest was quoted earlier. His wider argument concerns the kinds of cosmopolitan identity that might develop from an initial patriotic or nation-centred affiliation. As is usual in Bhabha's work, he rejects in near absolutist terms the merits of such an affiliation. His particular target is the version of cosmopolitan identity promoted by the political theorist and Aristotle scholar Martha Nussbaum. Nussbaum suggests that cosmopolitan attachment arises when 'the "self" [located] at the center of a series of concentric circles' moves successfully and productively through these circles. The task of 'the citizen of the world' is to work through 'familial, ethnic, and communal affiliation' to an identification with 'humanity as a whole', and for Nussbaum this is overall a positive development (Bhabha 1995: 6). Bhabha rejects the formulation given by Nussbaum and among other things confounds her neat stratifications by pointing to *The Remains of the Day*. In his opinion,

The brilliance of Ishiguro's exposition of the ideology of service lies in his linking the national and the international, the indigenous and the colonial, by focusing on the anti-semitism of the inter-war period, and thus mediating race and cultural difference through a form of difference – Jewishness [45] – that confuses the boundaries of class and race and represents the *insider's outsidedness*.

(Bhabha 1995: 14, emphasis original)

Striking a different and more cogent note, finally, Lazarus reads Ishiguro's first three novels as impassioned acts of protest against contemporary conditions that inhibit the formation of community. He argues that the cognitive and emotional impacts of these works are not harmed by the individual acts of betrayal committed by their chief protagonists. We glimpse behind 'the unseeing eyes and unknowing thoughts' of these characters a larger socio-utopian 'yearning for fellowship or collectivity'. 'The sadness that suffuses Ishiguro's work is finally of the order of philosophy' (Lazarus 2005: 432). Furthermore, for Lazarus, these concerns are rehearsed in the works of many important writers who tend to be sidelined by postcolonial studies. The works of these unjustly neglected authors suggest, in Lazarus's opinion, the need for an 'alternative theory' of postcolonial literature, one that questions entrenched shibboleths and outmoded ways of thinking (435).

FURTHER READING

Excellent introductions to the field of postcolonial literature can be obtained from Lazarus (2004), Desai and Nair (2005) and McLeod (2007). Parry (2004a, 2004b) gives a penetrating critique of some of its dominant trends and practices.

Ishiguro and psychoanalytic criticism

Psychoanalytic criticism tends to mistrust the surface claims of a text in favour of investigating its submerged or 'latent' meaning. One good example is the idea that jokes often reveal the deeper intentions of individuals who cannot say things in a direct way. A better example, one that has entered the general culture, is the idea that 'Freudian slips' tell us the 'true' intentions of speakers, maybe in ways they themselves cannot appreciate. This tendency to home in on the hidden or half-hidden meaning of language is also a feature of the psychoanalytic criticism of Ishiguro's fiction. In some cases, it helps to clarify how narrators and characters use the defence mechanisms of the ego – denial, projection, repression and so on – in their interaction with each other or just in the way they tell a story. Simplifying drastically, many of these readings start from the text and move 'inwards' to explore the conflicted operations of the psyche. Jacqueline Rose (1996) offers an account of *The Remains of the Day* that breaks the pattern – she moves outwards, as it were. Her reading will be reviewed first, followed by a survey of the pertinent commentary on *The Unconsoled*. Lacanian and other readings of Ishiguro's fiction will be surveyed in the rest of the sub-section.

Rose starts from Freud's correspondence with his good friend Wilheim Fliess (1858–1928), who often acted as a sounding board for his ideas. Among the salient features of this correspondence, Rose observes that Freud actually distinguished fantasies (*Phantasien*) from dreams. Dreams 'travel back from perception to [the] unconscious' but fantasies are 'progressive': they always head 'for the world' that they appear 'to have left behind'. Freud was also convinced that he would soon discover 'the source of morality'. As Rose relates it, it took him a quarter of a century to pull together the different strands of his thinking about these issues. His conclusion was that: 'guilt for crimes not committed', 'unconscious wishes' and 'troubled identifications' are all things that form 'the basis, the emotive binding, of social groups'. Rather than flee reality, therefore, fantasy is from the outset of Freud's thought associated with 'the question of how subjects tie themselves ethically to each other and enter a socially viable world' (J. Rose 1996: 3). It 'plays a central, constitutive role in the modern world of states and nations'. Moreover, 'it always contains a historical reference in so far as it involves, alongside the attempt to arrest the present, a journey through the past' (4–5).

For Rose, understanding fantasy like this allows great insight into why the 'modern definition of Englishness' puts as its centrepiece the Second World War. It allows us to understand why it proclaims a loud no to 'appeasement', to the iniquity represented by Nazism (69) [160]. *The Remains of the Day* presents this ethical project with great clarity through Darlington. However, Rose argues that in its journey through the past, the novel also ties Englishness with other situations normally thought of as distant to it – with South Africa, and with the Israel/Palestine situation. The 'literary map of the [English] world' is customarily drawn to deny these references (64). Nevertheless, the novel resists this move by telling the story of how Stevens's elder brother, a soldier, was killed during the Boer War. He 'died quite needlessly' during 'a most un-British attack on civilian Boer settlements' (*ROD* 40); and Stevens's father subsequently has to serve the general who ordered this carnage. If we consider that the 'immediate legacy' of the Second World War is the founding of the state of Israel, then, Rose argues, these two 'zones of influence' actually 'make their presence felt underneath or even at the surface' of Ishiguro's novel (J. Rose 1996: 64, 69). If appeasement is the key and 'what is at issue is silence, something failing to pass into speech', she is concerned with the 'continuing investment in apartheid' by certain sectors of British industry and society (67). She also asks rhetorically: 'What does it do to our modern definition of

Englishness if we place appeasement on one side and on the other the ongoing drama of Israel/Palestine?' (69).

The Unconsoled is Ishiguro's most openly experimental novel and most of the commentary on it is inflected with psychoanalytic concepts, although a, so to speak, full-fledged treatment has yet to be tabled. When it first appeared many reviewers noted its oneiric or dream-like qualities (Menand 1995; Rorem 1996) [66]. Barry Lewis adds that events in the novel appear to follow the logic exemplified by Freud's concept of displacement (Lewis 2000: 105). Displacement is one of the distorting operations that occur when we dream; and dreams are, for Freud, basically a kind of disguised wish-fulfilment where dream-thoughts latent in the unconscious are given manifest articulation. Lewis argues that 'displacement of space' is especially important in The Unconsoled. He asserts that: 'The unnamed town through which Ryder wanders has the sinister narrow alleys of a painting by Giorgio di Chirico and the impossible geography of a print by M. C. Escher' (108). Gary Adelman adds that the 'artistic aim' of the novel is to 'externalize the central character's interior life by means of doubles' (Adelman 2001: 178). Peter Childs suggests that '[t]he book's title in itself seems to be a variant on "the unconscious"' (Childs 2005: 137). He calls The Unconsoled, 'Ishiguro's most explicit treatment of creative misremembering and the anxiety [113] the individual pours into trying to come to terms with the past' (139). Natalie Reitano (2007) contends on her part that Ryder's narrative contains elements of a trauma recovery process. She investigates the process by referencing the work of Giorgio Agamben and Dominic LaCapra.

In addition to the above, Ishiguro's work has attracted a number of readings from critics who take their intellectual bearing from Jacques Lacan (1901–81). Lacan is considered by some to be the true intellectual heir of Freud. The workings of language feature greatly in Lacan's reconfiguration of Freud's ideas, so he tends to have a significant impact in literary and cultural studies, whereas the picture in psychoanalytic therapy is more complex. For the purposes of this sub-section, a brief recount of Lacan's main concerns is helpful before we move on to the individual readings. Freud, we may recall, had offered a structural model of the mind as an entity made up of ego, id and superego. Extending and reconfiguring this model, Lacan focused attention on the intersection between mind, language and reality both interhuman and material. For Lacan, the three structural orders that explain all psychoanalytic phenomena are the *symbolic*, the *real* and the *imaginary*, all of which have a specific technical meaning divorced from our everyday understanding of these terms. These three orders are central to Lacan's thought, and of the three the symbolic is the one most crucial for psychoanalysis: it determines subjectivity. Becoming a subject means that one is inserted into the symbolic order; it has a pre-established dimension. One characteristic of this order is that meaning is continually being deferred, a rough analogy being the idea that an entry for a word in a dictionary leads merely to another entry and so on. No entry (or signifier) has a meaning in isolation from the rest. Meaning derives from the system of mutual differences between all signifiers in a culture or language. Resulting from this premise, Lacan also has a unique way of explaining how desire operates. In a useful elaboration, Dylan Evans notes that desire for Lacan is diametrically opposed to what we understand as 'need'. A need can be met and as a result 'ceases to motivate the subject until another need arises'. In contrast, desire 'can never be satisfied'. It is 'constant in its pressure, and eternal'. Put in a nutshell: 'The realisation of desire does not consist in being "fulfilled", but in the reproduction of desire as such' (Evans 1996: 37).

Among the criticism in this area, Renata Salecl's account of *The Remains of the Day* is probably the most well known. Interestingly, Salecl speculates that the title of the novel is directly related to Freud's notion of 'days residues', and this is confirmed in a recent interview by Ishiguro [9, 111]. Salecl notes that in Freud's theory of dreams, days residues are 'the events, the residues of the previous day, that acquire a new meaning in dreams because of the unconscious structure in which they get embedded'. She suggests that 'By reading Stevens's memories with the help of this Freudian concept, it can be said that the remains of the day concern primarily the memory of his relationship with Miss Kenton' (Salecl 1996: 182). Salecl's conjecture is confirmed by Ishiguro in an interview with the *Paris Review* in which he says that the title came to him during a writers' festival he attended in Australia. He relates that at one point he enjoyed taking a break at the beach with several friends and writers including the Dutch poet Judith Herzberg. Among the things that came up in conversation, the group played a 'semi-serious game' of trying to find a title for his 'soon-to-be-completed' novel. Ishiguro says that he kept having to explain that it was about a butler:

> Then Judith [Herzberg] mentioned a phrase of Freud's, *Tagesreste*, which he used to refer to dreams, which is something like 'debris of the day'. When she translated it off the top of her head, it came out as 'remains of the day'. It seemed to me right in terms of atmosphere.
>
> (Hunnewell 2008: 52)

As for the novel proper, Salecl offers the provocative argument that in its thematic arrangement, love is not set against professionalism [142, 149], as it might appear to many readers. What Stevens actually desires are 'the masks of decency, professionalism, and asexuality' that seem to block him from his desire. In Salecl's opinion,

> It is useless to search in Stevens for some hidden love that could not come out because of the rigid ritual he engaged himself in – all

of his love is in the rituals. Inasmuch as it can be said that he loves Miss Kenton, he loves her from the perspective of submission to the codes of their profession.

(Salecl 1996: 185)

Salecl reaches this conclusion by referencing Lacan's explanation of how the ego-ideal operates. In Salecl's words, '[t]he ego-ideal is the place in the symbolic with which the subject identifies. It is the place from which the subject observes him- or herself in the way he or she would like to be seen'. For Stevens, this point or place is more or less made up by 'the principles or code of the butler's service' (184). So in the terms set by Salecl's argument it is cogent to claim that he loves the rituals of his job. Love arises in the first place only because of his devotion to duty and vocation.

Pursuing this line of thought, Richard Rushton notes that Salecl's argument implies a 'renunciation of all self-interest' on Stevens's part. It implies that Stevens 'sacrifice[s] [himself] to the ego ideal'. It appears from this standpoint that he is the 'very opposite of a narcissist', that he devotes himself to pleasing another person rather than himself. For Rushton, nevertheless, the 'satisfactions' that Stevens derives from the ego-ideal 'are deeply narcissistic'. Returning to Freud's work on this topic, Rushton argues that, for Stevens, 'it is no less than the ego itself that is put in the place of the ego ideal' (Rushton 2007: 114). He 'clearly derives a sense of supreme fulfilment and enjoyment from his devotion to the ideal'; but this isn't surprising because his devotion dovetails nicely with 'the narcissistic strivings of his own ego'. In this regard, Rushton contends, Stevens 'lives a life of terror' (115). His example is one of three different 'modes of terror' (109) that Rushton delineates as part of a wider discussion of certain analytic claims made by the French theorist Jean Laplanche.

Apart from Salecl, Charles Sarvan also relates Lacan's notion of the symbolic to Ishiguro's writing, in particular to Masuji Ono, the chief protagonist of *An Artist of the Floating World*. For Sarvan, Ono is 'caught in the webs of a symbolic order in which privileged but "contaminated" signifiers float free' (Sarvan 1997: 93). Ono has a way of undercutting himself by saying that words attributed to one person in a flashback sequence might have stemmed from someone else or even from himself. This trait exemplifies in Sarvan's opinion the 'associative' and 'metonymic' features of the symbolic order (95). For Lacan, the symbolic is additionally a stage that occurs when human development ventures beyond an obsessive preoccupation with the primary care giver. The key to this stage is a move from a dyadic relationship to one that involves three parties. Sarvan ventures in this context that 'Ono's symbolic stage' (his narrative) works to entangle 'the addressee/reader' in the fictional present. It is characterized by 'isolation, evasion and lack of clarity' (99) [43].

In much the same way, Molly Westerman applies the ideas outlined above to Stevens in *The Remains of the Day*. Quoting Lacan, she says that Stevens is 'caught in the rails ... of metonymy'. This means that he is 'eternally stretching forth towards the *desire for something else*'. Westerman notes that at the end of the novel, Stevens promises to develop the skill of bantering. His 'obsession grasps for a new object'. It moves from item to item hence leaving 'his symbolic structures more or less in place' (Westerman 2004: 169, emphasis original). In this context, Westerman argues, the 'ambivalence and inconsistencies' in Stevens's language tell us what he himself doesn't know. It shows us 'how his experience as a split subject is constituted, and how it constitutes him' (157).

Adopting a different slant from these accounts, Karl Jirgens prefers to use Lacan's concept of the '*real*' to clarify Stevens's 'ironic and dialogical self-portrayal' (Jirgens 1999: 221, emphasis original). Lacanian inflections can also be found in Earl Ingersoll's reading of *Never Let Me Go*, which he says 'allows us to explore an otherness that in the end may serve as a reflection of our innermost experiences as "normal" human beings' (Ingersoll 2007: 55). Taken together, the readings outlined so far can be usefully contrasted with Ben Winsworth's account of *The Remains of the Day*. Winsworth deploys in his reading a theory proposed by the British psychoanalyst D. W. Winnicott, namely that a distinction can be made between the 'true' self and the 'false' self (Winsworth 1999: 259). His understanding of otherness (the 'false' self) arguably departs from the readings above and offers an alternative point of view on this issue.

Returning to *Never Let Me Go*, Keith McDonald also deploys Lacan's theory of the subject to explain the novel. Furthermore, he links it to a critique of narrative genre, in this case to autobiography. Referring to the final scene where Kathy returns to Norfolk and 'surrenders to a fantasy in which those she has lost return to her', McDonald suggests that the field she stands in acts as a figure for what the novel itself has been doing all this while. The novel 'represents the symbolic field, where past things surface, and the reader and narrator exist at either side of this landscape, each looking for traces of lives lost' (McDonald 2007: 81–2). For McDonald, this situation showcases the 'autobiographical exchange' that 'occurs, to some degree, in all texts' (75). The traditional idea that autobiography is a bounded form privileging 'authenticity and empirical authority' is thus questioned and undermined by the novel (80) [111]. As a 'speculative memoir' in which 'autobiographical exchange is both pervasive and effective', *Never Let Me Go* invites us to abandon the notion of authenticity and to rethink our customary notions about form and genre (75).

Eluned Summers-Bremner also discusses *Never Let Me Go* but is more concerned with the Lacanian distinction between humans and animals [157]. She notes that animal communication 'operates entirely within the field of the biological'. In contrast, human language 'exiles human beings from direct access to our instincts, rendering our primal impulses conflicted, [and] prone to endless meanings' (Summers-Bremner 2006: 146). Language understood in this sense confers a fundamental impasse on human experience, one that Never Let Me Go pits as its 'central problem', namely how we deal with death [82], with the fact that for all of us it is pre-given and by definition unthinkable from 'within the bounds of reason'. For Summers-Bremner, Ishiguro's willingness to address this issue gives Never Let Me Go a trenchant edge over current formulations about posthumanity [85, 156], which tend to concentrate on issues involving science and technology. Until they come to terms with the concerns raised in the novel, however, these formulations are 'doomed to be forever wishful' (154).

Finally, Deborah Britzman turns to the work of the British psychoanalyst Melanie Klein, which she uses to examine Never Let Me Go. She reads the novel as 'an occasion for thinking about reading as an allegory of psychic development'. In particular, it 'may be read as a commentary on the internal world of object relations, where Ishiguro's characters stand in relation to our affective representations' (Britzman 2006: 307).

FURTHER READING

Wright (1991) gives an excellent introduction to psychoanalytic criticism. Vice (1996) brings together several important readings in this area. Fink (1995) and Evans (1996) provide useful expositions of Lacan's theory of the subject.

Ishiguro as an international writer

This sub-section testifies to the geographical reach of Ishiguro's work, and to a sense in which his fiction is seen as representing certain large social and cultural trends. Ishiguro's work has been taken up in comparative literature, in Asian diasporic literature, and in the field of US multiculturalism. It has been linked to East Asian cultural analysis conceived in broad terms. Partly because of Ishiguro's self-ascription as an 'international' writer [20] who wishes to write novels where thematic considerations take precedence over historical and social reference (Ishiguro and Oe 1991: 115; Shaffer and Wong 2008: 145), his work has drawn attention from the burgeoning new field of cosmopolitan studies. Related to this development, it has also been drawn into the study of an emergent middle-class consciousness that considers professionalism to be a new transnational ethic. As will be clear from the survey below, Ishiguro's fictional project arguably tracks an ongoing convergence in some of these fields and domains. We will start with a review of the pertinent general considerations before moving on to the listed topics.

One way to understand what motivates the investigation of the themes identified above is to attend to an argument proffered by Bruce Robbins.

Robbins contends that a pressing ethical and theoretical project of our times is a better understanding of the transnational socio-economic and cultural influences that surround us. He argues that:

> We are connected to all sorts of places, causally if not always consciously, including many that we have never traveled to, that we have perhaps only seen on television – including the place where the television itself was manufactured. It is frightening to think of how little progress has been made in turning invisibly determining and often exploitative connections into conscious and self-critical ones, how far we remain from mastering the sorts of allegiance, ethics, and action that might go with our complex and multiple belonging.
>
> (Robbins 1998: 3)

When We Were Orphans is arguably a work that explores and articulates this thesis. It frames its concerns under the heading proposed by Robbins, and in fact uses the same word, 'connectedness' (*WWO* 6) [72] in order to rewrite Dickens's *Great Expectations* [70, 118]. This idea is backed by the general stance of other Ishiguro works, by *The Gourmet* [99], by *The Saddest Music in the World* [101] and by the short story, 'A village after dark' [97]. The appeal to readers to differently imagine their attachments and affiliations is keenly suggested at one point in *When We Were Orphans* when the chief protagonist says that the Shanghai International Settlement [77, 99] is basically his 'home village' (*WWO* 256). In literary historical terms, such an emphasis can be considered a geographical extension of E. M. Forster's 1910 novel, *Howards End*, whose motto is the phrase that it famously uses as an epigraph, 'Only connect … '.

The claim that *When We Were Orphans* explores what transcultural or transnational fellow feeling might entail has been endorsed by a number of commentators. Brian Finney argues that 'In Ishiguro's fiction to be orphaned, to be deprived of parental security, becomes a trope for transnational identity, for doing without a fatherland or motherland' (Finney 2002: par. 2). Timothy Weiss asserts that 'It would be an exaggeration to claim that the novel conceives of identity as nomadic, but its title metaphorically suggests the difficulty of locating identity … It also suggests that place and identity are discontinuities rather than persistent unities' (Weiss 2004: 139). Concurring on this issue, Lisa Fluet adds that '[t]he detective careerism advocated by Banks … holds out the possibility of international "well-connectedness" as a substitute for national feelings of membership' (Fluet 2003: 112). Also sharing this emphasis, Shao-Pin Luo argues that despite its problematic status as an enclave created by imperialism, the International Settlement is a powerful and compelling metaphor:

The International Settlement in *When We Were Orphans* may yet provide a transcultural vision for a possible world of redemption. Even as it remains utopian and illusory, and in reality, as an adult Banks realizes ... an imperialist enclave on Chinese territory, an international hybrid space holds the only hope we have in this world, in order to live side by side, in harmony.

(Luo 2003: 79)

Apart from *When We Were Orphans*, these concerns have also been raised in the critical discussion on *The Unconsoled*. Due to its unwieldy dimensions and psychological complexity, this work has not attracted the attention that it deserves. Reviewers of the novel tend to focus on the central protagonist's (Ryder's) abrogation of his family responsibilities. On this point, Katherine Stanton allows that 'the sacrifice of an emotional life to a sense of professional duty' is an important theme for Ishiguro (Stanton 2006: 10). Nevertheless, she argues that the myriad tasks that Ryder gets saddled with work against our understandable tendency to circle the wagons when confronted with complex challenges. The unconsummated status or 'non-finality' (8) of these tasks is precisely the point being made, namely the range of legitimate calls on our attention. In this respect, the novel 'alerts us to the pervasiveness of claims on us ... of the difficult necessity of deciding among our many pressing obligations' (12). Stanton summarizes her argument in the following manner:

I take Ryder's insignificant duties (to attend a dinner party, to support a local cause, to listen to a struggling musician rehearse, and so on) as the source of the significant ethical point the novel is making. Representing as an everyday problem the tension between a singular and a universal responsibility, the novel invites us to treat the problem of multiple demands *as* a problem to be struggled over.

(Stanton 2006: 5, emphasis original)

For Stanton, therefore, *The Unconsoled* is a work that 'expand[s] our capacities for ethical agency and political action across the shifting borders of the nation and into a cosmopolitical field' (8).

Without making these larger socio-political connections, John Carey has suggested that *The Unconsoled* 'is about stress, a problem of epidemic proportions in our culture that modern fiction largely ignores' (Carey 2000b: 163). In a separate discussion of this feature of the novel, Robbins takes the point that it deploys a 'shared vocabulary of everyday over-commitment, overload [and] harriedness' [153] in order to communicate with far-flung readers. However, he notes that it also plays with our customary notions of time and space. The city that it describes could be home and everywhere, local as well as foreign. The novel doesn't specify the language used, there are 'no translation problems' and 'no maps, street plans, or calendars'. By combining 'a citiscape of classical abstraction' with the non-stop demands made of Ryder, the novel 'creates the atmosphere of a prolonged anxiety dream'. But in the same breath, Robbins contends, 'it also jokes ambiguously about the plenitude of additional commitments that it would be possible to take on, and the importance one's works and days might then assume, if only the usual limits of time and space did not apply'. In the process, Ishiguro allows readers to imagine what it might mean if they had 'the *freedom* to overcommit' (Robbins 2001b: 430, 437, emphasis original). Among other things, Robbins pays attention to Gustav, a porter in the novel who has a dual characterization as Ryder's father-in-law. He argues that the novel enjoins an inclusive society that is at the same time cosmopolitan and non-parochial. It suggests that 'in order to cohabit with less indecency in a world of immigrants, refugees, and strangers ... we need a broader and more inclusive civility, and the civility of the city can be a daily model and training site for it' (439–40).

Robbins extends his meditation on civility and the common good in a recent discussion of *Never Let Me Go*, which he reads as an allegory of how public services operate in the modern welfare state. The novel's chief protagonist, Kathy, is a 'carer' (*NLMG* 3). The book features a school where clones are taught to accept their fate as spare parts for original humans. For Robbins, these aspects of the novel allow it to function as a metaphor for social class and the hypocrisies that surround it [118]: as an 'organ-donation gulag' it is 'tucked away from public view and yet not kept fully secret' (Robbins 2007: 200). Robbins doesn't mention *The Gourmet* [99] but the line of development from the play to the novel supports his conjecture that the novel can be read as a commentary about social stratification. Robbins's wider point is that many deeply loved novels attain that status because they are what he calls upward mobility stories. These stories were made possible *by* the modern welfare state – because it encompasses in complex ways our most cherished hopes and dreams. Despite its achievements, however, Robbins suggests that the bleak final scene of *Never Let Me Go* looks ahead to some unfinished business (232–3). The history that went into the making of a sense of the common good (common welfare) is precious, it defines the West. Nevertheless, for Robbins, it is also an 'incomplete project' (242). If readers are to remain faithful to those dreams that they seek in art, that project should be shared or broadened to a 'planetary' level; it needs to encompass the rest of humanity outside the West (243).

In the case of *The Unconsoled*, Natalie Reitano argues in contrast that the positive gloss it gives to cosmopolitan affiliation is undercut by its manner of approach. Reitano allows that Ryder's behaviour brings across to readers the 'urgency of worldly (cosmopolitan) responsibility' (Reitano

2007: 380). However, she argues that he also undermines it because the situation described in the novel is so abstract and so unconnected to any 'national or historical context'. Without such contextualizing references, the socio-political vision promoted by the novel becomes 'fantastically outsized and perversely limited'. In this regard, Reitano contends, Ishiguro 'takes to task ... his own version of the universal' (362). He puts into the novel a vision of what cosmopolitan identity might entail but he also criticizes it.

As can be seen above, Ishiguro's recent work takes seriously his self-ascription as an 'international' writer [20]. Among other things, he addresses the hotly contested issue of globalization. This aspect of his work has generated a number of readings – Robbins (2001a), Fluet (2003), Trimm (2005) – which seek to connect his fiction with the growth of a global middle-class consciousness. More specifically, these accounts investigate the issue of professional ethics, of the body of ideas that underpin the self-understanding of individuals in this class. In some respects, these readings echo the discussion of Stevens undertaken in legal circles: the concern there is whether Stevens is a good model or exemplar of lawyerly professionalism [135, 159].

Robbins's account of *The Remains of the Day* is influential and deserves attention. For him, the novel is important because it provides insights into an emergent '*middle*-class internationalism' (Robbins 2001a: 17, emphasis original). It points to the idea of connectedness described above. His hope is that in the future it will generate a concerted effort to redress global social inequality, to tackle a situation where '20 per cent of the [world's] population consumes 86 percent of the resources' (18) [102]. On the face of it, Robbins notes, *The Remains of the Day* indicts the version of professional ethics espoused by Stevens. However, he outlines two considerations that might give us pause to question that viewpoint. First, he argues, there is a 'real historical possibility' that Darlington might have been right about the freezing of German war reparations during the inter-war period (27) [152, 160]. It is conceivable that this act could have prevented the Second World War. In addition, Robbins points to a recollection by Stevens's close friend, Mr Cardinal, about the 1923 conference held at Darlington Hall. In a conversation with Stevens, Cardinal recalls that he heard a man – Senator Lewis – accuse Darlington in public of being a useless, bungling amateur. Cardinal says that he was right to call him that; he wants Stevens to use his influence with Darlington so that he won't become too close to the Nazis. For Robbins, the novel endorses Cardinal's stance on this issue. He would soon be killed by the war and hence speaks 'with the authority of his imminent death' (27). In light of these considerations, Robbins asserts that:

> Something is clearly going on if the term *professionalism* can refer both to Stevens's ideological self-mystification and, at the transnational level, to something like a solution. This double reference opens up the logical though still mysterious possibility that

professionalism like the butler's might somehow belong to a new transnational ethic.

(Robbins 2001a: 28, emphasis original)

In addition, Robbins offers two other observations to back up his argument. He notes that the character Harry Smith in *The Remains of the Day* embodies 'the clearest, most democratic antithesis' to Stevens's sense of professionalism. Smith's name suggests that he represents the 'common man' (28). He is passionate about fighting Hitler and about the importance of representative democracy at home, but he is also equally passionate about the need to preserve the Empire. In the novel, he criticizes another character (Dr Carlisle) for supporting the idea that 'all kinds of little countries' should be allowed to go 'independent' (*ROD* 192). If supposedly the biggest critic of professionalism also champions 'imperialism', Robbins argues, the novel may not be so 'antiprofessional' after all (Robbins 2001a: 28). In addition, he asserts that the relationship between Miss Kenton and Stevens should not be framed as a tussle between the demands of work and the demands of private life. Their love develops from their deeply shared passion for the professional codes to which they *both* devote their lives. For Robbins, this aspect of their relationship is actually a cultural phenomenon of our times. It points to a 'historically emergent eroticizing of expertise and of the social bonds for which expertise stands' (29). In this regard, *The Remains of the Day* allows great insight into current global conditions. It gives hope that cosmopolitan identification will have a progressive impact on the world, that it won't become another way to repeat the damage caused by 'social hierarchy' (23).

Lisa Fluet also tackles this topic in a reading of *When We Were Orphans* which she uses to investigate American middle-class culture. She first draws a link between Raymond Williams's study of Victorian class society and Ishiguro's fiction, which for her is an 'ironically belated meditation' on the themes raised by Williams (Fluet 2003: 109). Among other things, Williams had argued that the upper servants of Victorian estates possessed divided and unexamined beliefs that are also a feature of the self-understanding of certain 'contemporary middle-class service professionals' (Fluet 2003: 100). Fluet sees this feature embodied obviously in Stevens in *The Remains of the Day* and more piquantly in Banks in *When We Were Orphans*. In a sense, both Banks and Stevens have to resolve the contradictions inherent in their situation, one that is indicative of the 'fundamentally bifurcated psychic life of modern agency' or modern personhood (110). Our senses tell us that even devoted selfless work might not do much in the larger scheme of things; it doesn't alter the essentially iniquitous nature of the society we 'pretend' to buy into (108). But at the same time, Fluet argues, we also need to hold such 'self-awareness' and even 'self-loathing' at bay (110). Readers might cock a snook at Stevens's conviction that in serving the 'the hub of this world's wheel' (*ROD* 126) [46], he accomplishes a lot. Nevertheless, as

Fluet sees it, that 'inherent powerlessness' also applies to us. Responsible 'utilization' of our services by individuals 'closer to "the hub" of social action' describes our lot in life (Fluet 2003: 110). We too labour under the same dispensation. For all his limitations, therefore, Fluet argues that Banks's careerism makes him potentially a force for social progress. His 'servant complex' lays the groundwork for Fluet's meditation on the work of the American social theorist and activist Barbara Ehrenreich (106).

On the topic of professionalism, Ryan Trimm adds that Dr Carlisle is radically different from Stevens. The novel indicates that Carlisle went to Moscombe in 1949 as a physician dispatched under the new National Health Service set up the previous year (*ROD* 210). For Trimm, he represents a vision of modernity in which 'professionals play a mediatory role between larger institutional systems they represent and a specific community they serve'. Seen in this context, Moscombe signifies a 'modern, bureaucratic, and socialist imagined community, one whose welfare state offers an institutional version of the *Gemeinschaft* ideals figured in a country village'. The affection and respect that the villagers show for Carlisle thus extends 'beyond the communal level of Moscombe'; it represents 'faith in the new postwar national social contract' (Trimm 2005: 143).

In addition to these approaches and concerns, Ishiguro's work has also been taken up in the field of comparative literature. The biggest influence here is arguably Rebecca Walkowitz, whose commentary on Ishiguro stands out as among the most insightful and illuminating. For Walkowitz, Ishiguro is an author who exemplifies 'new world literature' or 'comparison literature' (Walkowitz 2007: 218). His fiction exemplifies what she calls 'cosmopolitan style' (Walkowitz 2006: 20). Among its attributes, she argues that Ishiguro likes to use the trope of the 'echo' (2007: 223). He offers an 'ongoing critique' of 'uniqueness' and he also mulls over 'global paradigms such as the network, the tradition, and the scale' (218). Furthermore, Walkowitz asserts that his writing encourages us to think of translation [11] as something positive rather than negative. Instead of leading to '*cultural homogenization*' as some critics argue, it can lead to its opposite, to greater diversity and dialogue between the world's cultures and nationalities (216, emphasis original). Ishiguro uses the terms 'rephrasing' [19] and 'conversation' to describe his relationship with readers, so perhaps the echo trope identified by Walkowitz stems from this method of approach (Kenney 1995: 47).

With regard to the translation issue, Megumi Arai is however more uncompromising. Arai argues that *A Pale View of Hills* and *An Artist of the Floating World* present readers with a 'true-to-type and yet curiously unrealistic Japan' (Arai 1990: 30). Etsuko's stiff, formal English brings to mind certain 'English translations of Japanese novels'. They transport the reader into 'the Westerner's image of Japan – the Japan of Ozu, Kawabata, and Tanizaki seen through Western eyes'. In consequence, and '[f]or the Western reader':

[T]here is nothing unpredictable or disturbing about this Japan; it is exactly a picture of what one would expect post-war Japan to be like. Ishiguro of course presents this picture as that of Japan seen through the eyes of a woman apparently alienated from her own country, thus preventing the reader from expecting a realistic representation of that country. The reader is therefore never certain whether he is looking at Ishiguro's picture of Japan itself or at his idea of Japan as seen through Westernized eyes.

(Arai 1990: 30)

Apart from the debate over new world literature and the effects of translation, Ishiguro's work is also addressed in the field of Asian-American literature [34, 124]. An interesting anecdote here is the one related by Tomo Hattori. Hattori describes a question posed at an Asian-American panel held during a conference of the Modern Language Association of America. As Hattori describes it, one of the presenters was asked to 'explain' Ishiguro. Ishiguro's work was not referenced even in passing in the presentations. At the mention of his name, however, 'the session dissolved into a free-ranging discussion on the definition of Asian American literature, and Ishiguro's name became the test of that boundary' [131]. Furthermore, the panellist who fielded the question said that 'Ishiguro is a baffling and enigmatic case of a writer who neither writes about his own ethnicity nor about ethnic themes' (Hattori 1998: 218). Hattori takes this incident as an opportunity to discuss widely held assumptions about the field. He argues that it assumes Asian diasporic writers have a natural impulse to write '"in character" as an ethnic subject', to proffer 'ethnic autobiography' (217). Under this interpretive dispensation, 'Ethnic writers who do not write about their own ethnicity are seen as baffling and enigmatic in their resistance to what is assumed to be their "natural" impulse to write about ethnic national selfhood' (219). Such a template takes for granted the idea that writers and texts must be discussed under a 'pluralist' idiom of inclusion [53, 125]. But in the process, Hattori argues, it fails to recognize certain attendant dangers; it neglects the possibility that 'US ethnic groups' might become 'apologists for the further penetrations of the world by American capital, culture, and political ideology' (228).

Slightly tangential to this discussion but pertinent to its founding assumptions, Kwame Appiah contends that liberalism on one side and multiculturalism on the other are not necessarily at loggerheads. In an important article cast as a contribution to political philosophy, Appiah offers an account of *The Remains of the Day* that forms part of a wider discussion of the work of John Stuart Mill. Reading Stevens 'against the grain', he says that for all his faults he chose and lived the life of a butler, a model professional. Appiah argues that 'This picture of self-creation places identity at the heart of human life. Liberalism, I am suggesting, takes this picture seriously and tries to construct a state and society within which it is possible' (Appiah 2001: 315, 329). In Appiah's opinion, therefore, the founding principles of liberalism – 'liberal faith in allowing people to make their own lives' (330) – and the ethico-political commitments of various discourses of identity are not necessarily incompatible.

For Sheng-mei Ma, nevertheless, Etsuko's narrative in *A Pale View of Hills* fleshes out a problem that he sees as endemic to 'Asian Diaspora' writing (Ma 1998: 40). Using this term allows him to usher Ishiguro into a broadly US cultural context. For Ma, Etsuko is deluded about her innocence when she mis-remembers Keiko in place of Mariko as the one who went on a day-trip to Inasa, the hill-park overlooking Nagasaki Bay: this incident is a 'selective, if not fabricated, moment of happiness' that Etsuko assumes in order to 'defuse' her role in Keiko's suicide (54–5). Etsuko's delusion underpins Ma's charge that Asian minority (and Asian-American) writers have a tendency to paint first-generation migrants in self-orientalizing terms as incipiently 'schizophrenic' figures, thus endorsing the prejudice that they have a tendency to do crazy things (41).

Ma expands his critique in a subsequent essay to include the trajectory of Ishiguro's work from *A Pale View of Hills* to *The Unconsoled*. Because Ishiguro resorts to 'pop psychology' or the 'banality' of the minority person's 'divided self' in his portrayal of Etsuko, Ma complains that he fails to take on the burden of self-representation (Ma 1999: 81) [34]. Ethnic minority characters do not feature in his novels after *A Pale View of Hills*, and for Ma this points to a 'suppression of ethnicity' because Ishiguro fails to address his position as 'an Asian minority living in the West' (72, 81). Ma suggests that the use of White protagonists in *The Remains of the Day* and *The Unconsoled* is a reaction against 'Orientalist' responses to Ishiguro's earlier work (80). As 'universalist parables beyond identity politics', however, their increasing stylization and abstraction imply that Ishiguro has undergone a '*reactionary* cooptation into a dream world of postethnicity' (74, 72, emphasis original).

On this issue, Adam Parkes registers the concerns raised by Ma but suggests that the 'best writing on Ishiguro's handling of such issues … is marked by a certain caution'. That hesitancy 'serves as further testimony to the narrative and stylistic subtlety on which so many readers have remarked' (Parkes 2001: 76). As examples of such readings, Parkes cites the reviews of Ishiguro's work written by Ihab Hassan (1990) and Hermione Lee (1990). As to the question of Etsuko's blameworthiness, Michael Wood argues that the novel is 'not very interested in settling this sort of question at the level of the literal'. It would be surprising if Etsuko did not people the universe with doubles who point the finger of guilt at her and shout out her culpability as regards the treatment of Keiko. For Wood, it isn't surprising that Etsuko enters a 'blasted landscape where not being a good mother and killing your child are the same unspeakable thing, where it takes only one dead woman, not the 39,000 men and women massacred outright by the Nagasaki bomb, to turn the universe into an allegory' (M. Wood 1998: 180–1). As a survivor of two unspeakable tragedies, it would be surprising if she didn't act this way.

In contrast to its deliberation within American multiculturalism, another category of readings – Oyabu (1995), Rothfork (1996, 2004), Zinck (2004) and Weiss (2004) – relate Ishiguro's work to East Asian cultural and philosophical practices. Kana Oyabu argues that Ishiguro's early works are 'crosscultural' fictions inflected in part by Eastern metaphysics (Oyabu 1995: 261) [106]. John Rothfork argues that Ishiguro's first three novels 'need to be read as related' so that we can appreciate *The Remains of the Day* as a work that articulates 'a Buddhist criticism of Confucian ethics' (Rothfork 1996: 82). In contrast, *The Unconsoled* is 'better explained by Confucianism than by postmodern views and methods'. By '[s]huffling images' of Ryder into and out of various characters that he encounters in the novel (Boris, Hoffman, Gustav, Brodsky), Ishiguro, according to Rothfork, guides readers to the 'Confucian recognition' that individual development cannot take place in a vacuum [130]: it can only occur within the 'human relationships' that bind us to one another and to society (Rothfork 2004: par. 2).

Pascal Zinck on his part compares Ishiguro's early fiction with the Japanese literary tradition known as *shishosetsu* or self-novel [11]. He says that while Ishiguro's work should not be appraised according to the 'strictures' of this form, his first two novels do 'show ... affinities with the rhetoric of confession' that underpins it. For Zinck, 'the narrator's restricted scope, the palindromic structure of Ishiguro's fiction, the absence of an ending and a plot pared down to a minimum can all be traced back to the *shishosetsu*'s aversion to teleology' (Zinck 2004: 145). Weiss in turn draws on Buddhist concepts to elucidate *When We Were Orphans*, which according to him exemplifies 'emptiness'. Referring to the non-realist narrative techniques used in the novel, Weiss argues that Ishiguro 'defamiliarizes conventional conceptions of place and identity, pushing them towards the indefinable; [as a result] a certain oriental composition of mood is all that remains'. The reader may ponder questions about the nature of place and identity. But '[w]hen you think about them long enough, you may find that they begin to float away' (Weiss 2004: 144).

Finally, brief mention should be made of the commentary on Ishiguro published in English in Japan-based journals. These include the accounts offered by Yoshioka (1988), Arai (1990), Wain (1992), Klein (1994, 1995) and Mallett (1996). Arai's views on the translation 'impression' of Ishiguro's early work were cited above. Putting aside Arai's concerns, the readings referenced here tend to focus on Ishiguro's early writing and to adopt a belle-lettrist approach to criticism. They offer keen insights into style, structure and use of language. As to the question of how Ishiguro is received in Japan, Chu-chueh Cheng in an essay cites a thought-provoking news article written by Norimitsu Onishi. Onishi's commentary appeared in the *International Herald Tribune* and claims that Ishiguro's name when mentioned in the Japanese press is cited using the phonetic characters for foreign words (*katakana*) rather than the characters taken from Chinese (*kanji*) [17]. The same is applied to Alberto Fujimori, the former president of Peru who is of Japanese descent, and this is done in order to indicate their 'alien' status. In this regard, Cheng argues, Ishiguro is 'globally exotic'. He is 'alien to Britain, Japan, and the rest of the world' (Cheng 2005a: note 13).

FURTHER READING

Willett (1998) provides a good introduction to some key issues in the international debate on multiculturalism. Cheah and Robbins (1998) do the same for cosmopolitan studies. Lechner and Boli (2000) and especially L. Weiss (1997) give illuminating insights into globalization related issues and controversies.

Other readings

Apart from the approaches reviewed above, *The Remains of the Day* has been taken up in a number of areas – pedagogy, management theory, legal ethics – that involve what philosophers call practical reasoning: the use of reason to decide what to do and how to act. This is a testimony to the novel's extraordinary fecundity and potent impact on readers. This sub-section surveys these responses and also looks at the way in which Ishiguro's work is addressed in human rights and feminist discourse, and in the wider philosophical discussion about ethics. *Never Let Me Go* is starting to attract some attention pertaining to these and other areas. Given the ongoing advances in biotechnology, it will potentially have a great impact on the wider cultural debate about the shifting parameters of human nature or human-ness. These responses will be reviewed in the final part of the sub-section.

For Anthony Lang and James Lang, *The Remains of the Day* is both a historical novel and a teaching text; it is extremely useful for the international relations (IR) classroom. They assert that it is useful for IR courses because it allows students to 'understand more accurately the role that theory plays in forming and analyzing practice' (Lang and Lang 1998: 209). One important feature of the novel is the insight it gives into the 'value-laden' character of theory (210). In addition, Lang and Lang cite the work of Cynthia Enloe, which they credit for unveiling the gendered assumptions underpinning several practices in public life, including the way in which international diplomacy operates. One finding that arises from her work is that the promotion of diplomats in many instances is based upon an evaluation not of himself but of his partner, who is assessed on her ability to facilitate informal exchange, on whether she can 'provide an atmosphere conducive to productive interaction'. The authors argue that Stevens plays this role in *The Remains of the Day* (Lang and Lang 1998: 213).

Outside the political science arena, Knights and Willmott also use *The Remains of the Day* as a case study in their investigation of how power and inequality function in the workplace. Cast as a contribution to the field of management, Knights and Willmott assert that the novel provides 'an exceptionally sensitive account of power and inequality at work' (Knights and Willmott 1999: 88). They use Stevens's situation in the novel to prefigure their discussion of the more sophisticated analysis of power relations offered by Steven Lukes. Using Stevens as an example, they offer their own modulation of Lukes's three-dimensional model of power (95–8). They also discuss Max Weber's ideas about bureaucracy in relation to *The Remains of the Day*, as well as Frederick Taylor's ideas about scientific management (130–4). The authors' conclusion is that the study of power and inequality in the workplace is 'no less central to the study of management and organization than it is to other aspects of society' (117).

In addition to these accounts, *The Remains of the Day* has also been taken up in the area of legal ethics where it is basically read as a meditation on professionalism [135, 142]. The main focus in these accounts is on the dilemma that Stevens faces when asked by Darlington to dismiss two Jewish maids. His rationalization of his actions as permissible under an ethics of impersonal service is examined by Wendel (1995), Atkinson (1995), Luban (1996) and Pang (2005). These authors situate the novel in the context of contemporary debates about the role of lawyers in society. Luban notes as well that the novel has featured on the curriculum of a number of ethics teachers at American law schools (Luban 1996: 297).

For W. Bradley Wendel, *The Remains of the Day* is the 'literary equivalent' of certain situations which force lawyers to 'confront head-on their competing duties as advocates and as officers of the court' (Wendel 1995: 162). In situations where lawyers are asked to represent 'unsavory clients', Wendel observes that 'the dominant picture of legal ethics' allows the adoption of an amoral view, one that puts into practice 'the principle of nonaccountability': 'In this amoral view, lawyers are Teflon professionals – none of their clients' slime sticks to them' (165). Stevens's initial attitude towards Darlington exemplifies this position. Wendel examines the reasons (analogous to the ones cited by Stevens) for adopting such a 'role-differentiated' notion of morality – in which one's role in society is invoked as an excuse for some conduct or behaviour that would 'ordinarily be subject to ethical condemnation' (162). Stevens had so rationalized when he undertook unpleasant tasks on behalf of Darlington. He said that his job was to serve him unswervingly, and through him, humankind. Wendel discusses consequentialist and non-consequentialist arguments for adopting such a position as well as the wider pressure put on the legal profession to practise 'whole law' (174). He suggests that overall there *is* a need to question the prevalent stance on this issue.

Referring to a point in the novel where Stevens proclaims the importance of 'loyalty *intelligently* bestowed' on an employer (*ROD* 201, emphasis original), Wendel concludes that: 'Stevens pondered throughout his service to Lord Darlington whether Darlington was worthy of loyalty. Lawyers, if they wish not to be "lesser butlers", should ask the same of their clients' (Wendel 1995: 190).

Rob Atkinson echoes Wendel's argument in certain respects but also highlights other considerations like the importance of dialogue between different parties and the fit between theory and practice. He asserts that in the debate on this issue lawyers face two great difficulties:

> On the one hand is the risk of embracing, individually or collectively, flawed perfectionist ideologies of professionalism, mirages that seduce us with the promise of either moral nonaccountability or easy moral answers. On the other hand is the risk of discarding all forms of professionalism as discredited ideology or hypocritical cant, thus despairing of meaningful professional lives.
>
> (Atkinson 1995: 180)

For Atkinson, a careful analysis of *The Remains of the Day* offers a plausible solution to this predicament, 'a mediating, tragic vision of professionalism, somewhere between the perfectionist and the nihilistic. It is a professionalism that accepts the imperfection – indeed, the imperfectability – of both individuals and institutions without rejecting the possibility of virtuous professional lives and cultures' (180). In this context, Atkinson suggests that greater dialogue between the different parties involved can help alleviate the difficulty faced by Stevens. Analogous to the relationship between Stevens and Darlington, greater dialogue is needed between 'professionals and their principals' (196). Analogous to the relationship between, interestingly, Stevens and his father, greater dialogue is also needed between 'professionals and their peers' (205). As an example, Atkinson offers the following rewrite or 'reconstruct[ion]' of what Stevens could have said to Darlington when asked to dismiss the two maids. He wonders 'what might have been' (196) if Stevens had said:

> I'm terribly sorry, sir, but I consider it part of my duty, in discharging an employee, to give an account of why he or she is being dismissed ... Moreover, I have a duty to my employer not to convey to anyone, of whatever station, the impression that my employer has acted without good reason, much less arbitrarily or dishonorably.
>
> (Atkinson 1995: 197)

Only about a third of Atkinson's imagined proclamation is cited here. It is worth noting that he offers a manner of responding to literature that is different from all the other accounts surveyed so far in this volume. His creative insertion of a 'missing' scene in the novel departs from the usual analysis undertaken through expository prose.

In addition, Atkinson suggests that Stevens and Miss Kenton exemplify respectively two 'very different, if not quite antithetical' schools of thought on the issue of lawyerly professional responsibility, namely 'neutral partisanship' and 'moral activism' (216). In the novel, Stevens and Miss Kenton had 'unfulfilling professional lives', yet 'we are left with the impression not so much that their theories failed them, but that they failed their theories and, more fundamentally, their employer and each other'. Atkinson insists that in a 'moral' crisis situation both theories allow their adherents to 'remonstrate with the employer, to recommend the morally appropriate, not merely the legally permitted, course of action' (216). In a larger sense, he asserts that their 'dual failure is attributable not so much to internal inconsistencies or other weaknesses in these particular theories, as to weaknesses in this kind of theory as the basis for moral life' (217). Their failure underscores a more general issue, namely that all normative theories involve an agent who must judiciously apply them to particular cases, thus raising questions about the fit between the general and the particular. In addition, Atkinson contends that inter-generational differences in *The Remains of the Day* actually help to illustrate this point. 'Stevens astutely points out that his father's generation was given to telling stories about professional excellence, whereas Stevens's own generation preferred general theorizing. What his own story marvelously illustrates, however, is the way the two must fit together' (218).

From a literary scholarship perspective, the best account in this area is arguably the one offered by David Luban, who contends that Stevens and Senator Lewis in the novel model radically different versions of professionalism. Stevens exemplifies a 'professionalism of deference' while Lewis exemplifies a 'professionalism of expertise'. Luban prefers the former because the latter comes close to a form of nihilism. It tends to reduce all practical questions to 'a technical question having no moral dimension'. In this regard, it echoes certain ideas expressed by the sociologist Max Weber, who says that modern rationality [163] – the modern world – is marked by a 'disenchantment' akin to a loss of faith. In this world, 'moralism' and 'loyalty' are 'archaic holdovers from an age of superstition' (Luban 1996: 304–6).

Furthermore, Luban contends that both models of professionalism can lead to an 'anesthesia of conscience', one in which 'innocent moral impulse' is suppressed. Pressed to choose between the two, Luban notes that he would select Stevens's version. Nevertheless, he prefers a third version that he dubs the professionalism of '*presumption*', one that assumes the responsibility of 'counseling and even correcting an employer's bad moral judgment' (306, emphasis original).

More importantly, Luban pays attention to Darlington, whom the other accounts surveyed so far tend to overlook. In the novel he is called an amateur by Senator Lewis, but Luban argues that, seen in the proper context, Darlington's 'amateurism' might have prompted the right course of action (310). Luban prefigures in this context an influential argument made by Bruce Robbins (2001a), which is discussed in Part 3, 'Ishiguro as an international writer'. Drawing on illuminating historical research, Luban argues that Darlington's 'generous instincts' captured the 'despair and outrage of the German people who would soon acclaim Hitler as their savior'. He contends that 'the course of history' might have been different if professionals such as Senator Lewis had listened to Darlington (312):

> In 1921, led by the vengeful French, the Allies set war reparations [142, 160] for an already ruined Germany at a staggering 132 billion marks – about $33 billion at a time when national economies were far smaller than they are today. When Germany defaulted on her payments, France occupied the Ruhr industrial heartland ... These events occurred in January, 1923, just two months before Ishiguro sets Lord Darlington's conference. The conference, in other words, takes place in the midst of an international crisis. The German government was printing money as fast as it could to pay the reparations demanded by the Treaty of Versailles. Not surprisingly, hyperinflation set in ... Three months after the conference at Darlington Hall the exchange rate plummeted to 160 thousand marks to the dollar; four months later, a single dollar could buy more than 4 *trillion* marks. In Bavaria, Adolf Hitler's National Socialist Party had grown to 55,000 members and in November 1923 he attempted his infamous Beer Hall Putsch. Though it failed, the German people were, for the first time, turning a willing ear to Hitler's message of hate and vengeance.
>
> (Luban 1996: 309–10)

While Darlington is a manifestly problematic figure because of the way he treats his servants, Luban argues that in this one deployment of his 'unprofessional' conscience he was commendable. The lesson to draw from this is that 'when professional morality commands us to do something revolting to the nonprofessional conscience, the default assumption should be that the nonprofessional conscience has it right and that professional morality is too clever for its own good' (315). In addition, Luban believes that Ishiguro set his imaginary peace conference in 1923 because he 'wanted to choose a time' when Darlington 'may have been right' (310). His conjecture hints at the research that Ishiguro might have done on this project

[111]. If so, its unobtrusive placement in the novel heightens our appreciation of the craft that went into its writing.

Finally, Calvin Pang also discusses Stevens as an example of the professional life gone awry because he fails to grant proper weight to his private life. 'This diminution allows him to squeeze personal morals, values and judgment from his work, and ultimately constricts his map of professionalism.' For Pang, he functions as a cautionary example of 'our addictions to achievement, control, and overwork' (Pang 2005: 409) [140]. This point about stress in the workplace raises a literary-interpretive concern not addressed by Pang, namely the connection between *The Remains of the Day* and *The Unconsoled*. In the account of the latter given in Part 2, the porter Gustav is read as a burlesque of Stevens's father, who can be said to die from overwork in *The Remains of the Day*. The highpoint of this burlesque arguably occurs when Gustav performs a 'Porters' Dance' (*UC* 396) [62], one that involves him juggling several suitcases while dancing on a table-top.

Aside from the American legal ethics tradition, *The Remains of the Day* has also been assayed in connection with the work of the French philosopher Jean-Paul Sartre, in particular with the investigation of bad faith (*mauvaise foi*) undertaken in his major work, *Being and Nothingness*. Compared with his earlier construal as a flawed but redeemable embodiment of lawyerly professionalism, Stevens is arguably more negatively perceived in this area. In an early review of the novel, philosopher Galen Strawson suggests that Stevens echoes the famous examples used by Sartre to illustrate what he means by bad faith (a waiter in a café and tradesmen in general). Quoting from Sartre's text, Strawson replaced the word 'grocer' in the relevant passage with the word 'butler' in order to make his point. Part of the citation is reproduced below. The insertions in square brackets are Strawson's comments:

> Let us consider this waiter in the café [47]. His movement is quick and forward, a little too precise, a little too rapid. He comes towards the patrons with a step a little too quick. He bends forward a little too eagerly; ... his gestures and even his voice seem to be mechanisms ... He is playing [or acting]. But what is he playing? ... He is playing at *being* a waiter in a café. He is playing with his condition in order to *realize* it. This obligation is not different from that which is imposed on all tradesmen [or servants]. Their condition is wholly one of ceremony. The public demands of them that they realize it as a ceremony; there is the dance of the butler, of the tailor, of the auctioneer, by which they endeavour to persuade their clientele that they are nothing but a butler, an auctioneer, a tailor.

(Strawson 1989: 535)

It is in this context that Strawson criticizes Stevens for his obsession with 'acting' a role and for failing to attend to his private life. He asserts that Stevens manages to elicit love from Miss Kenton but is unable to acknowledge it. He 'loves in return, while managing – by sheer force of *mauvaise foi* – to be entirely unaware of this fact' (1989: 535). This line of argument has recently been extended by Michel Terestchenko, who notes that Sartre's concept can be taken in a 'weak' way or a 'strong' way. The former arises from the fact that all of us are compelled to act or 'play roles' in our 'social life' and to move from one role to the next. When we 'volunteer to play a part and invest all our energies in it', however, the strong version of bad faith sets in and brings about 'a radical negation of our freedom' (Terestchenko 2007: 82). In this regard, Terestchenko argues, Stevens violates 'the essential ontological basis of human beings – their freedom, which demands that a radical distinction be made between the private individual and the professional persona, so that they may always come back to their selves and heal their self-division'. Stevens's willingness to theorize about this condition – his discourse on dignity – shows how far he has 'internalize[d]' the rules of the 'dominating class' (83). Ultimately, for Terestchenko, his 'professional ethics of obedience to orders' is abhorrent and unconscionable; it is a kind of 'corpselike obedience', a term that Adolf Eichmann had used during his trial in Jerusalem (87).

Echoing this more sceptical response to Stevens's conception of his role, Michael Meyer also uses his situation to illustrate what he calls '[t]he more egalitarian idea of human dignity' [45, 102] characteristic of our era. Cast as a contribution to the international debate on human rights, Meyer argues that:

> Roughly put ... human dignity is that special moral worth and status had by a human being. One has human dignity regardless of not only (hereditary) social position, but also race, gender, nationality, ethnicity or other markers of social hierarchy. This egalitarian account of 'human dignity' is arguably a moral high-water mark of modern ethical and political thought.
>
> (Meyer 2002: 196)

Meyer contrasts this idea with the classical understanding of dignity derived from Aristotle. He acknowledges that because of his social position, Stevens possesses 'social dignity' or 'the dignity of office'. Nevertheless, the 'pre-modern world of natural and hereditary hierarchy' represented by Darlington Hall doesn't provide 'suitable ground' for the more egalitarian vision that he seeks to elucidate (203–4). Meyer's formulation of the issue is in turn questioned by David Medalie, who says that it basically makes Stevens 'identical with his social status'. For Medalie, this move is problematic because wider social changes have made him an 'anachronistic figure' (Medalie 2004: 53). In his meeting with Harry Smith, for instance, Smith uses the word 'dignity' to mean something totally different from Stevens. In Medalie's opinion, 'The fact that dignity can be employed in the service of such disparate ideologies – one determined to keep things as they are, the other to change them for the better – shows how protean a concept it is, conservative or radical as the case may be' (56). Ultimately, *The Remains of the Day* suggests that dignity is 'fluid in status and meaning' because 'the sociopolitical relations which inform it are themselves in a constant state of change' (55).

In other areas of philosophy, *The Remains of the Day* is referenced in passing by Michael Hardimon in his investigation of what role obligations entail (Hardimon 1994: 348). It is discussed briefly by Russell Hardin in connection with the issue of trustworthiness (Hardin 1996: 29). For Karen Scherzinger (2004), the novel exemplifies several ideas associated with the social theorist Victor Turner, in particular his views about pilgrimage, rituals and rites of passage.

Taken as a whole, Ishiguro's work has not attracted much attention from feminist critics or from a feminist interpretive perspective. The two outstanding exceptions are the readings proposed by Linda Raphael (2001) and Ruth Forsythe (2005). Raphael argues that while we only get a single narrator in *The Remains of the Day*, Stevens's 'masculine discourse' also allows access to 'the feminine responses facing it'. In the 'space' between these two discourses 'lies one that would be true to Stevens's inner life' and needs, but he doesn't possess the language to 'express his feelings' (Raphael 2001: 172). Referring to Ishiguro's professed desire to write 'international novels' [19], Raphael adds interestingly that Ishiguro achieves this goal 'not only by focusing on one individual's complicity with particular national myths, but by juxtaposing these mainly male myths with a nonmythical feminine discourse' (172). She elaborates this idea with particular emphasis on Miss Kenton's (reported) language, presence and role in the novel. This point chimes with assessments of the 1993 Ivory film adaptation that say one of its strengths is the greater attention given to Miss Kenton [161]. The idea that Ishiguro probes and questions a restrictive notion of national identity has become part of the gathering critical consensus on *The Remains of the Day* [44, 126]. Raphael's reading is a rare and substantial extension of this thesis. It points to an underexplored feminist dimension to the novel that arguably merits greater critical attention.

Forsythe's focus of attention is on *A Pale View of Hills*. She explores the key mother–daughter relationship in the novel and argues that it 'compounds' the various types of ambiguity already found in the text (Forsythe 2005: 100). For her, the novel demonstrates that the terms 'mother' and 'daughter' cannot be understood 'merely by unearthing the identity of the individuals' occupying those roles. Instead they are co-constituted by a relationship where 'perspectives vary and needs compete, [hence] often resulting in silence and restlessness' (107).

As for *Never Let Me Go*, one reviewer suggests that the novel offers 'the finest expression of moral disquietude' over bioscience advances since the publication of Aldous Huxley's *Brave New World* over seventy years ago. In this regard, it registers a shift in ethical parameters because advances in medical science threaten the Kantian maxim that individuals should not be 'a means to the ends of others' (Burley 2005: 427). Extending this observation, various commentators have investigated what that putative shift in ethical parameters might mean. They argue that the novel captures different positions in the wider cultural debate over human nature or human-ness [83]. Myra Seaman argues that as an example of contemporary popular cultural notion of the 'posthuman', *Never Let Me Go* 'shares more' with the medieval understanding of this subject than with its 'historical peers', which is to say with 'theoretical and scientific posthumanist discourses' (Seaman 2007: 258) [85, 138]. The novel opposes 'the loss of certain individually bounded identities celebrated by theoretical posthumanism', which trains its sights on the 'liberal' humanist notion of the subject (246, 258) [112]. It also opposes the reduction of human beings to 'the "all mind" hard drive promised by techno-science' (258). What it shares with the medieval notion of the posthuman is the idea that 'vulnerability' is an 'essential' part of 'humanness', and this is also an idea that has a religious or spiritual resonance (250) [88]. Human vulnerability is expressed in the clones' acknowledgement and exploration of their emotional selves and in their belief that 'they might have a future, despite all the evidence to the contrary' (268–9). 'By focusing the novel on the experiences and feelings of the clones ... Ishiguro makes clear that their identity is no different from that of the humans who created them' (265). Referring to the art-exchanges held at Hailsham, Seaman adds that art [82] is shown to be 'necessary to human expression and self-understanding, especially in the midst of a culture in which the greatest demonstration of humanness – of human superiority – is assumed to be scientific, rather than artistic' (269). Seaman's reading chimes with the argument made in Part 2 that 'science' is pushed to the background in this novel. Her account is probably the first to connect Ishiguro's work with the academic study of the middle ages.

In a related vein, Leona Toker and Daniel Chertoff also focus on the novel's 'consciousness-raising potential' (Toker and Chertoff 2008: 178). They argue that *Never Let Me Go* reshapes the dystopian fiction genre [8, 118] to elicit sympathy for Kathy and her peers. It highlights the organ transplant and donation issue, and also the potential abuse of these practices in countries around the world. The novel achieves these goals because among other things the reader 'is made to feel complicit with the social structure that [it] conjures up'. She is 'provoked into self-scrutiny'. Ishiguro's ability to present these issues in a suitably 'aestheticized' form also adds to the effectiveness of the work (177–8).

Rebecca Walkowitz asserts on her part that the novel can be read on one level as an endorsement of certain arguments calling for a change in the way we treat animals [137]. She argues that the human donation system in *Never Let Me Go* is underpinned by an 'unquestioned hierarchy' drawn between humans and animals. At 'many points in the text' we are asked nevertheless to pay attention to this line of thinking. The drawings made by one of the clones, Tommy, allow us to appreciate for instance how 'strategies of abstraction' operate in this area. The result is that some entities are classified as individuals and others are classified as expendable (Walkowitz 2007: 224).

Striking a different note from the readings above, Mark Jerng compares public arguments for and against cloning and suggests that certain normative pressures underpin these arguments. Both sides deploy ideas about pro-creation and about 'the sanctity of the parent–child relation'. They reference family-dynamic paradigms that are missing from *Never Let Me Go* (Jerng 2008: 377). For Jerng, the novel challenges these 'circular narratives' (381) by measuring the human not in terms of some story of internal development but through the quality of the interaction or the 'relationality' that arises between the clones. In this regard, it 'foregrounds an ethical project to discover how cloning might change how we relate to each other' (391).

Film adaptation

The film adaptation of *The Remains of the Day* was directed by James Ivory and produced by Ismail Merchant, with a screenplay written by Ruth Prawer Jhabvala. It stars Anthony Hopkins as Stevens and Emma Thompson as Miss Kenton. It also features James Fox, Christopher Reeve and Hugh Grant, and was nominated for eight Academy awards, winning three. In their adaptation of other modern novels such as E. M. Forster's *A Room with a View* (released in 1986) and *Howards End* (released in 1992), the Merchant Ivory team had acquired a reputation for promoting ersatz nostalgia and fostering an idealized picture of England. This did not change with *The Remains of the Day*. Despite being pertinent to only a small fraction of the population, that iconic picture still plays a large part in the imagination of many individuals. For historian David Cannadine, it plays a paradoxical or 'non-reasoning' role in the national cultural milieu. It says in effect that 'the only paradise we seek to regain is the one which was never ours to lose in the first place' (Cannadine 1997: 100). As suggested in Part 2, '*The Remains of the Day*', this idealized cultural mythology was precisely what Ishiguro wanted to question and explore. Thus from the outset there was always the possibility of a great rift developing between the book and its filmic avatar [65], even allowing for changes integral to the process of translating prose fiction into film. As one critic puts it, the movie 'seems to have appealed to a certain nostalgia for an idealized England of the past – ironically, the very nostalgia against which Ishiguro's novel cautions us (Parkes 2001: 78).

Ishiguro himself is relatively sanguine about such differences. With a German or a French translation, he states in an interview that he would 'expect a certain fidelity' to the original English text. But with film the situation is different. He has to accept that 'there is this other thing that is called James Ivory's *The Remains of the Day* which is a cousin of my *The Remains of the Day* but it is a different work of art' (Shaffer and Wong 2008: 148–9). Ishiguro adds that after a spell writing for television early in his career, he wanted to write novels 'completely unique to the reading experience ... to use purely literary techniques'. As such he thought that the novel was 'entirely unfilmable' because it is 'entirely internal' (Steinberg 1995: 106).

Even so, reviewers and commentators have charged Merchant Ivory with various errors of omission and commission. In a spirit of fidelity to the original, the consensus appears to be that the movie overloads on sentiment and diminishes many important themes and ideas. Nevertheless, upbeat comments or assessments have been tabled by Parkes (2001), Alleva (1993) and G. Rose (1996). Rose provides arguably the most provocative analysis of the film. She questions whether the ersatz nostalgia promoted by the Ivory adaptation necessarily lessens its theoretical and even philosophical interest. In the discussion below, the critical or censorious readings will be recounted, first followed by a review of the more positive commentary.

One recurrent theme in the commentary on the film was that it watered down the political concerns of the novel. In Bert Cardullo's opinion, the movie 'recasts Ishiguro's exquisitely balanced tale more as doomed romance than as political allegory' (Cardullo 1995: 618) [102]. Sarah Gibson argues that the novel mounts among other things a critique of Thatcherite identity politics [5, 52]. In this context, the English landscape is 'deconstructed' as part of the novel's examination of 'Englishness'. This feature is, however, erased in the film, and as a result, Gibson argues, the audience ends up adopting a 'tourist position' in the sections depicting Stevens's motor-car journey (Gibson 2004: 65). Adam Parkes concurs with reviewers who complain that the movie downplays the important theme of dignity. He asserts that, 'There was no need, surely, to omit Harry Smith's contribution to the debate on dignity, unless one wanted to ... mute the note of political protest that runs through the novel' (Parkes 2001: 78).

Related to this issue, commentators also debated arguably the major change that Merchant Ivory made to the novel. Instead of being narrated by Stevens, events in the movie are portrayed through an 'objective camera' perspective that is the filmic equivalent of third-person narration. The opening scene is accompanied by the sound of Emma Thompson's Miss Kenton reciting her letter to Stevens into the film-text, and, a while later, by excerpts from Stevens's reply to her letter. Earl Ingersoll asserts that this voiceover disrupts the 'delicate' ambiguity of the novel. In the book we only get Stevens rendering quotes from Miss Kenton's letter; we eventually 'doubt the accuracy' of his reading, 'as Stevens himself does'. In the film, however, Ingersoll remarks, the reading of the letter into the film-text establishes its bona fide status with a far greater authority (Ingersoll 2001: par. 11) [108].

Compared with Ingersoll, Stanley Kauffmann is more uncompromising about this issue. He argues that the novel's '[first-person] perspective is not merely a literary device' that can be willy-nilly set aside:

> Ishiguro's aim was to show a man so encapsulated in protocols that all the major events of his life, political and emotional, happen on the periphery of that life. We see, through his eyes, more clearly than he does what is happening around him. Ishiguro means this, I believe, as a comment on England. The film fractures his intent.
>
> (Kauffmann 1993: 33)

Parkes states as well that because they shun the voiceover technique (for Stevens), Merchant Ivory 'denied themselves the novel's primary means of expressing the theme of dignity: the private musings of Stevens's narrative (Parkes 2001: 79). Edward Jones adds that in fairness they do try to incorporate first-person stance through the periodic use of a 'subjective camera' (the use of shots simulating the perspective of an individual consciousness so that audience, character and camera 'see' basically the same thing). However, when they do this, the effect is to emphasize 'the male gaze directed at Miss Kenton from upper windows, porthole windows in the servant quarters, and, indeed, at one point, through a keyhole'. In tandem with their 'exchange of looks, stares, and glances', this aspect of the film highlights the 'frustrated-love' theme but weakens 'the social criticism found in the novel' (Jones 2001: 100). Cardullo argues in this regard that a technical balance between first- and third-person stance is difficult to achieve. He suggests that the solution is:

> not to use a first-person camera throughout, to show only what the narrator can see and never the narrator himself, nor to employ large chunks of first-person voiceover narration; what the camera eye must do as much as possible is *see as the narrator in the book does*, see as if it were using the narrator's eyes.
>
> (Cardullo 1995: 617, emphasis original)

In addition to the debate about the use of camera perspective, Bruce Robbins argues that setting the movie in the 1930s instead of the 1920s discounts the possibility that Darlington could have been right. It disregards the possibility that a freezing of German war reparations [142, 152] might have prevented the onset of the Second World War. This change is extremely 'disturbing', for if the stakes were indeed so high, Robbins claims, it is 'much harder to argue' that Stevens's 'extreme, almost inhuman devotion to his professional duty ... [is] a self-evident piece of self-delusion' (Robbins 2001b: 433). In such a situation, his professional commitment to Darlington might have been the right thing.

Another adjustment made by the film is that it omits one of two colonial stories or anecdotes told by the novel [53]. Jacqueline Rose spots this variation and again links it to the theme of dignity. She notes that the depicted anecdote is the one that Stevens's father likes to tell. It involves a butler in India who killed a tiger without fuss so that it wouldn't 'disturb the equipoise of a colonial tea-party' (J. Rose 1996: 67). The one *not* represented is the revelation that Stevens's elder brother, a soldier, was killed during the Boer War. He 'died quite needlessly' during 'a most un-British attack on civilian Boer settlements' (*ROD* 40); and subsequently Stevens's father has to serve the general responsible for the carnage when he visits his employer, Mr Silvers. In so doing, Rose argues, '[t]he film simply gets rid of the story which is the hardest to tell – dignity as mute suffering as opposed to heroic risk'. It downplays the novel's concern with appeasement [133], with what happens when something fails to 'pass into speech' (J. Rose 1996: 67). In this sense, it violates one of the main planks of British cultural identity, namely that the easier course of action is not necessarily the right choice in matters involving the nation. Rose's larger concern is with how these ideas link up with the current Middle East impasse, in particular the Israel/ Palestine situation that is one of the legacies of the British Empire.

In the early stages of production, the book was slated for adaptation by Nobel laureate Harold Pinter, but subsequently Ivory rejected his screenplay in favour of Jhabvala's. For Cardullo, this is an 'unfortunate' development because Pinter has 'proved himself adept at adapting novels with first-person narrators' (Cardullo 1995: 617). He gives as examples some of Pinter's projects such as *The Go-Between* (1970), *The Proust Screenplay* (1977) and *The Heat of the Day* (1989). According to Edward Jones, Pinter was offered co-credit for the screenplay when the picture was released but he declined the offer (Jones 2001: 99). Jones managed to obtain a copy of Pinter's script and he asserts that, compared to the Ivory–Jhabvala treatment, it 'cuts closer to the bone' and 'more deeply into Ishiguro's novel' (107). Among the differences between the two, he states that Pinter's script doesn't collapse Lewis and Farraday into one character, as the film does (103). Near the close of the novel, Stevens confesses to a stranger he meets on the beach at Weymouth that while Darlington 'made his own mistakes' he couldn't even say that about himself. 'Really,' he says, 'one has to ask oneself – what dignity is there in that?' (*ROD* 243). Jones notes that these pivotal remarks are spoken in the film by a man who gives Stevens a lift to his stalled car. It comes at a point quite a while before the end of the movie. For Jones, this amendment is 'the most damaging' among those made by the film, because it alters substantially 'the letter and spirit of Ishiguro's novel' (Jones 2001: 101). In contrast, Pinter's script preserves the novel's inquiry into 'what measure of "discovery" Stevens can lay claim to'. Jones states that 'Pinter has Stevens say and poignantly repeat during this sequence on the beach, "I think I've given all I have to give. I gave it all to him, you see"' (101). Without a completed movie based on Pinter's script, Jones concedes that, 'we cannot know, of course, how well it might have worked'. In a 'cinema of the mind', nevertheless, he asserts that 'it is provocative to speculate on what Pinter's late collaborator, Joseph Losey, might have done with his friend's tougher, more direct, and less ornate screen treatment' of the book (105–6).

Apart from the above, more positive accounts of the movie have also been given. Parkes writes insightfully that 'If the complexity of Stevens's narrative is diminished in the movie, Miss Kenton emerges from the shadows to which Ishiguro's narrator consigns her'. Parkes notes that Emma Thompson's Miss Kenton is forcefully and compellingly portrayed. She is a 'warm-hearted, generous woman for whom the passing years bring increasing frustration'. In contrast, the 'novel's point' seems to be that Miss Kenton 'remains in the shadows because the narrator is unable to acknowledge her as a substantial, living person'. Comparing the two versions 'enables us to appreciate that the novel's exploration of Stevens's sense of loss need not rule out an attempt to imagine what Miss Kenton might be like if she were permitted to live' (Parkes 2001: 81) [155]. It heightens our understanding of the novel. On this score, Ingersoll adds as well that '[b]ecause of its obviously pictorial nature, the film reminds the spectator – as the novel may not reveal to its reader – how exclusively male the world of Darlington Hall is' (2001: par. 19). We might add here that emotional sterility is raised as an issue when Darlington asks Stevens to convey to his godson information about 'the facts of life' (ROD 82). Stevens fails miserably in this mission and the comedy comes at his expense; but given the patriarchal dominance noted by Ingersoll, that comedy also has a larger socio-critical thrust.

Also sharing this emphasis, Richard Alleva contends that the novel is 'almost as predictable as its hero'. He points out that everything Stevens says is meant to be taken in the obverse. If he says that Darlington was a high-minded gentleman, 'you know … [he] will turn to be an incipient Fascist'. If he says that 'his feelings for Miss Kenton were entirely professional, then you must suspect suppressed sexual longings'. Alleva argues that

> It's a stunt and you soon learn the mechanics of the stunt. But it's
> a stunt with a humanistic purpose: cramped inside Stevens's bland

monologue is Kazuo Ishiguro mischievously indicting Stevens –
and through Stevens anyone who fails to live his own life.

(Alleva 1993: 15)

On this score, Alleva prefers the movie because to him it isn't a stunt: the
movie 'immediately' transmits the episodes and incidents of the story-line; it
is told in a linear fashion instead of skipping back and forth in time;
most importantly, the audience doesn't follow the story 'through the veil of
Stevens's language' (1993: 15).

Arguably the most provocative and intellectually demanding reading of the
film is the one offered by Gillian Rose, who marshals the film into a wider argument about contemporary cultural and philosophical malaise. Rose highlights
the way in which the movie 'explores the ethics of the dedicated service of the
head butler ... to a Lord, who tries, from 1923, to lead the British political
class to support the Nazi movement, and then the Hitler government'. Stevens 'finds himself in the contradiction of the ethic of service'. The movie
shows that 'the dilemma of this inspired and blinkered service ... arises out
of and issues in a personality which is loveless, and which wards off and
refuses love' (G. Rose 1996: 51–2). Meera Tamaya has suggested separately
that in the novel the intimate tone of the narrative 'beguiles the reader into
a curious complicity with Stevens' point of view' (Tamaya 1992: 50). The
point that Rose makes echoes Tamaya's and highlights the film's ability to
entice audiences because it 'centres on the drama of the relation' between
Stevens and Miss Kenton, unlike in the novel where 'the political framework and the butler's story are more evenly balanced' (G. Rose 1996: 52).

Rose argues that such a rendition surpasses other renditions of fascism
such as the 1993 movie *Schindler's List*, in which a sheen of 'sentimentality'
prohibits meaningful engagement with the topic (47). In contrast, Ivory's
adaptation 'breaks the barrier of passive sobriety or sentimentality of witness' (52). Caught unawares by its seductive rendering of 'violence in which
not one blow is cast', the film 'dramatises the link between emotional and
political collusion', meaning that we understand from our emotional collusion with Stevens our implication in the forms of violence inculcated in our
own culture – our ability to deny this link is broken down by the film (51,
53). As a result, Rose argues, the movie 'induces active recognition in oneself of the nihilism of disowned emotions, and the personal and political
depredations at stake' (52). In the 'crisis of identification' thus induced, a
'dissolution of particular identity' is attained together with a 'vision of the
universal' (53–4). Instead of following the conventional pattern of seeking
satisfaction for individual interest or engaging in identity politics, we
glimpse through the film what it means to go beyond that.

This last point has wider implications for Rose, who argues that in contemporary continental philosophy all appeals to universal (representative)
notions of 'justice, freedom, and the good' are disqualified 'for being

inveterately "metaphysical", for colonising and suppressing their others with the violence consequent on the chimera of correspondence' (7). It does this because it stays fixed on the line of reasoning that says Auschwitz – the violence wrought on European Jewry in the Second World War – is the end-product and telos of modern rationality [151]. On this account of how modern reason operates, representation in philosophy (the logic of meaning itself), art (mimetic art) and politics are all considered to be irredeemably totalitarian. Rose argues, however, that this line of reasoning shows how mourning is endemic to our culture; it laments 'the loss of securities which, on its own argument, were none such' (11). For her, 'Only the persistence of always fallible and contestable representation opens the possibility for our acknowledgement of mutual implication in the fascism of our cultural rites and rituals' (41). To proceed otherwise is to abdicate one's responsibility to promote and foster the growth of community.

Finally, one of the most intriguing aspects of the book–movie connection is the possibility that Ishiguro might have 'rewritten' certain aspects of *The Remains of the Day* in response to the adaptation – and put it into his 1995 novel, *The Unconsoled*. One of the most striking changes made by the film concerns a scene where Stevens dallies in the corridor outside Miss Kenton's room: she has just received a letter informing her of the death of her aunt; Stevens is unwilling to go in to offer his condolences because he might 'intrude upon her private grief' (*ROD* 176). Later in the novel, however, Stevens tells us that he actually mis-remembered this scene. His hesitation outside Miss Kenton's room occurred a few months later when he failed to intercede after she received a marriage proposal from her future husband (*ROD* 212, 215, 226–7). In the amended, presumably more truthful account of this episode, Stevens recalls that there was 'no real evidence' that he could hear Miss Kenton crying. Nevertheless, he remembers being 'quite certain' that if he were to knock on her door and enter her room, he would 'discover her in tears' (226–7). This event – Stevens's inept dawdling in the corridor – is obviously one of the key events of his life, something he spends time mulling over. It is crucial to the emotional impact of the novel. In the movie, however, the ambiguity and tension attached to the episode is shattered and potentially belittled. As Cardullo describes it:

> In Ivory's film, as you might guess, the door does get opened and Stevens discovers Miss Kenton in tears, only to advise her that some household article wants dusting! Further, after the butler departs, the camera remains on Miss Kenton, regarding her heart-broken face in a way that Stevens could never bring himself to do.
>
> (Cardullo 1995: 619)

In *The Unconsoled*, Ishiguro arguably offers a sly burlesque of the entire imbroglio through a hotel porter, Gustav, who after the accidental death of the pet hamster of his daughter Sophie dallies outside her bedroom door wondering whether he should go in to express solicitude. In his account of this episode, Gustav claims that he has some '*understanding*' with his daughter that explains why he doesn't express his feelings. Furthermore, he says, she knows this 'arrangement' and respects it (*UC* 82, 85, emphasis original).

Chronology

1954	Kazuo Ishiguro born 8 November in Nagasaki, Japan.
1960	Family moves to Guildford, Surrey. Father joins British government research project on the North Sea.
1973	Completes schooling. Takes up sundry jobs including grouse-beater for the Queen Mother at Balmoral Castle, Scotland.
1974	Travels in the US and Canada for several months.
1974–8	Attends University of Kent at Canterbury. Graduates with a BA (Honours) in English and Philosophy.
1976	Community worker in Renfrew, Scotland.
1979	Resettlement worker with Cyrenians; works with the homeless.
1979–80	Attends creative writing course at University of East Anglia, Norwich. Tutors include Malcolm Bradbury and Angela Carter.
1981	Three short stories published in *Introduction 7*.
1982	Publishes *A Pale View of Hills*.
1983	Wins Winifred Holtby Memorial Prize. Nominated by *Granta* magazine as one of twenty best young British writers. Obtains UK citizenship.
1984	*A Profile of Arthur J. Mason* broadcast in Britain.
1986	Publishes *An Artist of the Floating World*. Shortlisted for Booker. Wins Whitbread Book of the Year award. Marries Lorna Anne MacDougal. *The Gourmet* broadcast in Britain.
1989	Publishes *The Remains of the Day*. Wins Booker Prize for fiction. Harold Pinter buys film option rights. Ishiguro returns to Japan as guest of Japan Foundation.
1992	Daughter, Naomi, born in March.
1993	*The Remains of the Day* released by Columbia Pictures. Movie nominated for eight Oscars. Ishiguro again included in *Granta*'s twenty best young British writers list.

1994	Member of jury at Cannes Film Festival.
1995	Publishes *The Unconsoled*. Receives OBE for services to literature.
1998	Named Chevalier de l'Ordre des Arts et des Lettres by the French government.
2000	Publishes *When We Were Orphans*. Shortlisted for Booker.
2001	'A village after dark' published in the *New Yorker*.
2003	*The Saddest Music in the World* released by IFC Films.
2005	Publishes *Never Let Me Go*. Shortlisted for Booker. *The White Countess* released by Sony Pictures.

Bibliography

Adelman, G. (2001) 'Doubles on the rocks: Ishiguro's *The Unconsoled*', *Critique*, 42 (2): 166–79.

Adorno, T. (2000) [1974] *Minima Moralia: reflections from damaged life*, trans. E. Jephcott, London: Verso.

Alleva, R. (1993) 'Stunts', *Commonweal*, 17 December: 14–16.

Annan, G. (1989) 'On the high wire', Review of *A Pale View of Hills, An Artist of the Floating World* and *The Remains of the Day*, *New York Review of Books*, 7 December: 3–4.

Appiah, K. A. (2001) 'Liberalism, individuality, and identity', *Critical Inquiry*, 27 (2): 305–32.

Arai, M. (1990) 'Ishiguro's floating worlds: observations on his vision of Japan and England', *General Education Review* (Japan), 22: 29–34.

Atkinson, R. (1995) 'How the butler was made to do it: the perverted professionalism of *The Remains of the Day*', *Yale Law Journal*, 105: 177–220.

Barthes, R. (1973) *Mythologies*, trans. A. Lavers, St Albans: Paladin.

—— (1998) [1981] *Camera Lucida: reflections on photography*, trans. R. Howard, New York: Hill and Wang.

Benedict, R. (1989) [1946] *The Chrysanthemum and the Sword*, reprint edn, Boston: Houghton Mifflin.

Bhabha, H. (1995) 'Unpacking my library again', *Journal of the Midwest Modern Language Association*, 28 (1): 5–18.

Bickers, R. (1999) *Britain in China: community, culture and colonialism 1900–1949*, Manchester: Manchester University Press.

Boehmer, E. (1995) *Colonial and Postcolonial Literature*, Oxford: Oxford University Press.

Bowlby, J. (1991) *Loss: sadness and depression*, London: Penguin.

Brandmark, W. (n.d.) *Kazuo Ishiguro* [pamphlet], London: British Council.

Britzman, D. P. (2006) 'On being a slow reader: psychoanalytic reading problems in Ishiguro's *Never Let Me Go*', *Changing English*, 13 (3): 307–18.

Brookner, A. (1995) 'A superb achievement', Review of *The Unconsoled*, *Spectator*, 24 June: 40–1.

Bryson, B. (1990) 'Between two worlds', *New York Times*, 29 April: sect. 6, p. 38+.

Burley, J. (2005) 'A braver, newer world', Review of *Never Let Me Go*, *Nature*, 26 May: 427.

Cannadine, D. (1997) [1989] *The Pleasures of the Past*, London: Penguin.

Cardullo, B. (1995) 'The servant', *Hudson Review*, 47 (4): 616–22.

Carey, J. (2000a) 'Fiction – books', Review of *When We Were Orphans*, *Sunday Times*, 2 April: 45.

—— (2000b) *Pure Pleasure: a guide to the twentieth century's most enjoyable books*, London: Faber and Faber.

Carpi, D. (1997) 'The crisis of the social subject in the contemporary English novel', *European Journal of English Studies*, 1 (2): 165–83.

Chaudhuri, A. (1995) 'Unlike Kafka', Review of *The Unconsoled*, *London Review of Books*, 8 June: 30–1.

Cheah, P. and B. Robbins (eds) (1998) *Cosmopolitics: thinking and feeling beyond the nation*, Minneapolis, MN: University of Minnesota Press.

Cheng, C. (2005a) 'Making and marketing Kazuo Ishiguro's alterity', *Post Identity*, 4 (2), http://hdl.handle.net/2027/spo.pid9999.0004.202 (accessed 2 August 2008).

—— (2005b) 'Chic clichés: the reinvention of myths and stereotypes in Kazuo Ishiguro's Novels', *EnterText*, 5 (3): 148–86, http://arts.brunel.ac.uk/gate/entertext/issue_5_3.htm (accessed 2 August 2008).

—— (2006a) 'Anachronistic periodization: Victorian literature in the postcolonial era or postcolonial literature in the Victorian era?', *Postcolonial Text*, 2 (3): 1–13, http://postcolonial.org/index.php/pct/issue/view/11/showToc (accessed 2 August 2008).

—— (2006b) 'Glimpsing history through stories: the Second World War remembered in Kazuo Ishiguro's novels', *InterCulture*, 3 (3), http://www.fsu.edu/~proghum/interculture/vol3.html (accessed 2 August 2008).

Childs, P. (2005) *Contemporary Novelists: British fiction since 1970*, Basingstoke: Palgrave.

Chira, S. (1989) 'A case of cultural misperception', *New York Times*, 28 October: 13.

Chisholm, A. (1986) 'Lost worlds of pleasure', Review of *An Artist of the Floating World*, *Times Literary Supplement*, 14 February: 162.

Clewell, T. (2004) 'Mourning beyond melancholia: Freud's psychoanalysis of loss', *Journal of the American Psychoanalytic Association*, 52 (1): 43–67.

Colley, L. (1992a) *Britons: forging the nation, 1707–1837*, New Haven, CT: Yale University Press.

—— (1992b) 'Britishness and otherness: an argument', *Journal of British Studies*, 31: 309–29.

Connor, S. (1996) *The English Novel in History 1950–1995*, London: Routledge.

Coster, G. (1991) 'Another country', *Weekend Guardian*, 1–2 June: 4–6.

Cumings, B. (1993) 'Japan's position in the world system', in A. Gordon (ed.) *Postwar Japan as History*, Berkeley: University of California Press, 34–63.

Cuningham, H. C. (2004) 'The Dickens connection in Kazuo Ishiguro's *When We Were Orphans*', *Notes on Contemporary Literature*, 34 (5): 4–6.

Davis, R. G. (1994) 'Imaginary homelands revisited in the novels of Kazuo Ishiguro', *Miscelánea*, 15: 139–54.

Desai, G. and S. Nair (eds) (2005) *Postcolonialisms: an anthology of cultural theory and criticism*, New Brunswick, NJ: Rutgers University Press.

Dower, J. W. (1999) *Embracing Defeat: Japan in the aftermath of World War II*, London: Allen.

Doyle, W. (1993) 'Being an other to oneself: first person narration in Kazuo Ishiguro's *The Remains of the Day*', in E. Labbé (ed.) *L'Altérité dans la littérature et la culture du monde anglophone*, Le Mans: Presses de l'Université du Maine, 70–6.

Ekelund, B. G. (2005) 'Misrecognizing history: complicitous genres in Kazuo Ishiguro's *The Remains of the Day*', *International Fiction Review*, 32 (1–2): 70–90.

Évain, C. (2004) 'Digressions, palimpsests and nostalgia in *An Artist of the Floating World*', *Études britanniques contemporaines*, 27: 23–38, 179.

Evans, D. (1996) *An Introductory Dictionary of Lacanian Psychoanalysis*, London and New York: Routledge.

Fink, B. (1995) *The Lacanian Subject: between language and jouissance*, Princeton, NJ: Princeton University Press.

Finney, B. (2002) 'Figuring the real: Ishiguro's *When We Were Orphans*', *Jouvert*, 7 (1), http://social.chass.ncsu.edu/jouvert/v7is1/ishigu.htm (accessed 2 August 2008).

Fluet, L. (2003) 'The self-loathing class: Williams, Ishiguro and Barbara Ehrenreich on service', *Keywords*, 4: 100–30.

Forsythe, R. (2005) 'Cultural displacement and the mother–daughter relationship in Kazuo Ishiguro's *A Pale View of Hills*', *West Virginia University Philological Papers*, 52: 99–108.

Fort, C. (2004) '"Playing in the dead of night": voice and vision in Kazuo Ishiguro's *A Pale View of Hills*', *Études britanniques contemporaines*, 27: 39–53, 179–80.

Francken, J. (2000) 'Something fishy', Review of *When We Were Orphans*, *London Review of Books*, 13 April: 37.

François, P. (2004) 'The spectral return of depths in Kazuo Ishiguro's *The Unconsoled*', *Commonwealth Essays and Studies*, 26 (2): 77–90.

Freud, S. (1957) [1917] 'Mourning and melancholia', in J. Strachey (ed.) *Standard Edition of the Complete Psychological works of Sigmund Freud*, 14: 243–58.

George, R. M. (1996) *The Politics of Home: postcolonial relocations and twentieth-century fiction*, Cambridge: Cambridge University Press.

Gibson, S. (2004) 'English journeys: the tourist, the guidebook, and the motorcar in *The Remains of the Day*', *Journeys*, 5 (2): 43–71.

Gilroy, P. (1987) '*There Ain't No Black in the Union Jack*': the cultural politics of race and nation, London: Unwin.

—— (1990) 'One nation under a groove: the cultural politics of "race" and racism in Britain', in D. T. Goldberg (ed.) *Anatomy of Racism*, Minneapolis, MN: University of Minnesota Press, 263–82.

Gluck, C. (1997) 'The "end" of the postwar: Japan at the turn of the millennium', *Public Culture*, 10: 1–23.

Griffiths, M. (1993) 'Great English houses/new homes in England?: memory and identity in Kazuo Ishiguro's *The Remains of the Day* and V. S. Naipaul's *The Enigma of Arrival*', *SPAN*, 36: 488–503.

Grossman, L. (2005) 'Living on borrowed time', Review of *Never Let Me Go*, *Time*, 4 November: 62.

Gurewich, D. (1989) 'Upstairs, downstairs', Review of *The Remains of the Day*, *New Criterion*, 8 (4): 77–80.

Guth, D. (1999) 'Submerged narratives in Kazuo Ishiguro's *The Remains of the Day*', *Forum for Modern Language Studies*, 35 (2): 126–37.

Hall, L. (1995) 'New nations, new selves: the novels of Timothy Mo and Kazuo Ishiguro', in A. R. Lee (ed.) *Other Britain, Other British: contemporary multicultural fiction*, London: Pluto Press, 90–110.

Hammond, P. (ed.) (1997) *Cultural Difference, Media Memories: Anglo-American images of Japan*, London: Cassell.

Hardimon, M. O. (1994) 'Role obligations', *Journal of Philosophy*, 91 (7): 333–63.

Hardin, R. (1996) 'Trustworthiness', *Ethics*, 107: 26–42.

Harrison, M. J. (2005) 'Clone alone', Review of *Never Let Me Go*, *Guardian*, 26 February: final edn, p. 26.

Hartley, L. P. (2002) [1953] *The Go-Between*, New York: New York Review of Books.

Hassan, I. (1990) 'An extravagant reticence', *The World and I*, 5 (2): 369–74.

Hattori, T. (1998) 'China man autoeroticism and the remains of Asian America', *Novel*, 31 (2): 215–36.

Head, D. (2002) *The Cambridge Introduction to Modern British Fiction 1950–2000*, Cambridge: Cambridge University Press.

Heidegger, M. (1962) *Being and Time*, trans. J. Macquarrie and E. Robinson, New York: Harper.

Henke, C. (2003) 'Remembering selves, constructing selves: memory and identity in contemporary British fiction', *Journal for the Study of British Cultures*, 10 (1): 77–100.

Hewison, R. (1987) *The Heritage Industry: Britain in a climate of decline*, London: Methuen.

Holmes, F. M. (2005) 'Realism, dreams and the unconscious in the novels of Kazuo Ishiguro', in J. Acheson and S. C. E. Ross (eds) *The Contemporary British Novel*, Edinburgh: Edinburgh University Press, 11–22.

Howard, B. (2001) 'A civil tongue: the voice of Kazuo Ishiguro', *Sewanee Review*, 109 (3): 398–417.

Hunnewell, S. (2008) 'Kazuo Ishiguro: The art of fiction, no. 196', *Paris Review*, 184: 23–54.

Huxley, A. (1977) [1932] *Brave New World*, New York: Flamingo–HarperCollins.

Ingersoll, E. G. (2001) 'Desire, the gaze and suture in the novel and the film: *The Remains of the Day*', *Studies in the Humanities*, 28 (1–2): 31–47, http://find.galegroup.com/itx/start.do?prodId = AONE (accessed 10 July 2008).

—— (2007) 'Taking off into the realm of metaphor: Kazuo Ishiguro's *Never Let Me Go*', *Studies in the Humanities*, 34 (1): 40–59.

Ishiguro, K. (1981a) 'A strange and sometimes sadness', in *Introduction 7: stories by new writers*, London: Faber and Faber, 13–27.

—— (1981b) 'Waiting for J', in *Introduction 7: stories by new writers*, London: Faber and Faber, 28–37.

—— (1981c) 'Getting poisoned', in *Introduction 7: stories by new writers*, London: Faber and Faber, 38–51.

—— (1982a) *A Pale View of Hills*, London: Faber and Faber.

—— (1982b) 'In conversation with Timothy Mo', *The Fiction Magazine*, 1 (4): 48–50.

—— (1983a) 'A family supper', in T. J. Binding (ed.) *Firebird 2: writing today*, Harmondsworth: Penguin, 121–31; also in M. Bradbury (ed.) (1988) *The Penguin Book of Modern British Short Stories*, Harmondsworth: Penguin, 434–42; and in *Esquire* (March 1990): 207–11.

—— (1983b) 'Bomb culture', *Guardian*, 8 August: 9.

—— (1983c) 'The summer after the war', *Granta*, 7: 119–37.

—— (1984) *A Profile of Arthur J. Mason*, television programme, Channel 4, London.

—— (1985) 'October, 1948', *Granta*, 17: 177–85.

—— (1986a) *An Artist of the Floating World*, London: Faber and Faber.

—— (1986b) 'Introduction' to Y. Kawabata, *Snow Country and Thousand Cranes*, trans. E. G. Seidensticker, Harmondsworth: Penguin, 1–3.

—— (1986c) *The Gourmet*, television programme, Channel 4, London.

—— (1989) *The Remains of the Day*, London: Faber and Faber.

—— (1991) 'T by Kazuo Ishiguro', in S. Spender (ed.) *Hockney's Alphabet*, London: Faber and Faber for the Aids Crisis Trust.

—— (1993a) *The Gourmet* [filmscript], *Granta*, 43: 89–127.

—— (1993b) 'Letters to Salman Rushdie – Kazuo Ishiguro', in S. MacDonogh (ed.) *The Rushdie Letters: freedom to speak, freedom to write*, Kerry: Brandon, 79–80.

—— (1995) *The Unconsoled*, London: Faber and Faber.

—— (2000a) *When We Were Orphans*, London: Faber and Faber.

—— (2000b) 'There was a liberating feeling', *Guardian*, 28 November: 5.

—— (2001) 'A village after dark', *The New Yorker*, 21 May: 86+.

—— (2005) *Never Let Me Go*, London: Faber and Faber.

Ishiguro, K. and K. Oe (1991) 'The novelist in today's world: a conversation', *Boundary 2*, 18 (3): 109–22; also in B. W. Shaffer and C. F. Wong (eds) (2008) *Conversations with Kazuo Ishiguro*, Jackson, MS: University Press of Mississippi, 52–65.

The Island (2005) DVD, Dreamworks, Glendale, CA (with Warner Bros), dir. by M. Bay.

Israel, N. (2006) 'Tropicalizing London: British fiction and the discipline of postcolonialism', in J. F. English (ed.) *A Concise Companion to Contemporary British Fiction*, Oxford: Blackwell, 83–100.

Iyer, P. (1991) 'Waiting upon history', Review of *The Remains of the Day*, *Partisan Review*, 58: 585–9.

Jaggi, M. (1995) 'Dreams of freedom', *Guardian*, 29 April: 28.

Jameson, F. (1971) *Marxism and Form: twentieth-century dialectical theories of literature*, Princeton, NJ: Princeton University Press.

—— (1993) 'In the mirror of alternate modernities', foreword to K. Karatani, *Origins of Modern Japanese Literature*, translation edited by B. Bary, Durham, NC: Duke University Press, vii–xx.

—— (2005) *Archaeologies of the Future: the desire called utopia and other science fictions*, London: Verso.

Jerng, M. (2008) 'Giving form to life: cloning and narrative expectations of the human', *Partial Answers*, 6 (2): 369–93.

Jirgens, K. E. (1999) 'Narrator resartus: palimpsestic revelations in Kazuo Ishiguro's *The Remains of the Day*', *Q/W/E/R/T/Y*, 9: 219–30.

Jones, E. T. (1993) 'Harold Pinter: a conversation', *Literature-Film Quarterly*, 21 (1): 2–9.

—— (2001) 'On *The Remains of the Day*: Harold Pinter remaindered', in S. H. Gale (ed.) *The films of Harold Pinter*, Albany, NY: State University of New York Press, 99–107.

Jones, R. C. (2000) 'Books', Review of *When We Were Orphans*, *The Times*, 6 April: 15.

Karatani, K. (1993) *Origins of Modern Japanese Literature*, translation edited by B. Bary, Durham, NC: Duke University Press.

Kass, L. R. (2002) *Life, Liberty, and the Defense of Dignity: the challenge for bioethics*, San Francisco: Encounter.

Kauffmann, S. (1993) 'An elegy', *The New Republic*, 6 December: 32–3.

—— (1995) 'The floating world', *The New Republic*, 6 November: 42–5.

Kelman, S. (1991) 'Ishiguro in Toronto', in L. Spalding and M. Ondaatje (eds) *The Brick Reader*, Toronto: Coach, 71–7; also in B. W. Shaffer and C. F. Wong (eds) (2008) *Conversations with Kazuo Ishiguro*, Jackson, MS: University Press of Mississippi, 42–51.

Kenney, M. (1995) 'Stung by critics, "*Remains*" author rethinks his style', *Boston Globe*, 18 October: city edn, sect. Living, p. 47.

Kerr, S. (2005) 'When they were orphans', Review of *Never Let Me Go*, *New York Times*, 17 April: late edn, sect. 7, p. 16.

King, B. (1991) 'The new internationalism: Shiva Naipaul, Salman Rushdie, Buchi Emecheta, Timothy Mo and Kazuo Ishiguro', in J. Acheson (ed.) *The British and Irish Novel since 1960*, New York: St Martin's, 192–211.

King, F. (1982) 'Shimmering', Review of *A Pale View of Hills*, *The Spectator*, 27 February: 24–5.

—— (1989) 'A stately procession of one', Review of *The Remains of the Day*, *The Spectator*, 27 May: 31–2.

Klein, R. D. (1994) 'Reflections and echoes: Ono's life in the floating world: part I – reflections', *Bulletin of Hiroshima Jogakuin University*, 44: 33–54.

—— (1995) 'Echoes and reflections: Ono's life in the floating world: part II – echoes', *Bulletin of Hiroshima Jogakuin University*, 45: 75–90.

Knights, D. and H. Willmott (1999) *Management Lives: power and identity in work organizations*, London: Sage.

Krider, D. O. (1998) 'Rooted in a small space: an interview with Kazuo Ishiguro', *Kenyon Review*, 20 (2): 146–54; also in B. W. Shaffer and C. F. Wong (eds) (2008) *Conversations with Kazuo Ishiguro*, Jackson, MS: University Press of Mississippi, 125–34.

Kumar, K. (2001) '"Englishness" and English national identity', in D. Morley and K. Robins (eds) *British Cultural Studies: geography, nationality and identity*, Oxford: Oxford University Press, 41–55.

Lang, A. F., Jr. and J. M. Lang (1998) 'Between theory and history: *The Remains of the Day* in the International Relations classroom', *PS: Political Science and Politics*, 31 (2): 209–15.

Lang, J. M. (2000) 'Public memory, private history: Kazuo Ishiguro's *The Remains of the Day*', *Clio*, 29 (2): 143–65.

Lazarus, N. (ed.) (2004) *The Cambridge Companion to Postcolonial Literary Studies*, Cambridge: Cambridge University Press.

—— (2005) 'The politics of postcolonial modernism', in A. Loomba, S. Kaul, M. Bunzl, A. Burton and J. Esty (eds) *Postcolonial Studies and Beyond*, Durham, NC: Duke University Press, 423–38.

Lechner, F. J. and J. Boli (eds) (2000) *The Globalization Reader*, Malden, MA: Blackwell.

Lee, H. (1990) 'Quiet desolation', Review of *A Pale View of Hills*, *An Artist of the Floating World*, and *The Remains of the Day*, *The New Republic*, 22 January: 36–9.

Lehmann, J. (1978) *The Image of Japan: from feudal isolation to world power, 1850–1905*, London: Allen.

Lewis, B. (2000) *Kazuo Ishiguro*, Manchester: Manchester University Press.

Littlewood, I. (1996) *The Idea of Japan: western images, western myths*, London: Secker and Warburg.

Lodge, D. (1992) *The Art of Fiction*, London and New York: Penguin.

Lowenthal, D. (1991) 'British national identity and the English landscape', *Rural History*, 2 (2): 205–30.

—— (1998) *The Heritage Crusade and the Spoils of History*, Cambridge: Cambridge University Press.

Luban, D. (1996) 'Stevens's professionalism and ours', *William and Mary Law Review*, 38: 297–317.

Luo, S. (2003) '"Living the wrong life": Kazuo Ishiguro's unconsoled orphans', *Dalhousie Review*, 83 (1): 51–80.

Lütticken, S. (2007) 'Unnatural history', *New Left Review*, 45: 115–31.

Lyne, S. (2002) 'Consuming Madame Chrysanthème: Loti's "dolls" to *Shanghai Baby*', *Intersections*, 8, http://intersections.anu.edu.au/issue8/lyne.html (accessed 2 August 2008).

Ma, S. (1998) *Immigrant Subjectivities in Asian American and Asian Diaspora Literatures*, Albany: State University of New York Press.

—— (1999) 'Kazuo Ishiguro's persistent dream for postethnicity: performance in whiteface', *Post Identity*, 2 (1): 71–88.

McCombe, J. P. (2002) '"The end of (Anthony) Eden": Ishiguro's *The Remains of the Day* and midcentury Anglo–American tensions', *Twentieth-Century Literature*, 48 (1): 77–99.

McCrum, R. (2006) 'What's the best novel in the past 25 years?', *Observer*, 8 October, http://books.guardian.co.uk/departments/generalfiction/story/0,,1890247,00.html (accessed 4 August 2008).

McDonald, K. (2007) 'Days of past futures: Kazuo Ishiguro's *Never Let Me Go* as "speculative memoir"', *Biography*, 30 (1): 74–83.

Macfarlane, R. (2000) 'The bookies' Booker', *Observer*, 5 November: 11.

Machinal, H. (2004) 'The strange case of Christopher Banks in Kazuo Ishiguro's *When We Were Orphans*', *Études britanniques contemporaines*, 27: 55–66, 180.

McLeod, J. (ed.) (2007) *Routledge Companion to Postcolonial Studies*, London: Routledge.

Mallett, P. J. (1996) 'The revelation of character in Kazuo Ishiguro's *The Remains of the Day* and *An Artist of the Floating World*', *Shoin Literary Review* (Japan), 29: 1–20.

Marcus, A. (2006) 'Kazuo Ishiguro's *The Remains of the Day*: the discourse of self-deception', *Partial Answers*, 4 (1): 129–50.

Marsden, G. (1990) 'Introduction', in G. Marsden (ed.) *Victorian Values: personalities and perspectives in nineteenth-century society*, Harlow: Longman, 1–12.

Martin, B. (1998) 'Multiculturalism: consumerist or transformational?', in C. Willett (ed.) *Theorizing Multiculturalism: a guide to the current debate*, Oxford: Blackwell, 121–50.

Mason, G. (1989a) 'Inspiring images: the influence of the Japanese cinema on the writings of Kazuo Ishiguro', *East West Film Journal*, 3: 39–52.

—— (1989b) 'An interview with Kazuo Ishiguro', *Contemporary Literature*, 30 (3): 334–47; also in B. W. Shaffer and C. F. Wong (eds) (2008) *Conversations with Kazuo Ishiguro*, Jackson, MS: University Press of Mississippi, 3–14.

Massie, A. (1990) *The Novel Today: a critical guide to the British novel 1970–1989*, London and New York: Longman.

Mayes, T. and M. Rowling (1997) 'The image makers: British journalists on Japan', in P. Hammond (ed.) *Cultural Difference, Media Memories: Anglo-American images of Japan*, London: Cassell, 115–38.

Medalie, D. (2004) '"What dignity is there in that?": the crisis of dignity in selected late twentieth-century novels', *Journal of Literary Studies*, 20 (1–2): 48–61.

Menand, L. (1995) 'Anxious in dreamland', Review of *The Unconsoled*, *New York Times Book Review*, 15 October: 7.

Meyer, M. J. (2002) 'Dignity as a (modern) virtue', in D. Kretzmer and E. Klein (eds) *The Concept of Human Dignity in Human Rights Discourse*, The Hague: Kluwer Law International, 195–207.

Milmo, C. (2000) 'We were never opium importers, insists firm named in Ishiguro novel', *Independent*, 1 June: 5, http://www.independent.co.uk/arts-entertainment/books/news/we-were-never-opium-importers-insists-firm-named-in-ishiguro-novel-714854.html (accessed 3 August 2008).

Miner, E. (1958) *The Japanese Tradition in British and American Literature*, Princeton, NJ: Princeton University Press.

Miyoshi, M. (1991) *Off Center: power and culture relations between Japan and the United States*, Cambridge, MA: Harvard University Press.

Moretti, F. (1988) [1983] *Signs Taken for Wonders: essays in the sociology of literary forms*, trans. S. Fischer *et al.*, rev. edn, London: Verso.

Morton, K. (1986) 'After the war was lost', Review of *An Artist of the Floating World*, *New York Times*, 8 June: sect. 7, p. 19.

Mouer, R. and Y. Sugimoto (1990) [1986] *Images of Japanese Society: a study in the social construction of reality*, London and New York: Kegan Paul International.

'Nagasaki' (1995) *The New Encyclopaedia Britannica: Macropaedia*, 15th edn.

Naugrette, J. (2004) '*When We Were Orphans*, or the postponement of home', *Études britanniques contemporaines*, 27: 67–82, 180–1.

Newton, A. Z. (1995) *Narrative Ethics*, Cambridge, MA: Harvard University Press.

Nixon, R. (2005) 'Environmentalism and postcolonialism', in A. Loomba, S. Kaul, M. Bunzl, A. Burton and J. Esty (eds) *Postcolonial Studies and Beyond*, Durham, NC: Duke University Press, 233–51.

Nunning, A. F. (2005) 'Reconceptualizing unreliable narration: synthesizing cognitive and rhetorical approaches', in J. Phelan and P. J. Rabinowitz (eds) *A Companion to Narrative Theory*, Oxford: Blackwell, 89–107.

Oates, J. C. (2000) 'The serpent's heart', Review of *When We Were Orphans*, *Times Literary Supplement*, 31 March: 21–2.

O'Brien, S. (1996) 'Serving a new world order: postcolonial politics in Kazuo Ishiguro's *The Remains of the Day*', *Modern Fiction Studies*, 42: 787–806.

Oyabu, K. (1995) 'Cross-cultural fiction: the novels of Timothy Mo and Kazuo Ishiguro', unpublished thesis, University of Exeter.

Page, N. (1991) 'Speech, culture and history in the novels of Kazuo Ishiguro', in M. Chan and R. Harris (eds) *Asian Voices in English*, Hong Kong: Hong Kong University Press, 161–8.

Pang, C. G. C. (2005) 'Introductory remarks to professionalism and personal satisfaction', *Clinical Law Review*, 11 (2): 405–11.

Parkes, A. (2001) *Kazuo Ishiguro's The Remains of the Day*, New York: Continuum.

Parry, B. (2004a) *Postcolonial Studies: a materialist critique*, London: Routledge.

—— (2004b) 'The institutionalization of postcolonial studies', in N. Lazarus (ed.) *The Cambridge Companion to Postcolonial Literary Studies*, Cambridge: Cambridge University Press, 66–80.

Patey, C. (1991) 'When Ishiguro visits the west country: an essay on *The Remains of the Day*', *Acme*, 44 (2): 135–55.

Pégon, C. (2004) 'How to have done with words: virtuoso performance in Kazuo Ishiguro's *The Unconsoled*', *Études britanniques contemporaines*, 27: 83–97, 181–2.

Petry, M. (1999) *Narratives of Memory and Identity: the novels of Kazuo Ishiguro*, Frankfurt: Peter Lang.

Phelan, J. (2005) *Living to Tell about it: a rhetoric and ethics of character narration*, Ithaca, NY: Cornell University Press.

Phelan, J. and M. P. Martin (1999) '"The lessons of Weymouth": homodiegesis, unreliability, ethics, and *The Remains of the Day*', in D. Herman (ed.) *Narratologies: new perspectives on narrative analysis*, Columbus: Ohio State University Press, 88–109.

Phillips, C. (ed.) (1997) *Extravagant Strangers: a literature of belonging*, London: Faber and Faber.

Pillière, L. (2004) 'The language of repression: a linguistic approach to Ishiguro's style', *Études britanniques contemporaines*, 27: 99–109, 182–3.

Pollack, D. (1992) *Reading against Culture: ideology and narrative in the Japanese novel*, Ithaca, NY: Cornell University Press.

Prendergast, C. (2000) *The Triangle of Representation*, New York: Columbia University Press.

Pynchon, T. (2000) [1984] *Slow Learner*, London: Vintage-Random.

Quandt, J. (2003) 'Purple majesty: James Quandt talks with Guy Maddin', *Artforum International*, June: 156–61, 206.

Raphael, L. S. (2001) *Narrative Skepticism: moral agency and representations of consciousness in fiction*, Madison: Fairleigh Dickinson University Press.

Reitano, N. (2007) 'The good wound: memory and community in *The Unconsoled*', *Texas Studies in Literature and Language*, 49 (4): 361–86.

Richards, L. (2000) 'January interview, Kazuo Ishiguro', *January Magazine*, October, http://januarymagazine.com/profiles/ishiguro.html (accessed 4 August 2008).

Robbins, B. (1998) 'Introduction part one: actually existing cosmopolitanism', in P. Cheah and B. Robbins (eds) *Cosmopolitics: thinking and feeling beyond the nation*, Minneapolis, MN: University of Minnesota Press, 1–19.

—— (2001a) 'The village of the liberal managerial class', in V. Dharwadker (ed.) *Cosmopolitan Geographies: new locations in literature and culture*, New York and London: Routledge, 15–32.

—— (2001b) 'Very busy just now: globalization and harriedness in Ishiguro's *The Unconsoled*', *Comparative Literature*, 53 (4): 426–41.

—— (2007) *Upward Mobility and the Common Good: toward a literary history of the welfare state*, Princeton, NJ: Princeton University Press.

Romney, J. (2004) 'He's not unhappy, just obsessed', Review of *The Saddest Music in the World*, and *Van Helsing*, *Independent*, 9 May, http://www.independent.co.uk/arts-entertainment/film-and-tv/film-reviews/the-saddest-music-in-the-world-15brvan-helsing-12a-562853.html (accessed 4 August 2008).

Rorem, N. (1996) 'Fiction in review', Review of *The Unconsoled*, *Yale Review*, 84 (2): 154–9.

Rorty, R. (1995) 'Consolation prize', Review of *The Unconsoled*, *Village Prize Literary Supplement*, October: 13.

Rose, G. (1996) *Mourning Becomes the Law: philosophy and representation*, Cambridge: Cambridge University Press.

Rose, J. (1996) *States of Fantasy*, Oxford: Clarendon Press.

Rothfork, J. (1996) 'Zen comedy in postcolonial literature: Kazuo Ishiguro's *The Remains of the Day*', *Mosaic*, 29 (1): 79–102.

—— (2004) 'Confucianism in Kazuo Ishiguro's *The Unconsoled*', *QLRS*, 4 (1), http://www.qlrs.com/essay.asp?id=394 (accessed 30 January 2008).

Rushdie, S. (1991) *Imaginary Homelands: essays and criticism 1981–1991*, London: Granta.

Rushton, R. (2007) 'Three modes of terror: transcendence, submission, incorporation', *Nottingham French Studies*, 46 (3): 109–20.

Salecl, R. (1996) 'I can't love you unless I give you up', in R. Salecl and S. Zizek (eds) *Gaze and Voice as Love Objects*, Durham, NC: Duke University Press, 179–207.

Sarvan, C. (1997) 'Floating signifiers and *An Artist of the Floating World*', *Journal of Commonwealth Literature*, 32 (1): 93–101.

Sauerbereg, L. O. (2006) 'Coming to terms – literary configurations of the past in Kazuo Ishiguro's *An Artist of the Floating World* and Timothy Mo's *An Insular Possession*', *EurAmerica*, 36 (2): 175–202.

Scanlan, M. (1993) 'Mistaken identities: first-person narration in Kazuo Ishiguro', *Journal of Narrative and Life History*, 3 (2 and 3): 139–54.

Scherzinger, K. (2004) 'The butler in (the) passage: the liminal narrative of Kazuo Ishiguro's The Remains of the Day', *Literator*, 25 (1): 1–21.

Seaman, M. J. (2007) 'Becoming more (than) human: affective posthumanisms, past and future', *JNT: Journal of Narrative Theory*, 37 (2): 246–75.

Sexton, D. (1987) 'Interview: David Sexton meets Kazuo Ishiguro', *The Literary Review*, January: 16–19; also in B. W. Shaffer and C. F. Wong (eds) (2008) *Conversations with Kazuo Ishiguro*, Jackson, MS: University Press of Mississippi, 27–34.

Shaffer, B. W. (1998) *Understanding Kazuo Ishiguro*, Columbia: University of South Carolina Press.

—— (2001) 'An interview with Kazuo Ishiguro', *Contemporary Literature*, 42 (1): 1–14; also in B. W. Shaffer and C. F. Wong (eds) (2008) *Conversations with Kazuo Ishiguro*, Jackson, MS: University Press of Mississippi, 161–73.

—— (2006) *Reading the Novel in English 1950–2000*, Oxford: Blackwell.

Shaffer, B. W. and C. F. Wong (eds) (2008) *Conversations with Kazuo Ishiguro*, Jackson, MS: University Press of Mississippi.

Sim, W. (2005) 'Kazuo Ishiguro', *Review of Contemporary Fiction*, 25 (1): 80–115.

—— (2006) *Globalization and Dislocation in the Novels of Kazuo Ishiguro*, New York: Mellen.

—— (2008) 'Aesthetic innovation and radical nostalgia in Kazuo Ishiguro's *When We Were Orphans*', in N. Murphy and W. Sim (eds) *British Asian Fiction: framing the contemporary*, Amherst, NY: Cambria Press, 329–49.

Sinclair, C. (1987) 'The land of the rising son', *Sunday Times Magazine*, 11 January: 36–7.

Smith, A. M. (1994) *New Right Discourse on Race and Sexuality: Britain 1968–1990*, Cambridge: Cambridge University Press.

Smith, J. L. (1995) 'A novel taste of criticism', *The Times*, 3 May: 17.

Squier, S. M. (2004) *Liminal Lives: imagining the human at the frontiers of biomedicine*, Durham, NC: Duke University Press.

Stanton, K. (2006) *Cosmopolitan Fictions: ethics, politics, and global change in the works of Kazuo Ishiguro, Michael Ondaatje, Jamaica Kincaid, and J. M. Coetzee*, New York: Routledge.

Steinberg, S. (1995) 'Kazuo Ishiguro: "a book about our world"', *Publishers Weekly*, 18 September: 105–6.

Strawson, G. (1989) 'Tragically disciplined and dignified', Review of *The Remains of the Day*, *Times Literary Supplement*, 19–25 May: 535.

Streitfeld, D. (1990) 'The author's life as a salesman; Ishiguro, on tour with no time to write', *The Washington Post*, 9 October: final edn, p. E1.

Strongman, L. (2002) *The Booker Prize and the Legacy of Empire*, New York: Rodopi.

Su, J. J. (2002) 'Refiguring national character: the remains of the British estate novel', *Modern Fiction Studies*, 48: 552–80.

Summers-Bremner, E. (2006) '"Poor creatures": Ishiguro's and Coetzee's imaginary animals', *Mosaic*, 39 (4): 145–60.

Suter, R. (1999) '"We're like butlers": interculturality, memory and responsibility in Kazuo Ishiguro's *The Remains of the Day*', Q/W/E/R/T/Y, 9: 241–50.

Tamaya, M. (1992) 'Ishiguro's *Remains of the Day*: the empire strikes back', *Modern Language Studies*, 22: 45–56.

Terestchenko, M. (2007) 'Servility and destructiveness in Kazuo Ishiguro's *The Remains of the Day*', *Partial Answers*, 5 (1): 77–89.

Teverson, A. (1999) 'Acts of reading in Kazuo Ishiguro's *The Remains of the Day*', Q/W/E/R/T/Y, 9: 251–8.

Thompson, J. (1993) *Fiction, Crime, and Empire: clues to modernity and postmodernism*, Chicago, IL: University of Illinois Press.

Toker, L. and D. Chertoff (2008) 'Reader response and the recycling of topoi in Kazuo Ishiguro's *Never Let Me Go*', *Partial Answers*, 6 (1): 163–80.

Tonkin, B. (2000) 'Artist of his floating world', *Independent*, 1 April: 9.

Trimm, R. S. (2005) 'Inside job: professionalism and postimperial communities in *The Remains of the Day*', *Literature Interpretation Theory*, 16: 135–61.

Trocki, C. A. (1999) *Opium, Empire and the Global Political Economy: a study of the Asian opium trade*, London: Routledge.

Veyret, P. (2004) 'Did Mr Stevens write any Christmas cards? Purloined memories in *The Remains of the Day*', *Études britanniques contemporaines*, 27: 111–25, 183.

—— (2005) 'The strange case of the disappearing Chinamen: memory and desire in Kazuo Ishiguro's *The Remains of the Day* and *When We Were Orphans*', *Études britanniques contemporaines*, 29: 159–72.

Vice, S. (ed.) (1996) *Psychoanalytic Criticism: a reader*, Cambridge: Polity Press.

Vinet, D. (2004) 'Fugal tempo in *The Unconsoled*', *Études britanniques contemporaines*, 27: 127–41, 183–4.

—— (2005) 'Revisiting the memory of guilt in Ishiguro's *When We Were Orphans*', *Études britanniques contemporaines*, 29: 133–44.

Vogel, E. F. (1989) 'Foreword' to R. Benedict [1946] *The Chrysanthemum and the Sword*, reprint edn, Boston: Houghton Mifflin, ix–xii.

Vorda, A. and K. Herzinger. (1993) 'Stuck on the margins: an interview with Kazuo Ishiguro', in A. Vorda (ed.) *Face to Face: interviews with contemporary novelists*, Houston, TX: Rice University Press, 1–36; reprint of 'An interview with Kazuo Ishiguro', *Mississippi Review*, 20 (1991): 131–54; also in B. W. Shaffer and C. F. Wong (eds) (2008) *Conversations with Kazuo Ishiguro*, Jackson, MS: University Press of Mississippi, 66–88.

Wain, P. (1992) 'The historical-political aspect of the novels of Kazuo Ishiguro', *Language and Culture* (Japan), 23: 177–204.

Walkowitz, R. L. (2001) 'Ishiguro's floating worlds', *ELH*, 68: 1049–76.

—— (2006) *Cosmopolitan Style: modernism beyond the nation*, New York: Columbia University Press.

—— (2007) 'Unimaginable largeness: Kazuo Ishiguro, translation, and the new world literature', *Novel*, 40 (3): 216–39.

Wall, K. (1994) '*The Remains of the Day* and its challenges to theories of unreliable narration', *Journal of Narrative Technique*, 24 (1): 18–42.

Walton, J. (1995) 'Arts interview: the artist formerly known as populist', *Daily Telegraph*, 6 May: AB4.

Weiss, L. (1997) 'Globalization and the myth of the powerless state', *New Left Review*, 225: 3–27.

Weiss, T. (2004) *Translating Orients: between ideology and utopia*, Toronto: University of Toronto Press.

Wendel, W. B. (1995) 'Lawyers and butlers: the remains of amoral ethics', *Georgetown Journal of Legal Ethics*, 9 (1): 161–90.

Westerman, M. (2004) 'Is the butler home? Narrative and the split subject in *The Remains of the Day*', *Mosaic*, 37 (3): 157–70.

Wilkinson, E. (1991) *Japan versus the West: image and reality*, London: Penguin.

Willett, C. (ed.) (1998) *Theorizing Multiculturalism: a guide to the current debate*, Oxford: Blackwell.

Williams, R. (1973) *The Country and the City*, New York: Oxford University Press.

—— (1977) *Marxism and Literature*, Oxford: Oxford University Press.

Winsworth, B. (1999) 'Communicating and not communicating: the true and false self in *The Remains of the Day*', *Q/W/E/R/T/Y*, 9: 259–66.

Wong, C. F. (1995) 'The shame of memory: Blanchot's self-dispossession in Ishiguro's *A Pale View of Hills*', *Clio*, 24 (2): 127–45.

—— (2000) *Kazuo Ishiguro*, Horndon, UK: Northcote House.

—— (2001) 'Like idealism is to the intellect: an interview with Kazuo Ishiguro', *Clio*, 3 (3): 309–25; also in B. W. Shaffer and C. F. Wong (eds) (2008) *Conversations with Kazuo Ishiguro*, Jackson, MS: University Press of Mississippi, 174–88.

—— (2005) 'Kazuo Ishiguro's *The Remains of the Day*', in B. W. Shaffer (ed.) *A Companion to the British and Irish Novel: 1945–2000*, Oxford: Blackwell, 493–503.

Wong, S. C. (1993) *Reading Asian American literature: from necessity to extravagance*, Princeton, NJ: Princeton University Press.

Wood, F. (1998) *No Dogs and Not Many Chinese: treaty port life in China 1843–1943*, London: Murray.

Wood, J. (1995) 'Ishiguro in the underworld', Review of *The Unconsoled*, *Guardian*, 5 May: 5.

—— (2005) 'The human difference', Review of *Never Let Me Go*, *New Republic*, 16 May: 36–9.

Wood, M. (1995) 'Sleepless nights', Review of *The Unconsoled*, *New York Review of Books*, 21 December: 17–18.

—— (1998) *Children of Silence: on contemporary fiction*, New York: Columbia University Press.

Wormald, M. (2003) 'Kazuo Ishiguro and the work of art: reading distances', in R. J. Lane, R. Mengham and P. Tew (eds) *Contemporary British Fiction*, Cambridge: Polity, 226–38.

Wright, E. (1991) *Psychoanalytic Criticism: theory in practice*, London: Routledge.

Wright, P. (1985) *On Living in an Old Country: the national past in contemporary Britain*, London: Verso.

Wroe, N. (2005) 'Living memories', *Guardian*, 19 February, http://books.guardian.co.uk/departments/generalfiction/story/0,,1417665,00.html (accessed 4 August 2008).

Yoshioka, F. (1988) 'Beyond the division of east and west: Kazuo Ishiguro's *A Pale View of Hills*', *Studies in English Literature* (Japan): 71–86.

Zinck, P. (2004) 'The homeless writer or the remains of Japan in Kazuo Ishiguro's early fiction', *Études britanniques contemporaines*, 27: 143–61, 184.

—— (2005) 'The palimpsest of memory in Kazuo Ishiguro's *When We Were Orphans*', *Études britanniques contemporaines*, 29: 145–58.

—— (2006) 'Superheroes, superegos: icons of war and the war of icons in the fiction of Kazuo Ishiguro', *Refractory*, 10, http://blogs.arts.unimelb.edu.au/refractory/category/browse-past-volumes/volume-10/ (accessed 4 August 2008).

Index

HOW TO DO YOUR
RESEARCH
PROJECT